Critical Essays on
Native American
Literature

Critical Essays on Native American Literature

Andrew Wiget

G. K. Hall & Co. • **Boston, Massachusetts**

Published by G. K. Hall & Co.
A publishing subsidiary of ITT

Critical essays on Native American literature.

(Critical essays on American literature)
Includes bibliographies and index.
1. Indian literature — North America — History and criticism —
Addresses, essays, lectures. 2. American literature — Indian authors —
History and criticism — Addresses, essays, lectures.   I. Wiget, Andrew.
II. Series.
PM156.C75   1985   897   84-19210
ISBN 0-8161-8687-1

This publication is printed on permanent/durable acid-free paper
MANUFACTURED IN THE UNITED STATES OF AMERICA

CRITICAL ESSAYS ON AMERICAN LITERATURE

This series seeks to anthologize the most important criticism on a wide variety of topics and writers in American literature. Our readers will find in various volumes not only a generous selection of reprinted articles and reviews but original essays, bibliographies, manuscript sections, and other materials brought to public attention for the first time. This volume on Native American Literature, edited by Andrew Wiget, is a welcome addition to our list. There are reprinted reviews and articles by the founders of the field, including Henry Rowe Schoolcraft, Franz Boas, Melville Jacobs, Claude Lévi-Strauss, as well as essays by leading contemporary scholars, Barbara Babcock, Lawrence J. Evers, Elaine Jahner, and Kathleen M. Sands, among others. In addition to an extensive introduction by Professor Wiget, there are original essays by Dexter Fisher, Lawrence J. Evers, and A. LaVonne Brown Ruoff. We are confident that this volume will make a permanent and significant contribution to American literary study.

James Nagel, GENERAL EDITOR

Northeastern University

CONTENTS

The Study of Native American Literature: An Introduction

Robert Spiller was only uttering the conventional wisdom when he opened his *Literary History of the United States* by trumpeting: "The literature of this nation began when the first settler from abroad of sensitive mind paused in his adventure long enough to feel he was under a different sky, breathing a new air, and that a New World was all before him with only strength and Providence for guides."[1] One might smile today at this naive combination of cultural vanity and a vague geographical determinism, but to those subscribing to such popular views in 1969, the Pulitzer Prize for Fiction must have come as something of a shock, at best a novelty. It was awarded to N. Scott Momaday for *House Made of Dawn*, a complex and affecting novel of one Pueblo Indian's failure to succeed in the urban jungle dominated by Anglo-American values and institutions. Momaday has explicitly acknowledged his debt to two cultural traditions: the Kiowa heritage to which he feels himself intimately linked through the memory of his grandmother, Aho, and the Euroamerican world to which he gained access through formal education at the highest level under the tutelage of Yvor Winters.[2] If Abel, the protagonist of Momaday's novel, ominously seems to sustain the stereotype of the beaten Indian "caught between two worlds," it is equally true that his creator's bicultural inheritance has proved to be an invaluable personal and artistic resource.

Given the historical antipathy toward American Indians and the pressures which in any case shape the institutional canon of American literature, the recognition afforded Momaday's novel, even its very existence, demanded an explanation that could account for its successful fusion of materials from two very different cultural traditions. Such criticism was not immediately forthcoming, but today the study of Native American literature is maturing as a genuinely interdisciplinary enterprise. Before *House Made of Dawn* called attention to literature written in English by Native Americans, the interest of scholars had been directed primarily to the traditional tribal oral literatures and had been carried on under the rubric of anthropology, linguistics or folklore. Many of the most important pieces in this volume, and much of the present essay, address this body of material. And because of the relationship between indigenous tribal literary tradi-

1

tions and contemporary Native American writing informed by Euroamerican models, literary scholars have come to depend on these other disciplines. The essays in this volume reflect the historical collegiality of this field and represent a critical heritage hard won from four centuries of preoccupation with the indigenous peoples of this continent. I have included among the contents essays on Eskimo and Mayan peoples, not only because the method of exposition in those essays makes a unique contribution to our way of understanding Native literatures, but because a harmony of perspectives exists within the cultural pluralism of Native America that transcends pre-invasion linguistic and post-invasion political boundaries.[3]

Even prior to that invasion, Europeans were preoccupied with the inhabitants of the western hemisphere, though such beings were then mere hypotheses.[4] Contact so heightened this interest that on Columbus' second voyage (1493) Fray Ramon Pane joined the crew for the express purpose of gathering ethnographic information on the now extinct Taino, collecting their folklore in order to study their religion and anticipating by nearly two hundred years the first Anglo-American efforts at collecting Native American oral literature. Throughout the sixteenth century Spanish priests, like Fray Bernardino de Sahagun, whose *History of the Things of New Spain* (or Florentine Codex) incorporated a good deal of Aztec oral literature, labored side by side with their Aztec converts, like Alva Ixtlilxochitl, to record and understand the indigenous cultural heritage. Simultaneously, however, the conquest continued apace, and this increased cultural understanding was put at the service of political and religious factions arguing for their own policy options. At mid-century Sepulveda and Las Casas met at Valladolid to debate whether or not the Indians were human, the declaration of humanity entitling one not only to baptism but to the ownership of property which could not be appropriated by force.[5] Spain was not alone in this, though the English-speaking colonies had few quibbles about the humanity of the Indians, and the expedient measures taken to displace, debilitate, or destroy them are too well-known to be recapitulated here.[6] More important for our concern is that the preoccupation with reducing the Indian required a notion of unidirectional acculturation across the frontier of ideas. Colonists might exchange with the Indians that which was useful for subsistence or commerce, but they would not accept Native beliefs or values without risking expulsion from white communities. As a result, however much attention they might have given to Native customs and economy, most Euroamericans paid little heed to oral literature, and those who did, perhaps because they learned the language of the people among whom they were living — one thinks here of missionaries like John Eliot, Roger Williams, John Heckewelder, and David Zeisberger — appropriated these elements of Native culture, as had the Spanish, for their own sectarian or ideological purposes.

Basking in the self-congratulation of a more reasonable age, Benjamin Franklin could smile at the composure and evident generosity of the Indians in the face of these assaults on the literature in which they had dramatized their most cherished values. In his "Remarks Concerning the Savages of America" (1784), Franklin preserved a marvellous record of one such encounter between a Swedish minister and the Susquehannah Indians. The minister narrated the Biblical story in outline, emphasizing in good Pauline terms how Christ had repaired the damage of sin brought by the original sin of Adam:

> When he had finished, an Indian orator stood up to thank him. "What you have told us," says he, "is all very good. It is indeed bad to eat apples. It is better to make them into cider. We are much obliged by your kindness in coming so far, to tell us these things which you have heard from your mothers. In return, I will tell you some of those we have heard from ours."[7]

The Indian then proceeded to tell the missionary his people's creation story of The Woman Who Fell From the Sky, (an Earth-Diver variant, see Fenton, this volume), and how from her corpse sprang all the edible plants. When the "disgusted" missionary angrily asserted that such stories were "mere fable, fiction, and falsehood" and the Biblical account "sacred truth," the Indian was offended by this evident lack of open-mindedness. Whether this incident represents an accurate report, Franklin's humorous elaboration of a real occurrence, or sheer invention, it reflects the clarity of vision with which both sides understood the function and value of cultural narratives in the ideological conquest of North America.

The one literary dimension of Native American expressive culture to which eighteenth-century colonists did attend was public speaking, perhaps because, in Franklin's democratic Enlightenment perspective, Native government was "the model of reason and order . . . by counsel of the sages: there is no force, there are no prisons, no officers to compel obedience, or inflict punishment. Hence they generally study oratory, the best speaker having the most influence."[8] Jefferson's *Notes on the State of Virginia*, published like Franklin's "Remarks" in 1784, similarly drew attention to Native oratory with his oft-cited admiration for the speech of Logan, a Delaware, to Lord Dunsmore in 1774. Despite the historical argument surrounding the circumstances of the speech, Jefferson had no hesitancy whatsoever in challenging "the whole orations of Demosthenes or Cicero and of any more eminent orator, if Europe has furnished more eminent, to produce a single passage, superior to the speech of Logan."[9] Such effusiveness is hardly the mark of careful criticism, and the reader of Jefferson's *Notes* will find the full discussion of Logan's achievement carefully couched as evidence in a larger argument against the contention of Buffon, the most renowned naturalist of his day, that the climate of America had debilitating effects on both indigenous and transplanted inhabitants.[10] Both the *Notes* and Franklin's "Remarks," published just a year after the cessation of the War for Independence, need to be read together as part of a larger enterprise to valorize America and attract European settlement and invest-ment.[11] In other words, even to the end of the eighteenth century, and despite a positive reevaluation of Native American cultural expression, their literary attainments were still not appreciated in literary terms, but bent to alien purposes.

This did not change until the second decade of the nineteenth century, when the War of 1812, the final chapter of the American Revolution, ac-complished two critical changes in public attitudes. First, it sufficiently alienated the United States from England that Americans began to seek for the roots of their cultural heritage on this continent. If Stanley Smith could cry out in the English press, "In the four quarters of the globe, who reads an American book?," his remarks were anticipated by others like Walter Chan-ning, who in 1815 identified as "the second cause of the barrenness of Amer-ican literature, viz. the dependence of Americans on English literature to the consequent negligence of the exertion of their own intellectual powers."[12] Channing went further, however, in asserting that "this country has a literature notwithstanding all that has been said in this paper to the contrary. But it is not the least indebted for it to the labour of its colonies. I now refer to the oral literature of the aborigines." Channing's praise of Native American literature was founded on an appreciation of Indian language which he probably acquired second-hand. Though they appeared "so ridiculous in the English dress as to be a new cause for English satire and merriment," he found these vocabularies "the very language of poetry." Subscribing to a natural theory of the origins of language, he believed Indian languages to be sublime because the world they described was sub-lime, the "objects" denominated therein "the very element of poetry." Channing's transmutation of an anti-British attitude into a neoprimitivist indigenism is related, it seems to me, to the second important cultural con-sequence of the War of 1812, the privileging of what were perceived to be Native American cultural values. The War saw the defeat of the tribes of the Trans-Appalachian frontier and established the absolute military suprem-acy of the United States east of the Mississippi River. For the moment, Indian peoples no longer posed a threat to America's sense of order, civiliza-tion, or destiny. No longer a presence to be accounted for, the sentimentaliz-ing of the vanishing American—a theme renewed at the end of the cen-tury—became in the hands of Cooper, Sigourney, Child, and Stone, the stuff of the imagination for smug seaboard audiences. For the assured agent on the frontier, confident in his nation's military supremacy and cultural superiority, Indians became objects for management or study.

One such man was Henry Rowe Schoolcraft, a geologist turned Indian Agent in Michigan Territory in the second quarter of the century. School-craft empathized with the plight of the Ojibwa he lived among, learned their language, married a young Ojibwa woman, and commenced a study of their oral literature and customs which he published in 1839 as *Algic Re-searches, Comprising Inquiries Respecting the Mental Characteristics of the North American Indians* (New York: Harper & Bros.). Like the mass of educated men in his day, Schoolcraft had so thoroughly internalized the mawkish romantic style then popular that his presentations of these tales and legends are frequently verbose. Like other of his contemporaries who had studied European folklore in the context of emerging romantic nationalism, he accepted a racial/national bias which began by accounting for certain current traits of "national character" by reference to "ancient" lore, and which ended by distributing the achievements of mankind variously among the nations of Europe, accounting the non-European peoples destitute. Though in all these he was remarkably ordinary, the project upon which he had embarked was unprecedented in the extent and nature of the collection and in the public audience for Native American literature it created both in government and among the citizenry generally. In the preface to *Algic Researches*, edited for inclusion in this volume, Schoolcraft groped towards issues of critical importance for the study of that literature. By calling it "vernacular and homogenous" he understood that it had its origins in folk tradition, though he could identify specialist-reconteurs, "individuals who related the tales [who] were also the depositories of historical traditions." He anticipated Franz Boas in attempting to identify the areal distribution of tales, though he adopted a psychogenetic approach which attributed this phenomenon to the psychic unity of the Indian race. He could distinguish variants, however, on the basis of recurrent motifs (though he did not use that term), noting of the tales that "there are distinctive tribal traits, but the general features coincide." And in suggesting that the narratives were meant to hold up models of appropriate and inappropriate behavior, he offered a rude kind of functionalist interpretation, which he pointed up with the examples of Pontiac, addressing the Wyandots with a tale "admirably adapted in its incidents to the point he had in view," and of Manabozo, the trickster / culture hero in whom he found a unique combination of "high exploits" and "low tricks."

In the wake of *Algic Researches*, Schoolcraft committed himself to a longer, encyclopedic endeavor which eventually appeared later in the 1850s. In the same period, the American Ethnological Society was founded (1842) and Lewis Henry Morgan's classic ethnography, *The League of the Ho-de-no-sau-nee or Iroquois* was published (1851). In a significant move, Congress shifted the jurisdiction over the Bureau of Indian Affairs (BIA) from the Department of War to the new Department of the Interior in 1849. After the Civil War, which had curtailed study of Indian peoples, Congress authorized several Geological Surveys of the Far West. Many, like that led by Major John Wesley Powell through the Colorado River drainage, brought back important information about the culture and condition of Indian peoples. This swelling of interest in Indian cultures, which not unexpectedly coincided with increased interest in Indian lands, led to the establishment of the Bureau of American Ethnology (BAE) in 1879 with Powell as its first director.[13] Institutional interest in the American Indian

consolidated into two camps. Representatives from the BAE, frequently
army officers or medical men attached to reservation posts, sometimes
Eastern gentleman adventurers, included the likes of J. O. Dorsey, Washington Matthews, James Mooney, Frank Cushing, Jesse Fewkes, and Alice
Fletcher, many of whom frequently enlisted the aid of educated Indians. In
addition, there emerged a class of private citizens, well-educated and frequently associated with the new professional societies, museums, and state
history associations. Typical of the second group is Morgan, already well-
known for his Iroquois work, whose subsequent *Ancient Society* (1871) asserted a sequence of cultural evolution from savagery through barbarism to
civilization. Another principal figure was Daniel Brinton, a Philadelphia
doctor active in the American Philosophical Society and an internationally-
known linguist. Brinton's most significant contribution was the publication
of the *Library of Aboriginal Literature* throughout the 1880s. This multi-
volume series of native works in bilingual format, each volume augmented
by notes on style and culture, included a collection of Aztec poetry, poorly
translated by Brinton; the Delaware historical epic, the *Walam Olum*;
Horatio Hale's version of the Iroquois Condolence Ritual, and several other
pieces. In calling the volume of Mesoamerican poetry the *Rig Veda Ameri-
canus*, the whole a "library," and a concurrent monograph "Aboriginal Authors and Their Productions," he clearly meant to elevate these oral literary
traditions to distinction. In the Annual Reports and Bulletins of the BAE, in
the publications of the American Museum of Natural History and the Field
Museum, of the American Folklore Society and the American Anthropological Association, these nonacademics shaped a course of study for Native
American oral literature founded on Native language acquisition, bilingual
presentation of texts, and dictated records. Almost from the beginning none
of these principles was attained in full, however, and reports paid little attention to individual reconteurs or to the context of the performance.

In 1892 at Clark University, Brinton examined A. F. C. Chamberlain,
the first Ph.D. candidate in anthropology trained at an American institution.[14] Chamberlain's instructor had been a young German emigré brought
to Clark from an editorial position at *Science* magazine — Franz Boas. Boas
did not stay at Clark. A few years later he left to establish the anthropology
program at Columbia, from which institution he did more than any other
individual over the first three decades of this century to provide a theoretical foundation and methodological rigor for the infant American academic
anthropology, which was burgeoning in the flurry of renewed interest in the
American Indian. If the existence of a "Boasian school" is problematic for
some, there is little doubt about the value of contributions made to the
study of Native Americans and their literature by Boas and his students, who
included the likes of A. L. Kroeber, Robert Lowie, Edward Sapir, Frank
Speck, Leslie Spier, Paul Radin, Ruth Benedict, Gladys Reichard and a host
of others. A co-founder of both the American Anthropological Association
and the American Folklore Society, Boas magnified his impact by editing

the latter's journal from 1908–25 and by founding the *International Journal of American Linguistics* (IJAL) in 1917.[15]

The dominant explanation for cultural differences in the 1890s was psychogenic evolutionism, which assumed that cultural elements of similar form, despite their origins in distant cultures, nevertheless originated in similar mental concepts. Its method was to isolate elements from their cultural context, order them according to some predetermined principle of formal complexity, and then argue comparatively toward a pattern of universal evolution of cultures that would place each item individually and each culture in sum at a particular point on a single scale of comparison. As a result of fieldwork among the Eskimo and among the North Pacific coast tribes, Boas found in Native American oral literature the kind of detailed evidence he needed to rebut this theory of culture change on the grounds that similar forms might have different meanings specified by different contexts. The contrast between recurrent elements of folklore (motifs) and the variable details with which each tribe or teller elaborated the tale supported his own preference for attributing apparently similar data to historical diffusion rather than a psychologically-based polygenesis.[16] By questioning the apparently similarity of phenomena—"Totemism," he noted, "is an artificial unit, not a natural one"[17]—he anticipated the contemporary distinction between Western analytic categories and indigenous or ethnic genres. The contrast between motif and detail made possible studies of historical and geographical distribution of motifs and motif sequences and an explanation for the causes of variation.[18] Similarly, it honed in Boas a perspective on acculturation which focussed on those elements most resistant and those most susceptible to change,[19] and drew attention at the same time to the ambiguous role of the storyteller as the focus of both innovation and tradition. Finally, because of Boas' conviction that language was the key to understanding human experience, he insisted on native language acquisition and trained a generation of scholars in field linguistics whose transcriptions and translations, however much maligned in this age of machine recording, were far preferable to the summary and paraphrase which was then commonplace in other circles.[20] This linguistic focus made possible the first legitimate studies of style in oral literature. All of these issues he addresses in the "Mythology and Folk-Tales of the North American Indians," edited and reprinted for this volume, which seems very modern despite the lapse of nearly three-quarters of a century and despite its preoccupation with the solar and psychogenetic theories of Bastian, Wundt, Ehrenreich, and others.

Boas' encyclopedic interests were everywhere motivated by the search for pattern, but unlike the evolutionists, for Boas the pattern was not simply formal, but explicitly historical and multi-dimensional, integrating relationships between language, environment, material culture, kinship systems, mythology, and religion into a number of cultural themes which cohered into a holistic pattern expressing a unique relationship between a community and its environment.[21] The essay included here by William Fenton, another of Boas' students, is an excellent example of such an illuminating thematic study. Boas' work in oral literature is analogous to that of the critic of written literature who struggles with similar problems of genre, style, theme, convention, source study, and influence. The principal difference in the tasks is that Boas and his students were responsible for gathering the literature as well as studying it and for developing a perspective not on a single piece but on the equivalent of entire national literatures. Viewed in this light, the formative influence of Boas on the subsequent study of Native American oral literature cannot be exaggerated.

Throughout the 1930s, 1940s and into the early 1950s the study of Native American literature more and more fell to the hands of professional folklorists, whose path of inquiry, as mandated by Stith Thompson at the University of Indiana, approximated the Finnish historical-geographic studies of distribution and variation, which considerably refined the kind of diffusion analysis Boas and his students had done.[22] Cultural anthropologists, having long since put psychogenesis to rest, were deeply divided however. Some busied themselves with renovating the classic functionalism of Malinowski and Radcliffe-Brown; others recorded life histories in order to define the relationship between culture and personality. In this latter effort, psychoanalytic theory played a major role. Freudian criticism of Native American oral literature frequently seems as arbitrary and heavy-handed as some Freudian literary criticism, and its narrow focus on sexuality, a distinctly European preoccupation, appears ethnocentric in other cultural contexts.[23] For a short time, such criticism focussed on the inevitable deviance theories of creativity; one remembers the interest in Hosteen Klah, the Navajo singer and transvestite. Jungian criticism fared somewhat better and produced a few popular classics.[24] Advocates of both kinds of psychologism began sinking in a sea of speculation, however, and psychological criticism of Native American literature, oral or written, has been a marginal activity at best.[25] In the early 1950s, several important moments of cross-disciplinary communication occurred which revitalized the study of Native American literature. For one, cultural anthropologists brought to academic folklorists preoccupied with texts a renewed commitment to understanding the function of folklore in its social context. For another, the influence of structural linguistics offered anthropology an opportunity to develop a less speculative, more methodologically rigorous model of the mental dimensions of culture, and cognitive anthropology was born. Together, these two emphases made possible the redirection of concern with Native American literature away from historical and geographical studies to the study of folklore in the moment of performance.

Cognitive anthropology shifted the definition of culture away from material items like cups, dances, legends, and bumper stickers to the conceptual categories by which members of a culture organized those elements of experience. It is not difficult to point to the source of this momentous redefinition: analogies from Saussurean structural linguistics are ubiquitous. Structural linguistics represented language as an activity in which discernible but unarticulated rules governed the transformation of an unexpressed phon*eme* into a number of expressed phon*etic* variants. The particular transformation from the -emic level of *langue* or idealized language to the -etic level of actual use or *parole* was determined by the different contexts in which the phoneme was scheduled to appear. Culture, by analogy, was conceived similarly as the set of rules governing appropriate behaviors, and meaning was seen to reside not in the behaviors themselves, but in the relationship between concept, behavior, and context. As the abstracted sound relationship was called a *phoneme*, the abstracted unit of meaning was called the *sememe*, from the Greek for "sign." Understanding the linguistic analogy enables one to sort out the variety of approaches to oral literature born in this period, and the strengths and weaknesses each entails.

At least through the mid-1970s, the most important of these was structuralism, the most preeminent form of which was introduced by Claude Lévi-Strauss in 1955 with the publication of "The Structural Study of Myth," a significant portion of which is included here. Though most of his fieldwork was done in Brazil and he knew North American Indians only through the anthropological literature, his proofcase for the application of his method of analysis to tribal literature, included here, was a Zuni myth. Despite its daunting use of charts and formulae, the method is nevertheless straightforward. Making an explicit appeal to the linguistic analogy, Lévi-Strauss argued that just as one analyzes everyday speech to discover the rules governing the selection of phonetic variants and thus arrives at an understanding of the phonemic level of language, so also must the oral literary text be analyzed according to units of meaning or "terms" (a, b) which recur in conjunction with certain narrated actions or "functions" (F_x, F_y). These thematic term-function relations can be abstracted further until one is left with an irreducible and apparently irreconcilable pair of relations. These are mediated by a third term, which is not altogether new but which is treated in the narration as a transvaluation of one of the two original terms (thus "a" becomes "a^{-1}"), a process of inversion which reverses the prior term-function relationship (so $F_y[b]$ becomes $F_{a-1}[y]$). This produces his mathematical formula for inversion. The function of mythical thought, Lévi-Strauss concludes, is to "provide a logical model capable of overcoming contradictions." There was, in other words, a mythic paradigm, which to his mind functioned like a phonological law, that worked changes on conceptual categories and established thematic relations between them through the narrative structure.[26]

The notion Lévi-Strauss reiterates continually — that culture is a form of intervention man is continually raising up to overcome existential dilemmas of binary form — is an attractive one. Lévi-Strauss lacked any external verification for his assumption, however, that this binary structure was a function of mental processes innate to man; others had postulated that such binary structures are more deeply rooted in the physical reality of our bilateral symmetry than in any mental structure.[27] Further, his identification of units of meaning within the text was entirely subjective, despite the show of rigor; this was a problem inherent in any formalist approach which depended upon one's own categories for identifying such units. Even terms as widely-accepted as "motif" become plastic under pressure and are at best a shorthand, incapable of the precision that Lévi-Strauss imagines. Consequently, the more abstract his formulations become in disclosing the tale's deep structure, the greater difficulty he has in establishing its relationship to the actual story of this particular text, a problem exacerbated by his lack of interest in the actual language or "texture" of the narration.[28] Having initiated a dialectical mode of analysis, the results inevitably bear out the assumptions under which the analysis was begun. In the end, when he attributes these results to the peculiar character of mythic, Zuni thought, he confuses his analytical procedure with Zuni creative processes. And since he does not establish the Zunis' own sense of these issues to corroborate his work, when pressed he would have to argue that his analysis had disclosed an *un*conscious process, the creators of the myth not knowing themselves how they create the meaning they do. Despite these objections, as a method of explication Lévi-Strauss' particular brand of structuralism has proved an important tool. His paradigms of mediation and inversion are particularly well-suited to the studies of marginal figures, like Barbara Babcock's study of the Trickster included here.

The appearance of an English translation of *The Morphology of the Folktale* in 1958 introduced Western scholars to another form of structuralism.[29] The 1928 study by the Russian Formalist, Vladimir Propp, offered a syntagmatic analysis of the ways in which thirty-one functions of the role-players in Russian fairy tales could be sequenced. He further described how some function-sequences (Lack-Lack Liquidated, or Interdiction-Violation) provide the basic structure of shorter narratives and how their embedding could create longer narratives. The model was soon applied to Native American materials. B. N. Colby tried to establish a grammar of Eskimo folktale narration, while Alan Dundes, by applying Propp's method, found no structural differences between narratives Indians had classified as myths and those they had classified as tales.[30] This led Dundes to conclude that distinctions between these genres must involve criteria like setting, credibility, style of narration, and context of performance.

The publication in 1959 of Melville Jacobs' lengthy study of Clackamas Chinook oral literature was overshadowed by the English translation of Propp, and then, too, it was a formal study in an era of structural analysis. But its significance is no longer a question, especially a chapter entitled "Variability in Play Structures" which has been retitled for this volume in Burkean terms to reflect what Jacobs argues is the essentially dramatic nature of oral narrative. Jacobs argues that to appreciate the significance of these narratives one must obtain a clear sense of their dramatic structure in which junctures between "scenes" and "acts" are occasionally marked by linguistic features and the dramatic units themselves are grouped into patterns of five, the Chinook "sacred" number. In this short chapter Jacobs' imagination and humanistic bent took a cue from Boas' observation that "sacred" numbers have less a religious than a stylistic function, deriving from the "aesthetic values of rhythmic repetition." (See Boas essay, this volume.) More importantly, Jacobs' suggestion — which he did not develop — that structural units of plot might be identical to linguistically-marked units of discourse was a significant insight, for neither Lévi-Strauss nor Propp nor any other structural analyst could make this explicit connection between the deep-structure of a text and the actual language of performance. Thus Jacobs prepared the way for the series of landmark articles by Dell Hymes, establishing the validity and significance of this mode of analysis. And in imaginatively reassessing these performances not as narratives, but as dramas built around alternations of sound and silence, he anticipated the work of Dennis Tedlock, who argues in the same terms for new modes of text-making and a redefinition of oral performance as poetry.[31] Jacobs is the undisputed father of them both.

Whatever direction formal or structural analysis took, however far removed from the text it became, inevitably it was compelled to return to the language and context of the performance itself. Such a connection was explicit in Jacobs' dramatistic analysis, but it was also implicit in the difficulties of structuralists and in Dundes' observation that Proppian analysis cannot account for the differences Native Americans attributed to "myth" versus "tale." Dundes himself argued in the same year that all folkloric material, including Native American oral literature, could only be fully understood by how it functions in context, with the performer present to his or her audience.[32] In doing so, Dundes called attention to the second major cross-disciplinary impulse of the 1950s, one that would have enormous consequences for the study of Native American literature. The impact of anthropological functionalism on professional folklore was sounded by William Bascom's presidential address to the American Folklore Society in 1953, entitled "The Four Functions of Folklore."[33] Though the impact of functionalism has been variously evaluated,[34] Bascom's address chartered the study of folklore as public action, the representation or dramatization of meaning for the sake of accomplishing important social, cultural, or personal ends. The 1960s brought a string of important theoretical articles which continue into 1970s: Dundes on the relationship between text, texture, and context; Hymes on performance and setting; Ben-Amos on the fundamental difference between analytical categories and ethnic genres; Toelken and Tedlock on style; Bauman on the nature of performance.[35] A serious and enduring reconsideration of the relationship between the oral literary performance and its context was thus begun, which continues to provide fresh insights into the creativity of the performer of oral literature and the previously unidentified dimensions of his art.

In the last ten years, a new, genuinely interdisciplinary field of inquiry called the ethnography of speaking emerged from conversation among cognitive anthropologists interested in the manipulation and communication of symbols, sociolinguists interested in the social context of language use, and folklorists interested in a performance rather than a text model for oral literature.[36] The impact of the ethnography of speaking on the study of Naive American oral literatures has been tremendous. Unlike the historical and comparative studies of earlier folklorists, the ethnography of speaking is entirely synchronic, focussing on the performance(s) at hand and addressing the ways in which the stylistic resources of the language and indigenous aesthetic conventions are used to accomplish particular ends. Darnell's study of a particular Cree performance, included here, is a model of how setting and audience help shape the emergent structure of the performance of oral literature in a number of ways, including the adroit, spontaneous creation of a novel ending and the decision to omit certain incidents. Gossen's study offers a typology of Chamula Maya oral literature, which demonstrates that indigenous notions of genre are every bit as complex as European ones, encompassing several aspects of setting, style, form, and subject, and that they emerge from a continuum of style which evades simple distinctions between "ordinary" and "poetic" language. Indeed, only with the advent of the ethnography of speaking could the literary achievement of Native American tribal traditions become accessible in its own terms. In addition to the previously mentioned work of Hymes and Tedlock, which provides a substantial understanding of two Native American literatures, Warm Springs Chinook and Zuni, other important work has concerned the New York Iroquois, the James Bay Cree, and the Kuna of San Blas.[37]

In the 1970s, cultural events like Momaday's Pulitzer Prize and political events like the Wounded Knee occupation drew the attention of literary scholars to American Indians and their literature. The *literati*, however, seem always to have been fascinated. In the period just before World War I, Alice Fletcher's *Indian Story and Song* and Natalie Curtis' *The Indians' Book* had won popular acclaim, while Mary Austin was "reexpressing" traditional oral song in contemporary verse conventions. As this material entered journals like *Poetry*, it had a measurable impact on H. D., Pound, and the Imagists. The opening of the Southwest to rail touring and the wave of interest in American folk traditions capped this particular cycle of appreciation, which found its fullest expression in George Cronyn's collection, *The Path on the Rainbow* (1916). After the war, the Taos Pueblo land conflict and the members of the Mabel Dodge Luhan group there, who numbered among them D. H. Lawrence, made that community the Western boundary of the floodtide of neoprimitivism surging across America in the 1920s. Then Mary Austin came into her own as the principal spokesperson for "aboriginal American literature." In an article of the same name, she lamented that "the whole subject has been obscured by the obsessions, by a modish intellectual resistance to what is indigenous and underived, working against both appreciation and preservation of our aboriginal material." Because the literature of Native America was not being studied by literary scholars nor taught in the universities of the land, she continued, "It is still easier to know more of Beowulf than of the Red Score of the Delaware, more of Homer than of the Creation Myth of the Zuni . . . [and] the first-born literature of our native land, such as becomes among all other peoples a proud and universally accepted literary heritage, is still unmediated by the application of creative literary intelligence."[38] For her part, Austin tried to establish both formal and thematic connections between the verse forms of Native American oral literature as she perceived them and the landscape to identify what she called in her most significant work, *The American Rhythm* (1923).

If it is true that among the popularizers there were a few, like Mary Austin, who worked diligently to articulate a relationship between Native American literature and canonical American literature, for the most part these men and women were not scholars but salon members, caught up in one of the twentieth century's periodic infatuations with Indians.[39] But in the late 1940s and early 1950s, two anthologies, Margot Astrov's *American Indian Prose and Poetry* (1946) and A. Grove Day's *The Sky Clears* (1951), tried with some success to bring contemporary anthropological and literary understanding to bear upon Native literatures through extensive notes and introduction in the first case and a running commentary in the second. Nevertheless, it was not until Momaday's Pulitzer Prize for Fiction in 1969 that the attention of literary scholars was truly focussed upon this material. By the early 1970s panels were addressing this literature at the annual meetings of the MLA, within which a discussion group was formed, and articles began to appear in literary journals.[40] At the root of these discussions were attempts to determine what marked this literature as peculiarly Indian. Because of the multiple indices of identification associated with "Indian," ready, simple answers seemed frivolous. Might not the ascription of Indianness be based on subject matter? Then one could include Anglo-authored works, like Frank Waters' enormously popular *The Man Who Killed the Deer*, and many did. Or could Indianness at its narrowest be based on some biographical determinant such as blood quantum, degree of tribal enculturation, native language facility, and so forth? Despite fascination with occasional works proclaimed to be "conceived in Native Language X" but mentally translated for commitment to writing in English, such extraliterary criteria were eventually discounted, though their appeal remains. Complex answers, on the other hand, frequently seemed abstruse, tortured, and self-serving, because most of those concerned with Native American literature were trained under New Critical theory to forsake evaluation for description, context for text, and were unprepared to examine fundamental notions such as the criteria for canonicity, the relationship between an author and tradition, and modes of articulation between oral and written expression. Eventually the problem of identification began to focus on discovery of continuities of form, style, and theme between contemporary Indian writers and Native American tribal literature and experience.

In this atmosphere, Momaday's *House Made of Dawn*, unlike his *Way to Rainy Mountain*, drew some criticism for being an essentially Western literary form, because it did not seem to have antecedents in a particular tribal literary tradition. This presumably accounted for its not being read by Indians, that being another putative test of "Indianness."[41] By 1977 it could be contrasted with two other novels written by Native Americans. In that year, the Laguna Pueblo writer Leslie Silko published *Ceremony*, a novel in which the protagonist Tayo, like Momaday's Abel, was effectively alienated from his community and lacked an integrated sense of self. But *Ceremony* was different, as Elaine Jahner's essay in this volume illustrates, because it incorporated Navajo and Laguna myths as models for the reader's interpretation of how the protagonist comes to his healing. James Welch's *Winter in the Blood* (1974), hailed by the *New York Times* as "the best first novel of the season," featured a disaffected protagonist similar in some ways to Tayo and Abel. But unlike Abel of *House Made of Dawn*, who can only silently express his partial reintegration at the conclusion of the novel by joining the others running to renew the sun, Welch's character, as Kathleen Sands points out in her essay in this volume, is able to bring together the broken narratives of his life into a wholeness. In the end, the problems of interpretation associated with *House Made of Dawn* derive in great part from its urban setting and silent protagonist, both of which challenge critical assumptions about ethnographic Indianness, as much as they do from the complexity of its narrative structure. Larry Evers' essay, "Words and Place," suggests that Momaday's choice of an urban setting and a silent protagonist were meant to highlight those pantribal values associated with the word and with the land which were retained by many relocated Indians living in the cities. The need to demonstrate continuities of perspective and form between tribal and contemporary literatures and to effectively ground interpretation in a cultural context also provoked a number of ethnographic and historical studies. Evers' "The Killing of a New Mexican State Trooper" is among the best of these. Not simply an examination of the historical events that generated two, and perhaps three tellings now firmly a part of the canon of contemporary Native American literature, it is an impressive demonstration of how such knowledge can enable readers to appreciate the aesthetic value of the choices made by Silko, Ortiz, and Momaday.

LaVonne Ruoff's essay, written specifically for this volume, is an invaluable survey of Native American writing in English from its origins through the end of the nineteenth century. During that period of time, Na-

tive Americans frequently found their English-language fluency an unde-
niably distinctive trait: for some, like Samson Occum, it became as much a
burden as a blessing, being the very feature of his person that opened him
to exploitation; for others, like George Copway, it was a means of social
advancement, enabling him, for a moment at least, to glitter brightly in
New York literary circles. For most, English language fluency was bought
at the high cost of acculturation which undermined tribal values. At no
time was this negotiation of identity more widespread that at the turn of
this century, when educated Indians broached the issue in their writings
and, as Dexter Fisher observes in her essay here on Zitkala Sa and Mourning Dove, in their persons as well. Some cooperated with anthropologists to
coproduce "as-told-to" autobiographical narratives.[42]

The issues of coproduction and the translation and presentation of
texts had a substantial impact on the revaluation of Native American literature underway in the 1970s. In an essay included in this volume, Arnold
Krupat, one of the most original critics of Native American literature,
adopts a post-structuralist perspective on writing and a Marxist approach
to text production to assess the nature of the collaborative effort between
the Native language performer and the English language translator/tran-
scriber/editor.[43] Not only does he insist that the products of such a collaboration are not amenable to criticism in conventional Western terms, but he
reminds readers that conventions of Western criticism like "author" have
themselves been called into question. The virtue of bringing to bear upon
oral literatures the fruits of the most contemporary literary criticism is that
such an activity forces a reexamination of the most basic literary questions
of form, signification, and value. That reexamination, Krupat contends,
will prepare the way for the inclusion of Native American oral literature
into the institutional canon of American literature.

For the moment, however, the more immediate task is to discover the
relationships within Native American literature, especially those aspects of
continuity between tribally-shared matrices of meaning and value and the
work of the individual artist. Such work must necessarily address larger issues, such as the relationship between orality and writing as modes of presentation, and the relationship of structures of signification to the language
of presentation. And the informed reader will recognize from the contents
of this volume areas within the field which have not been given the attention they deserve. The privileging of narrative from Schoolcraft through
the present has meant that little attention has been given to rhythmic
structures, whether song in oral tradition or poetry in written tradition.
Nor do we have any reasonable understanding of how Native American
writers have made a space for themselves by distancing themselves from
writers of "Indian" books from Fenimore Cooper to Gary Snyder and
Jerome Rothenberg. While some authors have not been addressed in this
study because of the extensive critical literature associated with them
(Charles Eastman, for instance), many historically important writers—
Alex Posey, John Joseph Mathews, D'Arcy McNickle—still await critical

scrutiny of their literary achievement. But the work has begun in earnest. Though the European colonist of the sixteenth century could not conceive of it, the Native Americans he met were nevertheless an imaginative, insightful people, adept at word play, skilled in narrative, and possessed of a reverence for language. Today few could reiterate with impunity Spiller's vision of a sterile New World waiting in silence for the arrival of culture and literature from the east. "Father, hear me, a voice I am sending," the opening prayer of the Lakota Sun Dance, rises from the earth and joins that of the contemporary Hopi poet, Wendy Rose, in insisting:

> I won't go down
> in being unreal;
> I won't go down
> in being unheard.[44]

ANDREW WIGET
New Mexico State University

Notes

1. Robert Spiller et al., *The Literary History of the United States*, 3rd ed. (New York: Macmillan, 1963), p. xvii.

2. For Momaday's creative understanding of his family's impact see his memoir, *The Names* (New York: Harper and Row, 1976).

3. The best single bibliographic source for the cultures of native North America is George Peter Murdock and Timothy O'Leary, *The Ethnographic Bibliography of North America*, 5 vols. (New Haven: Human Relations Area Files, 1975).

4. See, for instance, Fredi Chiapelli, ed. *First Images of America*. 2 vols. (Berkeley: Univ. of California Press, 1976); Hugh Honour, *The New Golden Land: European Images of America from the Discoveries to the Present Time* (London: Allen Lane, 1975); and Ronald Sanders, *Lost Tribes and Promised Lands: The Origins of American Racism* (Boston: Little, Brown & Co., 1978).

5. The information about Fray Pane comes from A. I. Hallowell, "The Beginnings of Anthropology in America," *Contributions to Anthropology: Selected Papers of A. Irving Hallowell* (Chicago: Univ. of Chicago Press, 1976), p. 43. For Sepulveda and Las Casas, see Lewis Hanke, *Aristotle and the Indians* (Chicago: Regnery, 1959). For colonial powers generally, see Howard Peckham and Charles Gibson, *Attitudes of the Colonial Powers Towards the American Indian* (Salt Lake City: Univ. of Utah Press, 1969).

6. A good summary history of Indian-Euroamerican relations in the area that would become the United States is Arrell Morgan Gibson, *The American Indian: Prehistory to Present* (New York: D. C. Health, 1980). The principal bibliographies are by Francis Paul Prucha, *A Bibliographical Guide to the History of Indian-White Relations in the United States* (Chicago: Univ. of Chicago, 1977), and its supplement, *Indian-White Relations in the United States: A Bibliography of Works Published, 1975–1980* (Lincoln: University of Nebraska, 1982).

7. Benjamin Franklin, "Remarks Concerning the Savages of America," (1784) in Nancy B. Black and Bette S. Weidman, *White on Red: Images of the American Indian* (Port Washington, N.Y.: Kennikat Press, 1976), p. 104.

8. Franklin, "Remarks" p. 104.

9. Thomas Jefferson, *Notes on the State of Virginia*, Query VI, in *The Portable Thomas Jefferson*, ed. Merrill D. Peterson (New York: Viking, 1975), p. 99. See also James H. O'Donnell, III, "Logan's Oration: A Case Study in Ethnographic Authentication," the *Quarterly Journal of Speech*, 65 (1979), 150–56.

10. Jefferson contributed much to American anthropology, later serving simultaneously at one point in his career as president of both American Philosophical Society (1797–1815) and of the United States (1801–09). See Hallowell, p. 50 ff.

11. See Edna Sorber, "The Noble, Eloquent Savage," *Ethnohistory*, 20 (1972), 227–36. For Indian oratory in general, see C. W. Vanderwerth, *Indian Oratory* (New York: Ballantine, 1971).

12. "Essay on American Language and Literature," *North American Review*, 1 (1815), rpt. in *American Indian Culture and Research Journal*, 2 (1976), 3–7.

13. The best history of the Bureau of American Ethnology, and one which also provides a guide to its publications, is Neil M. Judd, *The Bureau of American Ethnology: A Partial History* (Norman: Univ. of Oklahoma Press, 1967).

14. Hallowell, "Anthropology in Philadelphia," *Contributions*, p. 150.

15. This assessment of Boas' career is garnered from: Gladys Reichard, "Franz Boas and Folklore" and A. L. Kroeber, "Franz Boas: The Man," both in *Franz Boas, 1858–1942*, Memoir 61, American Anthropological Association (Menasha, Wisc.: 1943); John J. Honigman, "The American Historical Tradition," Ch. 6, *The Development of Anthropological Ideas* (Homewood, Il.: Dorsey Press, 1976); and George W. Stocking, Jr., ed., *The Shaping of American Anthropology, 1883–1911: A Franz Boas Reader* (New York: Basic Books, 1974). Typical of Boas' contributions through his editorship at *JAF* are Robert Lowie, "The Test Theme in North American Mythology," *JAF*, 21 (1908), 97–148; T. T. Waterman, "The Explanatory Element in the Folk-Tales of the North-American Indians," *JAF*, 27 (1914), 1–54; and Gladys Reichard, "Literary Types and the Dissemination of Myths," *JAF*, 34 (1921), 269–307. All are essential reading.

16. See Boas, "Dissemination of Tales Among the Natives of North America," (1891) in *Race, Language and Culture* (New York: Basic Books, 1940), 437–45; and "Mythologies of the Indians," in Stocking, *Shaping*, 135–48.

17. "The Origins of Totemism," *Race*, p. 318.

18. Boas, *Tsimshian Mythology*, 31st Annual Report of the Bureau of American Ethnology (Washington, D.C.: GPO, 1916), 515–18; and "The Growth of Indian Mythologies," (1895), *Race*, 425–36. Reference to historical and geographical distribution of folklore usually implies a connection to the work of the Finnish school of folkloristics, but there is no evidence that Boas knew the monographic distribution studies of individual tale types of his contemporary, Kaarle Krohn, or those of Krohn's student, Antti Aarne, nor that he knew Krohn's summary methodological work, *Die Folkloristiche Arbeitsmethode*, 1926 (trans. Archer Taylor, 1971, *Folklore Methodology*). Though some of Krohn's work was published in Germany before Boas came to the United States, they seem to have worked separately.

19. See, for instance, his "Northern Elements in the Mythology of the Navaho," *American Anthropologist*, 10 (1897), 371–76.

20. See Franz Boas to W. H. Holmes, 24 July 1905: "The Documentary Function of the Text," in Stocking, 122–23; also several articles, including "Metaphorical Expression in the Language of the Kwakiutl," (1929), *Race*, pp. 232–39, and "Stylistic Aspects of Primitive Literature," (1925), *Race*, pp. 421–502. More influential than Boas in this regard was his student, Edward Sapir, whose pioneering work in language use, as in "Abnormal Speech Types in Nootka" (1915, rpt. 1963, *Selected Writings of Edward Sapir*, ed. D. G. Mandelbaum, Berkeley), laid the groundwork for modern ethnography of speaking and its concerns for style and performance.

21. Boas was succeeded in this work by his students, notably Ruth Benedict's *Patterns of Culture*. Katherine Spencer's *Mythology and Values: An Analysis of Navaho Chantway Myths*

(Philadelphia: American Folklore Society, 1957) owes as much to Boas' *Kwakiutl Culture as Reflected in Mythology* (Memoir 28 of the American Folklore Society, 1935) as it does to Harvard's Laboratory of Social Relations' Comparative Study of Values.

22. Thompson's dissertation concerned "European Tales Among the North American Indians" (Harvard, 1919). He later adapted it as part of his collection, *Tales of the North American Indians* (Harvard, 1929). Native American tales also comprised a major portion of his study, *The Folktale* (New York: Holt, Rinehart & Winston, 1946). The difference between his local adaptation of the Finnish method (n. 18, above) and the Boasian motif-distribution study is evident in comparing Thompson's own, "The Star Husband Tale," rpt. Alan Dundes, *The Study of Folklore* (1965), pp. 414–74, with Reichard's "Literary Types" cited in n.15.

23. For classic Freudian perspective see Géza Róheim, "Culture Hero and Trickster in North American Mythology," *Indian Tribes of Aboriginal America*, Selected Papers of the 29th International Congress of Americanists, 1949, ed. Sol Tax (New York: Cooper Square Publishers, 1967), 190–95. Karl Kerényi offers a Freudian interpretation of Tricksters as well; see Paul Radin, *The Trickster: A Study in American Indian Mythology* (1959; New York: Schocken, 1972), pp. 173–91. More culturally contextualized and more reasonable are two articles by Laura Makarius, "The Crime of Manabozo," *American Anthropologist*, 75 (1973), 663–75, and "Ritual Clowns and Symbolic Behavior," *Diogenes*, 69 (1970), 44–73.

24. Jung has written a long and very influential article based on a reading of the Winnebago Trickster stories, "On the Psychology of the Trickster Figure," which Radin included in his volume, *The Trickster*, and which influenced Radin's own interpretation.

25. Tendencies toward psychological speculation erupt occasionally in studies of the historical causes of variation in oral literature, especially when scholars have spent enough time with an individual or a community to convince themselves of their own insightfulness. See, for example, Gladys Reichard, "Individualism and Mythological Style," *JAF*, 57 (1944), 16–25; Theodore Stern, "Some Sources of Variability in Klamath Mythology," *JAF*, 69 (1956), 1–12, 135–45, 377–86; Morris Opler, "Three Types of Variation and Their Relationship to Culture Change," in *Language, Culture and Personality; Essays in Memory of Edward Sapir*, ed. Leslie Spier (Menasha, Wisc. 1941), 246–58; and Esther Goldfrank, "The Impact of Situation and Personality on Four Hopi Emergence Myths," *Southwestern Journal of Anthropology*, 4 (1948), 241–62. Most recently, and most radically, Alan Dundes has interpreted the Earth-Diver creation story as an anal manipulation story, "Earth-Diver: Creation of the Mythopoeic Male," *American Anthropologist*, 64 (1962), 1032–51.

26. Pierre and Elli Köngas Maranda usefully expand this formula through four permutations in *Structural Models in Folklore and Transformational Essays*, Approaches to Semiotics, No. 10, ed. Thomas Sebeok (The Hague: Mouton, 1971).

27. See Honigman, *Development of Anthropological Ideas*, pp. 329–30.

28. For attempts at reconciling these two "levels" of text, see my own "Form as Process in Folktale Narration: The Relationship between Deep and Surface Structures," *Folklore Forum*, Bibliographic and Special Series, 9, no.15 (1976), 83–101; and "Sayatasha's Night Chant: A Literary Textual Analysis of a Zuni Ritual Poem," *American Indian Culture and Research Journal*, 4 (1980), 99–140.

29. Vladimir Propp, *The Morphology of the Folktale* (1928, 1958; rpt. 1968, Austin: Univ. of Texas Press).

30. Benjamin N. Colby, "A Partial Grammar of Eskimo Folktales," *American Anthropologist*, 75 (1973), 645–62. Alan Dundes, *The Morphology of North American Indian Folktales*, Folklore Fellows Communications, No. 195 (Helsinki: Suomalainen Tiedeakatemia, 1964).

31. Essays by Hymes and Tedlock were not included in this volume because they have each made available recent collections of their work. Hymes's essays have been collected as '*In Vain I Tried to Tell You': Essays in Native American Ethnopoetics* (Philadelphia: Univ. of

Pennsylvania, 1981); see his comment therein on Jacobs, p. 152, n.4. Tedlock's work has been brought together under the title, *The Spoken Word and the Work of Interpretation* (Philadelphia: Univ. of Pennsylvania Press, 1983).

32. Alan Dundes, "Text, Texture and Context," *Southern Folklore Quarterly*, 28 (1964), 251–65.

33. *JAF*, 67 (1954), 333–49.

34. See the debate between Elliot Oring and Alf Wale in the 1977 volume of *JAF* concerning the impact of functionalism.

35. Dundes, "Text,"; Dell Hymes, "Models of the Interaction of Language and Social Setting," *Journal of Social Issues*, 23 (1967), 8–28; Dan Ben-Amos, "Analytical Categories and Ethnic Genres," *Genre*, 2 (1969), 275–301, rpt. Ben-Amos, ed., *Folklore Genres* (Austin: Univ. of Texas Pess, 1976), 215–42. J. Barre Toelken, "The 'Pretty Language' of Yellowman: Genre, Mode and Texture in Navajo Coyote Stories," *Genre*, 2 (1969), 211–35, substantially revised for inclusion in Karl Kroeber, ed., *Traditional Literatures of the American Indian* (Lincoln: Univ. of Nebraska Press, 1981), pp. 65–116; Dennis Tedlock, "On the Translation of Style in Oral Literature," *JAF*, 84 (1971), 14–33; Dell Hymes, "Breakthrough into Performance," in *Folklore: Performance and Communication*, ed. Dan Ben-Amos and Kenneth Goldstein (The Hague: Mouton, 1975), 11–74. Reprinted in *'In Vain I Tried to Tell You,'* 79–141.

36. Richard Bauman, *Verbal Art as Performance* (Rowley, Mass.: Newberry House, 1977); Richard Bauman and Joel Sherzer, *Explorations in the Ethnography of Speaking* (London: Cambridge Univ. Press, 1974); Américo Paredes and Richard Bauman, eds., *Towards New Perspectives in Folklore* (Austin: Univ. of Texas, 1973).

37. Michael Foster, *From the Earth to Beyond the Sky: An Ethnographic Approach to Four Iroquois Longhouse Speech Events*, National Museum of Man, Mercury Series, Canadian Ethnology Series, No. 20 (Ottawa: National Museum of Man, 1975); Robert J. Preston, *Cree Narrative: Expressing the Personal Meaning of Events*, Mercury Series, Canadian Ethnology Series, No. 30 (Ottawa: National Museum of Man, 1975); Joel Sherzer, *Kuna Ways of Speaking* (Austin: Univ. of Texas, 1983). Gossen's full-length study of the Chamula Maya is *Chamulas in the World of the Sun: Time and Space in Maya Oral Tradition* (Cambridge, Mass.: Harvard Univ. Press, 1974).

38. Mary Austin, "Aboriginal American Literature," in *American Writers on American Literature*, ed. John Macy (New York: Tudor, 1934), pp. 426–41. A useful biography is *I-Mary*, by Augusta Fink (Tucson: Univ. of Arizona, 1983).

39. Discussion of Southwest neoprimitivism is found in Arrell Morgan Gibson, *The Santa Fe and Taos Colonies: Age of the Muses, 1900–1942* (Norman: Univ. of Oklahoma, 1982) and Marta Weigle and Kyle Fiore, *Santa Fe and Taos: The Writer's Era, 1916–1941* (Santa Fe: Ancient City Press, 1982). Anglo-American imitators and popularizers of Indian oral poetry are the subject of Helen Addison Howard's poorly-titled *American Indian Poetry* (Boston: Twayne, 1979) and Michael Castro's *Interpreting the Indian* (Albuquerque: Univ. of New Mexico, 1983).

40. The papers by Sands and Jahner included here were originally delivered at sessions of the MLA devoted to American Indian literature. The first article on Native American oral literature to be published in *PMLA* was Jarold Ramsey's "The Wife Who Goes Out Like A Man, Comes Back as a Hero: The Art of Two Oregon Indian Narratives," *PMLA* 92 (1977). In 1976 *College English* brought out another important article, Kenneth Roemer's "Survey Courses, Indian Literature and *The Way to Rainy Mountain*," pp. 619–24, originally titled "Teaching Indianness."

41. See Michael Dorris' negative comments on Momaday and *House Made of Dawn* in the Newsletter for the Association for the Study of American Indian Literatures (March 1975), p. 1. Contrast the favorable treatment of *Rainy Mountain*'s "Indianness," n.40.

42. See Arnold Krupat's important essay, "The Indian Autobiography: Origins, Types

and Function," *American Literature*, 53 (1981), 21–42; rpt. in Brian Swann, ed. *Smoothing the Ground: Essays on Native American Oral Literature* (Berkeley: Univ. of California, 1983), 261–82.

43. See also Arnold Krupat, "Identity and Difference in the Criticism of Native American Literature," *Diacritics* (Summer 1983), pp. 2–12, and "Native American Literature and the Canon," *Critical Inquiry*, 10 (1983), 145–71.

44. Wendy Rose, "Unstoppable: Academic Poets' Cocktail Party, Berkeley," *Lost Copper* (Morongo Indian Reservation: Malki Museum Press, 1980), p. 31.

Historical and Methodological Perspectives

Preliminary Observations on the Tales

Henry Rowe Schoolcraft*

The following tales are published as specimens of an oral imaginative lore existing among the North American aborigines. In the long period of time in which these tribes have been subjects of observation, we are not aware that powers of this kind have been attributed to them. And it may be asked, Why the discovery of this peculiar trait in their intellectual character has not been made until the first quarter of the nineteenth century? The force of the query is acknowledged; and, in asserting the claim for them, the writer of these pages proposes first to offer to the public some proofs of the correctness of his own conclusions on this point.

*   *   *   *

The Indians could never be made to appreciate the offers of education and Christianity by one portion of the community, while others were arrayed against them in arms. Their idea of government was, after all, the Eastern notion of a unity or despotism, in which everything emanates from the governing power, and is responsible to it. Nor has their flitting and feverish position on the frontiers been auspicious to the acquisition of a true knowledge of their character, particularly in those things which have relations to the Indian mind, their opinions on abstract subjects, their mythology, and other kindred topics. Owing to illiterate interpreters and dishonest men, the parties have never more than half understood each other. Distrust and misapprehension have existed by the century together. And it is, therefore, no cause for astonishment, that the whole period of our contemporaneous history should be filled up with so many negotiations and cessions, wars and treaties.

These remarks are offered to indicate, that the several periods of our colonial and confederate history, and wars, were unfavorable to the acquisition of that species of information respecting their mental capacities and social institutions, of which it is our purpose to speak. The whole tendency

*Reprinted from Henry Rowe Schoolcraft, *Algic Researches, Comprising Inquiries Respecting the Mental Characteristics of the North American Indian, First Series, Indian Tales and Legends*, Vol. 1 (New York: Harper & Bros. 1839), pp. 31, 36–55.

of our intercourse with them has been, to demonstrate rather the physical than moral capabilities of the Indian, his expertness in war, his skill, stratagem, powers of endurance, and contempt of suffering. Indian fortitude has been applauded at the stake, and Indian kindness and generosity acknowledged in the wigwam, and in the mazes of the wilderness. Admiration had been excited by his noble sentiments of independence and exaltation above personal fear. Above all, perhaps, had he been accredited for intellect in his acuteness in negotiation and the simple force of his oratory. But the existence of an intellectual invention had never been traced, so far as it is known, to the amusements of his domestic fireside; nor could it well have been conjectured to occupy so wide a field for its display in legendary tales and fables.

My attention was first arrested by the fact of the existence of such tales among the Odjibwa nation inhabiting the region about Lake Superior in 1822. Two years previous, I had gone out in that quarter as one of the members of a corps of observation, on an exploratory expedition to the head waters of the Mississippi. The large area of territory which it was found this tribe occupied, together with their number and warlike character, induced the department of war to extend a military post to the Falls or *Sault* of St. Mary's, near the outlet of Lake Superior, in the year above named. I accompanied this force, and assumed, at the same time, an official relation to this tribe, as Agent of Indian Affairs, which led me to inquire into their distinctive history, language, and characteristic traits. It was found that they possessed a story-telling faculty, and I wrote down from their narration a number of these fictitious tales,[1] some of which were amusing merely, others were manifestly intended to convey mythologic or allegoric information. The boundaries between truth and fiction are but feebly defined among the aborigines of this Continent, and it was found in this instance, that the individuals of the tribe who related the tales were also the depositories of their historical traditions, such as they were; and these narrators wove the few and scattered incidents and landmarks of their history into the web and woof of their wildest tales. I immediately announced this interesting discovery in their moral character to a few friends and correspondents, who were alike interested in the matter; and a new zest was thus given to the inquiry, and the field of observation greatly extended. The result was the finding of similar tales among all the northwestern tribes whose traditions were investigated. They were also found among some of the tribes west of the Mississippi, and the present state of the inquiry demonstrates that this species of oral lore is common to the Algic, the Ostic, and some tribes of the Abanic stock. It is conjectured to exist among the rather extended branches of the Muskogee, and also the Cherokee, although no actual proof is possessed. And it becomes a question of interest to ascertain how far a similar trait can be traced among the North American tribes, and where the exceptions and limitations are to be found. To find a trait which must hereafter be deemed characteristic of the mental habits of these tribes, so diffused, furnishes a strong motive for extending inquiries farther and wider. It may be asked whether the South American aborigines possessed or still possess, this point of intellectual affinity with the tribes of the North. Did Manco Capac and Montezuma employ this means to strengthen political power, inspire courage, or console themselves under misfortune? Do the ice-bound and impoverished natives of the Arctic circle draw inspiration in their cruel vicissitudes from a similar intellectual source? What sound deductions can be drawn from a comparison of Eastern with Western fable, as thus developed? And, finally, is this propensity connected, in other of the American stock tribes, with a hieroglyphic system of notation, as we find it in the Algic, which will bear any useful comparison with the phonetic system of Egypt, the Runic of Iceland and Norway, or with any other mode of perpetuating the knowledge of events or things known to the human race?

A few remarks may be added respecting the character of the tales now submitted to inspection. And the first is, that they appear to be of a homogeneous and vernacular origin. There are distinctive tribal traits, but the general features coincide. The ideas and incidents do not appear to be borrowed or unnatural. The situations and circumstances are such as are common to the people. The language and phraseology are of the most simple kind. Few adjectives are used, and few comparisons resorted to. The style of narration, the cast of invention, the theory of thinking, are eminently peculiar to a people who wander about in woods and plains, who encounter wild beasts, believe in demons, and are subject to the vicissitudes of the seasons. The tales refer themselves to a people who are polytheists; not believers in one God or Great Spirit, but of thousands of spirits; a people who live in fear, who wander in want, and who die in misery. The machinery of spirits and necromancy, one of the most ancient and prevalent errors of the human race, supplies the framework of these fictious creations. Language to carry out the conceptions might seem to be wanting, but here the narrator finds a ready resource in the use of metaphor, the doctrine of metamorphosis, and the personification of inanimate objects; for the latter of which, the grammar of the language has a peculiar adaptation. Deficiencies of the vocabulary are thus supplied, life and action are imparted to the whole material creation, and every purpose of description is answered. The belief of the narrators and listeners in every wild and improbable thing told, helps wonderfully, in the original, in joining the sequence of parts together. Nothing is too capacious for Indian belief. Almost every declaration is a prophecy, and every tale a creed. He believes that the whole visible and invisible creation is animated with various orders of malignant or benign spirits, who preside over the daily affairs and over the final destinies of men. He believes that these spirits must be conciliated by sacrifices, and a series of fasts and feasts either follow or precede these rites, that by the one they may be rendered acceptable, and by the other, his gratitude may be shown. This constitutes the groundwork of the Algic religion: but superstition has ingrafted upon the original stock, till the growth is a upas of giant size, bearing the bitter fruits of demonology, witchcraft, and necromancy. To make the matter worse, these tribes believe that animals of the lowest, as well as highest class in the chain of creation, are alike endowed with reasoning powers and faculties. And as a natural conclusion, they endow birds, and bears, and all other animals with souls, which, they believe, will be encountered in other shapes in another state of existence. So far the advantages of actual belief come in aid of their fictitious creations, and this is the true cause why so much importance is attached to the flight and appearance of particular birds, who, being privileged to ascend in the air, are supposed by them to be conversant with the wishes, or to act in obedience to the mandates of the spirits: and the circumstance of this belief deserves to be borne in mind in the perusal of their tales, as it will be found that the words put into the mouths of the actors express the actual opinions of the natives on life, death, and immortality, topics which have heretofore been impenetrably veiled.

The value of these traditionary stories appeared to depend, very much, upon their being left, as nearly as possible, in their original forms of thought and expression. In the original there is no attempt at ornament. Great attention is paid, in the narration, to repeating the conversations and speeches, and imitating the very tone and gesture of the actors. This is sometimes indulged at the risk of tautology. Moral point has been given to no tale which does not, in the original, justify it; and it is one of the unlooked-for features connected with the subject, that so considerable a proportion of them possess this trait. It is due to myself, and to those who have aided me in the collection and translation of the materials, to say, that the advantages enjoyed in this respect have been of the most favourable character. The whole examination, extending, with intervals, through a period of seventeen years, has been conducted not only with the aid that a public station, as an executive officer for the tribes, has supplied, but with the superadded intelligence and skill in the language existing within the range of my domestic and affiliated circle. . . .

Astronomy and cosmogony constitute subjects of frequent notice [in these tales]; and this might naturally be expected from a people who are quick in their perceptions of external nature, and pass a large share of their time under the open sky. The phenomena of thunder, lightning, the aurora borealis, meteors, the rainbow, the galaxy of the milky way, the morning and evening stars, and the more prominent groups of the fixed and minor stars, are specifically named and noticed. The cardinal points are accurately distinguished. They entertain the semi-ancient theory that the earth is spheroidal, and the sun and moon perform their circuits round it. The visiters to these luminaries, described in the text, personify the former as a male and the latter as a female, under the idea of brother and sister. We are left to infer, from another passage, that they believe the sky revolves. Nothing, however, in the "open firmament," is a subject of more constant and minute observation, and a more complex terminology, than the clouds.

Their colour, shape, transparency or obscurity, movements, and relative position to the sun and to each other, constitute objects of minute notice and deep importance. A large proportion of the names of individuals in the Algic tribes is drawn from this fruitful source of Indian observation. The Great Spirit is invariably located in the sky, and the Evil Spirit, and the train of minor malignant Spirits, in the earth. Their notions of the position of seas and continents are altogether vague and confused. Nor has it been observed that they have any knowledge of volcanic action. The idea of a universal deluge appears to be equally entertained by the tribes of North and South America.[2] The Algics certainly have it incorporated in their traditionary tales, and I have found the belief in these traditions the most firmly seated among the bands the farthest removed from the advances of civilization and Christianity.

It is the mythology, however, of these tribes which affords the deepest insight into their character, and unfolds, perhaps, some of the clearest coincidences with Oriental rites and opinions. Were the terms Baalim and Magii introduced into the descriptions of their worship, instead of Manito and Meeta, this coincidence would be very apparent. Medical magic spread the charms of its delusion over the semi-barbaric tribes who, at a very early epoch, spread from the Persian and the Arabian Gulfs to the Mediterranean; and it would not be a light task to find branches of the human race who are more completely characterized by its doctrines and practices than the wide-spreading members of the Algic stock of this Continent. Their prophets, jugglers, and meetays [Midés] occupy the same relative importance in the political scale. They advise the movement of armies, and foretel the decrees of fate to individuals. They interpret dreams, affect the performance of miraculous cures, and preside over the most sacred rites. Oracles alike to chiefs and kings, warriors and hunters, nothing can be accomplished without their aid, and it would be presumptuous and impious to attempt anything, in war or peace, which they had decreed to be wrong. But our more immediate object is the class of oral fictions among the Western tribes, and for the growth and development of which their peculiar belief in the doctrine of spirits and magicians has furnished so wide a field. Come from what quarter of the world they may, the propensity to amusing and serio-comic fiction appears to have been brought with them. What traits, if any, of the original threadwork of foreign story remain, it would be premature, in the present state of these collections, to decide. The character and incidents of the narrations are adapted to the condition they are now in, as well as the position they now occupy. There is, it is true, a spirit of reminiscence apparent which pleases itself in allusions to the past; they speak of a sort of golden age, when all things were better with them than they now are; when they had better laws and leaders; when crimes were more promptly punished; when their language was spoken with greater purity, and their manners were freer from barbarism. But all this seems to flit through the Indian mind as a dream, and furnishes him rather the source of a pleasing secret retrospection than any spring to present and future exertions. He pines away as one that is fallen, and despairs to rise. He does not seem to open his eyes on the prospect of civilization and mental exaltation held up before him, as one to whom the scene is new or attractive. These scenes have been pictured before him by teachers and philanthropists for more than two centuries; but there has been nothing in them to arouse and inspire him to press onward in the career of prospective civilization and refinement. He has rather turned away with the air of one to whom all things "new" were "old," and chosen emphatically to re-embrace his woods, his wigwam, and his canoe.

Perhaps the trait that was least to have been anticipated in the tales is the moral often conveyed by them. But, on reflection, this is in accordance with the Indian maxim, which literally requires "an eye for eye, and a tooth for a tooth." And the more closely this feature of poetic justice is scrutinized, the more striking does it appear. Cruelty, murder, and sorcery are eventually punished, although the individual escapes for the time and his career may be long drawn out. Domestic infidelity meets the award of death in the only instance narrated. Religious vows are held inviolate. Respect for parents and for age, fraternal affection, hospitality, bravery, self-denial, endurance under fatigue or suffering, and disinterestedness, are uniformly inculcated. Presumption and pride are rebuked, and warnings given against the allurements of luxury and its concomitant vices. With a people who look back to some ancient and indefinite period in their history as an age of glory, an adherence to primitive manners and customs naturally occupies the place of virtue. The stories are generally so constructed as to hold up to admiration a bold and independent spirit of enterprise and adventure. Most of their heroes are drawn from retired or obscure places, and from abject circumstances. Success is seen to crown the efforts of precocious boys, orphans, or castaways. But whatever success is had, it is always through the instrumentality of the spirits or Manitoes — the true deities worshipped by all the Algic tribes.

The legend of Manabozho reveals, perhaps, the idea of an incarnation. He is the great spirit-man of northern mythology. The conception of the character reveals rather a monstrosity than a deity, displaying in strong colours far more of the dark and incoherent acts of a spirit of carnality than the benevolent deeds of a god. His birth is shrouded in allegoric mystery. He is made to combine all that is brave, warlike, strong, wise, and great in Indian conception, both of mortal and immortal. He conquers the greatest magician, overcomes fiery serpents, and engages in combats and performs exploits the most extravagant. He has no small share in the Adamic-like labour of naming the animals. He destroys the king of the reptile creation, is drawn into the mouth of a gigantic fish with his canoe, survives a flood by climbing a tree, and recreates the earth from a morsel of ground brought up in the paws of a muskrat. In contrast with these high exploits, he goes about playing low tricks, marries a wife, travels the earth, makes use of low subterfuges, is often in want of food, and after being tricked and laughed at, is at one time made to covet the ability of a woodpecker, and at another outdone by the simple skill of a child. The great points in which he is exultingly set forth in the story-telling circle, are his great personal strength, readiness of resource, and strong powers of necromancy. Whatever other parts he is made to play, it is the Indian Hercules, Samson, or Proteus that is prominently held up to admiration. It is perhaps natural that rude nations in every part of the world should invent some such mythological existence as the Indian Manabozho, to concentrate their prime exploits upon; for it is the maxim of such nations that "the race *is* always to the swift, and the battle to the strong."

In closing these remarks, it will not be irrelevant to notice the evidence of the vernacular character and antiquity of the tales, which is furnished by the Pontiac manuscript, preserved in the collections of the Historical Society of Michigan. By this document, which is of the date of 1763, it is shown that this shrewd and talented leader of the Algic tribes, after he had formed the plan of driving the Saxon race from the Continent, appealed to the mythologic belief of the tribes to bring them into his views. It was the Wyandots whom he found it the hardest to convert; and in the general council which he held with the Western chiefs, he narrated before them a tale of a Delaware magician, which is admirably adapted in its incidents to the object he had in view, and affords proof of his foresight and powers of invention. It is deemed of further interest in this connexion, as carrying back the existence of the tales and fables to a period anterior to the final fall of the French power in the Canadas, reaching to within a fraction more than sixty years of their establishment at Detroit.[3] While, however, the authenticity of this curious politico-mythologic tale is undisputed, the names and allusions would show it to be of the modern class of Indian fictions, were not the fact historically known. The importance of this testimony, in the absence of any notice of this trait in the earlier writers, has induced me to submit a literal translation of the tale, from the original French MS., executed by Professor Fasquelle.

Notes

1. Some specimens of these tales were published in my "Travels in the Central Portions of the Mississippi Valley" in 1825, and a "Narrative of the Expedition to Itasca Lake" in 1834, and a few of them have been exhibited to literary friends, who have noticed the subject. Vide Dr. Gilman's "Life on the Lakes," and Mrs. Jameson's "Winter Studies and Summer Rambles," received at the moment these sheets are going through the press.

2. Humboldt found it among the traditions of the Auricanians.

3. Although Quebec was taken in 1759, the Indians did not acquiesce in the transference of power, in the upper lakes, till the *raising of the siege* of Detroit in 1763. This is the true period of the Pontiac war.

Mythology and Folk-Tales of the North American Indians

Franz Boas*

I   Material

During the last twenty years a very considerable body of tales of the North American Indians has been collected. Before their publication, almost the only important collections available for scientific research were the Eskimo tales published by H. Rink, — material recorded in part by natives during the earlier part of the nineteenth century, and printed also in the native language in Greenland; the traditions collected by E. Petitot among the Athapascan tribes of northwestern Canada; the Ponca tales collected by J. O. Dorsey; a few Siouan tales recorded by Stephen R. Riggs; and the Klamath traditions collected by Albert S. Gatschet. The material published in Daniel G. Brinton's "Library of Aboriginal American Literature" also deserves notice. In all of these the attempt was made to give a faithful rendering of the native tales; and in this they differ fundamentally from the literary efforts of Schoolcraft, Kohl, and other writers. Owing to their scope, they are also much more valuable than the older records found in the accounts of missionaries and in books of travel and exploration.

Since those times, somewhat systematic collections have been made among a large number of tribes; and, although the continent is not by any means covered by the existing material, much has been gained to give us a better knowledge of the subject.

Two types of collection may be distinguished. The one includes tales taken down in English or in other European tongues directly from natives, or indirectly with the help of interpreters. Among American institutions, the Bureau of American Ethnology, the American Museum of Natural History, the Field Museum of Natural History (Field Columbian Museum) in Chicago, for a few years the Carnegie Institution of Washington, have worked in this field. Much material is also found in the "Journal of American Folk-Lore," and in the earlier volumes of the "American Anthropologist" and of the "American Antiquarian and Oriental Journal." The other type of collection contains tales taken down from dictation by natives, or recorded in the native language by natives, and later on revised and edited. So far, the latter form the smaller group.

With the increase of material, the demands for accuracy of record have become more and more stringent. While in the earlier period of collecting no great stress was laid upon the recording of variants and their provenience, — as, for instance, in Rink's collection, in which we have variants

*Journal of American Folklore, 27 (1914), 374–410. Reprinted from Franz Boas, Race, Language and Culture, copyright 1940 by Franz Boas, renewed 1968 by Franziska Boas Nicholson, by permission of Macmillan Publishing Co.

from different parts of the country combined into a single story, — we now desire that each tale be obtained from several informants and from several places, in order to enable us to gain an impression of its importance in the tribal lore, and to insure the full record of its contents and of its relations to other tales. Furthermore, the importance of the record in the original language has become more and more apparent. This is not only for the reason that the English translation gives a very inadequate impression of the tales, but also because often the interpreter's inadequage knowledge of English compels him to omit or modify important parts. Even the best translation cannot give us material for the study of literary form, — a subject that has received hardly any attention, and the importance of which, as I hope to show in the course of these remarks, cannot be overestimated.

It is doubtful whether all the records that have been collected in previous years are well adapted to this study, because the difficulty of taking down accurate rapid dictation from natives, and the difficulty which the natives encounter in telling in the traditional manner sufficiently slowly for the purpose of the recorder, almost always exert an appreciable influence upon the form of the tale. Owing to the multiplicity of American languages and to the exigencies of the situation in which students find themselves, the recorder has only rarely a practical command of the language; and for this reason the difficulty just mentioned cannot be readily overcome. Up to the present time, the most successful method has been to have the first record made by natives who have been taught to write their own language. After they have acquired sufficient ease in writing, the diction generally becomes satisfactory. A certain one-sidedness will remain, however, as long as all the material is written down by a single recorder. It has also been suggested that phonographic records be used, which may be written out from re-dictation; but so far, no extended series has been collected in this manner.

The experience of investigators in many regions suggests that the difficulty just mentioned is not as great as might be supposed. This is indicated by the fact that good informants often break down completely when requested to dictate descriptions of the events of everyday life. They will then state that they are well able to tell stories that have a fixed form, but that the slow dictation of descriptions to be made up new is too difficult for them. It would seem, therefore, that the form in which most of the tales are obtained must be fairly well fixed. Ordinarily a poor rendering of a story can easily be recognized by the fragmentary character of the contents, the briefness of sentences, by corrections and unnecessary repetitions. We also have many tales in which the same incident is repeated a number of times; and in those cases the form of the repetitions shows, on the whole, whether the narrator has a fairly good command of his subject. Furthermore, a great many native tales contain, besides the connected narrative, stereotyped formulas, which are always told in the same manner, and which are undoubtedly always given in correct form.

It has been the habit of most collectors to endeavor to find the "right" informant for tales, particularly when the stories refer to elaborate sacred rituals, or when they are the property of social groups possessing definite privileges. It may then be observed that certain tales are in the keeping of individuals, and are only superficially or partially known to the rest of the people. In these cases the recorder has often adopted the attitude of the Indian who possesses the most elaborate variant of the tale, and the fragmentary data given by the uninitiated are rejected as misleading. This view is based on the assumption of a permanence of form of tradition that is hardly justifiable, and does not take into consideration the fact that the esoteric variant which is developed by a small number of individuals is based on the exoteric variants afloat among the whole tribe. We shall revert to this subject later on.

This static view of Indian folk-lore is also expressed by the preference given throughout to the collection of purely Indian material unaffected by European or African elements, and by the reluctance of investigators to bestow as much care upon the gathering of the more recent forms of folk-lore as is given to those forms that were current before the advent of the Whites. For the study of the development of folk-tales the modern material is of particular value, because it may enable us to understand better the processes of assimilation and of adaptation, which undoubtedly have been of great importance in the history of folk-tradition.

II   Myth and Folk-Tale

In our American collections the two terms "myth" and "folk-tale" have been used somewhat indefinitely. This is a necessary result of the lack of a sharp line of demarcation between these two classes of tales. No matter which of the current definitions of mythology we may adopt, there will arise difficulties that cannot be settled without establishing arbitrary distinctions. If we define myths as tales that explain natural phenomena, and that may be considered in this sense as parts of an interpretation of nature, we are confronted with the difficulty that the same tale may be explanatory in one case, and a simple tale without explanatory features in another. The strict adherence to this principle of classification would therefore result in the separation of tales that are genetically connected, one being classed with myths, the other with folk-tales. It goes without saying that in this way unnecessary difficulties are created.

If we make the personification of animals, plants, and natural phenomena the standard of distinction, another difficulty arises, which is based on the lack of a clear distinction between myths, on the one hand, and tales relating to magical exploits that are considered as true and of recent occurrence, on the other, and also on the similarities between tales relating to the adventures of human beings and animals.

Of similar character are the obstacles that stand in the way of a definition of myths as tales relating to ritualistic performances.

In all these cases the same tales will have to be considered, in one case as myths, and in another as folk-tales, because they occur both in explanatory and non-explanatory forms, relating to personified animals or natural objects and to human beings, with ritualistic significance and without it. If we do accept any one of these definitions, it will therefore always be necessary to consider the two groups together, and to investigate their historical and psychological development without regard to the artificial limits implied in the definition. This difficulty cannot be met by assuming that the folk-tale originated from a myth and must be considered a degenerate myth, or by the hypothesis that conversely the myth originated from a folk-tale; for, if we do this, a theoretical point of view, that should be the end of the inquiry, is injected into our consideration.

For our purposes it seems desirable to adhere to the definition of myth given by the Indian himself. In the mind of the American native there exists almost always a clear distinction between two classes of tales. One group relates incidents which happened at a time when the world had not yet assumed its present form, and when mankind was not yet in possession of all the arts and customs that belong to our period. The other group contains tales of our modern period. In other words, tales of the first group are considered as myths; those of the other, as history. The tales of the former group are not by any means explanatory in character throughout. They treat mostly of the achievements of animals and of heroes. From our modern point of view, it might be doubtful sometimes whether such a tale should be considered as mythical, or historical, since, on account of the Indian's belief in the powers of animals, many of the historical tales consist of a series of incidents that might as well have happened in the mythological period; such as the appearance of animals that become supernatural helpers and perform marvellous exploits, or of those that initiate a person into a new ritual. It can be shown that historical tales may in the course of time become mythical tales by being transferred into the mythical period, and that historical tales may originate which parallel in the character and sequence of their incidents mythical tales. Nevertheless the psychological distinction between the two classes of tales is perfectly clear in the mind of the Indian. It is related, in a way, to the ancient concepts of the different ages as described by Hesiod.

For our analytical study we must bear in mind that the psychological distinction which the natives make between mythical and historical tales is, from an historical point of view, not more definitely and sharply drawn than the line of demarcation between myths and tales defined in other ways. The point of view, however, has the advantage that the myths correspond to concepts that are perfectly clear in the native mind. Although folk-tales and myths as defined in this manner must therefore still be studied as a unit, we have avoided the introduction of an arbitrary distinction through our modern cultural point of view, and retained instead the one that is present in the minds of the myth-telling people.

The mythical tales belong to a period that is long past, and cannot be repeated in our world, although the expectation may exist of a renewal of mythical conditions in the dim future. Only when we ourselves are transferred into the realm of mythical beings, that continue to exist somewhere in unknown parts of our world, may myths again become happenings. The mythological beings may thus become actors in historical folk-tales or in localized tradition, although they appear at the same time as actors in true myths. The Indian who disappears and is taken to the village of the Buffaloes is, in the mind of the Indian, the hero of an historical tale, although the Buffalo men are at the same time mythical personages. The novice initiated by the spirits of a secret society is taken away by them bodily; and when he re-appears among his tribesmen, he tells them his story, which deals with the gifts of mythical beings. The person who revives from a death-like trance has been in communion with the mythical world of the ghosts, although he has been allowed to return to our world and to follow his usual occupations.

It is therefore clear that in the mind of the Indian the appearance of mythical characters is not the criterion of what constitutes a myth. It is rather its distance in space or time that gives it its characteristic tone.

It appears from these remarks that in the study of the historical origin of myths and folk-tales of modern times, the widest latitude must be given to our researches. The types and distribution of the whole body of folk-tales and myths must form the subject of our inquiry. The reconstruction of their history will furnish the material which may help us to uncover the psychological processes involved.

I cannot agree with Bastian and Wundt,[1] who consider the discovery of the actual origin of tales as comparatively insignificant, because both, independently created and disseminated material are subject to the same psychological processes which may therefore be studied by an analytical treatment of the tales as they now exist. I do not see how this can be done without interpreting as an historical sequence a classification based entirely on psychological or other considerations, — a method that can never lead to satisfactory results, on account of the arbitrary, non-historical premises on which it is founded. If there is more than one classification of this type possible, the reconstructed psychological processes will differ accordingly; and we must still demand that the change from one type to another be demonstrated by actual historical evidence when available, by inferences based on distribution or similar data when no other method can be utilized. Here, as in all other ethnological problems, the principle must be recognized that phenomena apparently alike may develop in multitudinous ways. A geometrical design may be developed from a conventionalized realistic form, or it may develop directly through a play with elementary technical motives; a semi-realistic form may be a copy of nature, and may have been read into a pre-existing geometrical design; or both may have been borrowed and developed on new lines. A ritual may be a dramatic presentation of a myth, it may be an ancient rite to which a myth has become attached, or it may be a copy of foreign patterns. There is no *a priori* reason that tells us which has been the starting-point of a local development, for the modern forms may have grown up in any of these ways or by their joint action. At the same time, the psychological processes that come into play in one case or the other are distinct. For this reason we insist on the necessity of an inductive study of the sequence of events as the basis for all our work.

The results of these inquiries, however, do not touch upon another problem upon which much thought has been bestowed. The beings that appear as actors in mythological tales are creatures of the imagination, and differ in the most curious ways from the beings which are known in our every-day world. Animals that are at the same time men, human beings that consist of parts of a body or are covered with warts and blotches, beings that may at will increase or decrease in size, bodies that may be cut up and will readily re-unite and come to life, beings that are swallowed by animals or monsters and pass through them unharmed, are the ordinary inventory of folk-tales as well as of myths. Whatever is nowhere seen and whatever has never happened are here common every-day events.

The imagination of man knows no limits, and we must expect great varieties of form in mythical beings and happenings. While such diversity is found, there still exist certain features that occur with surprising frequency, — in fact, so often that their presence cannot be due to accident. The attention of many investigators has been directed to these similarities, which have led to the inference that those traits that are common to the myths and folk-tales of diverse peoples and races are the fundamental elements of mythology, and that our real problem is the discovery of the origin of those most widely spread.

It would seem that much of the conflict of current opinion is due to our failure to keep distinctly apart the two lines of inquiry here characterized, — the one, the investigation into the history of tales; the other, the investigation of the origin of traditions or ideas common to many or all mythologies.

III   Dissemination of Folk-Tales

Our first problem deals with the development of modern folk-tales. During the last twenty years the tendency of American investigators has been to disregard the problem of the earliest history of American myths and tales, and to gain an insight into their recent growth. The first step in an inductive study of the development of folk-tales must be an investigation of the processes that may be observed at the present time, and these should form the basis of inquiries into earlier history. Therefore stress has been laid upon the accumulation of many variants of the same tale from different parts of the country, and these have been made the basis of a few theoretical studies.

Not more than twenty-five years ago Daniel G. Brinton asserted that the similarity of Iroquois and Algonquian mythologies was due to the sameness of the action of the human mind, not to transmission. Since that time such a vast amount of material has been accumulated, proving definite lines of transmission, that there is probably no investigator now who would be willing to defend Brinton's position. A detailed study of transmission among the tribes of the North Pacific coast, and a brief summary of the similarities between Navaho and Northwest American folk-tales, were followed by many annotated collections containing parallels from many parts of America. The importance of dissemination was brought out incidentally in Dr. Lowie's investigation on the test-theme in American mythology and by Dr. Waterman's study of the explanatory element in American folk-tales.

Two rules have been laid down as necessary for cautious progress.[2]

First, the tale or formula the distribution of which is investigated, and is to be explained as due to historical contact, must be so complex, that an independent origin of the sequence of non-related elements seems to be improbable. An example of such a tale is the Magic Flight, in which we find a combination of the following elements: flight from an ogre; objects thrown over the shoulder forming obstacles, — first a stone, which becomes a mountain; then a comb, which becomes a thicket; lastly a bottle of oil, which becomes a body of water. It is hardly conceivable that such a group of unrelated incidents should arise independently in regions far apart.

The second rule is, that for a satisfactory proof of dissemination, continuous distribution is required. The simpler the tale, the greater must be our insistence on this condition. It must of course be admitted that simple tales may be disseminated over wide areas. It must also be admitted that in all probability tales known at one time have been forgotten, so that intermediate links in an area of geographically continuous distribution may have been lost. This, however, does not touch upon our methodological point of view. We desire to find uncontestable evidence of transmission, not alone the possibility or plausibility of transmission; and for this purpose our safeguards must be insisted on.

The study of the distribution of themes requires a ready means for their identification, and this necessitates a brief terminology: hence the attempts to establish a series of catch-words by means of which tales and incidents may readily be recognized. Frobenius, Ehrenreich, Lowie, and Kroeber[3] have contributed to this undertaking; but an elaboration of a satisfactory system of catch-words requires more penetrating study of the tales than those that have hitherto been made. Certain results, however, have been obtained from the study of the distribution of themes. The material that has been collected suggests that, as inquiry progresses, we may be able to discern various areas of distribution of themes. Some of these are known over large portions of the continent. For instance, the story of the Bungling Host — of a person who is fed by the magic powers of his host, who tries to imitate him and fails ignominiously — occurs from New Mexico on, all over the eastern part of North America, and is lacking only, as it seems, in California and on the Arctic coast. Similar to this is the distribution of the story of the Rolling Rock, which pursues an offending person, and pins him down until he is finally freed by animals that break the rock. Perhaps this does not extend quite so far north and south as the former story. While the Bungling-Host tale is known on the coast of British Columbia, the Rolling-Rock story does not reach the Pacific coast, although related tales are found in parts of California. Still other tales are essentially confined to the Great Plains, but have followed the trade-routes that lead to the Pacific Ocean, and are found in isolated spots from British Columbia southward to California. To this group belongs the story of the Dancing Birds, which are told by a trickster to dance with closed eyes, and then are killed by him, a few only escaping. Another story of this group is the characteristic Deluge story, which tells of the creation of a new earth by diving animals. During the Flood the animals save themselves on a raft. One after another dives, until finally the muskrat brings up some mud, of which the new earth is created. This story is known in a very wide area around the Great Lakes, and occurs in recognizable form on a few points along the Pacific coast. To this same group belongs the tale of the Star Husbands. Two girls sleep out of doors, see two stars, and each wishes one of these for her husband. When they awake the following morning, their wish is fulfilled. One of the stars is a beautiful man, the other is ugly. Eventually the girls return to earth. This tale is known from Nova Scotia, across the whole width of the continent, to the Western plateaus, Vancouver Island, and Alaska. Still other stories of the same area are those of the Blood-Clot Boy, who originates from some blood that has been thrown away, and who becomes a hero; the story of Thrown-Away, the name for a boy who is cast out, brought up in a magic way, and who becomes a hero; the Snaring of the Sun; and many others.

The second group has a decided Western distribution, and is found extensively on the Plateaus and on the Pacific coast; although some of the stories have also crossed the mountains, and are found on the Eastern Plains. To this group belongs the story of the Eye-Juggler; that is, of an animal that plays ball with his eyes, and finally loses them; of the ascent to the sky by means of a ladder of arrows; and the story of the contest between Beaver and Porcupine, Beaver inviting Porcupine to swim, while Porcupine invites Beaver to climb.[4]

A third area of distribution may be recognized in the peculiar migration legends of the Southwest and of the Mississippi basin, which have no analogues in the northern part of the continent.

The distribution of themes becomes the more interesting, the more carefully the tales are considered. Thus the widely spread of the Bungling Host may be divided into a number of types, according to the tricks performed by the host. On the North Pacific coast occurs the trick of knocking the ankle, out of which salmon-eggs flow; on the Plateaus, the piercing of some part of the body with a sharp instrument and pulling out food; on the

Plains, the transformation of bark into food; and almost everywhere, the diving for fish from a perch.[5] There is little doubt that as collection proceeds, and the distribution of themes can be studied in greater detail, the areas of dissemination will stand out more clearly than now. The greatest difficulty at present lies in the absence of satisfactory material from the Southeast and from the Pueblo region.

Ehrenreich[6] has attempted to extend these comparisons to South America and to the Old World; but many of his cases do not conform to the methodological conditions previously outlined, and are therefore not quite convincing, although I readily admit the probability of dissemination between the southern and northern half of the continent. I am even more doubtful in regard to the examples given by Dähnhardt[7] and Frobenius.[8] If Dähnhardt finds, for instance, that we have in North America a group of tales relating how Raven liberated the sun, which was enclosed in a seamless round receptacle, that the Chukchee tell of Raven holding the sun under his tongue, that the Magyar tell a similar incident of one of the heroes of their fairy-tales, it does not follow that these are the same tales. The Chukchee and Magyar tales are alike, and I should be inclined to search for intermediate links. Among the Chukchee the story has been inserted in the Raven cycle, and it seems probable that the prominence of the raven in their folk-lore is due to Northwest-coast influences, or that it developed at the same time in northeastern Asia and northwestern America. However, I do not think that the two tales are sufficiently alike to allow us to claim that they have the same origin.

Still more is this true of the alleged relations between Melanesian and American tales. Frobenius, who makes much of these similarities, calls attention, for instance, to the motive of the arrow-ladder, which occurs in Melanesia and in Northwest America. It seems to me that the idea of a chain of arrows reaching from the earth to the sky is not so complicated as to allow us to assume necessarily a single origin. Furthermore, the distance between the two countries in which the element occurs is so great, and there is apparently such a complete absence of intermediate links, that I am not convinced of the sameness of the elements. Even the apparently complicated story of the Invisible Fish-Hook, which was recorded by Codrington, and which is common to Melanesia and Northwest America, does not convince me. The fisherman's hook is taken away by a shark; the fisherman loses his way, reaches the shark's village, where a person lies sick and cannot be cured by the shamans. The fisherman sees his hook in the sick person's mouth, takes it out, and thus cures him. In this formula we have the widely-spread idea that the weapons of spirits are invisible to mortals, and *vice versa*; and the story seems to develop without difficulty wherever this idea prevails. The markedly close psychological connection of the incidents of the tale sets if off clearly from the Magic Flight referred to before, in which the single elements are quite without inner connection. Therefore the sameness of the formula, connected with the lack of intermediate geographical links, makes the evidence for historical connection inconclusive.

I repeat, the question at issue is not whether these tales may be related, but whether their historical connection has been proved.

Transmission between the Old World and the New has been proved by the occurence of a set of complex stories in both. The most notable among these are the Magic Flight (or obstacle myth), the story of the Island of Women (or of the toothed vagina), and that of the killing of the ogre whose head is infested with frogs instead of lice. The area of well-established Old-World influence upon the New World is confined to that part of North America limited in the southeast by a line running approximately from California to Labrador. Southeast of this line, only weak indications of this influence are noticeable. Owing to the restriction of the tales to a small part of America, and to their wide distribution in the Old World, we must infer that the direction of dissemination was from the west to the east, and not conversely. Every step forward from this well-established basis should be taken with the greatest caution. . . .

I have not considered in the preceding remarks the recent flux of foreign themes from Europe and Africa. A fairly large amount of European folk-lore material has been introduced into the United States and Canada. Among those Indian tribes, however, that still retain fresh in their memory the aboriginal mode of life, these tales are sharply set off from the older folk-tales. They are recognizable by distinctiveness of character, although their foreign origin is not always known to the natives. They belong largely to the fairy-tales of Europe, and most of them were probably carried to America by the French voyageurs. It is only in recent times that a more extensive amount of material of this kind has been accumulated.[9] Favorite stories of this group are "John the Bear," "Seven-Heads," and a few others of similar type.

In Nova Scotia and Quebec, where contact between the European settlers and the Indians has continued for a long period, the number of European elements in aboriginal folk-lore is much larger. They may have been derived in part from Scotch and Irish sources. Still the distinction between the types of aboriginal and foreign tales is fairly clear, even to the minds of the narrators.

In the Southern States, where a large Negro population has come into contact with the Indians, we find introduced into the aboriginal folk-lore, in addition to the fairy tales, animal tales foreign to America. Since many of these are quite similar in type to aboriginal American folk-tales, the line of demarcation between the two groups has tended to become lost. Some of the foreign details have been incorporated in the folk-lore of the Southeastern Indians, and their distinct origin has been forgotten by them. A similar assimilation of the animal tale has been observed in isolated cases in other districts, as that of a La Fontaine fable among the Shuswap of British Columbia, and perhaps of a European folk-tale among the Zuñi. For this reason we may conclude that the complete amalgamation is due to their identity of type. . . .

IV   Characteristics of Mythological Areas

We return to the discussion of the aboriginal lore as it is found in our times, disregarding those elements that can be proved to be of modern introduction. The material collected in different parts of the continent presents marked differences in type. These are due to several causes. In some cases the themes contained in the tales are distinct; in others the actors are different; the point of the stories shows certain local peculiarities; or the formal structure possesses local characteristics. Among these features, attention has been directed particularly to the first three, although no systematic attempts have been made to cover the whole field.

In the preceding chapter I have discussed the dissemination of tales, and at the same time pointed out that they are not evenly distributed over the whole continent. It does not seem possible to give a definite characterization of those themes that form the constituent elements of the folk-tales of these larger areas.

The actors that appear as the heroes of our tales differ greatly in various parts of the continent. While in Alaska and northern British Columbia the Raven is the hero of a large cycle of tales, we find that farther to the south, first the Mink, then the Bluejay, takes his place. On the Western Plateaus Coyote is the hero, and in many parts of the Plains the Rabbit is an important figure. In other regions, heroes of human form appear. These occur sporadically along the Pacific coast, but in much more pronounced form on the Great Plains and in the Mackenzie area, without, however, superceding entirely the animal heroes. Owing to this difference in the form of the actors, we find the same tales told of Rabbit, Coyote, Raven, Mink, and Bluejay, but also of such beings as culture-heroes or human tricksters among the Algonquin, Sioux, Ponca, and Blackfeet. There is almost no limit to these transfers from one actor to another. The story of the Bungling Host is, for instance, told of all these beings, and other themes are transferred from one to another with equal ease. Analogous transfers occur frequently in the case of other figures that are less prominent in the folk-tales. The sun is snared by Mouse, Rabbit, or beings in human form. Gull and a person appear as owners of the sun. Kingfisher, Water-Ouzel, or other birds, play the rôle of hosts. Chicken-Hawk, Gopher, Deer, or Eagle steal the fire. Fox, Opossum, or Rabbit dupe Coyote. In part, the animals that appear in tales are determined by the particular fauna of each habitat; but, even aside from this, numerous transfers occur. In how far these changes may be characteristic, aside from the changes of the main figure, has not yet been determined.

The third point in regard to which the materials of various areas show characteristic differences is their formal composition; for the impression that certain types of stories are characteristic of definite areas is not due mainly to the selection of themes that they contain, and of the actors, but to the fundamental ideas underlying the plots, and to their general composition — if I may use the term, to their literary style. . . .

In a way we may speak of certain negative features that are common to the tales of the whole American continent. The moralizing fable, which is so widely spread in Europe, Asia, and Africa, seems to be entirely absent in America. Professor Van Gennep has claimed that all primitive folk-tales must be moral.[10] This is true in so far as the plots of all primitive folk-tales find a happy solution, and must therefore conform to those standards that are accepted by the narrators.[11] This, however, is not the same as the moralizing point of the story, that is the peculiar character of the fable of the Old World. Although the American tale may be and has been applied by Indians for inculcating moral truths, this tendency is nowhere part and parcel of the tale. Examples of the moral application of a tale have been given by Swanton[12] from Alaska, and by Miss Fletcher[13] from the Pawnee. In none of these, however, has the tale itself the moral for its point. It is rather a more or less far-fetched application of the tale made by the narrator. The tale can therefore not be classed with the African, Asiatic, and European animal tales, the whole point of which is the moral that is expressed at the end. It seems to me very likely that the almost complete absence of proverbs among the American natives is connected with the absence of the moralizing literary form, which among the Indians seems to be confined to the art of the orator who sometimes conveys morals in the form of metaphoric expression.

The attempt has been made to characterize one or two areas according to peculiarities of literary form. It is perhaps easiest thus to describe the folk-tales of the Eskimo, which differ from other American tales in that the fanciful animal tale with its transformation elements does not predominate.[14]

In other cases, however, the formal elements can be given clear expression only when the tales are grouped in a number of classes. Most important among these are the serious origin tales, the trickster tales, and tales the incidents of which develop entirely or essentially in human society. As soon as this division is made, it is found possible to distinguish a certain number of well-defined types.

We shall take up first of all the origin myths. It is a common trait of most American origin myths that they deal with the transition from a mythological period to the modern age, brought about by a number of disconnected incidents, sometimes centering pre-eminently around the acts of one particular figure, sometimes by incidents distributed over a mass of tales that have not even the actions of one being as their connecting link. On the whole, the mythical world, earth, water, fire, sun and moon, summer and winter, animals and plants, are assumed as existing, although they may not possess their present forms, or be kept and jealously guarded in some part of the world inaccessible to the human race. We are dealing, therefore, essentially with tales of expeditions in which, through cunning or force, the phenomena of nature are obtained for the use of all living beings; and with tales of transformation in which animals, land and water, obtain their present forms. We do not find in North America the genealogical sequence of worlds, one generated by another, that is so characteristic of Polynesia. The idea of creation, in the sense of a projection into objective existence of a world that pre-existed in the mind of a creator, is also almost entirely foreign to the American race. The thought that our world had a previous existence only as an idea in the mind of a superior being, and became objective reality by a will, is not the form in which the Indian conceives his mythology. There was no unorganized chaos preceding the origin of the world. Everything has always been in existence in objective form somewhere. This is even true of ceremonials and inventions, which were obtained by instruction given by beings of another world. There is, however, one notable exception to this general rule, for many California tribes possess origin tales which are expressions of the will of a powerful being who by his thoughts established the present order. . . .

The statement here made needs some further restriction, inasmuch as we have quite a number of tales explaining the origin of animals and of mankind as the results of activities of superior beings. Thus we have stories which tell how men or food-animals were fashioned by the Creator out of wood, stone, clay, or grass; that they were given life, and thus became the beings that we see now. It is important to note that in these cases it is not a mere action of a creative will, but always the transformation of a material object, which forms the essential feature of the tale. Furthermore, I believe it can be shown that many of these tales do not refer to a general creation of the whole species, but that they rather supply a local or temporary want. For instance, the Creator carves salmon out of wood, but they are not fit to serve his purpose. This does not imply that no salmon were in existence before that time, for we hear later on in the same cycle that the real salmon were obtained by a party that captured the fish in the mythical salmon country. The Creator, therefore, had to make artificially an object resembling the real salmon that existed somewhere else, but his unsuccessful attempt resulted in the origin of a new species. . . .

There are also marked differences not only in the manner in which origins are accounted for, but also in the extent to which these elements enter into tales. While in a large collection of Eskimo stories only from thirty-five to fifty phenomena are explained, the number is infinitely greater on the Western Plateaus. In the essay quoted before, Waterman states that ninety-eight Eskimo tales contain thirty-four explanations, while in a hundred and eighty-seven Plateau tales, two hundred and twenty-five explanations are found. This quite agrees with the impression that we receive by the perusal of tales. In some cases almost every tale is an origin tale, in others these are few and far between. For the determination of this element as characteristic of various areas, we require, of course, extensive collections, such as are available from a few tribes only. It is particularly necessary that the tales should not be gathered from a one-sided standpoint, — as, for instance, for a study of celestial myths or of animal tales, — because this might give an entirely erroneous impression. That typical differences exist can be determined even now. It is particularly striking that in some regions, as on the Western Plateaus, the explanatory element appears often as the basis of the plot; while other tribes, like the Eskimo, have a number of very trifling origin stories almost resembling animal fables. If these are excluded from the whole mass of explanatory tales, the contrast between various groups in regard to the importance of the explanatory element becomes particularly striking.

Marked differences occur also in the selection of the phenomena that are explained. Among the southern Caddoan tribes the explanation of stars preponderates. Among the Plateau tribes the largest number of tales refer to characteristics of animals. Among the Blackfeet and Kwakiutl the mass of tales relate to ceremonials. Among the Southern tribes a great number are cosmogonic tales.

Related to this is also the more or less systematic grouping of the tales in larger cycles. It is but natural that in all those cases in which traits of animals form the subject of explanatory tales, the tales must be anecdotal in character and disconnected, even if one person should form the center of the cycle. It is only when the origin tales are brought together in such a way that the mythological concepts develop into a systematic whole, that the origin stories assume the form of a more complex cosmogony. This point may be illustrated by the long record of the origin legend of Alaska collected by Swanton,[15] in which obviously a thoughtful informant has tried to assemble the whole mass of explanatory tales in the form of a connected myth. Critical study shows not only the entire lack of cohesion of the parts, but also the arbitrary character of the arrangement, which is contradicted by all other versions from the same region. Unifying elements are completely missing, since there is no elaboration of a cosmogonic concept that forms the background of the tale. . . .

The contrast between the disconnected origin tales and the elaborate cycles is most striking when we compare the disjointed tales of the Northwest with the long connected origin myths of the East as we find them among the Iroquois and Algonquin, and even more when we place them side by side with the complex myths from the Southwest. . . .

On this basis a number of types of origins may be distinguished, — first, origins due to accidental, unintentional occurrences; second, the formation of the present order according to the decisions of a council of animals; third, development due to the actions of two antagonistic beings, the one benevolent and wishing to make everything easy for man, the other one counteracting these intentions and creating the difficulties and hardships of life; as a fourth type we may distinguish the culture-hero tales, the narrative of the migration of men or deities who wander about and set things right. At the present time it is hardly possible to group the origin stories quite definitely from these points of view. In the extreme north the disorganized tale seems to prevail. On the plateaus of the northern United States and in part of the plains, the animal council plays an important rôle. California seems to be the principal home of the antagonistic formula, although this idea is also prominent among some Eastern tribes; and culture-hero tales appear locally on the North Pacific coast, but more prominently in the south.

We shall next turn to a consideration of the trickster tales. In a sense these have been referred to in the previous group, because many of the trickster tales are at the same time origin tales. If, for instance, Coyote tricks the birds by letting them dance near the fire, and their red eyes are accounted for in this way, we have here an origin story and a trickster tale. At present we are not concerned with this feature, but rather with the consideration of the question whether certain features can be found that are characteristic of the whole cycle as developed in various regions. First of all, it seems of interest to note the degree to which the whole group of tales is developed. It is absent among the Eskimo, moderately developed in California, probably not very prominent in the aboriginal myths of the Southwest, but most prolific on the Northwest coast, the Northern Plateaus, and in the East. Whether it is a marked feature of the Athapascan area cannot be decided at present. Some of the heros of the trickster cycle have been noted before. Raven, Mink, Bluejay, on the Northwest coast; Coyote on the Plateaus; Old Man among the Blackfeet; Ishtiniki among the Ponca; Inktumni among the Assiniboin; Manabosho, Wishahka, and Glooscap among various Algonquin tribes, — are some of the prominent figures. Although a complete list of all the trickster incidents has not been made, it is fairly clear that a certain number are found practically wherever a trickster cycle occurs. I have already stated that one group of these tales is confined to the Western Plateaus, another one to the northern half of the continent. At present it is more important to note, that, besides these widely distributed elements, there seem to be in each area a number of local tales that have no such wide distribution. The characteristics of the tales appear most clearly when the whole mass of trickster tales in each region is studied. A comparison of the Raven, Mink, and Bluejay cycles is instructive. The background of the Raven stories is everywhere the greedy hunger of Raven. Most of the Raven tales treat of Raven's endeavors to get plenty of food without effort; and the adventures relate to his attempts to cheat people out of their provisions and to the punishment doled out to him by those who have suffered from his tricks. Quite different in type are the Mink stories. Here we find almost throughout an erotic background. Mink tries to get possession of girls and of the wives of his friends. Occasionally only a trick based on his fondness for sea-eggs is introduced. The Bluejay adventures may be characterized in still another way. Generally it is his ambition to outdo his betters in games, on the hunt or in war, that brings him into trouble or induces him to win by trickery. He has neither a pronounced erotic nor a notably greedy character. The tricks of the Plateau cycles are not so easy to characterize, because the deeds of Coyote partake of all the characteristics just mentioned. Coyote attempts to get food, and his erotic adventures are fairly numerous; but on the whole these two groups are considerably outnumbered by tricks in which he tries to outdo his rivals.

The identification of trickster and transformer is a feature which deserves special notice. I have called attention to the fact — borne out by most of the mythologies in which trickster and culture-hero appear as one person — that the benefactions bestowed by the culture-hero are not given in an altruistic spirit, but that they are means by which he supplies his own needs.[16] Even in his heroic achievements he remains a trickster bent upon the satisfaction of his own desires. This feature may be observed distinctly in the Raven cycle of the Northwest coast. He liberates the sun, not because he pities mankind, but because he desires it; and the first use he tries to make of it is to compel fishermen to give him part of their catch. He gets the fresh water because he is thirsty, and unwillingly spills it all over the world while he is making his escape. He liberates the fish because he is hungry, and gets the tides in order to be able to gather shellfish. Similar observations may be made in other mythological personages that embody the qualities of trickster and culture-hero. Wherever the desire to benefit mankind is a more marked trait of the cycle, there are generally two distinct persons, — one the trickster, the other the culture-hero. Thus the culture-hero of the Pacific coast gives man his arts, and is called "the one who sets things right." He is not a trickster, but all his actions have a distinct bearing upon the establishment of the modern order. Perhaps the most characteristic feature of these culture-hero tales is their lack of detail. Many are bare statements of the fact that something was different from the way it is now. The hero performs some very simple act, and ordains that these conditions shall be changed. It is only when the culture-hero concept rises to greater heights, as it does in the South, that these tales acquire greater complexity.

Here may also be mentioned the animal tales that belong neither to the trickster cycle nor to the origin tales. It is hardly possible to give a general characterization of these, and to distinguish local types, except in so far as the importance of the tale is concerned. In the Arctic and the adjoining parts of the continent, we find a considerable number of trifling animal stories that have hardly any plot. They are in part merely incidents descriptive of some characteristic of the animal. Some of these trifling stories are given the form of origin tales by making the incidents the cause from which arise certain bodily characteristics of the animals, but this is not often the case. In the more complex tales which occur all over the continent, the animals act according to the characteristic modes of life. Kingfisher dives, Fox is a swift runner, Beaver a good swimmer who lives in ponds, etc. Their character corresponds to their apparent behavior. Grizzly-Bear is overbearing and ill-tempered, Bluejay and Coyote are tricky. A sharp individual characterization, however, is not common.

We shall now turn to the third group of tales, those dealing with human society. These can only in part be characterized in the manner adopted heretofore. Some of their local color is due to the peculiar distribution of incidents which has been discussed before. On the whole, however, it is rather the plot as a whole that is characteristic. This may be exemplified by the incident of the faithless wife, which occurs all over the continent. The special form of the plot of the woman who has an animal or supernatural being or some object for a lover, whose actions are discovered by her husband who disguises himself in her garments and who deceives and kills the paramour and later on his wife, is most characteristic of the Northern area, reaching from northeastern Siberia and the Eskimo district southward to the Mississippi basin.

Individualization of form may also be illustrated by the widely distributed incident of the deserted child who rescues his people when they are in distress. The special form of the plot — in which the child makes his parents and uncles ashamed, is deserted and then helped by animals that send him larger and larger game until many houses are filled with provisions, and in which the people offer him their daughters as wives — is characteristic only of the North Pacific coast. On the Plains the deserted boy escapes by the help of his protector, and becomes a powerful hunter. The analysis of the plots has not been carried through in such detail as to allow us to do more than point out the existence of characteristic types in definite areas.

Much more striking in this group of tales is their cultural setting, that reflects the principal occupation and interests of the people. I have attempted to give a reconstruction of the life of the Tsimshian, basing my data solely on the recorded mythology. As might perhaps be expected, all the essential features of their life — the village, its houses, the sea and land hunt, social relations — appear distinctly mirrored in this picture. It is, however, an incomplete picture. Certain aspects of life do not appeal to the imagination of the story-tellers, and are therefore not specifically expressed, not even implied in the setting of the story. . . .

I have shown among the Kwakiutl the plot of most stories is the authentication of the privileges of a social division or of a secret society. Wissler has brought out a similar point in his discussion of Blackfoot tales,[17] many of which seem to explain ritualistic origins, the rituals themselves being in part dramatic interpretations of the narratives. The Pawnee and Pueblo stories reflect in the same way the ritualistic interests of the people. In this sense we may perhaps say without exaggeration that the folk-tales of each tribe are markedly set off from those of all other tribes, because they give a faithful picture of the mode of life and of the chief interests that have prevailed among the people during the last few generations. These features appear most clearly in the study of their hero-tales. It is therefore particularly in this group that an analogy between the folk-tale and the modern novel is found. The tales dealing with the feats of men are more plastic than those relating to the exploits of animals, although the animal world, to the mind of the Indian, was not so very different from our own. . . .

In the human tale the narrator gives us a certain amount of characterization of individuals, of their emotions, — like pity and love, — of their courage and cowardice, on which rests the plot of the story. The development of individual character does not proceed beyond this point. We do not find more than schematic types, which are, however, forms that occur in the every-day life of the people. On the contrary, the origin and trickster cycles deal with types that are either so impersonal that they do not represent any individual, or are merely the personification of greed, amorousness, or silly ambition. Wherever there is individuality of character, it is rather the expression of the apparent nature of the personified animal, not the character that fits particularly well into human society.

Considering the characteristic of the human tale as a whole, we may say that in all probability future study will show that its principal characteristics may be well defined by the cultural areas of the continent. How close this correspondence may be remains to be seen. The problem is an interesting and important one, because it is obvious that the tales, while readily adaptable, do not follow all the aspects of tribal life with equal ease, and a certain lack of adjustment may become apparent. This will serve as a valuable clue in the further study of the development of tribal customs and of the history of the distribution of tales. I have pointed out the probability of such incomplete adjustment in the case of the Kwakiutl, and Wissler has made a similar point in regard to the Blackfeet.

While much remains to be done in the study of the local characteristics of folk-tales in regard to the points referred to, a still wider field of work is open in all that concerns their purely formal character, and I can do no more than point out the necessity of study of this subject. On the basis of the material hitherto collected, we are hardly in a position to speak of the literary form of the tales. I am inclined to count among their formal traits the typical repetition of the same incident that is found among many tribes; or the misfortunes that befall a number of brothers, until the last one is successful in his undertaking. These have the purpose of exciting the interest and leading the hearer to anticipate with increased eagerness the climax. Quite different from this is a device used by the Tsimshian, who lead up to a climax by letting an unfortunate person be helped in a very insignificant way. The help extended to him becomes more and more potent, until the climax is reached, in which the sufferer becomes the fortunate possessor of power and wealth.

Another artistic device that is used by many tribes to assist in the characterization of the actors is the use of artificial changes in speech. Thus among the Kwakiutl the Mink cannot pronounce the sound *ts*, among the

Kutenai Coyote cannot pronounce *s*, among the Chinook the animals speak different dialects. Dr. Sapir[18] has called attention to the development of this feature among the Shoshoni and Nootka. . . .

V Recent History of American Folk-Tales

Our considerations allow us to draw a number of inferences in regard to the history of American folk-tales. We have seen there is no tribe in North America whose tales can be considered as purely local products uninfluenced by foreign elements. We have found that some tales are distributed over almost the whole continent, others over more or less extended parts of the country. We have seen, furthermore, that the tales of each particular area have developed a peculiar literary style, which is an expression of the mode of life and of the form of thought of the people; that the actors who appear in the various tales are quite distinct in different parts of the country; and that the associated explanatory elements depend entirely upon the different styles of thought. In one case the tales are used to explain features of the heavenly bodies; in others, forms of the land, of animals or of rituals, according to the chief interests of the people. It is fully borne out by the facts brought forward, that actors, explanatory tendencies, cultural setting, and literary form, of all modern American tales, have undergone constant and fundamental changes. If we admit this, it follows that the explanations that are found in modern tales must be considered almost entirely as recent adaptations of the story, not as its integral parts; and neither they nor the names of the actors reveal to us what the story may have been in its original form — if we may speak of such a form. Everything appears rather in flux. For this reason the attempt to interpret the history of the modern tale as a reflection of the observation of nature is obviously not justifiable. The data of American folk-lore do not furnish us with a single example that would prove that this process has contributed to the modern development of folk-tales. It would almost seem safer to say that the creative power that has manifested itself in modern times is very weak, and that the bulk of our tales consist of combinations and recombinations of old themes. At the same time the marked differentiation in the style of composition shows that the mainspring in the formation of the modern tale must have been an artistic one. We observe in them not only the result of the play of the imagination with favorite themes, but also the determination of the form of imaginative processes by antecedent types, which is the characteristic trait of artistic production of all times and of all races and peoples. I am therefore inclined to consider the folk-tale primarily and fundamentally as a work of primitive art. The explanatory element would then appear, not as an expression of native philosophy, but rather as an artistic finishing touch required for the tale wherever the art of story-telling demands it. Instead of being the mainspring of the story, it becomes in one case a stylistic embellishment, while in another it is required to give an impressive setting. In either case the occurrence of the explanation cannot be reduced to a rationalizing activity of primitive man.

In a sense these results of our studies of American folk-lore are unsatisfactory, because they lead us only to recognize a constant play with old themes, variations in explanatory elements attached to them, and the tendency to develop various types of artistic style. They do not bring us any nearer to an understanding of the origin of the themes, explanations, and styles. If we want to carry on our investigation into a remoter past, it may be well to ask, first of all, how long the present development of mosaics of different style may have continued; whether there is any proof that some tribes have been the originators from whom others derived much of their lore; and whether we have any evidence of spontaneous invention that may have influenced large territories.

Since historical data are not available, we are confined to the application of an inductive method of inquiry. We may ask how large a portion of the folk-tales of a tribe are its sole property, and how many they share with other tribes. If a comparison of this kind should show a large number of elements that are the sole property of one tribe, while others have only little that is their exclusive property, it would perhaps seem justifiable to consider the former as originators, the latter as recipients; and we may conclude either that their own older folk-tales have disappeared or that they possessed very few only. It is not easy to form a fair judgment of the originality of the folk-tales of each tribe in the manner here suggested, because the collections are unequally complete, and because collectors or narrators are liable to give preference to one particular kind of tale to the exclusion of others. It is always difficult to base inferences on the apparent absence of certain features that may be discovered, after all, to exist; and this seems particularly difficult in our case. Still it might be possible to compare at least certain definite cycles that have been collected fairly fully, and that occur with equal exuberance in various areas; as, for instance, the trickster cycles of the Plains. On the whole, I gain the impression that not a single tribe appears as possessing considerably more originality than another. . . .

VI Mythological Concepts in Folk-Tales

Our consideration of American folk-tales has so far dealt with their later history. The result of this inquiry will help us in the treatment of the question, What may have been the origin of these tales? It is obvious that in an historical inquiry for which no literary record of ancient mythology is available, we must try first of all to establish the processes that are active at the present time. There is no reason for assuming that similar processes should not have been active in earlier times, at least as long as the types of human culture were approximately on the same level as they are now. The art-productions of the Magdalenian period show how far back the beginning of these conditions may be placed; and so far we have no evidence that indicates that the American race as such has ever passed through a time in which its mental characteristics were different from those of modern man. The antiquity of cultural achievement in Mexico, the finds made in ancient shell-heaps, prove that for thousands of years man in America has been in possession of a type of cultural development not inferior to that of the modern, more primitive tribes. It may therefore be inferred that the processes that are going on now have been going on for a very long period. Constant diffusion of the elements of stories, and elaboration of new local types of composition, must have been the essential characteristic of the history of folk-tales. On the whole, invention of new themes must have been rare; and where it occurred, it was determined by the prevailing type of composition. . . .

Methodologically the proof of such independent origin of similar phenomena offers much more serious difficulties than a satisfactory proof of historical connection. The safeguards that must be demanded here are analogous to those previously described. As we demanded before, as criteria of historical connection, actual evidence of transmission, or at least clear proof of the existence of lines of transmission and of the identity of subject-matter, so we must now call for proof of the lack of historical connection or of the lack of identity of phenomena. Obviously these proofs are much more difficult to give. If we were to confine ourselves to the evidence contained in folk-tales, it might be an impossible task to prove in a convincing manner the independent origin of tales, because the possibility of the transmission of a single idea always exists. It is only on the basis of our knowledge of the limitations of areas over which inventions, art-forms, and other cultural achievements have spread, that we can give a basis for safer conclusions. On account of the sharp contrast between America and the Old World in the material basis of civilization, and the restriction of imported material to the northwestern part of the continent, to which we have already referred, we are safe in assuming that similar cultural traits that occurred in pre-Columbian time in the southern parts of the two continental areas are of independent origin. In more restricted areas it is all but impossible to give satisfactory proof of the absence of contact.

More satisfactory are our means for determining the lack of identity of apparently analogous phenomena. Historical inquiry shows that similar ideas do no always arise from the same preceding conditions; that either their suggested identity does not exist or the similarity of form is due to an assimilation of phenomena that are distinct in origin, but develop under similar social stress. When a proof of this type can be given, and the psychological processes involved are clearly intelligible, there is good reason for assuming an independent origin of the ideas.

A case in point is presented by the so-called "sacred" numbers. I am not inclined to look at these primarily as something of transcendental mystic value; it seems to me more plausible that the concept developed from the aesthetic values of rhythmic repetition. Its emotional effect is obviously inherent in the human mind; and the artistic use of repetition may be observed wherever the sacred number exists, and where it is not only used in reference to distinct objects, but also in rhythmic repetitions of tunes, words, elements of literary compositions and of actions. Thus the difference in favorite rhythms may account for the occurrence of different sacred numbers; and since the preference for a definite number is a general psychological phenomenon, their occurrence is not necessarily due to historical transmission, but may be considered as based on general psychological factors. The differences between the sacred numbers would then appear as different manifestations of this mental reaction. In the same way the idea of revival of the dead, or of the power to escape unseen, is a simple reaction of the imagination, and is not due, wherever it occurs, to a common historical source. These ideas develop naturally into similar incidents in stories that occur in regions widely apart, and must be interpreted as the effect of psychological processes that bring about a convergent development in certain aspects of the tales. An instructive example is presented by the tales of the origin of death. The idea of the origin of death is readily accounted for by the desire to see the dead alive again, which often must have been formulated as the wish that there should be no death. The behavior of man in all societies proves the truth of this statement. Thus the imaginative processes are set in motion which construct a deathless world, and from this initial point develop the stories of the introduction of death in accordance with the literary types of transformation stories. The mere occurrence of stories of the origin of death — in one place due to the miscarriage of a message conveyed by an animal, in others by a bet or a quarrel between two beings — is not a proof of common origin. This proof requires identity of the stories. We can even understand how, under these conditions, stories of similar literary type may become almost identical in form without having a common origin. Where the line is to be drawn between these two types of development cannot be definitely decided. In extreme cases it will be possible to determine this with a high degree of probability; but a wide range of material will always remain, in which no decision can be made.

The limitation of the application of the historical method described here defines also our attitude towards the Pan-Aryan, and Pan-Babylonian theories. The identification of the elements of different folk-tales made by the adherents of these theories are not acceptable from our methodological standpoint. The proofs of dissemination are not of the character demanded by us. The psychological basis for the assumption of an imaginative unproductiveness of all the races of man, with the exception of one or two, cannot be proved; and the origin of the myth in the manner demanded by the theories does not seem plausible.

The essential problem regarding the ultimate origin of mythologies remains — why human tales are preferably attached to animals, celestial bodies, and other personified phenomena of nature. It is clear enough that personification makes the transfer possible, and that the distinctness and individualization of species of animals and of personified phenomena set them off more clearly as characters of a tale than the undifferentiated members of mankind. It seems to me, however, that the reason for their preponderance in the tales of most tribes of the world has not been adequately given.

Notes

1. Wilhelm Wundt, *Völkerpsychologie*, v. 2, pt. 3 (Leipzig, 1909) p. 62.

2. See Boas, "Dissemination of Tales Among the Natives of North America," *Journal of American Folklore*, 4 (1891) pp. 13–20; Wundt, *Volkerpsychologie*, v. 2, pt. 3, p. 62; Van Gennep, *La Formation de Légendes* (1910) p. 49.

3. Leo Frobenius, *Im Zeitalter des Sonnengotts*; Paul Ehrenreich, *Die Mythen und Legenden der Südamerikanischen Urvolker*, pp. 34–59; Robert H. Lowie, "The Test-Theme in North American Mythology," *Journal of American Folklore*, 21 (1908) p. 101; A. L. Kroeber, "Catchwords in American Mythology," *Journal of American Folklore*, 21 (1908) p. 222; see also T. T. Waterman, "The Explanatory Element in the Folk-Tales of the North American Indians," *Journal of American Folklore*, 27 (1914) pp. 1–54.

4. See T. T. Waterman, pp. 1–54.

5. Franz Boas, "Tsimshian Mythology," *Thirty-First Annual Report of the Bureau of American Ethnology* (Washington, DC: GPO, 1916) pp. 694 ff.

6. P. Ehrenreich, *Mythen und Legenden* . . .

7. O. Dähnhardt, *Natursagen*, vols. I–IV, Indexes (Leipzig, 1907–12).

8. Leo Frobenius, *Die Weltanschauung der Naturvolker* (Weimar, 1898).

9. Most of this material has been published in the *Journal of American Folklore*, vol. 25–27 (1912–14); see also Rand, *Legends of the Micmacs* (New York, 1894).

10. Van Gennep, p. 16.

11. Friedrich Panzer, *Märchen, Sage und Dichtung* (Munich, 1905), p. 14.

12. John R. Swanton, "Tlingit Myths and Texts," *Thirty-Ninth Bulletin of the Bureau of American Ethnology* (Washington, DC: GPO, 1909).

13. Alice C. Fletcher, "The Hako," *Twenty-Second Annual Report of the Bureau of American Ethnology*, pt. 2 (Washington, DC: GPO, 1904).

14. Dr. Paul Radin states that the tales from Smith Sound published by Knud Rasmussen show that in Eskimo folklore the animal tale is as marked as among the Indians. This view does not seem to me warranted by the facts. The type of trifling animal tales recorded in Smith Sound has long been known, and differs fundamentally from animal tales common to the rest of the continent (article, "Eskimo," in Hastings' *Cyclopedia of Religions*).

15. Swanton, p. 80 ff.

16. Introduction to James Teit, *Traditions of the Thompson River Indians of British Columbia*, Memoirs of the American Folklore Society, 7 (1898).

17. Clark Wissler and D. C. Duvall, "Mythology of the Blackfoot Indians," *Anthropological Papers, American Museum of Natural History*, 2, p. 12.

18. Edward Sapir, "Song Recitative in Paiute Mythology," *Journal of American Folklore*, 23 (1910), pp. 456–57.

The Structural Study of [Zuni] Myth

Claude Lévi-Strauss*

To invite the mythologist to compare his precarious situation with that of the linguist in the prescientific stage is not enough. As a matter of fact we may thus be led only from one difficulty to another. There is a very good reason why myth cannot simply be treated as language if its specific problems are to be solved; myth *is* language: to be known, myth has to be told; it is a part of human speech. In order to preserve its specificity we must be able to show that it is both the same thing as language, and also something different from it. Here, too, the past experience of linguists may help us. For language itself can be analyzed into things which are at the same time similar and yet different. This is precisely what is expressed in Saussure's distinction between *langue* and *parole*, one being the structural side of language, the other the statistical aspect of it, *langue* belonging to a reversible time, *parole* being non-reversible. If those two levels already exist in language, then a third one can conceivably be isolated.

We have distinguished *langue* and *parole* by the different time referents which they use. Keeping this in mind, we may notice that myth uses a third referent which combines the properties of the first two. On the one hand, a myth always refers to events alleged to have taken place long ago. But what gives the myth an operational value is that the specific pattern described is timeless; it explains the present and the past as well as the future. This can be made clear through a comparison between myth and what appears to have largely replaced it in modern societies, namely, politics. When the historian refers to the French Revolution, it is always as a sequence of past happenings, a non-reversible series of events the remote consequences of which may still be felt at present. But to the French politician, as well as to his followers, the French Revolution is both a sequence belonging to the past — as to the historian — and a timeless pattern which can be detected in the contemporary French social structure and which provides a clue for its interpretation, a lead from which to infer future developments. Michelet, for instance, was a politically minded historian. He describes the French Revolution thus: "That day . . . everything was possible. . . . Future became present . . . that is, no more time, a glimpse of eternity."[1] It is that double structure, altogether historical and ahistorical, which explains how myth, while pertaining to the realm of *parole* and calling for an explanation as such, as well as to that of *langue* in which it is expressed, can also be an absolute entity on a third level which, though it remains linguistic by nature, is nevertheless distinct from the other two.

A remark can be introduced at this point which will help to show the

*Reprinted from *Structural Anthropology*, by Claude Lévi-Strauss, © 1963 by Basic Books, pp. 209–11, 218–31, by permission of the publisher.

originality of myth in relation to other linguistic phenomena. Myth is the part of language where the formula *traduttore, tradittore* reaches its lowest truth value. From that point of view it should be placed in the gamut of linguistic expressions at the end opposite to that of poetry, in spite of all the claims which have been made to prove the contrary. Poetry is a kind of speech which cannot be translated except at the cost of serious distortions; whereas the mythical value of the myth is preserved even through the worst translation. Whatever our ignorance of the language and the culture of the people where it originated, a myth is still felt as a myth by any reader anywhere in the world. Its substance does not lie in its style, its original music, or its syntax, but in the *story* which it tells. Myth is language, functioning on an especially high level where meaning succeeds practically at "taking off" from the linguistic ground on which it keeps on rolling.

To sum up the discussion at this point, we have so far made the following claims: (1) If there is a meaning to be found in mythology, it cannot reside in the isolated elements which enter into the composition of a myth, but only in the way those elements are combined. (2) Although myth belongs to the same category as language, being, as a matter of fact, only part of it, language in myth exhibits specific properties. (3) Those properties are only to be found *above* the ordinary linguistic level, that is, they exhibit more complex features than those which are to be found in any other kind of linguistic expression.

If the above three points are granted, at least as a working hypothesis, two consequences will follow: (1) Myth, like the rest of language, is made up of constituent units. (2) These constituent units presuppose the constituent units present in language when analyzed on other levels — namely, phonemes, morphemes, and sememes — but they, nevertheless, differ from the latter in the same way as the latter differ among themselves; they belong to a higher and more complex order. For this reason, we shall call them *gross constituent units*.

How shall we proceed in order to identify and isolate these gross constituent units or mythemes? We know that they cannot be found among phonemes, morphemes, or sememes, but only on a higher level; otherwise myth would become confused with any other kind of speech. Therefore, we should look for them on the sentence level. The only method we can suggest at this stage is to proceed tentatively, by trial and error, using as a check the principles which serve as a basis for any kind of structural analysis: economy of explanation; unity of solution; and ability to reconstruct the whole from a fragment, as well as later stages from previous ones.

The technique which has been applied so far by this writer consists in analyzing each myth individually, breaking down its story into the shortest possible sentences, and writing each sentence on an index card bearing a number corresponding to the unfolding of the story.

Practically each card will thus show that a certain function is, at a given time, linked to a given subject. Or, to put it otherwise, each gross constituent unit will consist of a *relation*.

However, the above definition remains highly unsatisfactory for two different reasons. First, it is well known to structural linguists that constituent units on all levels are made up of relations, and the true difference between our *gross* units and the others remains unexplained; second, we still find ourselves in the realm of a non-reversible time, since the numbers of the cards correspond to the unfolding of the narrative. Thus the specific character of mythological time, which as we have seen is both reversible and non-reversible, synchronic and diachronic, remains unaccounted for. From this springs a new hypothesis, which constitutes the very core of our argument: The true constituent units of a myth are not the isolated relations but *bundles of such relations,* and it is only as bundles that these relations can be put to use and combined so as to produce a meaning. . . .

[I]t cannot be too strongly emphasized that all available variants should be taken into account. If Freudian comments on the Oedipus complex are a part of the Oedipus myth, then questions such as whether Cushing's version of the Zuni origin myth should be retained or discarded become irrelevant. There is no single "true" version of which all the others are but copies or distortions. Every version belongs to the myth.

The reason for the discouraging results in works on general mythology can finally be understood. They stem from two causes. First, comparative mythologists have selected preferred versions instead of using them all. Second, we have seen that the structural analysis of *one* variant of *one* myth belonging to *one* tribe (in some cases, even *one* village) already requires two dimensions. When we use several variants of the same myth for the same tribe or village, the frame of reference becomes three-dimensional, and as soon as we try to enlarge the comparison, the number of dimensions required increases until it appears quite impossible to handle them intuitively. The confusions and platitudes which are the outcome of comparative mythology can be explained by the fact that multi-dimensional frames of reference are often ignored or are naïvely replaced by two- or three-dimensional ones. Indeed, progress in comparative mythology depends largely on the cooperation of mathematicians who would undertake to express in symbols multi-dimensional relations which cannot be handled otherwise.

To check this theory,[2] an attempt was made from 1952 to 1954 toward an exhaustive analysis of all the known versions of the Zuni origin and emergence myth: Cushing, 1883 and 1896; Stevenson, 1904; Parsons, 1923; Bunzel, 1932; Benedict, 1934. Furthermore, a preliminary attempt was made at a comparison of the results with similar myths in other Pueblo tribes, Western and Eastern. Finally, a test was undertaken with Plains mythology. In all cases, it was found that the theory was sound; light was thrown, not only on North American mythology, but also on a previously unnoticed kind of logical operation, or one known so far only in a wholly different context. The bulk of material which needs to be handled practically at the outset of the work makes it impossible to enter into details, and we shall have to limit ourselves here to a few illustrations. [A simplified chart of the Zuni emergence myth appears on p. 55.]

As the chart indicates, the problem is the discovery of a life-death mediation. For the Pueblo, this is especially difficult; they understand the origin of human life in terms of the model of plant life (emergence from the earth). They share that belief with the ancient Greeks, and it is not without reason that we chose the Oedipus myth as our first example. But in the American Indian case, the highest form of plant life is to be found in agriculture which is periodical in nature, that is, which consists in an alternation between life and death. If this is disregarded, the contradiction appears elsewhere: Agriculture provides food, therefore life; but hunting provides food and is similar to warfare which means death. Hence there are three different ways of handling the problem. In the Cushing version, the difficulty revolves around an opposition between activities yielding an immediate result (collecting wild food) and activities yielding a delayed result—death has to become integrated so that agriculture can exist. Parsons' version shifts from hunting to agriculture, while Stevenson's version operates the other way around. It can be shown that all the differences between these versions can be rigorously correlated with these basic structures.

Thus the three versions describe the great war waged by the ancestors of the Zuni against a mythical population, the Kyanakwe, by introducing into the narrative significant variations which consist (1) in the friendship or hostility of the gods; (2) in the granting of final victory to one camp or the other; (3) in the attribution of the symbolic function to the Kyanakwe, described sometimes as hunters (whose bows are strung with animal sinews) and sometimes as gardeners (whose bows are strung with plant fibers).

CUSHING		PARSONS	STEVENSON	
Gods, Kyanakwe }	allied, use fiber string on their bows (gardeners)	Kyanakwe, alone, use fiber string	Gods, Men }	allied, use fiber string
VICTORIOUS OVER		**VICTORIOUS OVER**	**VICTORIOUS OVER**	
Men, alone, use sinew (until they shift to fiber)		Gods, Men } allied, use sinew string	Kyanakwe, alone, use sinew string	

Since fiber string (agriculture) is always superior to sinew string (hunting), and since (to a lesser extent) the gods' alliance is preferable to their antagonism, it follows that in Cushing's version, men are seen as doubly underprivileged (hostile gods, sinew string); in the Stevenson version, doubly

CHANGE			DEATH
mechanical value of plants (used as ladders to emerge from lower world)	emergence led by Beloved Twins	sibling incest (origin of water)	gods kill children of men (by drowning)
food value of wild plants	migration led by the two Newekwe (ceremonial clowns)		magical contest with People of the Dew (collecting wild food *versus* cultivation)
		brother and sister sacrificed (to gain victory)	
food value of cultivated plants		brother and sister adopted (in exchange for corn)	
periodical character of agricultural work			
			war against the Kyanakwe (gardeners *versus* hunters)
food value of game (hunting)	war led by the two War-Gods		
inevitability of warfare			salvation of the tribe (center of the World found)
		brother and sister sacrificed (to avoid the Flood)	
DEATH			PERMANENCE

privileged (friendly gods, fiber string); while Parsons' version confronts us with an intermediary situation (friendly gods, but sinew strings, since men begin by being hunters). Hence:

OPPOSITIONS	CUSHING	PARSONS	STEVENSON
gods/men	−	+	+
fiber/sinew	−	−	+

Bunzel's version is of the same type as Cushing's from a structural point of view. However, it differs from both Cushing's and Stevenson's, inasmuch as the latter two explain the emergence as the result of man's need to evade his pitiful condition, while Bunzel's version makes it the consequence of a call from the higher powers — hence the inverted sequences of the means resorted to for the emergence: In both Cushing and Stevenson, they go from plants to animals; in Bunzel, from mammals to insects, and from insects to plants.

Among the Western Pueblo the logical approach always remains the same; the starting point and the point of arrival are simplest, whereas the intermediate stage is characterized by ambiguity:

LIFE (= INCREASE)		
(Mechanical) value of the plant kingdom, taking growth alone into account		ORIGINS
Food value of the plant kingdom, limited to wild plants		FOOD-GATHERING
Food value of the plant kingdom, including wild and cultivated plants		AGRICULTURE
Food value of the animal kingdom, limited to animals	*(but there is a contradiction here, owing to the negation of life = destruction, hence:)*	HUNTING
Destruction of the animal kingdom, extended to human beings		WARFARE
DEATH (= DECREASE)		

The fact that contradiction appears in the middle of the dialectical process results in a double set of dioscuric pairs, the purpose of which is to mediate between conflicting terms:

1.	2 divine mes- sengers	2 ceremonial clowns		2 war-gods
2.	homogeneous pair: dioscuri (2 brothers)	siblings (brother and sister)	couple (hus- band and wife)	heterogeneous pair: (grand- mother and grandchild)

We have here combinational variants of the same function in different contexts (hence the war attribute of the clowns, which has given rise to so many queries).

The problem, often regarded as insoluble, vanishes when it is shown that the clowns — gluttons who may with impunity make excessive use of agricultural products — have the same function in relation to food production as the war-gods. (This function appears, in the dialectical process, as *overstepping the boundaries* of hunting, that is, hunting for men instead of for animals for human consumption.)

Some Central and Eastern Pueblos proceed the other way around. They begin by stating the identity of hunting and cultivating (first corn obtained by Game-Father sowing deer-dewclaws), and they try to derive both life and death from that central notion. Then, instead of extreme terms being simple and intermediary ones duplicated as among the Western groups, the extreme terms become duplicated (i.e., the two sisters of the Eastern Pueblo) while a simple mediating term comes to the foreground (for instance, the Poshaiyanne of the Zia), but endowed with equivocal attributes. Hence the attributes of this "messiah" can be deduced from the place it occupies in the time sequence: good when at the beginning (Zuni, Cushing), equivocal in the middle (Central Pueblo), bad at the end (Zia), except in Bunzel's version, where the sequence is reversed as has been shown.

By systematically using this kind of structural analysis it becomes possible to organize all the known variants of a myth into a set forming a kind of permutation group, the two variants placed at the far ends being in a symmetrical, though inverted, relationship to each other.

Our method not only has the advantage of bringing some kind of order to what was previously chaos; it also enables us to perceive some basic logical processes which are at the root of mythical thought.[3] Three main processes should be distinguished.

The trickster of American mythology has remained so far a problematic figure. Why is it that throughout North America his role is assigned practically everywhere to either coyote or raven? If we keep in mind that mythical thought always progresses from the awareness of oppositions toward their resolution, the reason for these choices becomes clearer. We need only assume that two opposite terms with no intermediary always tend to be replaced by two equivalent terms which admit of a third one as a mediator; then one of the polar terms and the mediator become replaced by a new triad, and so on. Thus we have a mediating structure of the following type:

INITIAL PAIR	FIRST TRIAD	SECOND TRIAD
Life		
	Agriculture	
		Herbivorous animals
		Carrion-eating animals (raven; coyote)
	Hunting	
		Beasts of prey
	Warfare	
Death		

The unformulated argument is as follows: carrion-eating animals are like beasts of prey (they eat animal food), but they are also like food-plant producers (they do not kill what they eat). Or to put it otherwise, Pueblo style (for Pueblo agriculture is more "meaningful" than hunting): ravens are to gardens as beasts of prey are to herbivorous animals. But is also clear that herbivorous animals may be called first to act as mediators on the assumption that they are like collectors and gatherers (plant-food eaters), while they can be used as animal food though they are not themselves hunters. Thus we may have mediators of the first order, of the second order, and so on, where each term generates the next by a double process of opposition and correlation.

This kind of process can be followed in the mythology of the Plains, where we may order the data according to the set:

Unsuccessful mediator between Earth and Sky (Star-Husband's wife)

Heterogeneous pair of mediators (grandmother and grandchild)

Semi-homogeneous pair of mediators (Lodge-Boy and Thrown-Away)

While among the Pueblo (Zuni) we have the corresponding set:

Successful mediator between Earth and Sky (Poshaiyanki)

Semi-homogeneous pair of mediators (Uyuyewi and Matsailema)

Homogeneous pair of mediators (the two Ahaiyuta)

On the other hand, correlations may appear on a horizontal axis (this is true even on the linguistic level; see the manifold connotation of the root *pose* in Tewa according to Parsons: coyote, mist, scalp, etc.). Coyote (a carrion-eater) is intermediary between herbivorous and carnivorous just as mist between Sky and Earth; as scalp between war and agriculture (scalp is a war crop); as corn smut between wild and cultivated plants; as garments between "nature" and "culture"; as refuse between village and outside; and as ashes (or soot) between roof (sky vault) and hearth (in the ground). This chain of mediators, if one may call them so, not only throws light on entire parts of North American mythology — why the Dew-God may be at the same time the Game-Master and the giver of raiments and be personified as an "Ash-Boy"; or why scalps are mist-producing; or why the Game-Mother is associated with corn smut; etc. — but it also probably corresponds to a universal way of organizing daily experience. See, for instance, the French for plant smut (*nielle*, from Latin *nebula*); the luck-bringing power attributed in Europe to refuse (old shoe) and ashes (kissing chimney sweeps); and compare the American Ash-Boy cycle with the Indo-European Cinderella: Both are phallic figures (mediators between male and female); masters of the dew and the game; owners of fine raiments; and social mediators (low class marrying into high class); but they are impossible to interpret through recent diffusion, as has been contended, since Ash-Boy and Cinderella are symmetrical but inverted in every detail (while the borrowed Cinderella tale in America — Zuni Turkey-Girl — is parallel to the prototype). Hence the chart:

	EUROPE	AMERICA
Sex	female	male
Family Status	double family (remarried father)	no family (orphan)
Appearance	pretty girl	ugly boy
Sentimental status	nobody likes her	unrequited love for girl
Transformation	luxuriously clothed with supernatural help	stripped of ugliness with supernatural help

Thus, like Ash-Boy and Cinderella, the trickster is a mediator. Since his mediating function occupies a position halfway between two polar terms, he must retain something of that duality — namely an ambiguous and equivocal character. But the trickster figure is not the only conceivable form of mediation; some myths seem to be entirely devoted to the task of exhausting all the possible solutions to the problem of bridging the gap between *two* and *one*. For instance, a comparison between all the variants of the Zuni emergence myth provides us with a series of mediating devices, each of which generates the next one by a process of opposition and correlation:

messiah > dioscuri > trickster > bisexual being > sibling pair >
married couple > grandmother-grandchild > four-term group > triad

In Cushing's version, this dialectic is associated with a change from a spatial dimension (mediation between Sky and Earth) to a temporal dimension (mediation between summer and winter, that is, between birth and death).

But while the shift is being made from space to time, the final solution (triad) re-introduces space, since a triad consists of a dioscuric pair *plus* a messiah, present simultaneously; and while the point of departure was ostensibly formulated in terms of a space referent (Sky and Earth), this was nevertheless implicitly conceived in terms of a time referent (first the messiah calls, *then* the dioscuri descend). Therefore the logic of myth confronts us with a double, reciprocal exchange of functions to which we shall return shortly.

Not only can we account for the ambiguous character of the trickster, but we can also understand another property of mythical figures the world over, namely, that the same god is endowed with contradictory attributes — for instance, he may be *good* and *bad* at the same time. If we compare the variants of the Hopi myth of the origin of Shalako, we may order them in terms of the following structure:

$$(\text{Masauwu: } x) \simeq (\text{Muyingwu: Masauwu}) \simeq (\text{Shalako: Muyingwu})$$
$$\simeq (y: \text{Masauwu})$$

where x and y represent arbitrary values corresponding to the fact that in the two "extreme" variants the god Masauwu, while appearing alone rather than associated with another god, as in variant two, or being absent, as in variant three, still retains intrinsically a relative value. In variant one, Masauwu (alone) is depicted as helpful to mankind (though not as helpful as he could be), and in version four, harmful to mankind (though not as harmful as he could be). His role is thus defined — at least implicitly — in contrast with another role which is possible but not specified and which is represented here by the values x and y. In version 2, on the other hand, Muyingwu is relatively more helpful than Masauwu, and in version three, Shalako more helpful than Muyingwu. We find an identical series when ordering the Keresan variants:

$$(\text{Poshaiyanki: } x) \simeq (\text{Lea: Poshaiyanki}) \simeq (\text{Poshaiyanki: Tiamoni})$$
$$\simeq (y: \text{Poshaiyanki})$$

This logical framework is particularly interesting, since anthropologists are already acquainted with it on two other levels — first, in regard to the problem of the pecking order among hens, and second, to what this writer has called *generalized exchange* in the field of kinship. By recognizing it also on the level of mythical thought, we may find ourselves in a better position to appraise its basic importance in anthropological studies and to give it a more inclusive theoretical interpretation.

Finally, when we have succeeded in organizing a whole series of variants into a kind of permutation group, we are in a position to formulate the law of that group. Although it is not possible at the present stage to come closer than an approximate formulation which will certainly need to be refined in the future, it seems that every myth (considered as the aggregate of all its variants) corresponds to a formula of the following type:

$$F_x(a):F_y(b) \approx F_x(b):F_{a\text{-}1}(y)$$

Here, with two terms, *a* and *b*, being given as well as two functions, *x* and *y*, of these terms, it is assumed that a relation of equivalence exists between two situations defined respectively by an inversion of *terms* and *relations*, under two conditions: (1) that one term be replaced by its opposite (in the above formula, *a* and a^{-1}); (2) that an inversion be made between the *function value* and the *term value* of two elements (above, *y* and *a*).

This formula becomes highly significant when we recall that Freud considered that *two traumas* (and not one, as is so commonly said) are necessary in order to generate the individual myth in which a neurosis consists. By trying to apply the formula to the analysis of these traumas (and assuming that they correspond to conditions 1 and 2 respectively) we should not only be able to provide a more precise and rigorous formulation of the genetic law of the myth, but we would find ourselves in the much desired position of developing side by side the anthropological and the psychological aspects of the theory; we might also take it to the laboratory and subject it to experimental verification.

*   *   *   *

Three final remarks may serve as conclusion.

First, the question has often been raised why myths, and more generally oral literature, are so much addicted to duplication, triplication, or quadruplication of the same sequence. If our hypotheses are accepted, the answer is obvious: The function of repetition is to render the structure of the myth apparent. For we have seen that the synchronic-diachronic structure of the myth permits us to organize it into diachronic sequences (the rows in our tables) which should be read synchronically (the columns). Thus, a myth exhibits a "slated" structure, which comes to the surface, so to speak, through the process of repetition.

However, the slates are not absolutely identical. And since the purpose of myth is to provide a logical model capable of overcoming a contradiction (an impossible achievement if, as it happens, the contradiction is real), a theoretically infinite number of slates will be generated, each one slightly different from the others. Thus, myth grows spiral-wise until the intellectual impulse which has produced it is exhausted. Its *growth* is a continuous process, whereas its *structure* remains discontinuous. If this is the case, we should assume that it closely corresponds, in the realm of the spoken word, to a crystal in the realm of physical matter. This analogy may help us to better understand the relationship of myth to both *langue* on the one hand and *parole* on the other. Myth is an intermediary entity between a statistical aggregate of molecules and the molecular structure itself.

Prevalent attempts to explain alleged differences between the so-called primitive mind and scientific thought have resorted to qualitative differences between the working processes of the mind in both cases, while assuming that the entities which they were studying remained very much the same. If our interpretation is correct, we are led toward a completely different view — namely, that the kind of logic in mythical thought is as rigorous as that of modern science, and that the difference lies, not in the quality of the intellectual process, but in the nature of the things to which it is applied. This is well in agreement with the situation known to prevail in the field of technology. What makes a steel ax superior to a stone ax is not that the first one is better made than the second. They are equally well made, but steel is quite different from stone. In the same way we may be able to show that the same logical processes operate in myth as in science, and that man has always been thinking equally well; the improvement lies, not in an alleged progress of man's mind, but in the discovery of new areas to which it may apply its unchanged and unchanging powers.

Notes

1. Jules Michelet, *Histoire de la Révolution française*, IV, 1. I took this quotation from M. Merleau-Ponty, *Les Aventures de la dialectique* (Paris: 1955), p. 273

2. See *Annuaire de l'École pratique des Hautes Études*, Section des Sciences religieuses, 1952–1953, pp. 19–21, and 1953–1954, pp. 27–9. Thanks are due here to an unrequested but deeply appreciated grant from the Ford Foundation.

3. For another application of this method, see our study "Four Winnebago Myths: A Structural Sketch," in Stanley Diamond (ed.), *Culture in History: Essays in Honor of Paul Radin* (New York: 1960), pp. 351–62.

[The Dramatistic Structure of Clackamas Chinook Myths]

Melville Jacobs*

Folklore has long been regarded as the collection, comparison, and study of orally transmitted stories, with emphasis upon the word "stories." Since anthropological folklorists have rarely recorded in field situations which were living folklore sessions, and since they have stressed plots, themes, dramatis personae, and tale types, the impression has remained that folklore is everywhere storytelling which resembles the written short story or novel of Euroamerican culture. But if folktales are interpreted in the light of native usage, manner of recital, audience behavior, content, and design, they are often found to resemble the theater of Western civilization rather than its short story or novel. It may therefore be fitting to employ for folktales captions such as "skit," "one-act play," "two-act play," "comedy," "tragedy," and the like. If such captions are not taken literally,

*Reprinted from Melville Jacobs, *The Content and Style of an Oral Literature* (Viking Fund Publications in Anthropology, No. 26, New York, 1959), pp. 211–19.

they serve usefully for Clackamas and other folktales of the northwest states.

Clackamas narrators seem to have performed in the manner in which an actor of Western civilization gives solo readings of plays. I would add that a play-reading in the presence of an audience is to be regarded, for Clackamas, as a specially stylized and dramatic summarization of a story. Its full details are not recited. The audience projects into the recital its knowledge of such details.

In the study of Clackamas literature, one use of captions borrowed from Western theater arises from the need to describe the range of dramatic forms, from small to large and from comedy to tragedy. But it is hardly possible to classify them sharply in types; the forms intergrade. An oral literature may contain brief scenes at one extreme exemplified in the tiny Clackamas myth "Duck Was a Married Woman" (21) to multi-act dramas like those of Fire's grandson (13), Gi'ckux (34), and Ku'šaydi (40). Furthermore, some myths, such as the ones in which Awl Woman (27) and Hazel Gambler (29) are actors, display exceptional integration and an unusually well-contrived manipulation of elements of design. The framing of such plays contrasts, at one end of the continuum, with the sprawling formlessness, at the other end, of so effective a comedy-drama as "Fire and His Son's Son" (13) or a lengthy drama like that of the adventures of Gi'ckux (34).

Only the shorter Clackamas plays showed an obviously consciously fashioned unity and integration which held throughout. Longer plays were generally about as devoid of temporal or other unity as a historical novel which lacks a main actor or central location. On the other hand, some short plays were almost formless, and a long play, exemplified by the story of Ku'šaydi (40), sometimes had a remarkable degree of design.

Even without specialization of literary or theater personnel such as may develop in a society of wealth and social stratification, a Northwest oral literature displayed many kinds of aesthetic designs. Since in Clackamas literature it was usually the short plays that were painstakingly modeled, a reasonable deduction is that reworking of longer plays so as to produce integrated designs was more difficult for the non-specialists of a food-gathering society. In such a milieu everyone discussed and participated to the full in the literary heritage. Therefore creative addition, insertions, and subtractions must have been been more numerous for longer than for shorter plays. Shorter ones were less likely to be subjected to refashioning. They remained more rigidily designed because such forms could be more easily managed and contained less content for the community to discuss. Longer plays with more features of content remained relatively amorphous except for a few quite deliberately contrived structurings within segments, which could be easily accorded frames of the kind had by short plays. The subject of process of folkloristic change must be approached with the premise that a community subjected the content of long plays to discussions which allowed more recital alternatives than could be given to short plays. However, researches are needed to give proof or disproof for the premise that because there was less stylization in longer plays they witnessed more penetrating and rapid changes than shorter plays.

The presence of a few unstructured short plays (such as the moralizing tragedy which is myth 35) among many others that were short and well designed suggests two possibilities, neither of which seems subject to checking. One is that such a play was recently borrowed and had not yet been remodeled. Another is that Clackamas borrowed, on the one hand, from contiguous peoples whose myths were frequently neatly designed and, on the other, from adjoining peoples whose myths were, in some instances, as amorphous or simply chronological as myths 34 and 35.

Questions as to which plays were composites — welded or alloyed from short plays that were native or borrowed — and which plays were segments that had been dissected out of longer plays — probably often plays that had been borrowed — cannot be answered without comparative studies of cognates in neighboring groups.

Since plot content was decisive for community and narrator, formal features were those which the raconteur could insert or frame without injury to chronological or developmental presentation of events. Clackamas indulged their feeling for form and frame by employing structural and ornamental features which neither intruded upon nor distorted the content. They employed a traditional design or frame whenever they could. When they could not, they permitted description or chronology to take its course. Additional traits of design are seen in various motifs, each of which was applied to several plots.

Consciously applied stylization appeared in formal introductory sentences which were not so much prologues as curtain-raising devices. It is as if someone advanced to the front of the stage before theater footlights and uttered a sentence or two which pointed up what was going to happen, with the audience filling in a great amount of detail about the setting of the play which was about to start. Stylization also is shown in closing paragraphs, which were really epilogues. These were more detailed than introductions and were followed by a brief phrase which ended the performance. Stylization is exemplified by a variety of devices that expedited the plot. These included the pattern number five, which framed siblings and organized repetitive actions and sequences. The youngest-smartest motif is another example of design. Less consciously applied stylization is evident, principally in some of the shorter myths, in integration by means of unity of time and place; it is also apparent in some sequences of acts and some scenes within acts in longer myths. It appears in the genetic stages which expressed the development of a personality, as exemplified by Coyote in the long myth 9. It appears in progressive saturation with humor, or in intensification of frightfulness. The narrator never permitted a flashback — not once did a story pause to revert in time to an earlier situation.

Traits of design were applied with conscious manipulation to short myths or to single acts within extended narrative plots. Storytellers could design segments of plots, that is, short plays within larger ones; they were less able to apply canons of unity and consistency to lengthier plots. It was easy to proceed from one to another event, and often this was done without a special device to signal transition. An important feature of such chronological succession was the omission of matters — such as comments on journeys — which Euroamerican literature finds necessary to mention. Since Western drama might omit the very connections which Clackamas folklore ignored, a theatrical rather than novelistic quality of the latter is felt by us.

The components of gross structure in a short play or within a segment of a large play, and the very points of separation which I have regarded as spaces between scenes and acts, were marked by transitions which have never been carefully examined in field recording situations. These transitions took many forms. For example, a morpheme translated as "and now then, then next" could be employed, and was so employed in every northwest states language as far as I know. Again, there might be only an especially pointed pause with silence. If neither device appeared, only plot content itself effected transition to a succeeding portion of plot, or to the next scene or act. It is my impression that the stylization of such kinds of transitions is found over a wide area of the Northwest and is in no respect distinctive in Clackamas.

When field research has been conducted directly in English, that is, when the informant has translated mentally and dictated in English, pauses and transition points are not quite as evident as in dictations offered in the native language. Therefore an analysis into plot segments, whether termed "introductions," "acts," "scenes," or "epilogues," is sometimes not feasible for recordings made in English. For example, Ballard's and Adamson's folktales from western Washington Salish peoples, recorded directly in English, are in few instances such close translations that it is possible to analyze individual stories into segments which may be termed "acts" and "scenes." Not all texts are superior to dictated translations, but text dictations tend to be closer to original recital design. For practical purposes most folktales dictated and written in English cannot be used for design analysis.

An exception is Elizabeth D. Jacobs' field recording of Nehalem Tillamook tales from the Oregon coast. Her informant adhered with such unexampled fidelity to the original phrases and words in Salish that a stylistic study of the versions which she dictated in English might be comparable in validity to the better text dictations. English recording of such exactitude is rare. Mrs. Howard's texts, also, were fortunately so well dictated, as far as I can judge, that a design analysis which identifies acts and scenes is also possible.

The principal factors that permit valid analysis of gross design are, in the first place, degree of acculturative deterioration and conscientiousness of the informant, whether he dictated in his native language or translated directly into English, and, in the second place, quality of relationship between informant and anthropologist. Nowadays use of a tape recorder might minimize factors of relationship with the anthropologist who is present and might tend to encourage more responsible dictations in either the original language or English.

Emphases in the methodology of field text dictations, when the recording was with pen or pencil rather than a more impersonal tape machine, have long been such that plot content and linguistic features have been the central interests of research workers. I know of no anthropological folklorist or linguist who, in field research, made careful note of or even attempted to ascertain points of segmentation within a connected narrative which he was recording. Usually he later supplied paragraphing, sentencing, commas, and periods, where he judged them apt for purposes of an acceptable-looking publication. It is difficult to determine the spots for partitioning within narrations, because the raconteur usually proceeded without audible evidences of transition points other than the natural pauses that set apart successive situations and the connective morphemes which the language possessed. In other words, the story itself had its segments, evident to both narrator and audience, but the separations between segments were likely to be very brief periods of silence, not other kinds of signals.

Western civilization has much the same style of oral storytelling. When a Euroamerican tells a joke which contains several parts, he does not say, "End of the first part," and later, "End of the second." No matter how dramatically rendered, a monologue is unlikely to be offered with audible or easily recognized punctuation. Nevertheless, stories told by non-literate peoples may have their special punctuation which sets apart segments of content. In my judgment such markers, whatever they are, need to be indicated not by use of new symbols for markers as such but by showing content sequences like acts and scenes or by traditional paragraphing. The task is to determine the segments rather than to clutter the presentation with unsightly symbols, and to ascertain whether the segments add up to a more or less deliberate design.

I suggest that whatever they are, separations of content into acts and scenes in Clackamas literature functioned like phonemic or other junctures which scientific linguists have lately been noting. It is of interest that such linguists long failed to perceive or make formulations about the very presence or functions of junctures. If linguists, who have been in relatively considerable numbers, were deaf to the phenomena of juncturing, it is not surprising that the tiny fraternity of scientifically oriented folklorists, with their pen and pencil tools and their preoccupation with plot and motif analysis, paid no attention to implied pauses or plot transition points. Plot junctures were very likely evident to storyteller and audience, were manipulated by the storyteller, and framed plot content in gross segments. Resultant structuring should be described. In addition to the more familiar because more patently stylized introductions, epilogues, and endings, numbers, frequencies, and weights of plot segments (such as acts and scenes) should be noted where possible. If points of plot segmentation are assumed, the Clackamas stories can be shown to separate out into acts and scenes as well as introductory and closing formulas.

Informants should usually not be asked to develop awareness of features of transition in plot presentation. Junctures which set acts and scenes apart should not be noted with an informant's help, at any rate not in the course of a dictation. Instead, the narrators should be allowed to adhere as closely as possible to natural recital style, lest they be distracted or self-conscious about items for which earlier they had only subliminal sensitization. Since melodic line, pause, connection, or other indication of discourse segments may be either lacking or too varied to permit easy partitioning of a story, its plot movement is likely to offer the principal or sole means for plot segment analysis. I have used plot content alone for the following sample analyses, because I lacked other means of identifying plot segments.

Although I have attempted to analyze all the stories into acts and scenes, I present only a few analyses because this kind of dissection is sufficiently revealing. The stories used here were selected to show contrasted extremes of story length and structuring. There are stories of intermediate length, and in fact the continuum ranges from very short to long.

An example of a long story which is unique in its structure is Coyote's journey (9). This comedy-drama contains twenty more or less equal segments, each of which may be regarded as a scene, but the scenes do not group into acts. I have briefly characterized each scene so as to permit easy identification of the sequence.

Introduction
scene   1: Pheasant Woman.
        2: Coyote deflowers a girl.
        3: Coyote releases bees.
        4: Coyote is unable to reach dancing girls.
        5: Sturgeon's body scrapings.
        6: *a*. Back-somersaulting Fuel Carrier.
           b. His wife's pregnancy and Coyote's lesson.
        7: Coyote rapes a girl across the river.
        8: Fifteen females transport Coyote.
        9: Coyote doctors a girl.
       10: Coyote is inside a tree and summons Woodpeckers.
       11: Coyote dismembers himself.
       12: Coyote visits Snail and steals her eyes.
       13: Coyote borrows Skunk's noisy anus.
       14: Coyote enjoys fellatio.
       15: Coyote makes a cascade and berry sites nearby.
       16: Coyote kills Grizzly in her oven.
       17: Coyote defeats Land Swallower.
       18: Coyote cuts mouths.
       19: Coyote instructs in the use of salmon.
       20: Coyote defeats River Swallower.

The first fourteen scenes represent the younger Coyote and are largely humorous; the last six depict the deific Coyote and are less funny. His development from immature to mature is itself a stylization. Moreover, five-patterns are inclosed within scene 1, where the actors perform spirit-power song-dances five times; scene 8, where Coyote is carried by three successive groups of five females each; and scene 9, where doctoring songs, which are repeated five times, are only implied. The play's structure is amorphous apart from its series of equally weighted scenes, five-patterns, introduction, ending, and chronological succession of actions in one upriver direction. Coyote's development from pre-adult to adult is the only remaining important feature of gross structuring.

No other play resembles this one at all closely in design. Although some longer plays have about as many scenes, these group into acts. The ritual myth (8), which is as uniquely structured in its way as is the Coyote journey, has as many discrete scenes; and in that myth each is quite like the others in content, expression, and design. Only two of the scenes of the Coyote epic are alike, those of the Land and Water Swallowers. Scene 6 is distinctive because of its halves.

The next example of act and scene structuring is the Bear-Grizzly drama (14), which was a kind of novel in its range of content.

Act I, scene   1: Bear and Grizzly capture two girls.
                2: Bear kills his wife.

Act II, scene   1: Grizzly swallows his wife's eye.
                2: She bears a son.
                3: Work at the root patch.
                4: Work at the root patch.
                5: Work at the root patch.
                6: Work at the root patch.
                7: Work at the root patch.
                8: The females incinerate the male Grizzlies.

Act III, scene   1: Daughter hurls mother onto a rock bluff.
                2: Girl throws an old woman into the fire.
                3: Girl in a headman's house.
                4: Girl throws an old woman into the fire.
                5: Girl in a headman's house.
                6: Girl throws an old woman into the fire.
                7: Girl in a headman's house.
                8: Girl throws an old woman into the fire.
                9: Girl in a headman's house.
             10: Girl encounters Meadow Lark Woman.
             11: Girl kills her mother.

Act IV, scene   1: Girl marries a headman, raises two sons.
                2: She metamorphoses into a Grizzly.
                3: She devours inhabitants of five villages.

Five-patterns give special frames to Act II, scenes 3 to 7; to scenes 4 to 11 in Act III; and to scene 3 in Act IV. The patterning in Act III is unique in the collection because of the alternation of two five-patterns — the breakdown of Mrs. Howard's dictation only apparently, not actually, misses perfection of design by omitting one scene of each of these five-patterns. Scenes 10 and 11 really complete each five-pattern. The play also contains a developmental feature; the girl goes through three stages: immaturity, marriage and raising of sons, and dominance of hate and killing after the sons mature.

A third example is one of the most effective dramas, that of Grizzly and Water Bug (17). Except for two five-patterns, its design is about as sprawled and shapeless as any. The first five-pattern occupies scenes 2 to 6 in Act I. There is an especially long and climactic fifth episode, in scene 6. The second five-pattern is the headman's stylized shooting of five arrows at his Grizzly wife in scene 2 of Act II.

Act I, scene 1: Grizzly marries a headman.
2: Grizzly murders a group of women.
3: Grizzly murders a group of women.
4: Grizzly murders a group of women.
5: Grizzly murders a group of women.
6: Water Bug accompanies the fifth group.
7: Water Bug finds paddles and corpses.
8: Water Bug and Grizzly jockey all night.
9: Women flee homeward.

Act II, scene 1: Grizzly pursues fugitives.
2: Fugitives reach village and headman shoots Grizzly.
3: People bring corpses back to the village.

A fourth example of the prevailing kind of chronologically presented plot in a goodly number of scenes, within some of which are five-patterns, is the Wren comedy (25). Progressive saturation with the obscene and incongruous was perhaps the principal means employed for audience effect, and the five-patterns were minor devices. The play seems to have been excellently designed because of its piling-up of incongruities which were ludicrous. It may be segmented as follows.

Act I, scene 1: Wren insults five animals.
2: Wren enters and leaves Elk five times.

Act II, scene 1: Grandmother will carry a hind quarter only.
2: Grandmother uses a fragile packstrap while Wren journeys five times with heavy packs.
3: Wren finds his grandmother masturbating.
4: Wren sleeps with his grandmother.
5: Wren throws her away.
6: Blue Jay and Jay Bird haul her from the river.

Act II, scene 7: Three shamans try to revive her.
8: Blue Jay and Jay Bird sell her to Wren.

> 9: Wren plays with her, throws her away again.
> 10: Blue Jay and Jay Bird cannot revive her.

Each of the first four scenes is a five-pattern. A unique three-pattern appears in scene 7 of Act II. The story's impact was consequent upon pyramidings of burlesque situations until the climax in scenes 9 and 10.

A medium-length play which lacks a five-pattern, but whose aesthetic effect was largely a consequence of straight chronology leading to a climax of violence and tragedy, is the dog-wife myth (28). It seems to be framed in two acts and six scenes, as follows.

> Act I, scene 1: Wealthy girl marries her dog to a suitor.
> 2: He smells excrements about his bride.
> 3: Girl paddles past his village.
> 4: He shoots his dog bride.
>
> Act II, scene 1: He puts snakes into maple bark which the girl flavors.
> 2: She gives birth to snakes and dies.

There are two climaxes, one at the end of Act I, the other and terrible end in the final lines of Act II. The effect depended principally upon plot content, with a build-up to a frightful resolution and Draconian justice.

Chronological presentations exemplified in the preceding, with their slight framing and dependency upon plot for aesthetic effect, resemble many other comedies and dramas of varying lengths. These contrast with the much more structured horror drama of Awl Woman (27), which is of medium length.

> Act I, scene 1: A hunter turns his awl into Awl Woman.
> 2: She hides, works for him, is confronted by him.
>
> Act II, scene 1: Girl comes, Awl terrorizes then kills her.
> 2: Girl comes, Awl terrorizes then kills her.
> 3: Girl comes, Awl terrorizes then kills her.
> 4: Girl comes, Awl terrorizes then kills her.
> 5: Youngest girl comes, is helped by Meadow Lark Woman.
> 6: Girl kills Awl.
>
> Act III, scene 1: Hunter rushes home when his bow breaks.
> 2: He arrives, buries four corpses, explains Awl to girl, marries her.

This drama has unity of time and place, and presents few actors. It engages in no digressions. Act II is a five-pattern, with youngest-smartest and Lark plot expediter devices. Perhaps scene 2 of Act I had a five-pattern too, if five days passed before the hunter confronted Awl. Myths 1, 24, and 36 exhibited the same over-all design. These four stories exemplify a distinct type of play in which the frame itself pleased, I think, to a greater degree than in most other stories of the collection, but the four also had content which dominated the effect, as in amorphous plays.

Several very short myths are formless single-scene dramas. Examples are Coyote's waiting for Sleep (12), Bear's mourning (15), and Robin's weeping for her younger sister (44). These three have only one actor each, and unity of time and place. They are like one-stanza poems whose compactness and sheer simplicity produced an effect of pleasure in form like that stirred by the four myths cited above (1, 24, 27, 36).

A few plays contained a scene which was an entr'acte. The myth of Panther, Coyote, and Trout (6) has five acts, with two or more scenes in all acts but the first. Act IV contains, in scene 1, an explanatory side excursion in which antlers are tried on various animals. Another excursion in scene 6 accounts for snowbirds. Both scenes relieved tension, did some explaining, and contributed nothing to the main plot. They certainly went far from the central line of the story. A similar entr'acte appears in the comedy interlude of Blue Jay's slipping through ice in Act I, scene 5, of the Canoemaker-Seal Hunter myth (26). Act III of that myth is an entr'acte too, which distracted from tension maintained in the remainder of the drama. In general, however, these digressions were rare in the literature. They were not present in comedies. They bear earmarks of being secondary additions inserted in bygone times in order to alleviate tension or mounting audience feelings; they were asides that were entertaining or instructive or both. Reflection upon ways in which community discussions may have resulted in changes in story content warrants the observation that, all in all, the infrequency of entr'actes points to a strength of feeling for uninterrupted plot continuity. This is a feeling for form.

Although most plays lack perfect designs as wholes, apart from a straight plot line and climaxes, many or most stories contain one or more especially well designed scenes or an act which is a succession of scenes in a five-pattern. In other words, Clackamas could provide a perfect story frame if the recital occupied a short space of time. People were disinclined to work toward such perfection or to force plots in order to effect it in longer narrations. The ever-present feeling for design might be taken care of by the stylized short introduction, longer epilogue, formal ending, succinct style of speech, stylized selections and very limited numbers of descriptive items, chronological succession of plot situations, and some other traits that characterized story recitals.

Structures of tales are to a degree distinct from myths. Six tales are formless anecdotes, each in a single scene; the eight remaining tales have two or more scenes, but only one (which is in two versions, in texts 57 and 58) has as many as six. And every tale is relatively feeble in design. Neither youngest-smartest motif nor five-pattern appears. My deduction is that tales had not been subjected to long periods of community discussion and creative treatment, so that they lacked the introductions, epilogues, and endings which were minimal requirements in myth recitals and which granted such occasions a special luster.

Correlates of Cree Narrative Performance

Regna Darnell*

Folklore as a discipline has all too often existed in a vacuum from which texts are abstracted for the edification of outsiders about the cultural context of their performance. Recent collaboration between folklorists and anthropologists, much of which comes under the general rubric of sociolinguistics, has taken an important step toward correcting the limitations of such a perspective. Many students of traditional material have learned to expect and value different versions of the same story told by different individuals or by the same individual at different times depending on the nature of the social occasion. It has become clear that a living folk tradition has a potential for creativity and modification such that the most interesting text may be one which is adapted on the spot to a new audience or a new situation. The feedback between audience and performer may be crucial to the organization of a performance. The folklorist, as a result, can no longer rely solely on a tape recorder in front of an isolated informant, although that individual may be, in other contexts, an authentic performer of his folk tradition. Narrative performance is in essence *social* activity.

This paper will discuss in detail a single instance of creative performance by an old Cree man recognized by his community as a carrier and performer of traditional Cree cultural material. It will be shown that the old man organized the event in a traditional manner, was responded to as an authentic performer in his narration and accompanying conversation, and freely adapted his traditional material to the presence in the audience of outsiders (investigator and spouse, plus tape recorder). The old man was successful in this situation in maintaining the performance to the secondary audience — his Cree hosts and part of his own family — as a validation of his own status of traditional performer. This itself was enhanced, for the Indian portion of the audience, by the fact that he was performing in front of outsiders who wanted to know 'what it was really like' in the old days.

The tapes were recorded in Wabasca, Alberta,[1] in March 1971. The occasion came about almost by accident at the insistence of our hosts, a seventy-year-old Cree man (henceforth Father) and his daughter Marie-Louise who had served as a Cree instructor with the investigator at the University of Alberta that year. An extremely casual atmosphere was maintained throughout the visit and many traditional stories and anecdotes were recorded from the father. However, our host did not feel that he was the best person in the community to tell us these things, and preferred that we meet an old man who was nearly a hundred years old and knew much more about traditional Cree ways. We would have to pay him to sing and tell

*Reprinted from *Explorations in the Ethnography of Speaking*, ed. Richard Bauman and Joel Sherzer (New York: Cambridge Univ. Press, 1974) pp. 315–36, by permission of the publishers.

stories for us but it would be well worth our while. We agreed, primarily out of curiosity about the relationship of the two men, representing different generations, but to the outsider both 'old' and therefore both appropriate teachers and performers of traditional Cree materials.

Before turning to the old man's performance[2] it will be necessary to sketch the background in terms of our hosts and their relationship to traditional materials. Marie-Louise served as interpreter throughout.[3] Because of her experiences in teaching Cree she was aware of my interests in Cree and partially aware of the grammar of the language and how to explain it to a non-native audience. She was, moreover, multilingual, speaking some German and Chinese because she had lived in Germany and Hong Kong with her husband. She was interested both in linguistic differences and in the preservation of traditional Cree materials, although she had not herself lived on the reserve for many years.

Marie-Louise had never attempted to become a performer of traditional Cree materials but had considered the possibility that she might be able to do so. Certainly she was interested in hearing the stories again, which is the way most new performers declare their intent. She had sent her youngest child, a boy of six, to spend the winter on the reserve and go to school there so he would learn about his Indian heritage. His grandfather was somewhat discouraged by the boy's progress in the Cree language but enjoyed his company and taught him whatever he could. Father thought that the boy had difficulty speaking Cree because he spent most of his time with his aunt (Marie-Louise's sister) and her children. Most of the Cree he learned was in this context. Since these children also spoke English (they owned one of the dozen or so television sets in the community) he did not have to depend on Cree to communicate. Father believes that although all of the children in Wabasca speak English, a few have not learned Cree. Some children on the reserve actually do understand Cree but refuse to respond to it. Father noted that this is 'something very nasty that the Indian has, he is ashamed of himself.'

Thus, Father has a profound and self-conscious pessimism about the future of the Cree language and culture which may not actually be borne out in fact. There are many young people in Wabasca and other northern Alberta communities who are eager to learn traditional materials; some will even perform them in the absence of a better-qualified individual to do so. They must, however, always defer to an established performer. Clearly, then, there will be *at least* one more generation of traditional performers. Although the effects of culture change have been great, particularly in the areas of education, material culture, and religion (Wabasca has been a major center for Catholic missionaries for some time), individuals still have the option of moving through the traditional Cree life cycle, at least with regard to performance of oral material.

Our host, however, felt isolated from the younger portion of the Cree community because he lived alone and did not understand many of the new influences. He felt that the young people did not want to speak Cree and would be offended if they were expected to do so. He realized that this reflected the inferior position of Indians in the larger society, but did not himself understand why Indian people should have to communicate among themselves in a 'foreign language.' He recalled that when he was a young man, Indians all spoke Cree except if a white man was present who would not understand Cree. He agreed that many young Indians were now trying to learn Cree but thought that grownups would never be able to learn the way 'a person who grows up with' the language learns it. He agreed that such people might learn to speak Cree for purposes of everyday interactions, but did not see how they would be able to learn traditional Cree or maintain the old ways without having been taught from childhood.

Father was, in many ways, reluctant to talk about traditional Cree ways because he believed that people now did not respect them. At the age of seventy, he has watched Cree people turn away from the teachings of their elders and does not believe they share his values. He explained that in the old days, sons respected their fathers because the old men had 'special powers' and could protect their children. Today the powers have been lost and this sanction to authority no longer exists.

Father himself remains with the old ways and does not feel that he has a right to force his beliefs on others. He understands English because he studied it in school many years ago, but is very reluctant to use it. He understood his daugher's translations and our comments, often correcting or adding to her rendition of his remarks. For example, he frequently began his reply before the translation was completed. Our conversational Cree is at approximately the level of his English, a fact which increased his confidence in talking to us. Minimal communication could be sustained easily when his daughter was not present to translate, each speaking his own language and understanding the other. This situation did not seem to embarrass him.

Informally during our visit, Father told us a number of traditional Cree stories, frequently reminding Marie-Louise that he had told these same stories to her as a child. Marie-Louise was apparently quite concerned that we might be bored by the stories and commented that 'they are all quite similar.' She noted that she remembers them as being much more exciting when she was a child. She remembered the stories well enough to jump ahead in her translation on several occasions.

Her major difficulty as a translator in this informal context was whether or not to *perform* the stories. She was able to articulate this difficulty quite clearly, explaining that we could see Father's gestures and hear his tone of voice. She felt 'silly' both performing them and simply translating. Performance was inappropriate because she was a young woman and etiquette required that she simply listen to an old man. But the stories are meant to be performed and they lose their effect if told in a monotone. In practice, conversation was usually translated in the form: 'He says . . .'; for

example, 'He thinks Cree will die out.' Marie-Louise was not herself responsible for this opinion and was trying to clarify her father's views. However,
in a long narrative she frequently translated in the first person: 'I have seen
it happen.'[4] At many points she began to tell a story formally and lapsed into
a style with gestures and voice qualities which were not imitations of her
father's but her own way of rendering the story as performance. Father
seemed pleased by this.

Father's stories were extremely well told and organized. Many of these
were stories about Wisahkitchak, the culture hero, and how he made the
world into what it is now. For example:

> Wisahkitchak was walking around a lake.
> He came upon a large boulder.
> 'It seems you have been here a long time,' he said. 'I'll make you a present
>   of his fur robe.'
> He went on walking.
> It looked like rain. He became chilly.
> He had been foolish to leave his robe, he thought.
> He went back.
> He took it off the stone and teased the stone. 'What will you do?' he said.
> The rock chased him.
> He ran through the brush. The boulder just went faster.
> He ran up a large hill. Still it came.
> At the top he ran fast downhill. He tripped.
> The rock came and sat on him. It almost killed him.
> A night-hawk came along.
> Wisahkitchak begged for help. He promised the bird he would make it
>   beautiful if it got the rock off.
> The night-hawk flew very high.
> It made a strange sort of noise.
> When the bird made that rude noise, the rock flipped over.
> Wisahkitchak got up and stretched.
> The bird sat there and waited [for Wisahkitchak].
> Wisahkitchak took dirt and made stripes on its wings. It is a very attrac-
>   tive bird now.
> Then Wisahkitchak did something extra. He stretched the bird's mouth
>   and added yellow marks to it.
> Wisahkitchak always does things this way. He does something to undo the
>   good he has done.

Such stories are traditionally called *atayohgewin* or sacred stories.
Under the influence of the missionaries, many native people refuse to consider them religious in content. Secularization facilitates continued performance without cultural conflict. Father believes that the stories about
Wisahkitchak are fables which no one considers to be true. Wisahkitchak is
a kind of prankster, with the religious context of the Algonkian culture hero
having been lost. Another narrator on a different occasion insisted that the
term *atayohgewin* be translated 'fictitious stories.' He believed it was im-

portant to transmit these stories to the younger generation, but they had become completely secular for him. The attitude is commonly expressed in this area that 'we didn't have any religion before the white man came.'

Most individuals are quite articulate about the philosophical tightrope necessary to reconcile cultural pride and religious teaching. Stories are often followed by long discussions which fall outside any formal literary genre, being classified as 'just talk,' but interpreting themes of the stories in terms of present times. This is particularly common with another class of Cree traditional materials, *achimowan. Achimowana* are stories about the past; they include tales of the old days, in which the speaker disavows personal knowledge of what he tells through frequent use of the particle *-esa*. They also include stories about an individual's past experiences which are told first-hand, and recent events. They are, however, more formal than mere conversation and the audience is expected to defer to the performer until he concludes.

An example of this genre is the story Father told us as the only one he had ever heard about a real *wihtigo* (a man who becomes a cannibal). Belief in *wihtigo* spirits is still quite strong in this area. *Wihtigo* is used to threaten children. Individuals who eat too much may be rebuked or teased by calling them *wihtigo*; this usage is not serious. On the other hand, an individual who is extreme in behavior may be seen as a potential *wihtigo* and assiduously avoided.[5] Most native people do not like to talk about *wihtigo* spirits to white men because they know they are disbelieved. The stories about the *wihtigo* are considered to be true. Father pointed out that they 'do exist in people's minds and beliefs.' Besides, he did not think that people had the imagination to invent stories like these.

> People in the old days did not tell lies. It was not done. There was no reason to kill a man unless he had done something or unless there was something terribly wrong with him really. It's quite true that nowadays that it seems unbelievable, but these things did take place, years ago.

Therefore, Father thought that even if an outsider does not believe in *wihtigo* spirits, they are more real than the *atayohgewin* which occurred before the world was as it is now.[6]

After Father had concluded his story, we asked about the morality of killing the *wihtigo*. This provoked a long discussion between Marie-Louise and her father. Father explained that before Christianity came to North America the land was under an evil influence 'and that is why things happened as they did.' The person who became a *wihtigo* was a reincarnation of something evil. But today people have different beliefs and that is no longer possible. Today the Indians have lost the powers they used to have. People were fooled by the evils that existed then. What they took to be good was not actually good, it was evil in origin. Many people lived very good lives at that time, although, of course, many people did not. Father believed that things had changed very little.

The question which bothered both Marie-Louise and her father was whether or not the killing of a *wihtigo* was justifiable according to Christian morality. Father pointed out that the man in the story who had killed his uncle to protect the rest of the community had been very upset. Then one night he had a dream and heard someone say to him, 'All right, that's enough now; you have paid for your sins. You have saved a lot of lives.' Father continued: 'Then he stopped crying, but he didn't live very long after that.' The ambivalence of Marie-Louise was greater:

> I suppose, if you look at it that you are committing murder, it is a sin, isn't it? Even though you are saving a lot of lives, it's still . . . particularly if it's your uncle. But there's a lot at stake. If someone's going to kill you, you must defend yourself, right? That's only a natural law.

Father agrees with Christianized rationalization but doesn't think a man could possibly kill his own children, though Indian custom prescribed this as the only possible remedy for a *wihtigo*. Father's personal view is that he would rather let himself be killed by a child who became a *wihtigo*. Both Father and daughter explain the matter in white terms, although they still understand the reasons for the killing in traditional terms.

One difficulty in obtaining traditional Cree texts from Father was the existence of obscene elements in many of the Wisahkitchak stories. Marie-Louise told us that her father had never told her any dirty stories and insisted these stories were traditionally told only in all-male company. Neither was willing to comment on whether these stories were traditionally told to children. The definition of obscenity, like the morality of the *wihtigo*'s punishment, comes from the Catholic missionaries. Marie-Louise, who had refused, during the past year, to discuss obscenity in Cree with university students learning the language, in this situation was embarrassed even to discuss the stories. At one point, after some discussion in Cree, Father asked her if she wanted to hear a story which she knew contained obscene elements. She said 'no thanks' and provoked much laughter. When translating, she broke out of the semi-performance entirely when asked to say that someone burned his ass-hole. Her response was 'I can't say that' with much embarrassment and an unusually loud, nervous voice. Father agreed, after this, to take a shortcut in telling us these stories (which he obviously enjoyed but did not feel his daughter should hear); he decided to omit the parts that were 'not nice,' although he pointed out that this would make the stories quite brief.

Marie-Louise was so upset by the obscene references in the stories before Father agreed to cut them out, that she omitted a whole section of one Wisahkitchak story. After completing the initial translation, she decided to backtrack and tell us what she had left out.

> Once Wisahkitchak was walking and lamenting about his loneliness. 'Nothing ever happens. I never even make any rude noises at people.' That's where the accident happened. [Apparently Wisahkitchak made

rude noises at a fox who later paid him back when he had lost his eyes.]
One time when Wisahkitchak was crawling around looking for his eyes,
the fox saw him, you see, he was spying on him. The fox took a piece of
wood and would poke him in the eye with it, in the socket he would stick
it. And Wisahkitchak would cry out 'Twigs in my eyes.' [After this episode
Wisahkitchak finds the spruce tree, fashions himself new eyes, and proceeds on his travels.][7]

With this background, it is now possible to return to the formal setting
in which the community's oldest man was invited to come and tell a set of
honored but outside visitors about the old days and traditional Cree way of
life. Although the context of visiting anthropologist was not an entirely natural one in native terms, it was treated as such to a great extent by all participants. The narration and song performance became an excuse for various
observers to hear the old man's performance and to reaffirm both their
pride in what he said and their recognition of his position as revered elder.
The positioning of participants in Father's cabin illustrates the observance
of traditional Cree canons of performance demeanor.

When the old man and his wife (hereafter old woman) arrived, my
husband and I were sitting at the kitchen table talking to Marie-Louise and
her father. Father got up, found the largest and most comfortable chair in
the room, and escorted the old man to it. This chair was placed at the center
of the room. There were no general introductions, although the old man
was told who we were. At no time did the old man turn his body to face
Father or Marie-Louise although he turned his head toward them occasionally. His wife was then seated next to him, between him and the table where
we were sitting. The old woman aligned herself facing her husband with
her back turned toward Marie-Louise and Father; she sat very close to him
but not touching. The two old people thus formed a closed circle, reflecting
both the self-effacing public behavior expected of a married Indian woman
and the closeness of these two individuals.[8] The circle was further reinforced by both spouses crossing their legs toward each other, thereby closing
out the other participants. The old woman remained silent during most of
the afternoon; her husband frequently spoke for her. Her only contribution
to her husband's performance was to dance while he played the drum, at his
instruction.

Father remained at his original seat, which left him very much in the
background. As host and a younger man, he was obliged to defer to the
greater cultural knowledge of the old man. He listened carefully and attempted to help Marie-Louise in her translations. He seemed to feel that he
too was one of the listeners and therefore was learning more about his own
culture. Marie-Louise, because she was a much younger woman, felt that
she should be as unobtrusive as possible. She made a few polite remarks to
the old woman but avoided direct conversation with the old man. This was
reflected in her change of position to a point behind the old man's line of
vision. Because of her role as translator, Marie-Louise could not retire into

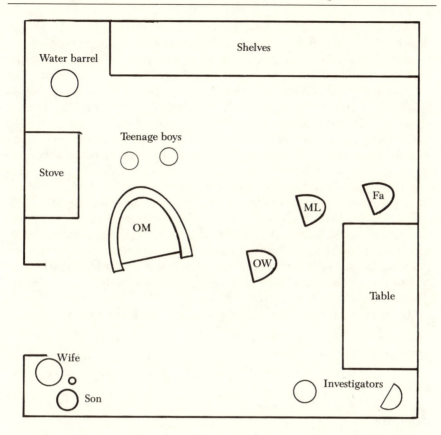

the background as a Cree woman of her age would normally do. Her role was reflected by her position between the old man and the white visitors. By turning her head, she could also consult her father behind her. Thus in terms of the group initially present, my husband and I constituted the primary audience and Marie-Louise and her father were observers from backstage. Their presence in a subsidiary position validated the old man's role of traditional performer in that they listened and accepted his right to speak for them and Cree people generally.

During the conversation (which continued for several hours) a number of other observers arrived. The old man's son and his wife came in, accompanied by a small child. They moved into the room, the husband first, positioning themselves squatting in the corner just inside the door.[9] They aligned their bodies facing the old man and listened carefully to him. The son greeted Father but did not otherwise speak to anyone in the room. His presence there was explained somewhat later by his father: this is the one child who remained at home with his parents. The old man referred to him as 'babysis' (the Cree diminutive suffix plus the English word baby), although telling us that he was fifty-three years old. During the old man's lifetime, this son could not become a household head in his own right and was socially subordinate in many contexts.

The last arrivals were two teenage boys. They stood for some time in the doorway, apparently hoping for an invitation to enter. Finally they moved into the room and positioned themselves behind the old man. Neither of them moved further into the room than the center of the old man's back. Both stood quietly without fidgeting and did not speak to anyone in the room. They were accepted by all native participants as appropriate listeners and learners as long as they did not interrupt the old man's speech. These young men were of the age where interest in old Cree traditions begins to manifest itself to identify potential future performers.

Before the old man could sing a traditional song or tell a story, a number of preliminaries had to be performed. These preliminaries had the function of making a gradual transition from the everyday world of Wabasca in 1971 to the mythological time framework in which traditional stories are situated. The old man could not simply plunge into his narratives. First he had to lead the audience through a progression of reference points.

1. He began by emphasizing the importance of his stories and the need to treat them seriously.

2. Then he presented personal biographical validation of his status as an old-fashioned or bush Indian.

3. Then he moved to a discussion of how Indian life was in the old days, many years ago.

4. From the Indian past in which things were much different than they are now, it was appropriate to move to mythological time. The traditional song, dealing with human powers in an old-style Indian world, made the transition complete; the song was formal traditional performance but still in real or everyday time.

5. With the story, the old man at last broke through from the normal world to the supernatural one.

Because he was speaking to virtual strangers, the old man first had to establish his relationship to the event. He did this by speaking of his relationship to Father, whom he spoke of as a younger brother: "I will tell stories for his sake. I love him just like a younger brother, just the same as if he was breast-fed by my mother.' Father accepted this fictive kin designation by occasionally speaking directly to the old man, for example, urging him to continue a narrative by calling him 'older brother' (a term of respect frequently used among unrelated or distantly related adult men). The old man then explained to Marie-Louise that her father thought a great deal of him, although he and his wife didn't know her well at all. Because we were introduced by Father and he wanted the old man to speak to us, it was acceptable for him to tell us seriously of the old Cree ways.

The old man was extremely concerned that his words be believed and that his audience respect the matters of which he spoke. Before any narrative event could proceed, he found it necessary to specify this. The old man wanted the stories written down and was not entirely confident that an accurate record of his important words would be made by the tape recorder. Marie-Louise was embarrassed by his insistence on this point, apparently not realizing that her father had said virtually the same things earlier the same day in speaking to us alone. As a result, she did not translate the old man's remarks literally:

OM: I'm going to tell them these sacred stories. I don't want them to repeat them wherever they go because maybe I'm lying [i.e., maybe they think I'm lying]. They should keep to themselves that story.

ML: He's telling it to you for your enjoyment.

OM: People get jealous for nothing [i.e., other Indians resent it when stories are told to white men]. I don't want every person to know what I'm telling.

ML: Some of the people have been cheated somehow; however he would like to tell you his story that he experienced in a dream.

OM: Many people ask me to tell stories but I don't do it often. I tell you because you are going to preserve our language.

ML: There are only certain people he would gladly tell stories to.

OM: These I'm telling stories to, I feel sorry for them. I feel sorry for your Dad, he sent you [Marie-Louise] here. I'll sing anyway, for sure I'm lying.

ML: [no translation]

This interchange reflects the traditional denial of competence which begins Cree narrative events. The speaker is not an individual but a performer of traditional material which is independent of his personal identity. Even if he speaks of his own dream visions, he is speaking of something outside himself. This is part of the formality of storytelling etiquette, and Mary-Louise is unsuccessful in shortening it by her failure to translate.

Father's version of concern for the integrity of the stories was equally intense although expressed less formally in a conversation about many topics, i.e., not as part of a recognized performance. He had always wanted to tell old Cree stories on tape, but some (Indian) man once accused him of being a liar and it hurt him. In spite of this, he would tell stories to us because we had come to hear about the Cree way of life from him. He had been approached by the Metis Association and by Indian Affairs and had refused: 'To make a man tell a story or to recount legends of the past that are discredited as lies later on or made like fairy tales, really does something to a man's pride.' Because many people find the old stories so unbelievable, many Indians have refused to tell them. Father believes that it is useless to talk about the kinds of powers that Indians used to have because no one believes it any more. He knows people who still have such powers; one of his uncles could make a fox fur stand up and dance. But mostly he is reluctant to tell such stories because people laugh.

Having established that the stories were to be taken seriously, the old man then told about his own life, situating himself in the world of the traditional Cree Indian. He mentioned his age — ninety-seven years and six months — several times. Marie-Louise became impatient and translated it saying, 'He said that before.' His wife was ninety-one years old. They had been married for seventy-three years. The old man stressed that he and his wife used to be very good-looking. He insisted that Marie-Louise translate his statement that they were now ugly. Marie-Louise apparently considered this boasting and attempted to ignore it (unsuccessfully). Twice the old woman had almost died. She was very stooped because she had been sick. The old man continued discussing his advanced age:

> Now *she* can only lie on one side.
> So can *I*.
> *We* are getting too old.

The parallelism which expresses the unity of the two old people and the old man's solicitousness for his wife (especially in referring to her before himself) was ignored by Marie-Louise in her translation. She seemed to feel that if the old man was to interpret Cree culture he should not insert personal biographical details. Father, however, appeared to accept the validating role of these statements.

In his lifetime, the old man explained that he had killed 403 moose. He retired from hunting in the bush more than thirty years ago when he was sixty-five, because he was too old. Father and Marie-Louise laughed politely at this, a way of affirming the old man's special status. His age and continued agility, both mental and physical, reinforced his performing role as an interpreter of old Cree ways. Frequently the old man commented that he was getting old, expecting a denial from the audience, both native and white. He noted that his weight was now less than two hundred pounds, that of course being a great weight for a Cree man. (The old man is an extremely impressive-looking individual because of his great height and heavy build, both accentuated by a bushy beard.)

The old man was much concerned to explain how strong he had been as a younger man. He used to be able to pack seven hundred pounds for a short distance. In his youth he was a wrestler and he had never been beaten. Father confirmed that he had seen the old man wrestle when he was about ten years old. Once he was all black and blue because a man grabbed him across the waist; that man was very strong. The old man then noted, in a formulaic apology, that the visitors would think he was a big liar: 'I'm getting carried away with my stories.'

The old man was also eager to establish that he did not drink. He used to many years ago but had not for the past eleven years. Drunkenness is, of course, a frequent criticism of Indians by white people, and most Cree people are sensitive about it. The old man expressed the matter in terms of its effect on his ability to control himself and behave in a respective manner. Again, Marie-Louise's translations reflect her view of the matter (she definitely drinks) but follow the Cree rather closely:

OM: Because maybe I make a mistake in my speech or maybe I will not talk right or I'll get mad or maybe I'll fall. That's the thing I'm scared of. I'd like to have my right mind as long as I live.

ML: He's talking about alcohol and that business . . . and he feels that he wants to keep his sanity and walk, you know, instead of staggering around. He might fall down and break his neck.

After placing his own life in the context of traditional Cree culture, the old man then felt obliged to discuss how different things were today than they had been in the past. Again, this is a theme elaborated on by almost all narrators as a preamble to their presentations of traditional materials. The audience is expected to respond with an affirmation of eagerness to listen and learn. The old man began with a formal narrative of his early experiences:[10]

> The first time I saw Wabasca, there were only eight houses.
> My father was alive then.
> He passed away eighty years ago.
> My mother passed away sixty-five years ago.
> She lies close by at the church.
> Of religion there was nothing.
> Of the church [building] there was nothing.
> They lived in tipis.
> They were very poor, these people.

The old man continued more conversationally, telling us that now there were almost three hundred houses but they were all scattered around in the Indian style, not like a town.

As a young man, he worked hard. Again the narrative become stylized:

> In the bush I walked to get food to eat.
> There wasn't much food around.
> Long ago there wasn't anything around to make a living with.
> I used a piece of wood to keep my clothing together
>   [there were no buttons then].
> The people were very poor.
> Many times people died by freezing because they couldn't keep warm.
> They used straw or rabbit fur to keep their feet warm.
> It's a wonder how people continued to live.
> I was very poor.

Many times I didn't have a blanket to use.
When I went hunting, I'd go to sleep watching the campfire.
I believe all this because I have seen it.
Anyone that didn't see it wouldn't believe what I am telling.
I am old.
I'm telling stories now.
Right now I'm in that thing [tape recorder] speaking.

All of this may be taken as affirmation of his right to speak of these things. Without the experiences, he would not have been in a position to speak of the traditional Cree way of life.

An earlier conversation with Father had brought out many of the same points, although not in the context of validating his own role as an authentic performer. He believed that young people should be made aware of what had gone on in the past. They have no idea how difficult life was then. He went trapping one spring with his uncle and they found only sixteen muskrats between them. They raised cattle and they survived by their wits. Whatever they had was handmade. Marie-Louise interrupted at this point to say that she didn't think young people would be interested in these things. Father agreed that young Indians today took everything for granted. This began a long digression on how Indians were ashamed of their own people and customs.

Father remembered that when he was ten years old he lived in Athabasca. They had a fairly good life. There was enough money and there were jobs to be had. People didn't have to rely on welfare. But the jobs that were available for Indians were backbreaking. He used to pull freight boats on the Athabasca River for the Hudson's Bay Company from daybreak to dusk. It was five hundred miles with a lot of falls; they had to unload the boats and carry the cargo around the falls. 'Those people were crazy.' They became useless slaves. A man was laughed at for carrying only a hundred pounds and there was great rivalry among the men. A trapper had an easier life because at least he had dogs. Very few people had horses. They hunted little animals and received maybe ten dollars for a muskrat pelt. Today, very few people still trap. The muskrats have almost disappeared because flooding has destroyed their food. It is now harder for an Indian to make a living in the traditional Cree way.

The old man's first formal acting was to sing a traditional song. His ritual opening was a statement that this was his own song. 'Someday I will be dead and you won't be able to listen to my songs. The night is long when I start singing my songs.' This is very much in the traditional context of teaching only those those who wish to learn and understand the importance of what is being taught. After the introduction, the old man backtracked and explained that his drum had to be heated so that it would have the proper tone. Father eventually heated the drum over his stove and returned it to the old man, who remained sitting at the center of the room throughout. Then the old man explained that he was trying to think of a song. This too was a formulaic apology. The old man, like most Cree elders, had only a few songs which were his by virtue of dreams or other supernatural validation.

The explanation of the special status of this song was Christian, though in line with the traditional Cree manner of learning and performing songs:

OM: I never used any lies. Right now I'm thanking God. I'm going to sing now.

ML: It's a religious song.

OM: Now, I want to respect what God left on this earth. Now, this song I'm going to sing respected Indians. They knew God existed. Also the priests knew God existed. So we go along with them.

ML: He's talking about religion now. He feels the song, uh, ceremonial chant, he's going to sing you about — Before the priests came, it wasn't . . . you know, Indians believed in God.

OM: There is lots on my mind. God is so good. I like some people better than others. But I love God more than I do man. Could be I'm not worth much, not very good [religious meaning].

The song he sang was an Indian one relating his own dream experience. In accordance with the secrecy usually accorded visions, he did not explain the meaning of his song.

After completing his song, the old man put down his drum and signalled by clapping his hands that the song was over. After some casual conversation he decided to tell a traditional Cree story, again from one of his dreams. Although the elements are found in many traditional stories, the old man did not tie his tale to any of the traditional cycles or heroes. The story was translated in segments decided for the most part by the old man, although Marie-Louise often misunderstood or interrupted because she could not translate. Her father in such cases attempted to clarify the meaning in Cree and occasionally in English. The old man listened carefully but did not understand more than a few words of English and never contributed to the discussion unless asked by Father in Cree. Marie-Louise did not speak directly to the old man when she had problems.

The difficulties in translation were multiple in cause. Marie-Louise was extremely nervous because she did not feel that she could translate adequately. Earlier the same day her father had told her that her translations of his stories were not good enough. In fact he didn't think her English was good enough to translate either.[11] Father felt that formal education was necessary to translate. He had been away to school but it was mainly religious, and he thought that was no education whatsoever. His total English repertoire had been 'yes,' 'no,' 'I don't know,' 'sure.' Later he learned more English but had not used it for many years. Marie-Louise had managed fairly well, however, as long as she was translating for her father.

The old man presented an entirely different situation. Marie-Louise's performance as translator was expected to measure up to his as storyteller. She was a young woman and therefore not anywhere near the same status as the man whose ideas she presumed to translate. She was very nervous about making a mistake, especially in light of her father's great deference toward the old man. Moreover, traditional Cree stories contain a great deal of archaic lexicon with which she was not familiar. She did not know the old man's style of speaking at all well and was often confused by him. His Cree was very terse in style and many times Marie-Louise failed to understand the logic behind his sequential statements. The old man assumed that anyone would know these things and did not elaborate. Although traditionally questions are appropriate at narrative segments and pauses, Marie-Louise was too nervous as translator to take advantage of this chance.

The narrative itself was somewhat rambling, partially because the old man grew tired of interruptions and consultations about translation. However, the narrative as interpreted for us by Marie-Louise and her father illustrates quite clearly the generational hierarchy of appropriate performance and of ritual knowledge. Only the old man, of the three, was an authentic performer in this context. Marie-Louise's father did not yet have the self-confidence to perform independently, particularly since his own children had shown little interest in traditional Cree culture. Our conversations with him showed clearly that he had the competence to perform traditional materials but did not feel comfortable doing so. His daughter showed even less knowledge of these stories and no desire to attempt performance. However, she knew much of the material and could easily step into such a role later in life if she found herself in an appropriate situation to do so (in practice, only if she returned to the reserve with her children).

The narrative itself will be presented in segments, with comments on its organization and segmentation:

> Once there was a person who was said to be strong.
> He was called Bear.
> He was about four feet fall, this much maybe [gesture].[12]
> He saw three men, who were very strong.
> He knew them from sleep [he saw them in a dream].
> He took them just like friends . . . his boys . . . his slaves.

Father began translating, with the statement about seeing the men in sleep, his practice of repeating for emphasis the main points made by the old man. He validated the claim that Indians used to have strange powers 'just like in the dream' described. A translation problem arose over the status of the main character's companions. Three different Cree words were suggested. The old man said 'boys.' Father said 'slaves' or 'boys.' Marie-Louise translated the narrative version as 'friends, companions.' She finally settled for 'They became his servants, more or less.' The Cree meaning of 'they recognized his superior status and therefore decided to follow and serve him' is not easily translated and none of the participants could solve this difficulty in English. The old man appeared not to understand what was causing the difficulty.

> The first time he [Bear] met people, he was walking.
> And he had only enough meat for lunch.
> All of a sudden, he came upon a wooded hillock.
> He was eating that meat.
> He thought he saw it [the hillock] coming toward him.
> He took a stick. At first he stuck it on the ground.
> Then he took a stick over there and he stuck it further toward the hillock.
> He saw this hillock; he thought it moved.

Marie-Louise at first translated the word glossed 'wooded hillock' as 'island.' Father initially accepted this as an adequate translation. But as the old man made it clear that there were bushes on the island, he tried to clarify. He told Marie-Louise somewhat impatiently that it was not *nimistihk*, 'island' but *mistagwakeyaw*. The problem was obviously that Marie-Louise did not know the meaning of this word. The old man explained to Father that it meant 'woods' or 'prairie.'[13] Marie-Louise finally decided that it was indeed an island but that it wasn't on water:

> It was, uh, what it means is that there was a group of trees, you see, and the person was pulling on this piece of land. Otherwise it was all plain, you know, without any trees.

Note here also that Marie-Louise has jumped ahead of the story. She refers to a man pulling on the 'island' although the old man has not yet mentioned this. This demonstrates that she knows the story motif and can therefore make sense out of the unfamiliar word by knowing what will come next. This too is a way in which young people learn traditional materials, particularly given the correction in use of the word which Father forced her into considering.

Marie-Louise became somewhat confused with the reasons that the little but strong man marked the ground with a stick. The old man simply repeated that the man put a stake in the ground. Father added that he marked it because he didn't believe that the ground was moving and wanted to be certain. Marie-Louise then explained to us that he thought it moved. Father continued in Cree:

> He thought that it [the hillock] was as if it moved. He marked it but he only continued to eat meat [i.e., he did not go on to investigate]. Next time he looked at it, he said, 'It's true, behold.'

With the direct quotation in his explanation, Father had broken into narrative performance himself. Although this reflected his enthusiasm to clarify, it was culturally inappropriate because the old man was the authentic performer and should have been deferred to. After his performance in Cree, Father attempted to explain in English, apparently feeling uncomfortable since he had been so aggressive.

He left that place.
He came upon a person who was sitting like this.
There was so much bush around there.
There was a man ten feet tall pulling on the hillock.
'Could you come with me?' that small, four-foot-high one said to the
    man.
'Yes, if you want, I will go with you,' he said to that strong man.
'Over here are two of my brothers that you will have to make friends
    with before I will go with you.
'You know, they are stronger than you are,' the tall man said this to him.

Marie-Louise's translation was much more explicit as to the attributes of the two men and the reason for their responses. This information would not, of course, have been necessary for an all-Cree audience. She explained that the tall man decided he might come because he knew that the man was 'only very small but that he was very strong.' That is, the man who was pulling the hillock had the power of choice and made his decision on the basis of strength (with its implication of courage) rather than taking account only of the man's small stature. Marie-Louise at several points confuses the attributes of the major character, referring to him as 'young' rather than 'small.' In both cases, of course, a potentially negative attribute must be overcome by the man before his adventures can proceed satisfactorily.

The decision which must be made by the tall man is reinforced by his statement that the small man must also persuade his brothers to join him. (Cree keeps these 'he's' straight by the use of proximate and obviative third person forms.) These are the three men whose appearance was previewed by the first segment of the narrative. Again, by recognition of the powers of the small man these men will choose to accompany him on his adventures.

So the tall man let go of the land he was pulling and went with the short man.
Then the short man heard a noise as if someone was breaking trees.
It was a very loud noise.
Finally they saw a man.
'What are you making?' that little one said.
'I came here with my brother, he asked me along,' this strong one said.
'Now will you come with me?' that little one asked him.
The man was making a rope by peeling logs and winding trees together.
The short man came and he made a rope out of them, more or less.
And he asked the man who was doing this [before] if he would come with him.
And this man agreed that he would.

There was great difficulty over explaining how the trees were made of rope. More interesting, however, is the manner in which the second brother was persuaded to join the expedition. The man who was pulling the hillock, the first brother, told the man who was winding trees, the second brother, that the small man with him had requested that he come. His positive feeling toward the small man was conveyed by his use of the term '(little) brother.' This honorific form made it clear that he had accepted the man in whose company he travelled, although he was very small. The second brother was given additional evidence of the little man's strength and courage when he performed the same task, that of winding trees into a rope. On this basis, he agreed to join them.

> And they left, the three of them.
> And then they looked for someone [else]. They still looked for one.
> That one they were going to find.
> The man they had just picked up, the one that was making the rope, was twelve feet tall.
>
> Next then they came upon that other man standing up.
> The man picked up a piece of stone, a rocky mountain.
> He took it and moved it, always in the same direction.
> Now the short man said to him, 'If you're not strong, why do you do that?'
> 'Rocky mountain people are living in the mountains they said I made,' the man said.
> This man said, 'I have been sent by the spirit who is named God to build these mountains because people in the future will be numerous and they will speak different tongues.
> 'The Frenchmen will speak French.
> 'The Englishmen will speak English.
> 'The Chipewy will speak Chipewyan.
> 'The Ukrainians will speak Ukrainian.
> 'And the Crees will speak their own language.
> 'And in the end a lot of hardship and bad luck will come upon all these different races.'

Father reinforced the conclusion by reiterating that the mountains were made so that people would be there. He also said that all the different peoples should use the land, just like they do now. Marie-Louise noted that people would survive in the future because of the mountains being there. She invented a closing line: 'And this is one of the stories that tells about how mountains were formed.' The old man's closing was quite different:

> Now it's down in the book [tape recorder] as it was said and when I was a child in Crane Lake area.

Marie-Louise ignored this. The old man continued:

> Now there's something else I was going to tell them. The man [who made the mountains] predicted that in the future people would start growing their beards again. Their beards would grow as they had done originally. In that time all men had whiskers and all women didn't. All the first people used to wear long gowns. If a couple were walking with their backs covered, with their backs to you, you would think they were the same. But if you were to call to them, they would turn around and one would have a beard. Then you could tell the difference.
>
> I know that they [the investigators] will live happily together for the rest of their lives and I might meet them in the next world.

The old man then clapped his hands to show that his story was finished.

This double ending is not unique in Cree narrations. The formal story ended with the third brother's predictions for the future. But the old man telling the story wanted to make some comment which was intended for his particular audience. In this sense it might be called the moral or epilogue. He was responding to the fact that my husband had a beard (as did he) and that another white man he knew well had a beard. This was a way for the old man to include these outsiders in his rendition of traditional Cree material. It also served as a gradual transition back to the everyday conversational world. The style of the Cree changed radically, with the dignity and solemnity of the sacred story broken. This made it possible for all the participants to talk about the story.

The old man's attempt to return gradually to the spatiotemporal framework of everyday life was not entirely successful. Both Marie-Louise and Father were thinking in terms of the performance of traditional material and did not easily switch into a lighter vein. Apparently sensing the disapproval, the old man and his wife went home soon afterwards.[14] Marie-Louise and Father were silent for some time afterwards, lost in meditation about the old Cree world. Later, Father commented that the old man had changed the ending, perhaps because he was nervous about telling a sacred story to a white man. He then agreed that the story had been finished but did not understand why there had been more after that.

Both Marie-Louise and her father failed to perceive the skill with which the old man had concluded his narrative. For him, the formal narrative device paralleled the one he had used in beginning his story. He completed his narrative in mythological time with a formal ending. He then used a character from the sacred story to bridge the gap between the supernatural and everyday worlds. As at the start of his story, the progression was gradual.

1. First he spoke of old Indians with beards, who had been very close to mythological times in the Indian past.

2. Then he referred to more recent Indians who did not have beards.

3. Next, the old man followed his own progression into the future, saying that Indians would have beards again.

4. Finally, he tied his narrative to the present and future activities of the individuals present in the particular interaction. He used the theme of the beard from his prediction of the future by a mythological character to comment about the visitors to whom he had been speaking. He gave his approval to the individuals (perhaps in the manner of a priest blessing his congregation) and referred to the (Christian) future in which he would see these people again.

Although the Cree of northern Alberta have been considerably influenced by missionaries, ethnic diversity, and depreciation of Indian culture and language by Indian and white alike, traditional Cree genres of formal speaking persist and adapt. The Cree language is still spoken in its traditional functional complexity. The performance situation described here makes it clear that Cree narrative is still changing and adapting. Although the old man of this performance is not the same performer his grandfather would have been, his cultural tradition has been sufficiently strong to remain viable under a very different way of life. The Cree narrative tradition is not a static thing; its strength lies in the ability to adapt to whatever lives its performers may come to live. There is, therefore, a continuous interaction between context of performance, individual performer, and culture change.[15]

Notes

1. The dialect spoken in Wabasca, the home reserve of the Big Stone Band, is Plains Cree. This area is close to the boundary between Plains and Woods Cree, marked by a switch from / y / to / th / in certain phonological environments.

2. The old man is referred to in this manner throughout because it is his age which determines his role as an authentic carrier of the tradition. In the eyes of native people his personal identity is subordinate.

3. Father's comments were made in Cree and translated loosely by Marie-Louise at this time. The tapes were later transcribed with more detailed translations. Quotations of Father's remarks are from Marie-Louise's translation.

4. This is the style of the narrator in traditional Cree stories. Actors in the stories are quoted directly with 'he said' or 'he thought' as in introduction.

5. For example, when a man accused of beating his wife fled into the bush with his family last year, my Cree hostess, a woman of about sixty, refused to let her husband go trapping until he was caught, 'because he might be a *wihtigo* now.'

6. However, this does not account for the traditional Cree stories in which a *wihtigo* and Wisahkitchak appear in the same narrative. Many performers deny the existence of these stories when asked to reconcile the two different time frameworks. Analytically we may assume that *wihtigo* is not an individual but a psychological state personified. This state could exist in mythological time and simultaneously in present time, just as the animal actors in the sacred stories do. Each individual manifestation is representative of the category but does not exhaust it — *wihtigo*, bear, etc. (The only exception is that children may be called Wisahkitchak if they are very cunning or play a practical joke; this is a simile based on common behavioral attributes, as is the reference to *wihtigo* for someone who eats too much.)

7. Only one narrator has ever attempted to explain to me why all the stories begin: 'Wisahkitchak was walking.' This narrator explained that because they were growing up, he would tell his child audience the beginning of the story. In the beginning, Wisahkitchak was sitting. Where he was sitting, there was nothing. There was only a piece of dirt. Wisahkitchak blew on it and it grew bigger. He wondered how big to make it. This piece of dirt was the world itself. Then Wisahkitchak made a coyote, Wisahkitchak told the coyote to run around the edge of the world and come back. He came back and told Wisahkitchak how big the world had become. This happened many times. Wisahkitchak kept blowing. He didn't have enough. While the coyote was gone, Wisahkitchak made more animals, mostly game animals and birds. Then he sent the coyote for what might be the last time. Wisahkitchak got tired of waiting for this little coyote. Then Wisahkitchak got up for the first time. He got up and went off walking to look for the coyote. This is the beginning of the story and the end. The rest of the stories about Wisahkit-

chak branch off on his travels; this story is the roots. Nobody has ever heard that Wisahkitchak stopped walking so he must still be looking for that coyote.

8. Father explained at some length that many Indians used to beat their wives or ran from one woman to another. These two old people had been married for seventy-three years and had been particularly close throughout their lives. On occasion they can be seen holding hands, a gesture very rare for Cree adults and unashamedly symbolic of their relationship.

9. The positioning of the old man's son and his wife raises some interesting questions as to the ability of a non-native to acquire culturally appropriate intuitions for behavior. My husband, who has had limited contact with Indian people, drew an initial diagram of positioning in this interaction in which he reversed the positions of the man and woman. The intuition he applied was a European one, in which a man would always permit his wife to enter a room before him and to sit closer to the center of the interaction. In this case, the son would then be in direct alignment with his father and the wife closer to the audience and other participants. I objected to this positioning as factually inaccurate as well as subjectively inappropriate to Cree culture. A woman is always considered secondary to her husband and her positioning will reflect this. Thus, the son entered the room and squatted unobtrusively on the floor to listen to his father. His wife followed him and stayed in the space remaining between him and the door. Their small child remained very close to her between the two parents. We tested our understanding of the role relationships involved by asking an unrelated native person working on the tape transcriptions to tell us where the two individuals would position themselves. She said without hesitation that the woman would follow her husband and remain behind him. The moral is that the anthropologist or other outsider can indeed learn to approximate the standards of the culture; there is no inherent reason why he cannot, given sufficient time and exposure to the culture, do so in a way which approximates that of the native member of the society.

10. Prose is used to record normal casual conversation. Formal or stylized speech is given in poetic lines to approximate the tone of the original.

11. This judgment was confirmed by other native speakers listening to the tapes. Marie-Louise had not used Cree regularly for some time, and although she frequently had heard formal narratives, she had probably never tried to translate them before.

12. The use of the proximate forms for the small but strong man throughout the narrative indicates the identification of the old man with this character. Although he himself was a large man by Cree standards, his feeling of inferiority toward the special powers Indians used to have (in mythological times as well as in the recent past) was unmistakable. The smallness, however, was balanced by strength which the old man felt he had, although he was otherwise a man of no special powers. The obviate forms used for the people met by the small but strong man show that the main character observes the events of the narrative as an outside observer. He is, so to speak, an eyewitness to great things which are part of the Cree heritage. The proximate—obviate distinction organizes the narrative in the sense that it eliminates confusion: the main hero who provides the plot line in his physical movement from one situation to another, is always the focus of the narrator's attention. The other people and events are further away and seen only in relation to the journey of the main character. The only exceptions come when the main character is not participating at all.

13. This part of the story reflects the recent migration of the Cree from the woodlands to the prairies. Many story motifs assume a wooded environment which is no longer familiar. This wooded hillock would, indeed, constitute an anomaly in the western Canadian prairies, perhaps the reason Marie-Louise does not know the word.

14. The old man was extremely concerned about the quality of his performance. In fact, he phoned about an hour later to ask how he sounded on the tape. By then we were expected to have discussed his performance and settled on an evaluation.

15. I would like to thank Marie-Louise Kortuem, Samuel Auger, and Noel Boscius for their patience and hospitality to a student of their traditional ways and of their language. Frances Thompson and Roy Cardinal aided in translation of the Cree text and Carl Urion in

the transcription. I am also grateful to A. L. Vanek, who has served as an aid and sounding board in many ways.

Field research was sponsored by the Boreal Institute of the University of Alberta. Transcription and analysis were supported by the Department of Indian Affairs and Northern Development (in conjunction with a course in Cree language) and the General Fund of the University of Alberta.

To Speak with a Heated Heart: Chamula Canons of Style and Good Performance

Gary Gossen*

This paper explores a central metaphor which Chamulas used to talk about and evaluate speaking. I shall attempt to show how this metaphor — heat — functions as a basic canon of native criticism of nearly all kinds of speech performances which Chamulas recognize, from ordinary language to formal ritual speech and song. Heat possesses great religious significance because its primary referent is the sun deity (*htotik k'ak'al* "Our Father Sun"), who created and now maintains the basic temporal, spatial, and social categories of the Chamula cosmos. Controlled heat, therefore, symbolizes order in both a diachronic and synchronic sense. Language is but one of several symbolic domains which Chamulas think and talk about in terms of heat metaphors. Ritual action, the life cycle, the agricultural cycle, the day, the year, individual festivals, political power, economic status — all are measured or evaluated in units which derive ultimately from "Our Father Sun," the giver of order. Canons of verbal style and performance will therefore be described as ideal patterns which extend, in homologous fashion, into the whole fabric of Chamula social life and expressive behavior. I hope, thereby, to show how certain Chamula ethical and esthetic values behave as a unitary normative code.

After describing the community and the categories of cosmology which give symbolic power to the heat metaphor, I shall briefly outline the categories of verbal behavior which Chamulas recognize. Within this folk taxonomy, which can be seen as a continuum of style in which the individual genres are expressed, I shall discuss patterns of formalism, style, redundancy, and dyadic construction which are part of adult linguistic competence. Nearly all criteria which Chamulas use to evaluate these esthetic patterns are also moral criteria which apply to other aspects of their society. Controlled cycles of heat provide the metalanguage of native criticism for evaluating what is well spoken and beautiful. The same cycles of

*Reprinted from *Explorations in the Ethnography of Speaking*, ed. Richard Bauman and Joel Sherzer (New York: Cambridge Univ. Press, 1974), pp. 389–413, by permission of the publishers.

metaphorical heat provide the criteria for the good and the desirable in the life cycle, social relations, and cosmology. This equivalence leads me in the final section to some speculation about a dimension of Chamula thought which might be called philosophy of language.

The Community: Heat and Cosmos

Chamula is one of the eleven municipios in the state of Chiapas, Mexico, which speak Tzotzil, which belongs to the Tzeltalan group of Maya languages. Genuine bilingualism is minimal; perhaps 5% of the population, mostly men, speak Spanish well as a second language. More than forty one-room primary schools (first four grades), built in the last twenty years, have so far failed in their goal of teaching Spanish to significant numbers of Chamula children.

Some 40,000 Chamulas live patrilocally in over a hundred scattered hamlets near the top of the Chiapas Highlands, at an average elevation of 7600 feet. All Chamulas engage to a greater or lesser extent in swidden agriculture. The subsistence base consists of maize, beans, squash, and cabbage, in approximately that order of importance. In the many cases in which their own land is insufficient to produce enough food, Chamulas engage in cottage industries, such as the manufacturing of charcoal, pottery, backstrap looms, or furniture. Chamulas are governed by a political hierarchy which is partly traditional (*Ayuntamiento Regional*, consisting of sixty-two positions or *cargos*) and partly prescribed by Mexican law (*Ayuntamiento Constitucional*, consisting of six positions, including that of the chief magistrate, or *Presidente*). A religious hierarchy consisting of sixty-one major positions supervises ceremonial activities and cults to the saints and also coordinates its ritual activities with those of the political hierarchy. Political authority on the local level lies in the hands of past cargo-holders and heads of segments of patrilineages. Religious authority in the hamlets is exercised by shamans, past religious cargoholders, and again by elder males in the patrilineages.

Chamula religion and cosmology form a complex syncretistic system which is the product of sixteenth-century Spanish Catholicism and pre-Columbian Maya cults to nature deities, particularly to the sun (now identified with Christ), the moon (now the same as the Virgin Mary), water spirits, and earth lords. The other saints, including the patron saint of Chamula, San Juan, are kinsmen of the sun (the son of the moon). Chamulas also believe in individual animal soul companions which share certain aspects of people's spiritual and physical destinies.

Basic to Chamula cosmological belief is that they live in the center of the universe. They view their home municipio as the only truly safe and virtuous place on the earth. As physical distance increases, and as linguistic and social groups become ever more unlike Chamula, danger lurks more threateningly. The edges of the earth are populated by demons, strange human beings, and huge wild animals. From there one can see the terrifying spectacle of the sun and moon deities plunging into and emerging from the seas every day on their respective vertical circuits around the island universe. Not only does the sun deity delimit the spatial limits of the universe, but he also determines the temporal units (days and solar years) by the duration and position of his path. It was the sun who established order on the earth. He did this in progressive stages, separately creating the first three worlds and then destroying them, for people behaved improperly. Chamulas say that behavior equivalent to that of the people in the first three creations may still be found at the edges of the universe and, occasionally, among bad Chamulas. It is only the Fourth Creation which has been successful. This is a moral world which Chamulas must constantly strive to defend from bad behavior and evil people. Language, particularly the oral tradition, is a crucial tool for the defense, continuity, and ritual maintenance of the Fourth Creation. Perhaps the most important trait of language which provides power in Chamula social life is its capacity to express metaphorical heat in controlled, predictable cycles. Competent language use, like the sun, is characterized by measured, controlled patterns of intensity. This is expressed in various forms of redundancy which comes from the "heated heart." According to Chamula exegesis, language shares the quality of cyclical heat with other ritual substances such as rum, incense, candles, and tobacco. It is therefore necessary to report in some detail the meaning of heat in Chamula cosmology.[1]

"Our Father," the sun, is a primary and irreducible symbol of Chamula thinking and symbolism. At once in the concept of the sun, most units of lineal, cyclical, and generational time are implied, as well as the spatial limits and subdivisions of the universee, vertical and horizontal. Most of the other deities and all men are related lineally or spiritually to the sun creator. Day and night, the yearly agricultural and religious cycles, the seasons, the divisions of the day, most plants and animals, the stars, the constellations, as well as language, are the gifts of the sun, the life-force itself. Only the demons, monkeys, and other negative supernaturals were logically prior to and hostile to the coming of order. These forces killed the sun early in the First Creation and forced him to ascend in the heavens, thus providing heat, light, life, and order. Hence, the Tzotzil words for "day" (k'ak' al) and "fiesta" (k'in), which provide fundamental temporal references for Chamulas, are directly related to the Tzotzil word for fire (k'ok') and the proto-maya word for sun, heat, and divinity (k'inh), respectively. It is also relevant that one of the several names for the sun creator is htotik k'ak'al or "Our Father Heat (day)."

The fundamental spatial divisions of the universe, the cardinal directions, are derived from the relative positions of the sun on its east — west path across the heavens:

east:	emergent heat (or day)
west:	waning heat (or day)
north:	side of heaven on the right hand (of the sun)
south:	side of heaven on the left hand (of the sun)

The principal temporal divisions of each day are also described in relation to the position of the sun on its path across the sky. For example, "in the afternoon" is generally expressed in Tzotzil as "in the waning heat (or day)." "In the mid-morning" is expressed as "the heat (day) is rising now." The fiestas, which are perhaps the most commonly used temporal markers within the annual cycle, are considered to be mini-cycles of heat. Their name (*k'in*, related to sun, heat, and divinity) implies the presence of the heat metaphor. Furthermore, one is able to specify almost any day in the year by referring to stages of, or days before or after, one of the more than thirty fiestas which are celebrated annually in Chamula. In referring to a certain day in relation to the fiesta cycle, one says, for example, *sk'an to ?ošib k'ak'al ta k'in san huan*, which means "It is three days before (until) the fiesta of San Juan." This is usually understood as I have translated it, yet the relationship of the words for fiesta to the words for heat and deity is such that it is possible to understand this as "three daily cycles of heat before a major (religious) cycle of heat."

In all of these temporal references, two themes emerge which are significant in understanding the heat metaphor in relation to language. First, heat is divine and primordial; its primary referent is the sun creator, giver of temporal, spatial, and social order. Second, heat, like its primary sun referent, is cyclical. Each day finished is both a cycle of heat completed and an affirmation of the holy integrity of the sun deity. The same can be said of each year, each agricultural season, each festival, each human life. Indeed it can even be said of the largest temporal units which Chamulas recognize: the four creations of man, of which we are now in the most successful, the Fourth. In all of these, cycles of heat express and confirm the most basic principles of patrifocal order. For example, male religious officials constantly partake of the heat metaphor in properly carrying out their duties. They are said to be "helping the sun (or the saints, the sun's kinsmen) to bear the burden of the year." This burden implies heavy financial responsibility, as well as sponsorship of highly redundant ritual actions throughout the year. These invariably involve ritual substances such as rum, tobacco, tropical flowers, incense, fireworks, candles, which express actual and metaphorical heat. Furthermore, the counterclockwise direction which religious officials invariably follow through ritual circuits is, according to Chamula premises, the horizontal equivalent of the sun deity's vertical orbit. Officials thus move as the sun moves in their microcosm of ritual space (see Gossen 1972a). Another critically important aspect of ritual action which relates to the sun is of course the language used to conduct it. Ritual language, prayer, and song are all laced with metaphors for heat, as expressing homage, praise, and petition to the sun deity and his kinsmen. The highly redundant style of the ritual genres expresses the sacred and cyclical heat of religious transaction.

Heat expresses order in everyday life as well as in ritual life. The daily round of domestic life centers on the hearth, which lies near the center of the dirt floor of nearly all Chamula houses. The working day usually begins and ends around the fire, men and boys sitting and eating to the right of the hearth (from the point of view of one who faces the interior from the front door), women and girls to the left of the hearth. Furthermore, men in this patrifocal society always sit on tiny chairs, thus raising them above the cold, feminine ground, and wear sandals, which separate them from the ground and complement their masculine heat. Women, on the other hand, customarily sit on the ground, which is symbolically cold, and always go barefoot, which, symbolically, does not separate them but rather gives them direct contact with the cold, feminine earth. Coldness, femininity, and lowness are logically prior to heat, masculinity, and height. This follows from the mythological account of the coming of order. The male sun was born from the womb of the female moon and was then killed by the forces of evil and darkness. This in turn allowed him to ascend into the sky to create the cosmos, cyclical time, and patrifocal order.

The individual life cycle is also conceived of as a cycle of increasing heart from a cold beginning. A baby has a dangerously cold aspect. The individual acquires steadily increasing heat with baptism and sexual maturity. The heat of the life cycle reaches a fairly high level with social maturity, which is expressed by marriage and reproduction. The acquisition of heat may be carried further through a cargo or shamanistic career. Death plunges one into the cold from whence one came. Thus, life and death are also elementary expressions of the hot–cold syndrome of Chamula values. Life-crisis rituals and cargo initiations include symbols of life (hot and integrative) and death (cold and disjunctive). Hot and cold are also fundamental categories in the bewildering complexity which characterizes Chamula theories of illness. In sum, in nearly all aspects of Chamula life, mundane and sacred, increasing heat expresses the divine and order-giving will of the sun himself. We shall see below that language is no exception to this rule.

KINDS OF VERBAL BEHAVIOR

A bewildering number of processes, abstractions, and things can be glossed as k'op, which refers to nearly all forms of verbal behavior, including oral tradition. The term k'op can mean the following: word, language, argument, war, subject, topic, problem, dispute, court case, or traditional verbal lore. Chamulas recognize that correct use of language (that is, the Chamula dialect of Tzotzil) distinguishes them not only from non-humans, but also from their distant ancestors and from other contemporary Indian- and Spanish-speaking groups. According to Chamula narrative accounts, no one could speak in the distant past. That was one of the reasons why the sun creator destroyed the experimental people of the First and Second creations. The more recent people learned to speak Spanish and then everyone understood one another. Later, the nations and *municipios* were divided because they began quarreling. The sun deity changed languages so that people would learn to live together peacefully in small groups. Chamulas came out well in the long run, for their language was the best of them all (they refer to Tzotzil as *baȼ'i k'op* or "true language"). Language, then, came to be the distinguishing trait of social groups.

The taxonomy of *k'op*, which appears in Figs. 1 and 2, was elicited several separate times from six male informants ranging in age from eighteen to sixty-five over the period of one year. It should be noted that no data from female informants are considered. This gives a definite but unavoidable male bias to this study. I used both formal question frames and informal discussion to discover the kinds of verbal behavior which Chamulas recognize.[2] The two figures should be more or less self-explanatory. The reader will probably note that I have not made an effort to describe the taxonomy as a grid of uniform or symmetrical criteria and distinctive features. Such a scheme would be a distortion of the way in which Chamulas view the taxonomy. For example: time is a relevant criterial attribute for distinguishing level-3 categories of "new words" and "recent words"; for other categories at the same level (3) of the taxonomy, place of performance is a defining feature ("court speech"); for still others at the same level (3) performer of the words is the relevant feature ("children's improvised games"). Similarly, heat appears as a stated defining attribute in the name of only one level-2 category ("speech for people whose hearts are heated"). We know, however, that genres of "pure speech" have greater metaphorical heat value than the intermediate category which bears its name. Therefore, although I use the term "level" in referring to the scheme, I do not attach any uniform "deep structure" information to it. Levels are used only as descriptive conventions. Although I frequently recorded taxa at level 5 in the field, I have not recorded them in this abbreviated version of the classification because responses at this level were far from consistent from informant to informant. I include level-5 items in a few of the brief genre descriptions below, but only when the majority of my informants recognized them. Much more useful than any abstract explanatory grid one might impose on the taxonomy are the Chamula explanations of the supercategories. These are included in Fig. 2.

"Ordinary language" (*loʔil k'op*) is restricted in use only by the dictates of the social situation and grammaticality or intelligibility of the utterance. It is believed to be totally idiosyncratic and without noteworthiness in style, form, or content; it is everyday speech. As one moves from left to right in Figs. 1 and 2, progressively more constraints of various sorts apply to what a person says (content) and how he says it (form). The intermediate category ("language for people whose hearts are heated") contains

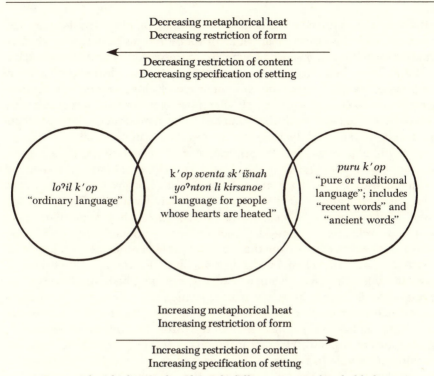

Decreasing metaphorical heat
Decreasing restriction of form

Decreasing restriction of content
Decreasing specification of setting

loʔil k'op
"ordinary language"

k'op sventa sk'išnah
yoʔnton li kirsanoe
"language for people
whose hearts are heated"

puru k'op
"pure or traditional
language"; includes
"recent words" and
"ancient words"

Increasing metaphorical heat
Increasing restriction of form

Increasing restriction of content
Increasing specification of setting

Fig. 1. A brief scheme of a Chamula folk taxonomy of verbal behavior

kinds of verbal behavior that are neither "ordinary language" nor "pure words." They are restricted with regard to form (that is, how people will speak), but they are unpredictable as far as content is concerned. A common Chamula explanation for this kind of emotional speech emphasizes the individual, idiosyncratic qualities of the performance: "It comes from the heart of each person." The term referring to all of these intermediate forms, "language for people whose hearts are heated," implies an elevated, excited, but not necessarily religious attitude on the part of the speaker. The state of excitement produces a style of verbal behavior in the intermediate forms that also occurs in the genres of "pure words." Yet, because content in the former depends on the individual whim of the speaker, these forms are not included by Chamula as a part of "pure words." It is only with the joint presence of prescribed content and form in genres to which all people ideally have equal access that we reach "pure words," on the right-hand side of the continuum shown in Figs. 1 and 2. As Chamulas told me, " 'Pure words' do not know how to change." The heat metaphor implies a transition into a more stylized form of speech, and continues from the intermediate category into the domain of "pure words," which contains the "genuine" Chamula genres of oral tradition. The implication is an obvious, but, I believe, important one: Chamula oral tradition ("pure words") is only a part of a continuum of styles of verbal behavior occurring in other, less standardized contexts. The classes of verbal behavior that are transitional carry vital information for making sense of what is "pure words." Furthermore, Chamula children begin to learn some of the transitional forms (particularly improvised games, songs, and emotional speech) long before they begin to experiment with "pure words." It therefore seems crucial to consider the whole of verbal behavior rather than just those genres having constant form and content. This will be discussed in greater detail on p. 00

Within "pure words," the criterion of time association is the most important one in distinguishing the secular forms ("recent words," associated with the present Fourth Creation) from those having greater ritual and etiological significance ("ancient words," associated with the First, Second, and Third creations). "Recent words" are colder for they do no refer to the full four-cycle creation period. "Ancient words" are hotter, for they were given and refer to events from the very beginning of order. Several apparent discrepancies in the scheme strike the non-Chamula observer. For example, certain stylistic features of "ancient words" may also be found in verbal aspects of "children's improvised games," which are thought to be idiosyncratic expressions of individual whims in the present. This does not constitute an internal inconsistency in the taxonomy, but rather illustrates an important aspect of Chamula language learning: children probably would not be able to recognize, understand, or learn the formal genres of "ancient words" if they did not experiment with the content, styles, rhythms, and syntax in their informal play behavior. Another example of apparent inconsistency is also instructive. Gossip might seem to the American or European observer to be excluded from anyone's oral tradition, for it cannot become truly "traditional" overnight. Tradition is, however, a relative thing. In Chamula, gossip does belong to "pure words" most of the time. Gossip, as the Chamulas see it, is not idiosyncratic or original in the way that intermediate types of verbal behavior are. Gossip is part of "true recent narrative" because it is a statement of fact, a segment of information known by several people in a single form, which ideally will be passed on as a whole. All, theoretically, have equal access to it. To illustrate: the gossip among women at a waterhole about the chief magistrate's oration to the Chamulas at a past festival is "true recent narrative," whereas the oration itself is not. The oration ("political oratory") belongs to the transitional category of "speech for people whose hearts are heated" because no one knew what he was going to say, only how he would say it. Another illustration may help to clarify the taxonomic criteria. Emotional speech ("speech for bad people") uses devices of cadence, repetition, syntax, and metaphor that are also found in "pure words," however, if a murder or some other noteworthy event followed the quarrel, an account of the entire event, including the language used in the quarrel, would probably be worthy of retelling as "true recent narrative."

1. *sk'op kirsano* "people's speech"

2. *loʔil k'op* "ordinary speech" or "conversational speech"

2. *puru k'op* "pure speech" or "true speech"

2. *k'op sventa šk'išnah yoʔnton yuʔun li kirsanoe* "speech for people whose hearts are heated"

3. *k'op sventa tahimol hʔolol* "children's improvised games"

3. *k'ehoh sventa hʔolol* "children's improvised songs"

3. *k'op sventa cavilto* "court speech"

3. *k'op sventa hʔopisialetik* "political oratory"

3. *k'op sventa čopol kirsano* "angry, emotional, or bad speech" or (LIT) "speech for bad people"

3. *ʔač' k'opetok* "new or recent words": associated with close time–space coordinates; Fourth Creation

4. *bac'i ʔač' k'op* "true recent narrative": folk history, gossip, tales, genealogies, other accounts of the recent past

4. *ištol k'op* "frivolous language": jokes, untrue narratives, puns, verbal dueling, proverbs, riddles

4. *tahimol* "games": traditional games, including verbal games and also verbal formulae which accompany other games

3. *ʔantivo k'opetik* "ancient words": associated with distant time–space coordinates; First, Second, and Third creations

4. *bac'i antivo k'op* "true ancient narrative": true accounts of the distant past, including "our" categories of myth, legend, and tale

4. *resal* (from Sp. *rezar* "to pray") "prayer": includes all ritual formulae directly addressed to supernaturals

4. *rioš* (from Sp. *dios* "God") "ritual speech": includes all ritual formulae not directed specifically to supernaturals

4. *k'ehoh* "song": includes drum, flute, and rattle music; also harp and guitar music; includes words and/or music

→ Increasing heat, formalism, redundancy, and invariance

Exegesis: *ta šk'o poh noʔos li kirsanoe* "the people simply talk"

Exegesis: *ta šlok' ta yoʔnton hu-hune* "it comes from the heart of each one"

Exegesis: *mu sna' shel sbaik* "they do not know how to change themselves"

Fig. 2. A folk taxonomy of Chamula verbal behavior

A CONTINUUM OF STYLE AS EXPRESSED
IN INDIVIDUAL GENRES

In this section I should like to discuss a continuum of style as it is expressed in individual genres of the taxonomy. The following are examples of gook (*lek*) speech performances by Chamula standards (cf. the taxonomy presented in Figs. 1 and 2). Space does not allow inclusion of examples of bad performance. Furthermore, I do not have such examples, labelled "bad" by Chamulas, for all of the genres. In most cases, an error in pattern of repetition (i.e., syntax, couplet sets, or sequence of dyadic sets) would render a given performance weaker as an example of its class. In presenting the "good" stylistic examples which follow I shall proceed from a cue suggested by the taxonomy itself: that increasing formalism, redundancy, and invariance are expressions of the order-giving metaphor of heat, and that "to speak with a heated heart" according to proper stylistic rules is the linguistic equivalent of doing the sun deity's will. In this way esthetics of language become subject to some of the same rules that apply to ethical social behavior.

There is, of course, much stylistic overlap between the genres, yet part and parcel of the genre's information and function is the way it is stated and performed. One of the main canons of good performance in all genres is proper cyclical patterning according to their respective rules; stylized, patterned speech is a symbol for the order-giving heat which is desirable in other classificatory domains as well. As the genres acquire greater ritual importance, they require greater heat of performance. This is expressed in greater metaphorical stacking and greater density of the semantic load. Hence, for a cargoholder to speak a formal genre well is to partake of the cyclical nature of the sun deity. Similarly for a child to speak verbatim lines well in a game is also to participate in the heat metaphor. In sum, 'to speak with a heated heart' means using prescribed redundant style competently.

Throughout, I shall emphasize that redundancy and invariance of syntax, information, and cadence are ways of saying, "These symbols matter." "Ordinary language" is typically cold in that it is believed to be idiosyncratic and non-redundant. Specialized genres are increasingly hotter as their time—space associations become greater. That is, "language for people whose hearts are heated" (emotional but idiosyncratic speech) marks the beginning of rising heat; "recent words" (genres associated with the Fourth Creation) are intermediate in kind and invariance of heat redundancy; "ancient words" (genres associated with the first three creations and distant time—space coordinates) form an extreme statement of metaphorical heat. Thus, greater time—space depth carries with it redundant stylistic associations which are themselves symbols for cyclical heat, the stuff of the cosmic order. In particular, dyadic constructions or couplets enter into these patterns of redundancy. These have been recognized cross-culturally as important stylistic devices. These dual or parallel constructions behave as elementary structures of Chamula formalism. A term which I have coined for the purposes of discussing Chamula style is "metaphorical stacking." By this I mean the tendency to repeat lines and themes for emphasis, in slightly different form; the greater the repetition, the more crucial the information. It is most typical of the more formal genres ("ancient words"), in which consecutive dyadic constructions restate important configurations of religious symbols time and time again, according to their importance for the maintenance of the social order. Elementary forms of metaphorical stacking occur in the less formal genres as well.[3]

"Ordinary Speech"

This has been discussed above. Here let me repeat simply that this is conventional speech. No one thinks about it as a special form, except to contrast the "correct" Chamula dialect with the "incorrect" neighboring Tzotzil dialects. It has no restrictions as to form and content except that it be intelligible, grammatical, and appropriate.

The Marginal Genres: "Speech for People Whose Hearts Are Heated"

"Language for people whose hearts are heated" represents the beginning of a continuum of restriction as to form, content, and setting in Chamula verbal behavior. It is more stylized than "ordinary language," yet it is not "pure words." This type of verbal behavior is distinguished from regular speech (*lo?il k'op*) in that "people's hearts are becoming heated" (*šk išnah yo?nton yu?un li kirsanoe*). I have discussed above the significance of heat in the Chamula value system. It has great positive value, for that which is "hot" is strong, mature, and life-giving. Yet heat is also dangerous when abused or uncontrolled, as drunken behavior demonstrates. The symbolic essence of heat is of course the sun deity, which is also the marker of cyclical time and order *par excellence*. It is therefore not surprising that repetition of phrases, metaphors, words, and ideas characterizes nearly all normative statements about the social order. It might be said that human social order depends upon repetition of rule-governed behavior as communicated and understood through language. Repetition and mastery of the use of language, furthermore, signal a child's successful socialization as well as adult mastery or cultural specialties. Repetition stands out as a distinctive feature of marginal genres. Speakers are excited, their hearts are hot, yet one does not know beforehand just what the speakers will say. And herein lies the critical difference which, according to Chamulas, excludes these genres from the stable genres which compose "pure words." The marginal genres show the redundant features of form and style which characterize the whole oral tradition, yet their content still comes from "within each one" (*šlok' ta huhune*); it is original and has not come intact from another source of another person. That explains why, from the Chamula point of view, the kinds of speech described in this section are neither "ordinary language" nor "pure words" but something in between. It should also be noted that the kinds of situations dealt with by these genres are either learning processes (as in children's games), challenges to the social order, or efforts to rectify it (as in court cases, scolding speech, and oration). Thus, the less formal part of the style continuum may be characterized by some variation in content and structure.

"Children's Improvised Games"
These games, including verbal and non-verbal components alike, tend usually to be imperfect children's imitations of adult behavior. The most typical verbal component of these games is related to language learning. It is verbatim repetition of words and phrases, often three or four times. (This style may also occur in emotional speech, court speech, and political oratory, the other less formal genres).

> lok' an me!   lok' an me!   lok' an me!
> Get out!   Get out!   Get out!
>
> (From a "children's improvised game")

This form of repetition is related not only to the other forms of "speech for people whose hearts are heated," but also to the genres of "pure words," as we shall see below.

"Children's Improvised Songs"
These songs are imperfect children's imitations of "song," a genre that occurs in "pure words." An important linguistic component of "children's improvised songs" is experimentation with metaphorical couplets, which are the most important stylistic building blocks of the formal genres of "ancient words." For example, the following song line came from a child's song of speculation about what animal soul he had. The small boy (four years old) sang it as he struck a cat with a stick:

> pinto čon un bi.
> Spotted animal (you are).
>
> pinto bolom un bi.
> Spotted jaguar (you are).

As an adult "song" the performance was imperfect on several counts. However, the couplet which the child used has a structure like hundreds which exist in more formal genres: same syntax in two lines, with a one-word synonym substitution in the second line.

"Court Speech"

"Court speech" refers to the language used by political officials, defendants, plaintiffs, and witnesses at court hearings that occur every day of the year except fiesta days. Verbal competence is absolutely crucial to anyone's success in court. Emotions, of course, play a vital part in all court happenings. The stylistic canons for "heated hearts" are nearly always apparent in "court speech." However, because each case is theoretically unique, one does not know beforehand what people will say, only how they will say it. The outstanding stylistic trait of "court speech" is parallel syntax. (This style occurs in emotional speech, political oratory, and narratives.)

> ?oy ša shayibuk velta ?elk'anik.
> Many times already you have stolen.
>
> šavelk'an čihe.
> You steal sheep.
>
> šavelk'an ti ?alak'e.
> You steal chickens.
>
> šavelk'an ti ?isak'e.
> You steal potatoes.
>
> šavelk'an ti ma?il e.
> You steal squash.
>
> šavelk'an ti k'u?il e.
> You steal clothing.
>
> šavelk'an ti ?itah e.
> You steal cabbage.
>
> šavelk'an ti tuluk'e.
> You steal turkeys.
>
> skotol k'usi šavelk'an.
> You steal anything.
>
> ?a? ša no?oš muyuk bu šavelk'an
>   be sbek' yat li kirsanoetik;
> The only things you don't steal
>   from people are their testicles;
>
> ?a? ša no?oš čalo?.
> And those you only eat.
>
> ("Court speech," from a court session in which
> the Presidente was chastising a female sheep thief)

Note that the repeated syntax, with one-word substitutions, is related to the metaphorical couplet and serves as an intensifier of the message. We will see below that, although this form of speech is idiosyncratic in content, its style of redundancy and parallelism is repeated throughout the oral tradition.

"Political Oratory"

"Political oratory" includes all public announcements made by religious and political officials outside ritual settings. Like "court speech," "political oratory" has highly predictable stylistic components; yet each performance is theoretically different, which is why it does not qualify as "pure speech." The stylistic devices that characterize it have already been discussed — parallel syntax, metaphorical couplets, redundancy of message, and verbatim repetition.

"Speech for Bad People"

The Chamula term for this genre is somewhat misleading, for this category of speech refers to any heated, emotional, drunken, or angry discussion. Heat is ideally desirable, for it represents the sun creator himself. Yet uncontrolled heat, that is, heat without measured cycles, is threatening. For example "speech for bad people" is so named for it sometimes leads to machete fights and killings if it is not handled with care. Therefore, emotional and excited speech is desirable if controlled and used in defense of the norm; it is undesirable if uncontrolled and used offensively against the norm. "Speech for bad people" thus refers to the excited language of those whose hearts "heat up," *possibly* to the point of no control.

The characteristic linguistic forms of this uncontrolled speech are as follows: multiple metaphorical restatements that may be in couplet form, but also in the form of longer restatements of sentence length, parallel syntax with one- and two-word substitutions, and simple verbatim repetition. Like other forms of the intermediate class, individual performances are unique and theoretically cannot be repeated. In this less formal style a repetition of ideas is expressed in non-parallel repetition. This style also occurs frequently in court speech, political oratory, and narratives. It is a form of metaphorical stacking.

> mi mu vinikukot, šaman ti ʔanč'e, penteho.
> If you were a man, you would buy a woman, you damned coward.

> čak'an ʔavahnil, pere moton šak'an.
> You want a wife, but as a gift you want (her).

> mu šak'an, kabron, mu šak'an šaman.
> You refuse to, you bastard, you refuse to buy (her).

> ("Speech for bad people," from an angry exchange between a man and his future son-in-law)

"Pure Words"

"Pure words" include those genres having constraints of three types: form, content, and social setting. Although less variation in form and content is permitted, generally the "semantic load" of words and phrases is greater in this more formal part of the style continuum than in the less formal styles discussed above. "Pure words" include the stable genres of Chamula oral tradition. As a unit, "pure words" carry a linguistic arsenal of defense for the Chamula way of life. Part of the strength of these genres seems to relate to the fact that the cyclical view of time, the very underpinning of the Chamula view of cosmic order, serves as an attribute that both unifies "pure words" and subdivides into two major classes, "recent words" and "ancient words." "Recent words" were learned or acquired in the present, Fourth Creation; "ancient words" relate to the coming and formal maintenance of the Chamula social order.

"Recent Words: True Recent Narrative"

"True recent narrative" includes "true" narrative accounts of Fourth Creation events that are worth repeating as a unit and to which all persons ideally have equal access. Stylistic traits of "true recent narrative" are familiar continuities from "speech for people whose hearts are heated." However, the joint presence of these traits with fixed content that is supposedly true qualifies these narratives as a genre of "pure words." Individuals may add emphasis in the telling of the event, but they should stick to the facts. Emphasis is given by greater or lesser density of stacking of metaphorical couplets. This serves speakers and listeners as a measure of what in the narrative is judged to be important and what is trivial. Greater redundancy of an idea, in the form of metaphorical couplets, parallel syntax, or longer semantic restatement, underlines the importance of the idea. The example which follows illustrates typical composition and a point of emphasis in a single couplet based on parallel syntax. The following fragment, from a text entitled "The Time of the Fever," tells of the influenza epidemic of 1918, which followed the Mexican Revolution. This is a particularly well performed passage, for it leaves little doubt in the listener's mind that the most important fact in the passage is that the epidemic was sent as a punishment from the sun.

> veno,
> Well, then,
>
> k'alal 'ital ti k'ak'al čamel ti vo'ne e
> When the fever came long ago
> pero veno ha? la smul ti hkaransa
> It was because of the crimes of the *carrancistas.*
>
> ?iliktal tahmek ta ?olon ?osil.
> It came from Hot Country

Parallel metaphorical couplet
{
> la la sčik'ik tal ti htotik e,
> Our Father, the Sun, brought it upon them,
>
> la la sčik'ik tal ti santoetik e
> The saints called it down upon them.
}

> pere ?ora tana ?un.
> But then something else happened.

"Recent Words: Frivolous Language"

What "true recent narrative" accomplishes with prose accounts of true breaches of the social order, "frivolous language" accomplishes with laughter. The genre actually consists of five subgenres (which might be called fifth level taxa in the context of Fig. 2). All of these express or refer to ambiguous or deviant behavior, and all elicit laughter from participants and onlookers. Laughter appears to underline the norm by placing the deviant or ambiguous item of behavior in sharp relief against the norm. Using this technique, they effect social control in informal settings and also in formal settings, when other means are not applicable. In all of the subgenres of "frivolous language" stylistic constraints are rigid, and great emphasis is given to multiple meanings. Form, content, social setting, and range of alternative meanings are more or less constant, thus qualifying them for inclusion in 'pure words.' Brief descriptions of the genres are given below.

"Lies." "Lies" are prose jokes which tell of admittedly untrue events. The subgenre might be glossed as a "tall tale." Nearly always there is a superficial theme which makes the "lie" sound like "true recent narrative," but there is always a second, usually sexual, theme which lies beneath the apparent surface theme. The laughter which "lies" elicit emphasizes by contrast what the norm is and should be. "Lies" share almost all stylistic traits with "true recent narrative." The difference is in the verity of the events reported and in the semantic dimension.

"Genuine Frivolous Talk.". This most widely used subgenre of "frivolous language" consists of hundreds of sets of suggestive words and phrases that have minimal sound shifts from one to the next. Words or phrases are spoken alternately by two players as a form of verbal dueling. The player who cannot respond to a challenge loses. As in "lies" there is a surface meaning and a second meaning or more. It is a characteristic form of boys' and men's joking behavior and frequently accompanies bantering about sexuality and sexual fantasies in this rather strait-laced society. It is a very popular form in which boys and young men strive to achieve excellence, for skill with language is highly prized and respected. There are few better indicators of adult political and ritual potential than virtuosity in this genre as an adolescent. The following is a typical exchange of "genuine frivolous talk" and is characterized by prescribed minimal sound shifts from one word or phrase to the next.

Boy I (challenging)	ʔak'bun ʔaviš.
	Give me your sister.
Boy II (replying)	ʔak'bo ʔaviš.
	Give it to your sister.
(From a verbal duel,	"truly frivolous talk")

"Obscure Words." Although glossed as "proverb," this subgenre of "frivolous language" has a different nature and apparently more complex role than proverbs have in western societies. Ultimately, Chamula "obscure words" make normative statements, but they do this by suggestion, never by actual explicit statement. In fact, they will often state the opposite of the norm. The reason for this is that their social setting demands circumlocution. They imply normative deviation by metaphor and try indirectly to correct it, and because the referent situation is usually obvious to offender, speaker, and others, they are remarkably funny. Both linguistic form and range of possible referent situations are more or less constant. Prescribed dyadic syntax, but not necessarily couplets, and dyadic semantic domains characterize the genre's style. (See Gossen 1973 for further examples.)

> ta štal li Ho? e,
> It is going to rain,
>
> pere ta štakih ta ?ora.
> But it will dry up right away.
>
> (An "obscure word" or proverb)

"Riddles." Chamula riddles behave as jokes and nearly always involve double meanings, usually emphasizing sexual or ambivalent topics which are points of stress in Chamula society. They are generally of two types, classified by linguistic form: fixed formulas and prose. In both cases, the form and content are more or less fixed, although the ambiguous referents (that is, "possible answers") may fluctuate within a given range of alternatives. Following is an example of the formula type. Like most of the other genres of "pure words," this type of riddle is characterized by dyadic syntax and corresponding meanings.

> hme? kumagre haval,
> My comadre is face up,
>
> kumpagre nuhul. k'usi ?un?
> My compadre is face down. What is it?
>
> Answer: teša.
>   A roof tile.
> (A "question word" or riddle)

"Buried Words." This subgenre behaves as a prose riddle, but is usually used to refer to specific situations, to describe and control specific cases of normative deviation. It uses the familiar parallel structures, discussed above, but the key words are nearly always sexual or scatological puns. Like "obscure words," "buried words" frequently call attention to some error in personal appearance or behavior. In a sense they tell an offender what is "wrong" by involving him in a suggestive guessing game. The humor underlies the norm but also mitigates potential hard feelings and quarrels.

"Recent Words: Games"

This genre includes verbal and non-verbal aspects of those games having definite rules and names. It is sometimes divided further into children's games, which are combined verbal and non-verbal performances, and adults' games, which are mostly verbal. The latter overlap with the subgenre of "frivolous language." In reference to children's games, it is important to note that they include rule-governed action of both a verbal and nonverbal nature. This implies that the verbal-non-verbal distinction is not particularly significant to Chamulas. It is rather the rule-governed aspect, the moral dimension, the predictability, which matter as criteria for inclusion of the genre in "pure words."

The verbal component is usually a combination of fixed lines of emotional speech and set formulae. The emotional lines accompanying the action are verbatim repetitions (usually in twos and threes) of key words and phrases. Frequently there are also set, redundant formulae, which must be said to make the game "correct." One such line comes from a kind of hide-and-go-seek game called Peter Lizard (*petul ʔokoč'*) in which the child playing Peter Lizard hides, while the other children try to find him, shouting:

> buyot?   buyot?
> Where are you?   Where are you?
>
> buyot, petul ʔokoč?
> Where are you, Peter Lizard?

When they find him (he helps by giving whistle signals), they pursue him and eventually trap him by piling on top of him. Thus, both actions and speech have constraints of form and content in true Chamula 'games.'

"Ancient Words: True Ancient Narrative"

This narrative genre shares many stylistic traits and performance aspects with "true recent narrative" (see above). The important difference between the two is content, this being related to the temporal dimension. Like all genres of "ancient words," "true ancient narrative" reports or refers to events of the first three creations. As such, most of the narrations are etiological and explanatory. Related to the role of "true ancient narrative" in stating the coming of the present order is a greater message redundancy than one finds in "true recent narrative." Items of assumed knowledge about the nature and establishment of order require more metaphorical stacking, for emphasis, than the threats to order which are reported in "true recent narrative." An example of this pattern follows. It is a fragment from a narrative about the Second Creation relating the origin of Ladinos[4] from the offspring of a Second Creation Ladino woman and her dog. Note the symmetry of this fragment, built of couplets.

	šinulan ʔanɛ́,
Parallel	The Ladino woman,
couplet	šinulan ɛ́eb;
	The Ladino girl;

	k'uyepal ʔoy?
Interrogative	How many were there?
couplet	čib sbi.
	Two of them.

	ɛ́'akal ta šanav,
Parallel	Behind her it walked,
couplet	ɛ́'akal ta sbeʔin:
	Behind her it travelled:

	šči ʔuk sɛ́i ʔ,
Semantic	She and the dog,
couplet	muyuk bu ta šanav stuk.
	She did not walk alone.

Not all texts are as symmetrical and redundant as this one, nor is symmetry necessarily present throughout a text. The fragment, however, illustrates a general tendency for all genres of "ancient words" to utilize greater stylistic redundancy than "recent words." This relates to the kind of information carried; it is crucial, basic knowledge that must be understood by all and formally maintained. Hence, still greater metaphorical heat is implied here than in genres previously discussed. Furthermore, "true ancient narrative" (and less frequently "true recent narrative") often is characterized by the more formal style of metaphorical restatement of an idea in couplets and multiples thereof. This metaphorical stacking for emphasis is present in the example below. Not accidentally, the heat of redundancy in three related couplets refers to none other than the sun deity himself.

Non-parallel	sakub lek ti banamil e.
metaphorical	The earth brightened.
couplet	lok' la talel ti htotik e.
	The sun came out.

	sakhaman ša la talel ti šohobale.
Non-parallel	Its rays came forth in soft white radiance.
metaphorical	
couplet	heč la ti htotik ta vinahel e yal la talel ta banamil
	So it was that the sun in heaven came down to earth

Non-parallel	ta la spas yan ti kirsanoetik e,
metaphorical	To make some other people,
couplet	melɛ́ah ti kirsanoetik e.
	To prepare mankind once again.

(From a text of "true ancient narrative")

"Ancient Words: Prayer"

"Prayer" is a ritual language addressed to supernaturals. It consists wholly of formal, bound couplets. I have never heard a "prayer" composed of smaller elements. Its use implies a ritual setting. Hence, still greater metaphorical heat is implied here than in genres previously discussed. All adult Chamulas know some "prayers"; religious specialists know hundreds. In all cases the components remain the same; highly redundant, metaphorical couplets with prescribed content and a more or less fixed order, the content and order of the couplets being determined by the specific ritual setting. This form also occurs constantly in "language for rendering holy" and in "song." Metaphorical stacking is used to emphasize religious symbols.

Parallel metaphorical couplet	lital ta yolon ?avok, I have come before your feet, lital ta yolon 'ak'ob. I have come before your hands.
Parallel metaphorical couplet	šči?uk hnup, With my wife, šči?uk hči?il, with my companion,
Parallel metaphorical couplet	šči?uk kol, With my children šči?uk hnič'nab. with my offspring.
Parallel metaphorical couplet	hbeh yoh kantila, But a feeble candle (I bring), lah yoh ničim, But a withered flower (I bring),
Parallel metaphorical couplet	muk'ta san huan, Great San Juan, muk'ta patron. Great Patron.

(From a "prayer of salutation" for San Juan)

The text illustrates a pattern of "ancient words": the greater the symbolic significance of a transaction, the more condensed and redundant will be the heated language used to conduct it.

"Ancient Words: Ritual Speech"

"Ritual speech" includes all ritual language not directed to supernaturals. Like "prayer," some kinds of "ritual speech" must be known by all adult Chamulas; religious and political specialists know the dozens of kinds required for their respective tasks. "Ritual speech" is used by ritual officials and laymen to talk among themselves on the elevated plane of the ritual setting. It is constantly present in Chamula life, from drinking ceremonies to installation of new ritual officials to bride-petitioning rites. Since it always accompanies ritual transactions, its content is as varied as these settings. The style (with some exceptions, such as drinking toasts) is very much like that of "prayer," and it is remarkably constant from one setting to the next. Like "prayer," it is built almost entirely of bound formal couplets, which are theoretically irreducible components for the composition of "ritual speech." The relationship of redundancy of style and content to the high symbolic significance of the transaction applies to "ritual speech" as it does to "prayer."

"Ancient Words: Song"

"Song" may be seen as the opposite end of a continuum of formalism and redundancy beginning with "ordinary language" (lo?il k' op). Again, the truly heated heart is speaking. "Song" has all of the formal stylistic attributes of "prayer" and "ritual speech," plus musical form and instrumental accompaniment (harp, guitar, and rattle). It is language so hot that it becomes, as it were, an essence, like the smoke of tobacco or incense. "Song" is present together with these other hot sacred substances at nearly all Chamula public rituals and at most private ones. No major Chamula ritual performance takes place without musicians. (Holy Week festivities are a near exception to this rule.) "Song" may be said to be the highest form of language addressed to supernaturals. The instruments are said to sing with heated hearts just as people do. "Song" is thus an extreme statement of metaphorical heat, for the musical form and heavily "stacked" couplet structure together make it possible to repeat them *ad infinitum* until the ritual events they accompany have concluded. Directed to the sun deity and his kinsmen (the saints), they are the pure essence of linguistic heat.

Parallel metaphorical couplet	sk'ak'alil la ?ak'inal e, It is the day of your fiesta, sk'ak'alil la ?apaškual e, It is the day of your joy,
Parallel metaphorical couplet	muk'ulil san huan e, Great San Juan, muk'ulil patron e. Great Patron.
Parallel metaphorical couplet	k'uyepal čihšanavotik ?o ta hlikel bi! How soon we are to be walking! k'uyepal čihšanavotik ?o ta htabel bi! How soon we are to be commencing the procession!

Parallel
metaphorical
couplet

> sk'ak'alil aničim ba,
> It is the day of your flowery face,
>
> sk'ak'alil ?aničim sat.
> It is the day of your flowery countenance.

Nonsense
syllables as
parallel
metaphorical
couplet

> la la li la lai la ?o
> la la li la lai la a
>
> la la li la lai la a
> la la li la lai la ?o

(A section from the first of the four "songs of praise for San Juan." San Juan is the patron saint of Chamula.)

LANGUAGE, STYLE, AND COSMOS

Throughout I have suggested that metaphorical heat gives some conceptual unity to the range of redundant style which Chamulas recognize as necessary and proper for good performance of the respective genres of their oral tradition. I also have suggested that the same metaphor operates as a fundamental organizational concept in Chamula thought, ethics, religion, and cosmology. This should hardly come as a surprise, for oral tradition, like any expressive domain, is a "social fact" which shares organizational principles with the society in which it lives.

In language itself, words and strict rules for combining them can generate infinite numbers of sentences. Chamula oral tradition is more invariant than the Tzotzil language in which it is expressed, for the traditional genres involve stylistic patterns which, by Chamula explanation, "do not know how to change" (*mu sna?shel sbaik*). Their traditional genres which "do not know how to change" also deal with assumptions and rules which themselves should not vary beyond given alternatives. This brings us to the fact, stated many times above, that oral tradition is primarily concerned with norms and limits of permitted variation within them. In this sense, Chamula oral tradition is a more or less invariant expressive system that provides information which helps people to deal with more or less invariant aspects of the social system. It therefore is fitting and consistent that the primary invariable aspect of Chamula cosmos — the sun deity — should provide a native metalanguage for talking about some of the invariable canons of language use.

These canons are expressed in a clear continuum from lesser to greater stylistic formality, invariance, and redundancy as one moves from ordinary discourse to "ancient words." The complexity of semantic reference also changes from one-word — one-referent relationships in ordinary discourse, through punning and verbal play with multiple ambiguous referents in the marginal genres and in "recent words," to highly complex ritual and religious symbolism in 'ancient words.' In every case the style of a genre of *k'op* has metaphorical value of its own, enabling a speaker to establish the mood and symbolic significance of his utterance by the way he speaks. The continuum of style is an approximation of the language-learning process itself. Children begin their mastery of *k'op* by learning to repeat single words correctly and relate them to the correct referents. Greater linguistic sophistication is required for using metaphoric restatement, parallel syntax, punning, and other forms of linguistic play. Mastery of formal dyadic couplets and other parallel structures, and the hundreds of alternative ways they can combine, plus the technique of "metaphorical stacking," are even more sophisticated techniques which Chamulas master only in the "masture heat" of adulthood.

Thus, the life cycle, language learning, stylistic complexity of language genre, context of performance, and metaphorical heat are all intimately related to sun primacy in Chamula thought. This characterizes the whole of *k'op* and not just formal genres. A piece of gossip in "true recent narrative" does not require great stylistic embellishment and redundancy because its message is not crucial to the formal maintenance of order. It usually deals only with a breach in the present social order. It corrects informally. In contrast, redundancy and formal dyadic style are required in order to give the proper emphasis to words which refer to ritual symbols, those objects and concepts which are highly imbued with multiple meanings. The diffuseness of the semantic referents of ritual symbols seems to require verbal representations which are analogous to the concepts themselves. For example, the sun is omnipotent and omnipresent. This makes intelligible the dozens of metaphors, sometimes stated consecutively and in dyadic structures, which are used to talk about him and to him. The sun deity's multiple aspects and the cycles of time which he represents make a kind of cyclically patterned style of speech appropriate for talking to him and of him. Like meets like. Similarly, "to speak with a heated heart" is to do justice to any specialized language use, for Tzotzil ("the true language") itself was a gift of the sun.[5]

Notes

1. More detail on Chamula world view and cosmology can be found in Gossen, "Temporal and Spatial Equivalents in Chamula Ritual Symbolism," in W. Lessa and E. Z. Vogt (eds.) *Reader in Comparative Religion*, 3rd ed., (1972), and Gossen, "Another look at world view: aerial photography and Chamula cosmology," in E. Z. Vogt (ed.) *Aerial Photography in Anthropological Field Research*, (1974). More extensive ethnographic data on Chamula appear in R. Pozas, "Chamula: un pueblo indio de Los Altos de Chiapas," *Memorias del Instituto Nacional Indigenista*, VIII, (1959), and Gossen, *Chamulas in the World of the Sun: Time and Space in a Maya Oral Tradition* (1974).

2. See Gossen, "Chamula genres of verbal behavior," in A. Paredes and R. Bauman (eds.) *Toward New Perspectives in Folklore* (1972) for methodology and complete descriptions of all genres. See Victoria R. Bricker on Tzotzil-speaking Zinacantan and Brian Stross on Tzeltal-speaking Tenejapa, both in R. Bauman and J. Sherzer (eds.) *Explorations in the Eth-*

nography of Speaking (London: Cambridge University Press, 1974), for comparative data on speech genres recognized in Maya Indian communities which are contiguous with Chamula.

3. *Grammatical parallelism* as I use it in this paper is one of the stylistic devices used to build *metaphorical couplets*. In particular it is the principal structural trait — same syntax in two consecutive lines, with one- and two-word substitutions in the second line — which characterizes what I call the *parallel metaphorical couplet*. Both this form and the *non-parallel metaphorical couplet* have dyadic semantic construction — same idea repeated with slightly different images in the second line. The two couplets differ in that the latter form does not have parallel syntax. There are other *dyadic constructions*, of which verbatim repetition, question and answer sets, verbal duel exchanges, and contrastive semantic sets (as in proverbs) are examples. Information in all of these dyadic constructions may be emphasized by means of the device which I call *metaphorical stacking*. Stacking is a form of message redundancy in which the speaker repeats critical information, usually in consecutive dyadic increments, until he achieves the desired emphasis. Metaphorical stacking is most typical of "ancient words," in which phrases referring to multivocal sacred symbols are the ones most commonly stacked for emphasis. However, stacking may also occur as an emphatic device in "recent words" and in the marginal genres. Stacks composed of consecutive dual constructions which "say" the same thing — or give different aspects of the same thing — may have as many as twenty lines (or ten couplets), the number depending upon the relative importance of the symbols being discussed.

4. Term used in Chiapas for people who are non-Indians from a cultural point of view.

5. My fieldwork in Chamula, state of Chiapas, Mexico, was undertaken at the suggestion of Professor Evon Z. Vogt, whose Harvard Chiapas Project is now approaching its fifteenth continuous year. I am grateful to him and numerous fieldworkers in this project for providing background linguistic knowledge and field facilities, as well as intellectual stimulation and encouragement while I was in the field. In the summer of 1965, I was supported by a National Science Foundation Cooperative Fellowship; in 1968–9 — the major portion of my fieldwork — I was supported by a predoctoral fellowship and an attached research grant from N.I.M.H. This financial support is gratefully acknowledged.

An Approach to
Native American Texts   Arnold Krupat[*]

Recent developments in post-structuralist hermeneutical theory, whatever their effect on the reading of Western literature, have had an enormously salutary effect on the reading of Native American literature. With the reexamination of such concepts as voice, text, and performance, and of the ontological and epistemological status of the sign, has come a variety of effective means for specifying and demonstrating the complexity and richness of Native American narrative. The movement away from structuralism's binary method necessarily rejected Claude Lévi-Strauss' opposition of the "myth" to the "poem," the one infinitely translatable, the other virtually untranslatable. In Lévi-Strauss' work, anything that might be considered the literature of "primitive" people always appeared as myth, its "content" available for transformation into abstract pairs while its "form," its actual language, was simply ignored or dismissed.

*Reprinted from *Critical Inquiry*, 9 (1982) 323–38.

Dell Hymes contributed significantly to the study of Native American texts by producing the conceptual structures of Native American narratives as a function of their particular linguistic structures, thus accepting Lévi-Strauss' insistence on their broad meaningfulness while rejecting his indifference to the actual terms of their presentation. Hymes has recently reminded us of what should have been obvious all along, that "the problems of understanding what Native American narrators have intended and expressed is difficult enough. It is far more difficult if, in a certain sense, we do not know what they said."[1] In all too many cases it is not possible to "know what they said," for what they said was never transcribed — or if transcribed, not preserved. All the more reason, then, to pay particularly close attention to those transcriptions (and, more recently, tapes) which do exist. Hymes himself, unusually learned in Native languages, has shown how informed scrutiny of transcriptions can reveal structural patterns which had been entirely obscured in English prose translation.

Beyond the considerable difficulty of knowing "what they said" lies the difficulty of knowing how they said it. Indian literature presents itself exclusively in the form of oral performances, not textual objects; no matter how scrupulous a transcription may be, it is inevitably a declension from the narrative as act. Attempting to recuperate the performative dimension, Dennis Tedlock worked directly from tape recordings to produce his well-known anthology from the Zuni, *Finding the Center* (1972). Tedlock used typographical variations to convey changes of pitch, volume, and pace; he also indicated the audience responses important to Native American narrative. Tedlock is perhaps foremost among those students of Indian literature wishing to move "toward an oral poetics."[2]

Unlike Tedlock, I do not believe that our textual culture, although presently restructuring itself to replace print with the printout, can develop an oral poetics. But this is not to say that the idea of an oral poetics can't be effective in checking our tendency to project alphabetic categories onto the nonalphabetic practice of Native Americans. We need to acknowledge the very nearly disabling fact that most of us (non-Indians, but a great many Indians, too) are going to experience Native American narrative art almost exclusively in textual form. This remains the case no matter how much Tedlock or his colleague Jerome Rothenberg may juggle typography. Yet we need to acknowledge as well that our desire for lost originals here is not the nostalgia of Western metaphysics but the price of Western imperial history. It is a result of the conquest and dispossession of the tribes that the signifier replaces the act; our script marked on the page is the pale trace of what their voices performed.

There is, nonetheless, every reason to attempt to understand both the texts we have and the performances we must at least try to imagine (some of them the better imagined because of the tape recordings of performances which we do have). I want to move here in the direction of a systematization by examining the concepts of (1) the mode of production of the text, (2) the author, (3) literature, and (4) canonicity to show how they may organize an approach to Native American texts.

1 THE MODE OF PRODUCTION OF THE TEXT

The concept of the mode of production — which includes the forces or means of production and the relations of production — derives from Marxist studies in which it designates the particular form of a given society's economic organization at a given time. Because the mode of production — the economic base — is considered largely to determine social relationships, and social relationships to determine consciousness and its material expressions, the importance of the mode of production to literary studies is clear. This is, of course, to assert what should be apparent but in a great deal of American liberal criticism is not — that texts are social and material, that they are made actively and by the expenditure of labor, and they they are commodities whose exchange value is not solely a question of the economics of publishing.

Important as this is for Euramerican writing, it is absolutely crucial for Native American texts, which cannot even be thought except as the products of a complex but historically specifiable division of labor. There simply were no Native American *texts* until whites decided to collaborate with Indians and make them. Nor is it unworthy of mention that they did not decide to make them until the late nineteenth century, when the American economy itself had shifted its base to making. Earlier, in the colonial period, trade was economically paramount. From the revolutionary period into the nineteenth century, America's wealth was based upon cultivation, not production: agri-culture and land "improvement" were, in Benjamin Franklin's phrase, "the way to wealth." So long as this remained the case, revolutionaries and Americans defined their lives against the Indian as wholly Other. They insisted, despite abundant evidence to the contrary, that the Natives were hunters, not farmers, and as noncultivators could have no culture — thus nothing worthy of textualization.

With a few exceptions, Indian texts did not begin to be produced until the 1830s, when the eastern tribes were forcibly removed west of the Mississippi. It was then that Indians, still popularly believed to have no culture of their own and so no capacity for cultural contribution, were accorded a history — one which began when a particular tribe resisted white encroachment. Indian resistance was not new, having commenced almost at the first moment of white invasion; what was new after 1830 was an interest in the Indians' own perspective on this "history." Thus the majority of these earliest Native American texts were attempts to preserve, complete, or correct the record inscribed by whites as a contribution to history. But most of what appears today in the anthologies as Indian literature — poems, tales, stories — was collected after the Civil War, very roughly from 1887–1934, inscribed by anthropologists determined to preserve this vanishing heritage for science.[3]

In particular, the rigorously trained workers sent into the field by Franz Boas after the turn of the century, conscious of their status as scientists, valued "translations that were 'direct' or 'close' or 'literal,' " as Tedlock has noted. These they "published with as few changes as possible from the sort of English used by interpreters or bilingual narrators."[4] This procedure led inevitably to the sort of "disaster" Tedlock quotes from Elsie Clews Parsons and Ruth Benedict. On the other hand, Frank Hamilton Cushing and other field workers who preceded Boas' students and who defined their scientific mission more loosely seem to have erred in a different direction, achieving a "style" in Tedlock's estimate, "more Victorian than Indian."[5] If the anthropological scientists produced either a florid "Victorian" style or a stiff, wooden style rather than an "Indian" style, what of the poets and humanists who have tried their hand at producing an Indian literature?

Early in this century, Mary Austin admitted her role in the production of the signifier by calling the Indian poems in her anthology, *The American Rhythm* (1923), *Reëxpressions of Amerindian Songs.*[6] That their style owes as much to imagist free verse as to "Indian" style is obvious, however, and the obvious result of Austin's contribution. More recently, William Brandon and, particularly, Rothenberg have extensively revised, even rewritten, Indian materials, thereby claiming to have achieved a more authentic Indian version than literal transcription and translation could provide. But it is difficult to avoid concluding once more that Indian style (whatever one conceives it to be) has been lost to the inscriber's cultural allegiance: Rothenberg's Indian poems appear, we may say, in post-modernist or *Alcheringa* style.[7]

But this is why the concept of the mode of production is of such importance, for it forces us to go beyond any given editor's account of (or silence in regard to) how a text was made in the direction of historical reconstruction. Indian *texts* are always the consequence of a collaboration; no matter what we wish to say about them, it is useful to know, as far as we can, just how they were made. How many workers, for example, were involved in the production of the final text, and what did each contribute to it? Do variants of a given version exist, and, if so, what were the differences in the production of each? How well did the various workers (Indian informant-speaker, white editor-transcriber, and also apparently in all cases, at least one translator, usually part-Indian and part-white) know each other's language? Under what auspices was the text produced, and what claims were made for it? Was its inscription sponsored by anthropological science and, if so, through a museum or a university? Was it paid for by the government or by a private individual? Was it sponsored historically or legally, in relation to a particular event or a particular claim? Was it sponsored poetically, religiously, morally, in the interest of revitalizing some aspect of American practice? What were the apparent intentions of the producers and what benefits did they derive from their collaborative project?

If questions like these seem uninteresting, I can only say that they are necessary so far as we aspire to some degree of rigorous understanding. If questions like these seem unliterary, I can only say that it is precisely upon their answers that any judgment of literariness will depend. Inquiry into the mode of production of most of the Native American texts conventionally studied as "scientific" — historical or anthropological — reveals complexities that seem far more accurately comprehended by a specifically literary hermeneutics. (The converse might also turn out to be true: thus the work of Hyemeyohsts Storm which presents itself as fiction might better be studied for its sociological or anthropological interest.) Jack Goody's observation that "most transcription transforms, often in complex ways; one can never be quite sure what utterance the 'text' represents," returns us to Hymes' concern for what Native American narrators actually said and marks the point of departure for the kind of work that must be done for Native texts.[8] Whatever Native American narrators may have said and however they may have said it, we will begin to understand what we have only when we recognize that the signifier's complex composition is the result of a historically specifiable mode of production — the result of not only the confrontation of two individuals but equally, in Fredric Jameson's words, "the confrontation of two distinct social forms or modes of production," a collective as well as an individual encounter.[9]

2 THE AUTHOR

All texts are materially produced, but not all texts have authors. Michel Foucault notes that a

> private letter may have a signatory, but it does not have an author; a contract can have an underwriter, but not an author; and, similarly, an anonymous poster attached to a wall may have a writer, but he cannot be an author. In this sense, the function of an author is to characterize the existence, circulation, and operation of certain discourses within a society.[10]

Foucault's statement has bearing upon the types and categories of use or exchange of any "discourse" and upon its consequent valuation: American Indian discourse, until very recently, has been notoriously lacking in its possession of named authors, and this has assuredly contributed to Euramerican neglect of it. As Foucault also notes, "Discourse that possesses an author's name is not to be immediately consumed and forgotten; neither is it accorded the momentary attention given to ordinary, fleeting words. Rather, its status and its manner of reception are regulated by the culture in which it circulates."[11] But can one attach an author's name to American Indian discourse? and if so, Whose? For its "status and its manner of reception" have always been tied to its presumptive anonymity, its lack of named authors.

In European and Euramerican culture, the rise of the author parallels the rise of the individual. Homologous with the bourgeois conceptualization of an opposition between the individual and society appears the corollary opposition between individual (private) and collective (public) production and composition. Individual composition means written composition, for only texts can have individual authors. From the eighteenth century forward, individual authors are protected by copyright laws. Authors are—the idea would seem to be obvious—the individual creators of the individual works which carry their name; accordingly, they are fully entitled to profit from the sale and circulation of their private property.

With the development of the conception of individual authorship, half of the etymological sense of the word "author," previously strong in ordinary understanding, dropped out of currency. "Author" is from the Latin *augere* which means both "to originate" and "to augment." But from the eighteenth and, most particularly, from the nineteenth century on, authors were regarded strictly as originators. Not Milton's desire to augment the tradition of elegy or epic, nor Pope's to say well what's oft been thought, but the will to original creation came to dominate literary projects. The authority of the author, in this view, derives not from his predecessors and their productions, nor from his contemporaries and theirs, but, instead, from his personality, his imagination, or, arriving at the ultimate mystification, from his genius which transcends the society that would seek to constrain it.

This particular methodology never developed in Native American culture, where the individual could not in any positive way be imagined to stand outside or against his society; where, as generations of whites lamented, there was an utterly deficient appreciation of the virtues of private property; and where, of course, there was no writing—and so no authors.

In studying this situation, John Bierhorst has spoken of the essential "anonymity" of Indian literature, for "the Indian poet does not consider himself the originator of his material but merely the conveyor. Either he has heard it from an elder or he has received it from a supernatural power. . . . Indian poetry, then, is usually attributed not to an individual but to his culture."[12] Or, at least, we must so attribute it. Thus in Indian narrative there was always augmentation, never origination; in Edward Said's sense, there might be some specifiable *beginning* for a particular song or story but never an attempt to assert its absolute *origin*. (This roughly parallels differences between various Native creation tales, where even in "the beginning" something always already exists, and the Judeo-Christian creation story in Genesis, which presents the absolute origination of the world through the solitary activity of God, the Author of Creation.)[13]

This posed a considerable dilemma for those who wished to write down Indian "literature." What was the Euramerican who published Indian poems to call himself? He was not their author, for he did not originate the material, and he could not admit to having augmented it without provoking the charge that he had thereby contaminated its authenticity. He was not merely the translator, for translators work from texts (sometimes in consultation with authors) and usually claim full competency in the language from which they are translating. Indian literature is not textual, and, to my knowledge, no Euramerican translator has ever tried to work entirely on the basis of his own competence in the Native language. Referring to oneself as the editor evades none of these problems, for the question arises, What editorial principle guided the final production of the text?

In the name of scientific accuracy, the late nineteenth- and early twentieth-century students of Boas, as I have noted, aimed for literalness in their translations, and contemporary commentators like William Bevis approve this commitment to "what they said." Poets from Austin to Rothenberg, on the other hand, have tended to see literalness as a bar to authenticity in translation. To get the actual feel of the thing (as they imagine it to have felt), they have taken great liberties in translation, seeking, in general, to convey "how they said it." Tedlock, at present, speaks well of this procedure. In any case, the "same" song or story at the hands of one or the other group of translators appears in very different forms. Thus we seem to have a situation parallel to that Frank Kermode summarizes as necessitating a choice between the search (vain, as Kermode thinks) for what the text "originally meant" and what it "originally means"—except that in Native American literature not just the meaning but the text itself is in question.[14]

Each of us may seek to resolve this sort of problem differently; nonetheless, the post-structuralist movement away from binary procedures should at least make it familiar, indeed, even attractive to consider. For Native American texts present concrete and actual instances of a kind that must remain hypothetical—however vigorously argued—within Western writing. E. D. Hirsch probably remains the most vigorous defender of the author and his intentions as the ethically and aesthetically privileged determinators of the text and its meaning, while Norman Holland and Stanley Fish claim that only the reader's activity constitutes the text. Critics as widely diverse as Raymond Williams and Wolfgang Iser have attempted to reconcile these opposed contentions. All of this, of course, bears upon our understanding of "author," and our understanding can be advanced by attention to Native American practice.

As Hymes writes:

> Comparative study of Native American narratives and analysis of fine individual narratives together make evident, behind the many varied linkages, shapings, and realizations of plots and motifs, the working of many reflective and articulate minds. In our own culture we would call such working with the received materials of our literary tradition authorship. We should do so in the case of Native Americans as well . . . in order to do justice to their accomplishments. But the notion, "author," is ours, not theirs.[15]

This seems just: yet "our" present "notion" of authorship has begun to describe something not so very different from "their" practice. We have come to recognize, for example, that even in our literature the force and authority of individual texts derives from what Said has called a system of *"affiliation . . .* an often implicit network of peculiarly cultural . . . associations between forms, statements, and other aesthetic elaborations on the one hand, and on the other, institutions, agencies, classes, and fairly amorphous social forces."[16] One way to specify some of the common problematics of Euramerican and Indian texts exists in what Williams calls the "recognition of the relation of a collective mode and an individual project." For, "the irreducibly individual projects that particular works are, may come in experience and in analysis to show resemblances which allow us to group them into collective modes."[17]

From this perspective we can see not only that the vaunted autonomy of the author in Western literature is not total but also that the anonymity of the Native American "conveyor" is not total either. We must not let the look of our writing entirely obscure for us the fact that it, too, is, in Kenneth Burke's still serviceable term, "dramatistic," a performance in which not only language but the human voice speaks, a voice at once individual and collective. In the same way, Indian narrators in successive performances don't only "convey" but comment, adding, deleting, and supplying emphases that alter as well as merely reproduce the already given.[18] We can see, therefore, that the Indian collective-anonymous "author" and the bourgeois individual-named "author" are no so much opposites as variants of the exercise of what (in Foucault's phrase) we may call the "author-function." But if this is so, we will have to think of literature as something other than the pure creation of the great author.

3 LITERATURE

The term "literature" today is undergoing a transformation as a result of two interrelated though very different developments. The first of these — that within advanced academic criticism — is fairly easy to describe and perhaps largely complete. But the second of these — that within the technology of microcomputers — is not so clear and probably only in its early stages. Though it exceeds the scope of this essay, I must remark that the shift from print to printout, from the library to the computer bank, is a real revolution; we are in the midst of a change to a genuinely new mode of production.

At present, critics like Paul de Man and Harold Bloom are expanding the specific nineteenth-century meaning of literature as "expressive and imaginative writing" to include all writing, thus causing the older etymological force of literature (from *littera*, "letter") to reemerge. All writing is imaginative and expressive, it has been claimed, because of the illimitable free play of signification inherent in the act of inscription itself, what de Man calls "the proliferating and disruptive power of figural language."[19] Yet the figural simply cannot be purged from writing; philosophers and social scientists cannot produce texts safe from figural disruption and self-decon-struction; neither, of course, can literary critics, whose texts, to use Bloom's terminology, are in any case misreadings or "misprisions" precisely as they are "strong" readings. Thus we are to believe that all writing is literature in the nineteenth-century sense merely, as in the older etymological sense, by being *writing*.

Indians, of course, did not write — at least they had no alphabet and marked no letters on paper. Perhaps, as Lewis Henry Morgan would con-clude, they had risen above the level of "savagery," yet they remained "bar-barians," analphabetically short of the supreme condition of "civilization."[20] Literature, product of the man of letters — poet, philosopher, historian, or divine — clearly could not exist among the culture-less, uncivilized children of nature, who did not write. When Thomas Jefferson, in a famous ex-ample, quoted the speech of Chief Logan, his purpose was to assert the ra-tionality and intelligence of Indians by showing them capable of eloquent oratory; but this was still deemed antecedent to a capacity for writing and for littera-ture.

By the early nineteenth century, literature came to mean not the entire culture of letters but, particularly, imaginative and expressive utterance — in writing, to be sure, but also, as Wordsworth noted, in the speech of com-mon men who might not be able to write. Romanticism's discovery of the "organic" Middle Ages (a period increasingly attractive as English society, industrializing, came to be considered "mechanical"), gave rise to an ex-panded awareness of oral literature as something other than a contradiction in terms. Once these ideas crossed the ocean, it became attractive (at least in the east) to think of Indians as standing in for America's missing feudal past, to hear their chants as poetic (rather than as satanic or as gibberish), as constituting a literature that remained only to be established in writing. While men like the Moravian Father John Heckewelder began this task even before the time of Indian Removal, very little was actually achieved until the last quarter of the nineteenth century when, as I have noted, most of what we find in the anthologies of Indian literature today was collected by anthropologists engaged in the practice of science. As the concept of the frontier yielded to that of the fieldwork, first the anthropologists of the Bu-reau of American Ethnology and the newly founded museums, and then the wave of anthropologists trained by Boas set out to preserve the material and ceremonial (but not the social and political) culture of the "vanishing race." Daniel Brinton, James Mooney, Alice Fletcher, Frances Densmore, Alfred Kroeber, Paul Radin, Robert Lowie, Parsons, Cushing, Boas himself, and others collected, recorded, transcribed, and translated — and some of what they got was considered literature.

These first recorders — to whom, whatever their limitations, we owe an enormous debt — had no uniform system of nomenclature for describing and cataloging the different materials they recorded, nor have we yet made much progress in this area. Horatio Hale, in 1883, published *The Iroquois*

Book of Rites, among which are compositions we might well call literature. Brinton, in 1890, published "Native American Poetry"; Cushing produced his *Outlines of Zuñi Creation Myths* in 1896, and in 1901 materials he thought better described as *Zuñi Folk Tales*. Fletcher thought she had got *Indian Story and Song from North America* (1900), and in the same year Mooney published *Myths of the Cherokees*, to follow his earlier *Sacred Formulas of the Cherokees* (1891). Edward Sapir simply used "text" as his term for his *Takelma Texts* of 1909, something which Boas had done by 1894 in his *Chinook Texts;* Boas also used "traditions," "folk tales," and "myths." Finally, to limit this listing, Densmore's important publications from 1913 to 1939 gave us the texts and notations for what she always regarded as Chippewa, Teton Sioux, Papago, Pawnee, Nootka, and Quileute "music."

Many of the same terms recur in work from the 1930s to the 1950s in the collections of Ruth Bunzel (1933), Ella Deloria (1932), Archie Phinney (1934) and, importantly, Melville Jacobs, who used the terms "myth," "text," and ultimately "oral literature" (*The Content and Style of an Oral Literature* [1959]). More recently, Hymes has used "myth," "text," "story," and "poem"; Tedlock's dissertation concerns *The Ethnography of Tale-Telling at Zuñi* (1968), while his *Finding the Center* collects *Narrative Poetry of the Zuni Indians*. Rothenberg subtitles *Shaking the Pumpkin, Traditional Poetry of the Indian North Americas,* and in another collection he has named Indian narrators *Technicians of the Sacred*. We may conclude with a return to the general category "literature" with Jarold Ramsey's *Coyote Was Going There* (1977), an anthology of *Indian Literature of the Oregon Country,* and Karl Kroeber's collection of *Traditional American Indian Literatures: Texts and Interpretations*.

Although there are presently some generally accepted criteria for distinguishing, say, a "myth" from a "tale," there are no parallel criteria for determining whether both or neither is literature. We can gain some sense of just how complex the situation was for the anthropological collector of what might be literary materials from Margot Liberty's description of the task facing Francis La Flesche, who himself was a Native American, among the Osage:

> There were seven degrees of the Nonhonzhinga Ieta or War Rites alone, and each gens had its own version of each of the seven. (These are not well defined or known except for the first, second, and seventh: having varied in order of recitation among the various gentes; and a majority having— despite La Flesche's best efforts—rolled under "the sheet waters of oblivion" long ago.) Those collected by La Flesche, who tried to get one from at least one gens in each of the two main tribal divisions or moieties (the Tzizhu or Sky division had seven gentes, and the Honga or Earth division fourteen gentes: the latter being split into the Honga and the Wazhazhe or Osage subdivisions, of seven gentes each) ran about 100 pages each of free translation. This yielded approximately a ten percent sample of . . . the War Rites alone. . . . I am suggesting here that the Osage ceremonial rec-

ord if reasonably complete in all versions of everything would run to some 40,000 pages of print, from fifty to eighty volumes of the dimensions of the typical 500–800 page Annual Report of the Bureau of American Ethnology.[21]

The temptation is great, on the one hand, to call none of this "literature" because it constitutes a "ceremonial record" of "rites"—except that a very good deal of this sort of thing has already a considerable history precisely as literature in translation. On the other hand, we might be tempted to call it all "literature," falling back upon Williams' broad definition of the word: "the process and the result of formal composition within the social and formal properties of a language."[22]

We have to consider yet another dimension to this problem before attempting a solution. My own work has dealt with Indian autobiographies. Ostensibly historical, these texts (e.g., *The Life of Black Hawk* [1833], *Geronimo: His Own Story* [1906], *Crashing Thunder: The Autobiography of an American Indian* [1926], and *Son of Old Man Hat* [1938]) also have important claims to literary consideration (although, because not merely their textualization but their very existence is a function of bicultural composite composition, they are not strictly instances of Native American literature per se). If Rousseau's *Confessions* or Cellini's *Autobiography* are part of literature, along with *Walden* and *The Education of Henry Adams*, on what grounds would we exclude these Indian texts? For even if it should turn out—which I am far from granting—that most of these texts aren't very good or interesting (evaluative criteria are particularly problematic, of course, and cross-cultural evaluative criteria even more so), that would still be insufficient reason for excluding them. For, in practice, the texts we teach and write about are those of a certain kind as well as of a certain quality. If Native American texts, as I shall presently argue, have claims to consideration as a literary kind, they necessarily have claims to consideration with similar texts of their kind (their quality to be judged differentially in relation to those texts).

The Western critic, by calling a text of any period or culture a "literary" text, announces a cognitively responsible decision to foreground the signifier with reference to its historical mode of production. Literary criticism, then, is a branch of the social sciences whose particular focus is texts read *as* literary; the reading constitutes an attempt to generate nontrivial results in the form of probabilistically verifiable theories or laws. A literary reading, whether of *Black Hawk* or *Hamlet*, meets the criteria for nontrivial effectivity in about the same way that any social science theory or law does, parsimoniously explaining much by little, and accounting for the phenomena under consideration not perfectly, but at least more cogently than before.[23] This is not possible when the composition of the signifier is treated in the idealizing synchronic mode, as *écriture* (no limits upon the play of signification). Since only logical (nonempirical) operations are involved in that case, probabilistic falsification is not accepted as disqualifying the results (e.g., Lévi-Strauss' famous indifference to whether his schema reveal how the minds of certain natives work or only how his own mind works), which are thus inevitably aesthetic or metaphysical (e.g. where only misreading is possible, criticism itself becomes literature). To speak of the mode of production of the signifier is to historicize and materialize its composition (and to allow its comparison to the economic mode of production in force).

Whatever the historical or anthropological uses to which Native American texts may be put, the complexity of the production of their signifiers — a complexity resulting not only from the nature of writing generally but from the historical specificities of their materialization — necessitates their treatment as literary texts. But in making this claim for them, I must make the further claim that they are entitled to consideration for inclusion among the canonic texts of American literature.

4 CANONICITY

The concept of "canon," or tradition, can be understood in two related ways. The first is simply as that which makes the text intelligible as a discursive type. Canon, here, means roughly the same thing as genre in either its "semantic" form (the modal perspective — comedy, romance, tragedy, irony — most readily associated with Northrop Frye) or its "syntactic" form (the structural perspective of Vladimir Propp or Tzvetan Todorov's early work), to use Jameson's distinction.[24] "Genres," as Jameson points out, "are essentially literary *institutions*, or social contracts between a writer and a specific public, whose function is to specify the proper use of a particular cultural artifact" (*TPU*, p. 106). But canon also can mean a selection from among genres — not merely *a* tradition of texts (Todorov's "fantastic" fictions, Annette Kolodny's or Nina Baym's women's domestic fictions) but the Great Tradition — those texts posited as the genuinely excellent by Matthew Arnold or F. R. Leavis, by T. S. Eliot or his violent critic Harold Bloom. Here we must speak of the official or pedagogical canon.

Understood in this second sense, the canon or canonicity is also institutional, but what is institutionalized is not so much functional propriety as cultural value. Practically speaking, the canon obviously presents what Williams has called "the *selective tradition:* that which, within the terms of an effective dominant culture, is always passed off as '*the* tradition', '*the* significant past' " (p. 39). Nor is this a neutral, innocent selection of "the best that has been thought and said," or a disinterested description of models given once and for all time (e.g., Tragedy, Comedy, the Novel). Rather, tradition, here, is "an aspect of *contemporary* social and cultural organization, in the interest of the dominance of a specific class. . . . a version of the past which is intended to connect with and ratify the present."[25] Any attempt to expand the canon — not merely add to it another "strong" poet but open it up to work deriving from other values — is an attempt to call into question the particular value it institutionalizes, and this (as the presently much maligned history of the 1960s showed) has important political implications.

By beginning with the mode of production of the text, I have begun at the logical theoretical beginning, but this is not the way in which most literary instruction in the schools is carried on. Rather, students commonly begin with a syllabus listing the selected texts of the canon; this identifies the great authors and defines the meaning of literature. Beyond some mention of history or biography as "background," instruction rarely moves outside the canon as a largely autonomous and self-enclosed system; any such move would run the risk of trespass upon other well-fenced fields. "Every relationship of 'hegemony' is necessarily a pedagogical relation," Antonio Gramsci observed; and the "pedagogical relation" in the schools is organized to ensure that the question of the mode of production can never arise.[26]

If the mode of production of Native American texts urges that they be considered literary texts, then they must be permitted entrance into a variety of literary canons. This means that Indian literature of apparently familiar types (creation and origin stories, etiological tales, invocations and prayers, lyrics of love or mourning, etc.) must be more frequently and abundantly taught, written about, and imitated along with their European and Euramerican counterparts. This means, as well, that the great body of Native American narrative which, until quite recently, has virtually been ignored by students and critics of literature, must be examined to determine, on the one hand, what the appropriate generic groupings among them might be and, on the other, the relation of these genres to the familiar Western narrative types. Some Native American narratives, for example, would be interesting to study in relation to the texts of Kafka, Borges, and Barthelme, and, theoretically, as possible types of essentially nonrepresentational, nonmimetic fiction.

The inclusion of Native texts in the canon of American literature could beneficially alter the pedagogical order in the schools (which, despite the distance of contemporary theory from the post-Kantian model I've sketched, seems largely to persist); by persisting in ignoring their mode of production we do more immediate and immediately discoverable violence to Native texts than to the standard, canonic texts of the Western tradition. By working with Native American texts among other types of what Jameson has called "hitherto marginalized types of discourse," critical theory may find significant opportunities to test and refine itself in practical application (*TPU*, p. 106). For obvious, but not necessary reasons, our major theorists, with the important exception of Said, are entirely Eurocentric. Attention to Indian literature would help move us away from our traditional practice of isolating the components of textual objects in the direction of what Williams calls "discover[ing] the nature of a practice and then its conditions" (p. 47). Here, we would not—I return to Jameson—oppose "the response of an individual subject to the collective realities of any moment of the past" or of another culture but instead establish "the quite different relationship of an objective *situation* in the present with an objective *situation* in the past."[27]

I believe that Native American texts will not only bid for entry into the broad canon of American literature but into the official, institutional canon as well. They will do so, if they do, not only because theoretical developments will prepare us better to understand them, nor simply because pluralists and democrats (I would count myself among them) will urge us to give them a fair shake. If the canon ratifies the present, as I have said, Native American literature cannot enter it until its values achieve or approach social ascendancy; nor can this occur until material conditions insist upon such ascendancy. But our material situation at present is such that the two major premises of Native American literature are already emerging in American culture and demanding attention. The first is that a global, ecosystemic perspective is the necessary condition of human survival and that such a perspective prohibits anthropocentrism. The second is that cultures — whether "advanced" or "primitive" — can sustain themselves without texts but that the absence (or abandonment) of print presents both possibilities and limitations. To the extent that American culture comes to base itself on these two premises will Native American literature establish itself in the canon.

Notes

1. Dell Hymes, "Reading Clackamas Texts," in *Traditional American Indian Literatures: Texts and Interpretations*, ed. Karl Kroeber (Lincoln, Nebr., 1981), p. 117.

2. See Dennis Tedlock, ed. and trans., *Finding the Center: Narrative Poetry of the Zuni Indians* (New York, 1972; rpt. Lincoln, Nebr., 1978); and Tedlock, "Toward an Oral Poetics," *New Literary History* 8 (Spring 1977) pp. 507–19.

3. These are the dates of the Dawes Severalty Act and the Wheeler-Howard (Indian Reorganization) Act. The first, an attempt to Americanize the Indian, marks the age of rescue anthropology or ethnographic salvage; the second, an attempt to legitimize tribal cultures as part of a wider cultural pluralism, marks the period when the greatest number of scientists were in the field. Native texts were recorded prior to 1887 and, to be sure, after 1934.

4. Tedlock, "On the Translation of Style in Oral Narrative," *Journal of American Folklore* 84 (Jan.-Mar. 1971) p. 118.

5. Ibid., p. 114.

6. Mary Austin, *The American Rhythm: Studies and Reëxpressions of Amerindian Songs* (1923; New York, 1970).

7. See William Brandon, ed., *The Magic World: American Indian Songs and Poems* (New York, 1971), Jerome Rothenberg, ed., *Technicians of the Sacred: A Range of Poetries from Africa, America, Asia, and Oceania* (Garden City, N.Y., 1968), and Rothenberg, ed., *Shaking the Pumpkin: Traditional Poetry of the Indian North Americas* (Garden City, N.Y., 1972). Rothenberg and Tedlock edit *Alcheringa*, a journal of ethnopoetics. Although received favorably at first, Rothenberg's practice has increasingly been criticized, most tellingly by William Bevis ("American Indian Verse Translations," *College English* 35 [Mar. 1974]: 693–703),

and most recently by William M. Clements ("Faking the Pumpkin: On Jerome Rothenberg's Literary Offenses," *Western American Literature* 16 [Nov. 1981]: 193–204).

8. Jack Goody, *The Domestication of the Savage Mind* (Cambridge, 1977) p. 158.

9. Fredric Jameson, "Marxism and Historicism," New Literary History 11 (Autumn 1979), p. 70.

10. Michel Foucault, "What Is an Author?" *Language, Counter-Memory, Practice: Selected Essays and Interviews,* ed. Donald F. Bouchard (Ithaca, N.Y., 1977), p. 124.

11. Ibid., p. 123.

12. John Bierhorst, introduction to *In the Trail of the Wind: American Indian Poems and Ritual Orations,* ed. Bierhorst (New York, 1971), pp. 4–5.

13. One reason why Indian oratory was initially easier for Euramericans to preserve was that the particular speech seemed to be the discourse of a single, prominent individual. Meanwhile, the notion of the great power of the individual Indian orator coexisted all through the nineteenth century with the exasperated recognition of the traditional and formulaic nature, the inevitably social and conventional nature, of any rhetorical act. Thus, many of the old Indian fighters recorded their exasperation that one or another "chief" could not come to what they felt was the point without recapitulating the history of his people or invoking the earth as our common mother.

14. Frank Kermode, *The Genesis of Secrecy: On the Interpretation of Narrative* (Cambridge, Mass., 1979), p. 99; see also pp. 125–26.

15. Hymes, "Discovering Oral Performance and Measured Verse in American Indian Narrative," *New Literary History* 8 (Spring 1977): 443. See also Hymes' comments on the Indian "author" in his "Breakthrough into Performance," in *Folklore: Performance and Communication,* ed. Dan Ben-Amos and Kenneth S. Goldstein (The Hague, 1975), pp. 11–74.

16. Edward Said, "Reflections on Recent American 'Left' Literary Criticism," *Boundary 2* 8 (Fall 1979) p. 26.

17. Raymond Williams, "Base and Superstructure in Marxist Cultural Theory," *Problems in Materialism and Culture* (London, 1980), p. 48; all further references to this work will be included in the text.

18. On this, see Tedlock's components in his introduction to *Finding the Center,* pp. xxv–xxvi, as well as in his "The Spoken Word and the Work of Interpretation," in *Traditional American Literatures,* ed. Kroeber, pp. 48–57.

19. Paul de Man, "The Epistemology of Metaphor," *Critical Inquiry* 5 (Autumn 1978): 30.

20. See Lewis Henry Morgan, *Ancient Society; or, Researches in the Lines of Human Progress from Savagery, through Barbarism to Civilization* (1877; New York, 1963).

21. Margot Liberty, "Francis La Flesche: The Osage Odyssey," in *American Indian Intellectuals,* ed. Liberty, Proceedings of the American Ethnological Society, 1976 (Saint Paul, Minn., 1978), p. 52.

22. Williams, *Marxism and Literature* (New York, 1977), p. 46.

23. This account is indebted to Marvin Harris' development of "cultural materialism" in *The Rise of Anthropological Theory* (New York, 1968) and in *Cultural Materialism: The Struggle for a Science of Culture* (New York, 1979), which, with Williams' "cultural materialism" (as developed particularly in *Marxism and Literature*), has been of great use to me. Neither Harris nor Williams has anything to say about Native American literature, nor, to my knowledge, has either commented in print on the other's use of the term "cultural materialism."

24. Jameson, *The Political Unconscious: Narrative as a Socially Symbolic Act* (Ithaca, N.Y., 1981), p. 107; all further references to this work, abbreviated *TPU,* will be included in the text.

25. Williams, *Marxism and Literature,* p. 116.

26. Antonio Gramsci, quoted by Evan Watkins in "Conflict and Consensus in the History of Recent Criticism," *New Literary History* 12 (Winter 1981), p. 359.

27. Jameson, "Marxism and Historicism," p. 57.

On Traditional Literatures

"This Island, The World on Turtle's Back"

William N. Fenton*

The Huron and Iroquois Indians were the aboriginal inhabitants of the lands bordering the lower Great Lakes, specifically Lakes Huron, Erie, and Ontario, and the St. Lawrence River, in what are now parts of Ontario and Quebec in Canada, part of Pennsylvania, and nearly all of New York State.[1] These peoples who spoke languages of the Iroquoian family always referred to their country as "This Old Island," of *Wendat E'hen*, in Huron, which they conceived as resting on the back of a turtle swimming in the primal sea. How the earth, various plants and animals, and the several celestial bodies and forces were created and put in operation; what special duties they were assigned of benefit to man; and how the first human beings on the earth learned to adjust to the situation as they found it comprise the subject and content of a myth that is one of the great intellectual display pieces of the New World. The Iroquois Indians had three such myths by which they marked their cultural history, and these were recited by their learned men at public gatherings or in the long lodge of a family that had kindled a fire and cooked a kettle of mush for the mythholder. The telling filled several days or nights, and great heed was paid to verbatim recall and recitation. Because of the inherent power of the myths, recitals were held only after the first frost when the earth sleeps. Though each authority claims fidelity for his version, each narrator had his own style. The published versions exhibit a remarkable consistency of plot and incident, but are nevertheless quite different in detail, and probably they differed slightly at each telling.

Our present concern is with the first of the three great myths, the Earth-grasper; the second is the Deganawidah epic of the founding of the League of the Longhouse people, to which we will turn momentarily; and *Kai'wi:yo:* "the good message," which is the revelation of Handsome Lake, the Seneca prophet, and which contains the ethos of present-day Longhouse culture, will occupy the greater span of attention because we know the most about it. I mention the three now because this is how Iroquois

*Reprinted from *Journal of American Folklore*, 75 (1962), 283–300, by permission of the American Folklore Society.

133

annalists see their own culture history: they speak of a time of Sapling before Deganawidah; of the period of the League's formation; and of the present since Handsome Lake. Naive as it may seem to sophisticated readers to employ the mythology of a primitive people for organizing the results of scientific inquiry, this is done deliberately in order to describe the culture in its own terms, for locked up in the three Iroquoian epics are the major institutions of their culture as well as the themes that guide behavior throughout their history and illuminate certain actions even today.

The isolation of themes or motifs and their use for classification and comparison of literatures has long been the standard method of systematic folklorists for storing and retrieving a huge body of information for use in a variety of problems, such as the dissemination of tales as evidence of historical relationships. These two interests — classification and comparison — have united literary folklorists and anthropologists for some seventy years. But the application of the theory of themes to the analysis of a culture is a more recent development that sprang from the association of anthropology and psychology, and it was first carried out rigorously by Morris Edward Opler on ethnographic and folkloristic materials from the Lipan Apache, the warlike raiders of the American southwest.[2]

Opler's idea struck me at the time he submitted it to a journal I was then editing as a useful scheme for organizing the materials of Iroquois culture, because he had succeeded in describing Apache ways in terms of their own internal consistencies, utilizing both the oral literature and his observations of their behavior. This came at a time when other ethnologists were losing interest in folklore studies, complaining that folklorists did not do anything with the tales except collect and present them. Opler's method offered a means of integrating folklore with the description of a culture; and the Iroquois have a large body of mythology, fiction, and tradition. If one could apply Opler's method, it might solve another problem: it might tell us something about the most durable aspects of culture, which are internal and are affairs of the mind. Why has Iroquois culture survived into the present century? In three hundred years of continuous contact with aggressive white people in the country's most populous state, several Iroquoian languages are still spoken from Brooklyn to Niagara. The voices of Seneca drummers rise from the swamps of Tonawanda and echo on the Allegheny hills. Masks are still carved in response to dreams, and the Falseface Society makes its spring and fall rounds. Work in high steel has replaced the adventure of the warpath. The kettle endures as a symbol of hospitality, although corn soup is cooked in aluminum ware instead of iron kettles hung over the fire, or in stone-propped earthen pots. The Seneca Nation is a republic, but at Tonawanda and Onondaga chiefs are elected by clan matrons and raised with the Condolence Council; and a fierce tradition of political independence contrasts with pride in a second generation educated in centralized schools with neighboring whites.

Besides having a rich mythology and folklore, the Iroquois have the best documented history of any primitive people; and they boast one of the largest ethnographic bibliographies. Historians have nevertheless failed in the attempt to describe Indian life from the viewpoint of the culture itself because the literature available to them was written by Europeans, and historians admit to evidence only written documents. Consequently, historians have denied the existence and questioned the authenticity of institutions like the League of the Iroquois on which the earliest sources are silent or give meager accounts of it indeed. The first full-scale description of the kinship system and of the League itself had to await the emergence of anthropology with L. H. Morgan at the mid-nineteenth century and to accompany the linguistic and folkloristic studies of Horatio Hale. By the writings of these two pioneer scientists it may be judged that the Iroquois social system, their political institutions, and their elaborate rites for installing chiefs were either invented for the amusement of anthropologists, or had eluded colonial administrators, missionaries, historians and explorers because they were too busy to write about them and because they were not trained as anthropologists. This is a perplexing problem because to admit the latter proposition is to deny change, and to deny it is contrary to the history of science. Is cultural persistence a response to boredom of nineteenth-century life on reservations? How are cultural institutions internalized in language and folklore? How can oral tradition be utilized for enriching documentary history and ethnographic observation? Do not the themes and motifs of folklore afford a model for finding analogies in other aspects of the culture? If so, what are they, how do they structure the culture, and how do they function as guides to individual behavior? What is the life of these themes? What is their role in tradition? What is their fate in culture change?

I raise these questions now in anticipation of presenting the history of Iroquois culture that will be stated in terms of its central themes and illustrated by the sketches of some typical careers of Iroquois persons who have since gone the long trail and whose lives epitomize Iroquois culture at its various periods. Before doing this, however, I propose in the present article to identify the themes that are to be found in the cosmology. So let us listen to "what our grandfathers were wont to relate."

Depending on how the tale opens, the Iroquois, like their Woodland neighbors and the Plains tribes, distinguish three types of narratives, which may be classified as myths, tales, and traditions. The first class relates of things and events "which truly happened" long ago, and in which the old people really believed; second, there is a great bag of tales which are pure fiction and open, "It is as if a man walked"; and third, there are human adventures which commence, "They went to hunt for meat." The latter often relate the experiences of individuals who founded medicine societies and may be distinguished from tribal history. It is an interesting but surprising commentary that the life of fiction is hardier than that of legendary material, but even trickster stories have vanished since 1930, as has the cosmology which we are about to hear.[3]

The myth of the Earth-grasper, or more commonly the Woman who fell from the Sky, exists in some twenty-five versions which all adhere to the same general plot and contain most of the essential elements. There is enough structural similarity between the Huron version first recorded by the Recollect Gabriel Sagard in 1623 — which was again heard in the next ten years by the Jesuit missionaries Brébeuf and Ragueneau — and the elaborate texts which Hewitt had from informants living at the close of the last century, to warrant our saying that one continuous mythological tradition confronts us, that it has three hundred years of recorded history, and that it extends into pre-Columbian times. This is no ethnological freak, nor is the relationship between early Huron versions and later Iroquois versions contrived.[4]

The essential elements in the cosmogonic myth number less than ten, but the longer versions contain fifteen or more component motifs which can be readily identified in Thompson's *Motif-Index of Folk-Literature*, 6 volumes (Bloomington, Ind., 1955–58). Martha Randle, editor of the Waugh Collection, lists nine essential points: (1) sky world; (2) uprooting of the light-giving tree; (3) casting down of the sky-woman; (4) animals diving for earth; (5) establishment of the earth on the turtle's back; (6) Sky-woman's daughter becoming mother of twins, Good- and Evil-minded; (7) Good-minded as culture hero liberating animals pent up by his brother and securing corn; (8) a cosmic duel with avowed fatal weapons — rushes or maize vs. flint or antler; and (9) the banishment of Evil-minded while Good-minded and Sky-woman retire to the sky-world, promising to return on the last day of the world.[5] This is the plot, but various episodes embellish the longer versions which include impregnation by the wind, twins quarreling in the womb, lodge-boy and thrown-away, constructive and destructive creation, a toad that hoards water until a flood issues from its belly or armpit, father search and son testing, experimental man making, and the theft of light. Peculiarly Iroquoian touches in this creation myth, which has a wide distribution in North America and Eurasia, are the dream-guessing contests in the sky-world; the struggle for power and control of the earth by a test of demonstrated mountain moving between Sky-holder or Good-minded and Hadu?i?, the hunchback mask being, who loses and becomes the Great Defender of mankind; the rite of returning thanks from the earth upward through the mid-pantheon of appointed forces to the sky-world; and the creation of the clans and moieties in the formative period of human society. When man is up against it, a fatherless boy from the fringe of the bush emerges to define the situation, propose a solution, and lead the community out of its dilemma. One senses that in this culture tradition has attuned the society to listen to the prophet.[6]

The prophet who would succeed among the Iroquois must speak in ancient tongues, he must use the old words, and he must relate his program to old ways. He is a conservator at the same time that he is a reformer. It will become apparent as one traverses the course of Iroquois culture history that its several reformations have been accomplished by such prophets. This is one of the reasons that Iroquois culture has endured so long; theirs is a tough tradition and a remarkably stable one. None enjoy greater prestige in this society than the men of intellect who perform fears of prodigious memory by relating the myths. These old men "who know everything" single out the young men who are seriously interested and able to learn and instruct them. Soon these young men are marked by the community. In recent years the ethnologist who sits at the feet of the professors of the tribal lore may soon find himself cast in this role. This is how Chief John A. Gibson became keeper of the lore of the Longhouse, and it is how J. N. B. Hewitt, himself a native Tuscarora, came to write it down. Because I succeeded Hewitt as ethnologist to the Iroquois at the Smithsonian Institution, I know something of both men.[7]

Chief John A. Gibson, who died in 1912, a lifelong resident of the Grand River Reservation in Canada, was unquestionably the greatest mind of his generation among the Six Nations. A young man when he was first installed as one of the eight Seneca chiefs to sit in the council of the Confederacy, as the League of the Iroquois tribes is called on the Grand River, this wide-awake and keen-witted Seneca chief attracted the notice of the senior member, one of the Onondaga fire-keepers. (It was the Onondaga chiefs who had taken the lead in rekindling the council fire that had burned for generations on the hills of central New York after they had removed to Canada following the American Revolution.) To keep the lore of the Longhouse alive, the elder Onondaga councilor decided to tutor his promising Seneca younger brother. Consequently the customs, traditions, and ceremonies that Gibson mastered were the ways of ancient Onondaga; and when the old man realized that he must lay aside his antlers of office and prepare to take up the long trail, he asked Gibson to stand in his place and lead the ceremonies at Onondaga Longhouse. This meant that for the rest of his life Gibson spoke Onondaga, although he occasionally preached in Seneca, his mother tongue. He was multilingual, his wife addressed him in Cayuga, he spoke to her in Onondaga, and they used these languages to their children who also learned Seneca from a grandmother. There were times when Chief Gibson performed rituals in Mohawk, he could converse with visiting Oneida chiefs, and he knew some Tuscarora. Besides, his English was excellent. Small wonder that the Gibson family were sought out by ethnologists and linguists as informants and as interpreters! The opportunities for learning Iroquoian languages on the Grand River before 1900 were better than they had ever been when the Six Nations were living scattered across New York State. This circumstance, coupled with real intellectual curiosity and a keen mind, enabled Gibson, who was not satisfied until he had traced a custom or a belief back to its earliest remembered antecedents, to become the greatest living source on Iroquois culture at the turn of the century when field ethnology commenced in earnest. His work with Hewitt on mythology and rituals and with Goldenweiser on social organization and political structure is unapproached by any other Iroquois informant.[8]

At the time that Hewitt worked with him, Chief Gibson had been totally blind for some twenty-six years as the result of a lacrosse injury at the age of thirty-one, an affliction which possibly freed his remarkable powers of memory and comprehension for intellectual pursuits. His version of the cosmology, which he dictated in Onondaga and which Hewitt wrote down in phonetic script in 1900 and afterward published,[9] is certainly one of the longest Iroquois texts extant, running to over 20,000 words and taking up some 145 pages in print. It is the best of the five versions that Hewitt collected and the one that I will follow, both because it is most complete and because Gibson's Onondaga deserves better treatment than Hewitt's pseudoscientific, biblical English. In making my own version for the general reader I will dip into the mush pots of Hewitt's other informants, if only to sample the flavor of their styles. But first a word about Hewitt himself.

I remember John Napoleon Brinton Hewitt, who died in October, 1937 at seventy-eight, because I had been to see him twice in the Smithsonian tower office I was later to occupy. Then I was a graduate student seeking help after my first fieldwork and Hewitt was an old man. He had married again late in life, and his wife, who claimed dowager rights in old Washington society, had gotten him up to look like a Smithsonian scientist: wing collar, Oxford gray coat, striped trousers, and white piping to his vest. He was the last of a notable group of self-taught students of the American Indian whom Major J. W. Powell had assembled soon after founding the Bureau of American Ethnology in 1879. Hewitt shared the added distinction with La Flesche, the Osage, of being a native Indian by Iroquois reckoning, since his mother was part Tuscarora; and he had grown up close to her tribal reservation near Niagara. Though he had planned to follow his Scottish father into medicine, by a series of mishaps, in 1880 at twenty-one he ended up working as secretary to Erminnie A. Smith, a Jersey socialite and folklorist, who employed him to assist her in collecting myths and interpreting among the Iroquoian tribes. Upon her death in 1886, Major Powell, who had already commissioned Erminnie Smith as temporary ethnologist, called Hewitt to the Bureau where he was to serve for fifty-one years. Hewitt soon added Mohawk, Onondaga, and Seneca to his quiver of Iroquoian tongues; and these and Tuscarora he recorded with painstaking accuracy in a phonetic orthography that, without the least difficulty, can be read back to native speakers today. He also became the leading authority on the League and its rituals. Being neither a trained linguist nor a schooled scientist, he had the good sense to concentrate on collecting texts, which is just as well, considering the state of theory in his day. His voluminous manuscripts, which are still largely in the original languages which he knew, are available for study today. The old men of the Seneca Nation and of

Six Nations Reserve may be gone, but Hewitt wrote down their words for all time.[10]

It is not that Hewitt lacked a philosophical turn of mind, for he was much interested in philosophy and in comparative religions, and his own justification for taking texts, or recording myths in the original languages, reveals this flair. He prefaced the *Cosmology* with this remark: "Upon the concepts evolved from their impression of things and from their experience with . . . their environment rest the authority of men's doctrines and the reasons for their rites and ceremonies. Hence arises the great importance of recording . . . [texts]."[11]

With this in mind I have gone through the four published versions of Hewitt's *Iroquoian Cosmology* looking for the concepts and themes which characterize the culture as I have come to know it from extensive fieldwork and reading. I have also noted literary devices by which the narrator leads his listeners. The versions differ to the extent that the narrators have different personal histories segmenting cultural history at earlier and later points of time, and close scrutiny tells us something about their personalities, as well as about culture change. Old John Skanawaati Buck in 1889 was closer to sources on the old culture than Gibson, but Gibson is far more complete and incorporates all the systems of his teacher without some of the cultural niceties. It is apparent from John Armstrong's short Seneca version of 1896 that the Senecas were mighty hunters and excellent naturalists familiar with habits of game on which they had recently depended. They knew star lore; he himself was an herbalist. The Seneca cast the patron of the False-faces in a more friendly role than the Onondaga, who emphasize the power struggle between the Creator and Haduiʔíʔ. Seneca versions may be expected to show tribal differences from Onondaga in detail and in literary devices but not in plot, and Armstrong's version is foreshortened and ends midcourse, raising questions of rapport between informant and folklorist. The Mohawk version of the cosmology comes from Seth Newhouse, the self-appointed chronicler of custom and law on the Six Nations Reserve, with whom Hewitt worked in 1897; it contains a number of Christian elements and manifests a passion for legitimacy notable in Canada today, as might be expected, since his people had been in contact with Anglican missionaries from the early eighteenth century. But it also illustrates and explains Mohawk usages not found elsewhere. I infer from Hewitt's papers that Newhouse was an opinionated person, that fancying himself an author he regarded Hewitt as competition, and hence the two savants had some disagreements.[12]

The longest version in Onondaga between Gibson and Hewitt — which comprises the *Iroquoian Cosmology; Second Part*, which I have analyzed into its constituent plots, incidents, and themes — incorporates most of the detail from the three earlier versions. What escapes us in this analysis and what I spare the reader can be used later "to shingle the bare poles of the longhouse" as chapter heads and illustrations. Notes and marginalia in my books say that I first read these myths in 1932 and 1933, as a fresh graduate student. But manifestly what I have now attempted was impossible then, and I shall try to convey to readers some of the thrill of rediscovery. In the years between, the whole field of Iroquois studies has expanded; and those of us who have done fieldwork have met to share experiences and ideas in the Conference on Iroquois Research, which has sent up its smoke when the leaves turn on the hills and on the fifth night of the new moon at Red House, New York.[13]

Hewitt was inclined, like many of the folklorists of his day, to derive myths from phenomena in nature; and he spent himself in the futile search for the original and ideal myth. But this commentary on his career, which was taken after I had personally reviewed traditions with informants and translated texts relating to the founding of the Iroquois League, nevertheless seems odd in the light of his own early realization that myths are composite cultural pieces and that they have varied histories in time and space. It is odder still, viewing what he wrote in 1903, that he did not follow Boas' lead and study their dissemination: "the great and fundamental fact [is] that all legends are the gradual result of combination from many sources by many minds in many generations."[14]

As among the factors that enter into myth formation—distribution and diffusion, the role of the narrator, and cultural drift between generations—the last two have greatest significance for a discussion of the cultural history of a single people. We can regard the myth of the Earth-grasper as a mirror of Iroquoian culture without denying that its principal motifs—celestial tree of light, the woman who fell from the sky, primeval water, earth diver, earth from the turtle's back, twins quarrel before birth, and lodge-boy and thrown-away—are at home in the mythology of neighboring Woodland peoples. Two of these—earth diver and rival twins—are known the breadth of the continent.[15] And indeed the notion of a primal sea out of which a diver fetches material for making dry land is among the most widespread concepts held by man, having a distribution, according to Earl W. Count, stretching from Finland across Eurasia, including India and southeastern Asia, and covering most of North America, suggesting that it diffused eastward to America when people settled the New World.[16] I am confident that as guardians of the lore of the Iroquois Longhouse, Chief John Gibson and Seth Newhouse would have been intrigued but not amazed to learn that their myth of the beginning of the world has such a distinguished world history; but they would claim priority for it in America, where they were certainly its greatest systematists. This drive toward synthesis which is so evident in the culture of the nineteenth-century Iroquois and which characterized their two greatest myths, the Myth of the Earth-grasper and the Deganawidah epic, represents in my opinion a response to the threat of the dominant culture by these narrators of ancient myths who seek to conserve as much of the old culture as possible within an ancient matrix. This is the whole history of the Longhouse movement, and it is exemplified among the Six Nations of Grand River by the career of Chief John A. Gibson, who was its greatest advocate.

The myth of the Sky-holder or Earth-grasper, according to Gibson and Hewitt, has three main parts which correspond to epochs. The first describes society of the Sky-world; the creation of the Earth upon the Turtle's back forms the second cosmical epoch; and the third is the World of Sapling, the period of primitive human society.

The sky-world is the upper surface of the visible sky. Here live manlike gods who have a culture like that of pre-Columbian woodland Indians who as persons manifest the emotional strengths and weaknesses of the Iroquois people of later times. In a clearing stands their village of typical bark-covered lodges which are extended to accommodate single maternal families. Newhouse said the lodges faced the rising sun and extended toward the sunset, a nice detail, but there was no sun yet. The only illumination is furnished by flowers on the tree of light which stands at the center beside the chief's lodge and for which he is named. Otherwise the environment consists of the familiar flora and fauna, specified or not, depending on the interest of the narrator. Entering the end doors, one finds along the interior walls of the lodges beds of rough bark where the occupants spread their mats to sleep and where they sit by day, each family having its own fire and compartment; these extend the length of the hallway to the opposite door.

After the morning meal the housemates go forth to their appointed tasks. The warriors are in the habit of going out to hunt in the mornings and of returning in the evenings. The older versions imply that this routine afforded the opportunity for a girl and a boy, who had been secluded or "downfended" after the old puberty custom, to get together: she goes over and combs his hair and somehow gets pregnant. The women of the family question her, but she refuses to tell. The lad meanwhile sickens and dies in a couvade over the birth of their daughter. He is buried on a scaffold in a spare room.

Gibson cleans up this incident and elaborates the plot by making the secluded youngsters siblings and putting them under the avuncular authority of the old man of the Sky-people, their mother's brother. Uncle becomes ill over some imagined omen, discloses the nature of death, and asks the Old Woman, his sister, to have him put up in a tree. The Iroquois love their dead, and the daughter or niece spends hours visiting the corpse and receives in one instance a wampum bracelet in token of paternity and in two instances instructions as to her marriage to the owner of the tree of light who is chief of a distant village.

The old wedding custom where the bride-to-be carries a basket of boiled bread by the forehead strap through the woods to the house of the groom, speaking to no one on the path, never ceases to fascinate Iroquois listeners, who thrill at the most detailed description. The bread, of sodden-corn flavored with berries, is a symbol of woman's skillful labor in raising and grinding corn in a wooden mortar. The forehead strap or tump line was as essential to woodland women for a variety of transport as her suburban-ite sister's automobile is today. The directions for her journey, the hazards of getting lost and crossing a stream over a floating maple log, and the tabu on speaking to strangers on the path all heighten her anxiety of leaving home to qualify as a woman in her husband's settlement. Distant patrilocal residence poses a theoretical problem for the ethnologist as well as for the bride, since the later theory of this society is matrilineal and matrilocal (the daughters should bring spouses home to mother's longhouse), a dilemma to which I will return. On arriving at the grassy clearing surrounding the village, etiquette prescribes that she shall go directly to his house and go right on in through the door to where the fire burns in the center of the lodge. There before the owner of the celestial tree she puts down her basket at his feet where he lies in his bunk, saying, "We two marry," and then sits opposite with the fire between them. He will lay down a string of white corn and say, "Soak it and make mush." This was all standard bridal custom for the Iroquois until the middle of the last century.

But the mush-making proves an ordeal. The bride is expected to strip and without flinching endure the pain of having her naked body spattered with boiling mush. Then she suffers the added indignity of having the blistered skin licked off by ferocious white dogs with abrasive tongues. She thus earns the admiration of her torture-loving listeners by surviving the test, and then is persuaded to engage in the most intriguing footsie gambit of aboriginal literature, in which she makes up her bed at the foot of his, and they sleep *pied à pied*. Only the soles of their feet touch, yet in some unexplained way, they sit up, their breathe mingle, and she becomes pregnant. Rather than seeking a sanctimonious interpretation of the act, as Hewitt was inclined, I am confident that many Iroquois would think this funny. To complete the bridal contract, the groom sends back dried venison, of which he has an inexhaustible supply; this he compresses by shaking it down in her packbasket. Despite its density, she is enjoined not to readjust her forehead strap going home. She reports his message to the town council, instructing them to remove the mats from their houses so that it may rain corn and fill them; and they distribute the magic meat which expands to fill the council house. Then she goes back to his village to live.

If the marriage of Awenha':ih "fertile flower" or "Sky-woman" to Ho-dä'he? "Standing tree," proprietor of the celestial tree and chief of the Sky-world, was not an unqualified success, at least it was not dull, and as an example of brittle monogamy, as Elsie Clews Parsons used to characterize the society of Hollywood, it is quite familiar to Iroquois listeners for whom the family means the maternal lineage. Confronted with the solid chain that runs from the eldest woman to the umbilical cord of the youngest infant-to-be, Iroquois spouses react sometimes as Sky-chief. A justifiable suspicion is augmented by jealousy, and it manifests itself in tests and in compulsive behavior. These ordeals are more or less reassuring, but since peace and domestic tranquility are always threatened and then broken by this strain of paranoia in the culture, individuals end in brooding and depression. Society employs several devices for diverting their minds: a game of ball, or a little dance, perhaps, while people try at random to guess his soul's desire as revealed in a dream. The other channel is active witchcraft. So when Sky-chief manifests symptoms of jealousy over his wife's blooming pregnancy, the community attempts to relieve his disturbed mind by guessing the word his soul desires. The dream feast, of which we read so much in the *Relations* of the Jesuit Fathers from Huronia, is held beneath the Tree of Light and attended by all the supernaturals of the pantheon except Wind. It has been foretold to Sky-woman what will be the verdict, so she counsels with her brother Earthquake, before returning to her spouse.

In myths of this length the sequence of events is not always clear. Part of the confusion arises from a device which narrators employ to post their listeners in advance of what is going to happen by letting them in on revelations that clairvoyants divulge to actors. It also builds up suspense. Thus in the Gibson version, Sky-chief has been holding a continuous dream feast dating back before his union with Sky-woman; she learns from her uncle's corpse, on a visit home, the nature of the dream which ordains and specifies her involvement. The dream that nobody has yet guessed, though they have diverted his mind, is a model of paranoid destruction: growing things shall wither, especially the flowers on the tree of light, which shall be uprooted so that he can shove them into the hole where he and his wife shall sit down on the brink, hang their feet over, and eat together. She is cautioned not to hesitate. Her name Awenha꞉ih "Ripe blossom" makes her an acceptable bride because it fits into his plans. In the Onondaga versions the key word is "Tooth," a reference to the flowers on the tree; and Fire-dragon or meteor guesses it. In one Seneca variant the key word is "excrement." The satisfied dreamer cries *Kuh!* (Onondaga) or *Gwah!* (Seneca), as he still does at the Midwinter Festival. Since it is a cardinal principle of Iroquois culture that the consequences of revealed dreams must be carried out, they proceed to fulfill them. They uproot the tree, and Sky-woman and Sky-chief sit down as directed to eat the food that she has placed beside them. Standing suddenly, he takes her by the nape of the neck and shoves her into space into which she is peering. Versions differ as to her curiosity or his rage, or whether he takes her by the left leg or shoves her with his foot. Life in the Sky-world ends with the casting down of Sky-woman and the resetting of the tree.

The second epoch, which is concerned with the creation of the world on the turtle's back, consists of some eighteen episodes and opens with the fall of Sky-woman, who becomes Earth-mother, the Old Woman, and the wicked Grandmother. She falls through the sky's crust into darkness. Old John Buck (Onondaga) said that she went provisioned for her journey into space with three ears of corn, dried meat, and firewood stuffed in her bosom and carrying her child on her back; but Gibson and Armstrong (Seneca) say that these cultural gifts were presented by Meteor and included miniature mortar and pestle, a small pot, and a soup bone, and that in falling she brought her own earth scraped from the sides of the hole.

The spectacle of the Sky-woman falling through space, assisted by waterfowl, to the back of the turtle swimming in the primal sea is a favorite subject with Iroquois artists, with notable examples by Jesse Cornplanter and Ernest Smith of the Seneca, and Tom Dorsey of Onondaga. Loon notices her; Bittern, whose eyes are ever on the top of his head, remarks that she indeed is not coming from the depths of the water; the ducks go up to guide her landing, while the council of animals sends various divers to fetch up mud from the depths. Muskrat alone succeeds, but comes up dead, paws and mouth full of mud; Turtle volunteers and Beaver with assistants plasters the mud on Turtle's carapace. Here Sky-woman is brought to rest, and immediately the earth starts expanding as she moves about and vegetation sprouts in her tracks. The process of the expanding earth will continue throughout creation. This cosmological notion of superimposed worlds from the tree of life, the sky-dome, and the first vegetation springing from the earth on the turtle's back has been reduced to curvilinear symoblism by generations of Iroquois women working in moosehair and quill embroidery and afterward in beads for decorating clothing.[17]

A daughter born to Sky-woman grows up rapidly and has a succession of animal suitors. On her mother's advice she accepts the fourth, the one with the dirty body who wears a deeply escalloped robe and leggings, who, naturally, is Turtle. He has several magic arrows, one having no point attached, which he keeps straightening, a characteristic motor habit of Iroquois arrow makers, and this one he leaves alongside of her body as she sleeps. In the Seneca version she is impregnated by the west wind while swinging at play on an uprooted tree; she descends to kneel on the grass, is entered by the wind, and is delighted. It does not take the old woman long to discover that her happy daughter is going to have a child. In this most unusual pregnancy she hears male voices quarreling within her body.

Of the twins who converse in the womb, the elder is born normally and becomes Sky-holder, alias Good-minded, Thrown-away, Sapling, the Creator, whose every act will symbolize and promote growth and fertility. The younger twin, the ugly one who is covered with warts and has a sharp comb of flint on his forehead, a motif that is memorialized in Seneca Falsefaces, seeks daylight and erupts through his mother's armpit, killing her. He is Flint (Ice), the Evil-minded, patron of winter, and author of monstrosities, bad luck and disaster. Flint becomes the favorite of his grandmother when he lies to her about cutting up his own dead mother, whom they bury in the doorway, and whose head they put up a tree for light. The theme of sibling rivalry dominates this period.

That grandmothers can be wicked and reject their grandsons is a hazard of growing up in a society that subscribes to the theory of matrilineal descent, inheritance, and succession. When Sky-woman tosses the elder twin into the brush to find shelter in a hollow tree, accepts the lying younger twin into her lodge, conspires against his elder brother, and then refuses to make bow and arrows for him, Thrown-away is driven to seek his father. As we shall see, the theme of the fatherless boy who becomes the hero permeates Iroquois folk history. One's father's line is always a second choice, after mother's brother, but father does impart certain culture gifts. Using a second magic arrow, which father has left, and a borrowed bow, Sky-holder shoots at a passing bird and parts the waters, revealing at the bottom of a lake his father's lodge, which he visits. Father Turtle, who holds-the-earth-in-his-two-hands, teaches the hero the arts of husbandry, the chase, and housebuilding; how to make fire; how to spit maize for roasting; and he gives the son several ears. In Seneca versions the father who is Wind offers as prize a flute and a heavy bag containing game animals to the winner among his four sons of a race around the earth. "So now the youth took up the bundle and packed it home by means of a burden strap." On arrival he announces having changed his name to "Maple Sprout" or "Sapling," in the Mohawk version. Sky-holder has also acquired a third magic arrow as proof against the water serpent and meteor, but it is not clear what use he made of it.

Sky-holder's acts of creation form the climax of this section. They are opposed and hindered by the evil grandmother, and they are offset by contrary acts of Flint. Here the growth principle is thwarted by frost, a dualism which symbolizes the alternation of seasons, and the contest goes on building up into a cosmic struggle for control of the earth. First comes the flora, starting with red osier for medicine, the grasses, shrubs, trees, and cultivated plants, including the sunflower for oil; Flint counters with thistle, poison ivy and other noxious weeds. Next come the birds, starting with Bluebird, the now extinct Passenger Pigeon that got immersed in bear oil so that afterward its squabs were fat. Handfuls of earth were cast into game animals. Flint makes a cosmic mistake by creating the bat which is, as an old Feather Dance song says, "the only animal that has teeth and yet flies." Rivers were created with two-way currents for man's convenience in travel; but Flint put in rapids and falls. Overcome by jealousy at the great ears of corn in Sky-holder's garden, Flint stunts them because man should not have it so good. Meanwhile Sky-holder is busy at man-making; and for the sake of balance, Old John Buck and Gibson have Flint making several species of apes which they obviously must have seen in zoological gardens but which quite enhance the narrative. When Sky-holder next looks around to view his creations, the game animals have disappeared, and only when Deermouse tells him does he discover where Flint has impounded them in a cave. Moving the rock, Sky-holder frees the game animals pent up by Flint, who tricks him afterward into releasing some monsters that might better have remained beneath the ground. Those that escaped in a thundering herd are the familiar game animals, but most of Flint's dangerously large animals remain imprisoned and are propitiated by the medicine societies of later times. This alternate impounding and release symbolizes hibernation and spring, as annually the animals go to earth and then reappear with young.

The climax is reached in a cosmic struggle of two phases between Sky-holder and his enemies to which the uncommitted game animals and humans are witnesses. In the first half he contends with his grandmother in the game of peach pits for which the "great bet" is the control of the earth. Each summons and exerts his *orenda* or magic power; each uses his own dice. For Sky-holder the dice are the heads of six volunteer chickadees who score for him "a clear field" (all of a color). Even today the duality of nature in the procession of summer and winter is dramatized at Green Corn and Midwinter festivals when the two halves of the longhouse community alternately symbolize the Master of Life (Sky-holder) and Sky-woman, one taking the eastern position, since east is life, and the other sitting west, which is winter and death, to contend in the Bowl Game.

In the second half, Sky-holder and Flint struggle to the death with avowed fatal weapons. Flint confesses that antler and flint will do him in and elicits from Sky-holder the secret that maize and rushes are his weakness. (Every Indian knew that antler would chip flint.) So Sky-holder goes around putting these objects up high and handy. Round the world they go heaving rocks and flinging mountains until, in some versions, nothing is left but their bones to be gathered by grandmother.

At this point occur two interruptions in most versions. A contest of power with the mask being, and the theft of light by Sky-holder and assisting animals, forestall the banishment of Flint and Sky-holder's return to the Sky-world.

The episode of the encounter between the Creator who is out inspecting his works and Hadu?i? ', the hunch-backed master of winds, patron of disease, gamekeeper and tutelary of the Falseface Society of later times, is deeply rooted in mythology and is evidently ancient. The dramatic incident underscores the importance that the Iroquois attach to this grotesque character who occupies a central place in their supernatural world, who is memorialized by hundreds of masks in museums, and who is celebrated by ceremonies among the Longhouse Iroquois today. A test of power evokes the familiar incident of moving a mountain while holding the breath, in which impetuous Hadu?i? ' smashes his nose in avid curiosity to see Sky-holder's success, thereby losing the contest. The forfeit is a promise not to harm the people but to rid the earth of disease, to dwell on the margins of the earth, and to coach the Falseface Society whose members shall call him "our dear grandfather." Powers to cure disease is given to those who wear masks and impersonate him, compensating for man's gift of tobacco in perpetual contract. He leagues with Sky-holder to rid the earth of Flint's monsters and promises not to harm the people. The ritual detail that is projected on mythology belongs to the description of later ceremonies. Here also belongs the use of tobacco "to send up one's words" to the supernaturals as in White Dog Sacrifice.[18]

The theft of light by Sky-holder and his animal helpers is a separate mythological episode having no contemporary counterpart. The plot is to secure the head of Earth-mother from a treetop where Sky-woman hung it, or put it in orbit for the use of man. Small mammals work together at canoe building, in voyaging, in guarding the boat, and in escape. Sky-holder makes his debut as Sapling in one version, but having no instep, uses antlers for climbing hooks; but Gibson has the Creator, Sapling's alter ego, manipulate his feet for shinning. Sapling's sudden descent with the head explains how the Sycamore tree got its scabs. Fox gets away with the sun in his mouth, and Black squirrel takes it over the treetops to the landing where the magic flight continues, Muskrat or Otter being clobbered with a paddle for talking back to the pursuing grandmother. Enormous variation in detail, in characters, and in episode indicate that this by no means uniquely Iroquoian motif is widespread in North America.

This epoch of creation closes by rapidly assigning roles to the actors in the midpantheon of service to mankind and returning others to the Sky-world. Earth-mother becomes "grandmother moon" and regulates women's affairs. Father Turtle, the Earth-grasper, becomes morning star, the Day-bringer. Sky-woman returns home, but their brother becomes "Elder brother the Day-Sun." Monsters are relegated to the mountains, and Thunders, "Our grandfathers whose voices reverberate from toward the sunset," keep an eye on them and bring rain to water crops until the end of time when they shall come from the east, foretelling the end of the world. The two brothers return to the Sky-world via the Milky Way, afterward the path of souls, which is forked to accommodate divergent careers and divided minds.

Sapling's world is the epoch of human society in the first times, which are described in some sixty pages, the final third of Gibson's text. It is a long period of enormous growth and expansion. Sapling, who in the older versions is an alias for the Creator, is the first man and culture hero; but various crises occur for which there are no traditional solutions, and this requires the Creator to make four returns in the guise of Sapling or the fatherless boy, a young man who proposes the clan system. The proposals draw heavily on the cultural memory of Gibson's sources, and I think that this explains the length of the myth and the compulsive character of its contents, which makes it a more rigid document than shorter, freer versions of John Buck and Armstrong, who were themselves, together with their audience, nearer to the old life. Gibson felt that his hearers needed to know.

I propose to reserve these rich cultural materials for appropriate use later on and confine the discussion here to structural, literary, and thematic considerations. Eight episodes are telescoped in as many paragraphs.

Odendonniha "Sapling" and *Awenhaniyonda* "Hanging Flower" are the first couple. They beget offspring and the people multiply. The Thunders water their crops when appealed to with tobacco.

The second coming of the Creator is occasioned by the need to teach the people the Four Ceremonies of thanksgiving which are sacred to the Creator and are the house-posts of later Longhouse festivals. The order of celebration and the content of the specified rituals is naturally that of Onondaga on Grand River. In general, the ceremonial cycle is balanced between a summer in-gathering of crops and a midwinter festival, coming after the hunt, marked by stirring cold ashes, kindling a new fire, dream guessing and renewal, and climaxed by the White Dog Sacrifice. Between festivals, it is the matron's duty to return thanks at dawn and dusk. Etiquette of hospitality or greeting and of departing is prescribed. The address of greeting and thanks to all the spirit-forces of the pantheon, the familiar Iroquois *Kanonyonk*, which opens all public gatherings, and prefaces every day of religious celebrations to this day, enumerates gifts that the Creator left on earth for man's use and enjoyment from the grass to the Sky-world.

The third coming of Sky-holder is occasioned by a typically Indian division of kindred into factions. Persons disappear; murder eclipses the sun. The elaborate ceremony for compounding murders and quickening the dead appears much later. Sapling seizes this opportunity to teach the first fruits ceremonies.

"For some time," we read, "the ceremonies were carried on correctly, and then again, there began to be disagreements." Disphoria over gossip becomes intense. The fourth, and since this is the magic number, the last appearance of the Creator is occupied by formal teaching of values afterward stressed in the Handsome Lake doctrine. Two aspects of ethnobotany receive attention. Herbal medicine, in which the Iroquois have a continuing interest, because they constantly suffer from real and imagined illnesses, depends on the necessity of botanical accuracy and must be imparted systematically, whereas symptomatology can remain vague as in their concept of "Disease, the faceless." The introduction of maize horticulture and the cycle of ceremonies attending its growth and maturation is accomplished by sending a pubescent boy and girl to find the "three sisters" (maize, beans, and squash) growing in the footprints of the gods, leading to the grave of Earth-mother and then having them report their discoveries to the town council. Inhumation has succeeded scaffold burial. Communal agriculture and mutual aid commence. From this episode two themes may be stated: only the pure may seek and find medicine and other cultural gifts; there shall be regular ways of organizing group activity, and these will become set in ritual.

A human being dies and the elders put the problem to the town council. An unknown young man, fulfilling the classic "no father" theme, proposes that they bury him. It is decided that in such events the elders shall choose a speaker to address the relatives, review with thanks the Creator's gifts, especially for herbal medicines that are used in sickness; and he shall anticipate that with the formation of clans the moieties shall function in turn to "lift up the minds" of the bereaved relatives. These things shall be the responsibility of elders.

Similarly woman's priority in matters affecting continuity of life is affirmed by placing control of these affairs in the hands of the matron of the *Ohwachira*, i.e., matrilineage. The Iroquois feel that this is consistent with the forces of nature. This statement is bound to provoke an argument among ethnologists and historians; indeed Gibson may have projected his own view on the past. In the legend of clan origin, a young man leads half of the families into crossing the river on a vine, the other half being left on the near shore. Camps on both banks are instructed that when their women go at dawn to water always to dip with the stream and to observe carefully and remember the behavior or character of the first bird or animal seen. These creatures become the eponymns of the familiar Iroquois clans, and, as we shall see, clan sets of personal names evolve.

A related problem that has to be settled by the elders is the establishment of a regular place of council, a concern that will crop up throughout history. The seating of the clans and their function in government occasions some movement across the council fire.

This long creation myth ends on two notes that provide the themes for understanding the stability and persistence of Iroquois culture during three centuries. The culture as ordained shall endure as long as does human society, the earth, its resources, and its products. This sentiment we shall encounter again and again throughout history, particularly in the Iroquois view of their agreements with the whites. "As long as the sun shines, the waters flow, and the grass grows" — so runs the line in the treaties. Related to it is the ending: "There shall always be tribes of people living on either side of the river."

The second note is the theme that culture is an affair of the mind: they thank the young man for the most important work that he has accomplished, in the creation of clan society, and they commemorate his contribution by giving him a new name, "He of the great mind."

A word about literary devices and style. The most conspicuous device that Gibson employs is the use of opening and closing lines for transition. "So-and-so began to travel from place to place" is the usual opening line of a fable, and Gibson employs it to introduce an incident. Another form of transition, which gives pause, after a series of actions, is: "So-and-so thought many things"; or "So-and-so returned to where his lodge stood." Typical ending lines are: "Now at that time they two went home"; or "Then he went elsewhere." Certain other connectors bind society to the future, as we have seen, as, for example, when after the Bowl Game the narrative concludes: "Human beings who dwell on the earth shall continue to relate it." Most of these devices refer to time and movement.

As Hewitt himself points out, the myth "is told partly in the language of tradition and of ceremony, which is formal, sometimes quaint, sometimes archaic, frequently mystical, and largely metaphorical." What this means is that when narrated in council or before a public gathering, the speaker would lapse into the high, intoned preaching style of council oratory which is an art in itself and which would markedly affect the impact if not the form of the myth. (A more intimate style of delivery characterizes the telling of tales by the fireside when a native folklorist impersonates the characters, and he and his audience live out the plot and incidents.) The figures of speech become concrete in the thought patterns of the Iroquois who regard the metaphors as fact. "Floating foam" is a figure that must have caught the fancy of some early storyteller. Rivermen know the flecks of foam beneath rapids; herbalists see it well to the surface when boiling roots; and women by the stream side observe it in dipping water. The "path" has many uses, referring to a course of action, to one's career, to the route of souls to the hereafter, as when the Creator says: "Where my path will have ended, there shall you find corn, beans, and squash growing from the grave of Earth-mother." I remember as a boy being entranced by Thornton W. Burgess's "bluebird that whistles off the snow"; but it is indeed bluebird in the *Iroquoian Cosmology* that gives the death cry — *Ko:weh´* (five times) — and frightens off the glacier, breaking up Flint's winter.

One final example. The ever-growing tree stands for life, status, and authority — for society itself. Uprooting the tree of peace and casting all evil weapons of war into a bottomless pit to be carried away by the stream, and then replanting the tree represents a kind of denial of reality so that life may go on. Thus we saw Sky-chief push all living things including his pregnant wife beneath the sky's crust and then replant the tree of heaven. Indian oratory is replete with this metaphor. Likewise a pine tree symbolizes chiefship, and the tree falls with the death of a chief; but the office continues, so the tree is raised up again with his successor. And finally, there is thought to be a giant elm at the center of the earth where the Masker rubs his rattle and derives his strength. We will find it again in art forms.[19]

We have seen that four is the magic number, imposing four tasks, so the listener always knows which will be the last. Suspense is created in other ways. Sky-holder directs Sapling, his alter ego, to go around and pick up antlers or flints as he sees them lying about and put them up handy. There is going to be a fight. Irony is conveyed when the wicked grandmother addresses Thrown-away, whom she hates, as "my dear grandson."

I will now summarize, as "Papa Franz" Boas used to say, by enumerating the main themes in Iroquois life as shown from concepts in the cosmology. I have reduced these to twenty.

1. *The native earth:* the earth, our mother, is living and expanding constantly imparting its life-giving force to all growing things on which our lives depend.

2. *Renewal:* the alternation of seasons and tasks is attuned to eco-

logical time as are the lives of plants and animals that rest when the earth sleeps.

3. *"It is us women that count"*: a chain of kinship connects all members of society running from the dead through our mothers to the smallest child whose life is separated from the spirit world as the thinness of a maple leaf, and even those yet unborn whose faces turn this way from beneath the ground. Consequently the Iroquois love their dead and cherish their children.

4. *Paternity is a secondary consideration: Agadoni comes after Ohwachira.* The fatherless boy becomes hero, but the boy rejected by his matrilineage may seek his father and learn.

5. *Twins are lucky,* and creative, but siblings fight. Only the pure who have been downfended or secluded succeed.

6. *The law of the kettle:* hospitality is a right and a duty to share. Throwing ashes is the negation of sharing, hospitality, friendship, peace, harmony and accord; but it is typically paranoid behavior that occurs all of the time in the culture.

7. *Home is where one customarily sits.* The bench or bed is the place of reflection and of council.

8. *Do not oppose the forces of nature:* going to water, traveling, making medicine, participating in ceremonial circuits.

9. *There is a regular way:* life and customary procedures are fairly established.

10. *Orenda* (supernatural power) adheres to animate and inanimate things, to aspects of the environment, and to sequences of behavior.

11. *Restraint is important:* one must not exert too much power and "spoil it." The equable person succeeds.

12. Acting the role by impersonation is a means of taking on power.

13. *Kanonyonk:* By continual and repeated greeting and thanks, the hierarchy of spirit-forces between the earth and sky that the Creator appointed to assist man in the enjoyment of the earth must be remembered and balanced in the fulfillment of their tasks.

14. *Dreams compel fulfillment:* Seeking the "word" that the soul desires, which once discovered must be fulfilled, involves diverting the mind by games, dances, and so on, and these prescribed ceremonies are subject to annual renewal for life,

15. The column of smoke, which carried the gods back to the sky-world, is a vehicle for sending up words. Smoke itself symbolizes thought, desire, community, and government. Tobacco is the "word" and closes the contract.

16. Earth-shakers are friendly spirits to be awed and propitiated: Turtle, Thunder, Haduʔiʔ', the Bigheads.

17. A man never refuses when asked, and he never shows fear.

18. *Things go by twos and fours:* forked path, divided mind, sex, seasons, moieties, life-death, balance of forces.

19. A pattern of reciprocity obtains between moieties for quickening life and faculties, for restoring society, and for all ceremonial associations of renewal.

20. Culture is an affair of the mind.

Notes

1. This paper was given as the address of the retiring president of the American Folklore Society in Philadelphia on 28 December 1960. *The People of the Longhouse* is the title of a general book on the Iroquois Indians of New York which the writer has in preparation for Farrar, Straus and Cudahy of New York.

2. Morris E. Opler, "An Application of the Theory of Themes in Culture," *Journal of the Washington Academy of Sciences*, 36 (1946), 137–166.

3. This is becoming true throughout the continent. See the author's "Folklore (American Indian)," *Encyclopaedia Britannica* (1960).

4. The cosmogonic myth is reported in detail in an account of Gallinée's visit to the Seneca towns in 1670 (see *Découvertes et Etablissements des Français dans l'ouest et dans le sud de l'Amérique Septentrionale. . . .*, ed. Pierre Margry, I [Paris, 1876], 360–362). Descendants of the Huron who were afterward called Wyandot were living at Detroit in 1872, when Horatio Hale of Clinton, Ontario, visited them and collected their ancient traditions (see Horatio Hale "Huron Folk-Lore," *Journal of American Folklore*, 1 [1888], 177–183). Later Marius Barbeau confirmed Hale's findings in his *Huron and Wyandot Mythology, Geological Survey Memoir* 80 (Ottawa, 1915), collated earlier variants from Sagard and the Jesuits to recent sources, and has recently published the Huron-Wyandot texts which he recorded phonetically from the last speakers of the language in Oklahoma in 1912 in his *Huron-Wyandot Traditional Narratives*, National Museum of Canada, Bulletin 165 (Ottawa, 1960). In his "Sketches of the Ancient History of the Six Nations," published in *The Iroquois Trail, or Foot-prints of the Six Nations*, ed. William M. Beauchamp (Fayetteville, N.Y., 1892), David Cusick prefaces his sketches with "A tale of the foundation of the Great Island (now North America), the two infants born, and the creation of the universe." To the same genre, if not to the same source, belong Elias Johnson, *Legends, Traditions, and Laws of the Iroquois, of Six Nations . . .* (Lockport, N.Y., 1881); Henry R. Schoolcraft, *Notes on the Iroquois, Proceedings of the American Philosophical Society*, 4 (1846), 611–633; Erminnie A. Smith, *Myths of the Iroquois*, 2nd Annual Report, *Bureau of American Ethnology* (1881), pp. 47–116; and the twentieth-century author and artist Jesse J. Cornplanter, *Legends of the Longhouse* (New York, 1938).

In addition to the latter three versions, for the Iroquois proper there are Seneca variants which were written down by New England missionaries at Buffalo Creek (see William N. Fenton, ed., "Seneca Indians by Asher Wright (1859)," *Ethnohistory*, 4 [1957], 305–307), and folklorists Jeremiah Curtin (see *Seneca Fiction, Legends, and Myths*, ed. Jeremiah Curtin and J. N. B. Hewitt, 32nd Annual Report, *BAE* [1918], p. 460); Harriet Maxwell Converse (see *Myths and Legends of the New York State Iroquois*, ed. Harriet M. Converse and Arthur C. Parker, New York State Museum, Bulletin 125 [Albany, 1908] pp. 31–38, and Arthur C. Parker, who was himself of Seneca descent (see Arthur C. Parker, *Seneca Myths and Folk Tales, Buffalo Historical Society Publications*, No. 27 [1923] pp. 59–73). And to complete the roster of Iroquoianists who collected the cosmogonic myth, F. W. Waugh found Oneida, Cayuga, and Tuscarora variants on the Six Nations Reserve (see Martha C. Randle, *The Waugh Collection of Iroquois Folktales, Proceedings of the American Philosophical Society*, 97 [1953], 629); and Reverend William M. Beauchamp, who with Hale was a charter member of this society, collected it at Onondaga (see William M. Beauchamp, *Iroquois Folk Lore Gathered from the Six Nations of New York*, Onondaga Historical Association, Syracuse, N. Y., [1922]). Not excerpted are the four versions—Mowhawk, Seneca, and two Onondaga—which comprise J. N. B. Hewitt's *Iroquoian Cosmology; First Part*, 21st Annual Report, *BAE* (1900), pp. 127–339; and *Iroquoian Cosmology; Second Part, with Introduction and Notes*, 43rd Annual Report, *BAE* (1928), pp. 449–819, which are my principal sources.

5. Randle, *The Waugh Collection of Iroquois Folktales*, p. 629.

6. Stith Thompson, *Tales of the North American Indians* (Cambridge, Mass., 1929); Thompson, *Motif-Index*; Earl W. Count, "The Earth-Diver and the Rival Twins: a Clue to the Time Correlation in North-Eurasiatic and North American Mythology," in *Selected Papers of the 29th International Congress of Americanists. Indian Tribes of Aboriginal America*, ed. Sol Tax (Chicago, 1952), pp. 55–62; Anthony F. C. Wallace, "Revitalization Movements," *American Anthropologist*, 58 (1955), 264–281; Anthony F. C. Wallace, "The Dekanawideh Myth Analyzed as the Record of a Revitalization Movement," *Ethnohistory*, 5 (1958), 118–130.

7. A. A. Goldenweiser, "The Death of Chief John A. Gibson," *AA*, 14 (1912), 692–694; William N. Fenton, "Simeon Gibson: Iroquois Informant (1889–1943)," *AA*, 46 (1944), 231–234; John R. Swanton, "John Napoleon Brinton Hewitt," *AA*, 40 (1938), 286–290.

8. Goldenweiser, Hewitt, *Iroquoian Cosmology; Second Part*, pp. 453–454.

9. Hewitt, *Iroquoian Cosmology; Second Part*.

10. See Swanton.

11. Hewitt, *Iroquoian Cosmology; First Part*, p. 134.

12. William N. Fenton, *Seth Newhouse's Traditional History and Constitution of the Iroquois Confederacy*, *Proceedings of the American Philosophical Society*, XCIII (1949), 153–157.

13. The history of the Conference on Iroquois Research, which has been held annually at Red House, N.Y., since 1945, is recorded in two places: William N. Fenton, *Symposium on Local Diversity in Iroquois Culture*, *BAE*, Bulletin 149 (1951), p. 4; and *Symposium on Cherokee and Iroquois Culture*, ed. William N. Fenton and John Gulick, *BAE*, Bulletin 180 (1961).

14. Hewitt, *Iroquoian Cosmology; First Part*, p. 139.

15. Thompson, *Tales of the North American Indians*, pp. 279–280.

16. Count (see fn. 6).

17. Following the lead of Frank G. Speck, who undoubtedly discovered the double-curved motif, Arthur C. Parker demonstrated among the Iroquois an even richer oral and decorative art involving symbolic trees and growing plants; cf. Arthur C. Parker, "Certain Iroquois Tree Myths and Symbols," *AA*, 14 (1913), 608–620.

18. J. N. B. Hewitt, "White Dog Sacrifice," in *Handbook of American Indians*, ed. F. W. Hodge, *BAE*, Bulletin 30 (1912), II, 939–944.

19. Parker, "Certain Iroquois Tree Myths and Symbols."

"A Tolerated Margin of Mess"[1]: The Trickster and His Tales Reconsidered[2]

Barbara Babcock*

No figure in literature, oral or written, baffles us quite as much as trickster. He is positively identified with creative powers, often bringing such defining features of culture as fire or basic food, and yet he constantly

*Reprinted from the *Journal of the Folklore Institute*, 9 (1975), 147–86.

behaves in the most antisocial manner we can imagine. Although we laugh at him for his troubles and his foolishness and are embarrassed by his prom-iscuity, his creative cleverness amazes us and keeps alive the possibility of transcending the social restrictions we regularly encounter.

From a literary point of view, society seems to create orders and rules for the very drama attendant upon their being broken. Literature's "heroes" are always those who depart from the norm. In our plays, our myths, and our stories we idolize, condemn, or laugh with and at the deviant. In short, as both Lévi-Strauss and Leach have stressed,[3] myth and other expressive media are preoccupied with those areas *between* categories, between what is animal and what is human, what is natural and what is cultural. Trick-ster and his tales exemplify this preoccupation, for at the center of his anti-nomian existence is the power derived from his ability to live interstitially, to confuse and to escape the structures of society and the order of cultural things.

More importantly, trickster expresses the ambiguous and paradoxical nature of power so derived. While trickster's power endows his group with vitality and other boons, it also carries the threat and the possibility of chaos. His beneficence, though central, results from the breaking of rules and the violating of taboos. He is, therefore, polluting (in Mary Douglas's sense of the term) and must remain marginal and peripheral, forever be-twixt and between. As a "criminal" culture-hero, he embodies all possibili-ties — the most positive and the most negative — and is paradox personified.

The essay which follows attempts to elucidate the paradox of trickster on a cross-cultural basis. In this regard, I have found it useful to examine critically various concepts of "marginality" and cultural negation, and to explore the range of powers available to those who play such an "outsider" role. The insights so derived I then apply generally to tricksters and trickster tales as a class, and specifically to a analysis of the tales of the Winnebago trickster, Wakdjunkaga. Finally, I address myself to the socio-cultural role or function of this particular paradox, this type of narrative.

I

The difficulties in defining "marginality" are compounded by the fact that the adjective "marginal" has become an all too encompassing rubric for grouping at times disparate phenomena; furthermore, few who use the term have done so with any precision. In the space of one brief introduction and one article,[4] for instance, the following social and literary types have been cited as instances of "marginal man": hobo, bum, outsider, expatriate, underground man, Okie, clown, alienated man, Bohemian, hippy, thief, "picaro," knight-errant, bastard, rogue, Don Juan, Prometheus, and Hermes.

The classic sociological definition was formulated by Robert Park and his student Everett Stonequist. The latter defined "marginal area" as "the boundary of two cultural areas where the occupying group tends to combine the traits of both cultures,"[5] and "marginal man" as "a personality type that arises at a time and a place where, out of the conflict of races and cultures, new societies, new peoples and cultures are coming into existence. The fate which condemns him to live, at the same time, in two worlds is the same which compels him to assume, in relation to the worlds in which he lives, the role of cosmopolitan and stranger."[6] He goes on to say that marginal man's "dual social connections will then be reflected in the type of life he leads, the nature of his achievements or failures, his conception of himself, and many of his social attitudes and aspirations. He will, in fact, be a kind of dual personality."[7] I should emphasize, however, that despite his title, *The Marginal Man*, and the implications of the preceding statements, Stonequist is "concerned finally and fundamentally less . . . with a personality type, than with a social process, the process of acculturation."[8]

More recently, Orrin Klapp, using the related term "deviant" has confused rather than clarified the issues by listing literally hundreds of social types under three major categories of heroes, villains, and fools in his social typology of the changing American character. He sees these as "three basic dimensions of social control in any society" and proceeds to analyze, if not reduce, their role in both everyday life and symbolic forms in terms of psychological and sociological functionalism — an error which he shares with most discussants of symbolic marginals and one which I will examine later in regard to interpretations of trickster figures. One value of his study, however, is that he points up the positive dimension of marginality, of being deviant in the sense of being better than or above the norms applied to group members or status occupants.

All too often "marginality," like "deviant," has connoted being outside in a solely negative sense, being dangerous to or somehow below "normal" boundaries. As such it promotes a dichotomy between good and evil which persistently confounds the analysis of the essentially ambiguous character of most literary marginals. In contrast to this either/or approach, we might better view this ambiguity as a necessary dualism and define marginality as being outside or between the boundaries of dominant groups for better *and* for worse. This may be saying nothing, for the notion of "boundary" is as multivocal or polyvalent (and as loosely used) as is "marginal." But, as an operational definition and point of orientation in these shifting concepts of "marginality," let it be said that a situation of "marginality" exists whenever commonly held boundaries are violated, be they those of the social structure, of law and custom, of kinship, family structure and sexuality, of the human person, or of nature.

Most current anthropological usage of the terms "marginality" or "marginal" is based on Van Gennep's concept of a tripartite structure or three-phase process of ritual consisting of separation, marginality or liminality, and reaggregation, as more recently examined and considerably amplified in Victor Turner's discussion of the ritual process. These different concepts of marginality point up a distinction that most discussions ignore, namely, the distinction between marginality as *phase* and as *type*. Van Gennep refers to a definite phase or span of time in a processual form and only indirectly to those persons who are in that phase or occupy that temporary state. Klapp, conversely, speaks of a definite type of individual or group of individuals while Stonequist uses the term to define both a type as well as the process and conditions generative of that personality and repeatedly confounds the two. At the risk of further confounding, I have used "marginal" as a generic term for all the interstitial and "antistructural" states specified in the following discussion. I therefore do not mean to imply simply Stonequist's definition of the term, and I have used "marginal" rather than "liminal" because I am not speaking specifically of *rites de passage*.

In his discussion of Hell's Angels, Beats, and Franciscans among others in the latter part of *The Ritual Process*, Victor Turner expands his definition and use of the term "liminal" from phase to generic type, that is, to social and personality types other than those initiands in a liminal ritual phase and to situations other than the "betwixt and between" period in a specific ritual process. To such marginal or liminal phenomena as ritual neophytes, court jesters, and participants in millenarian movements, he attributes the following common characteristics: they are persons or principles that (1) fall in the interstices of social structure, (2) are on its margins, or (3) occupy its lowest rungs. But in each case, he sees these as the products of a liminal cultural phase, thus retaining what he calls the "processual or diachronic profile."[9] In a recent lecture, "Passages, Margins, and Poverty," he has further qualified "liminality" and elaborated on the preceding three distinctions as follows (and as I paraphrase from lecture notes): (1) "Liminality" means midpoint in a status sequence, betwixt and between all fixed points of classification and, therefore, structurally if not physically invisible; (2) "Outsiderhood" means inhabiting a state permanently outside the social structure, either volitionally or nonvolitionally, and its constituency is to be contrasted with "marginals" in Stonequist's sense who are members of two or more groups, who are also "betwixt and between," but who, unlike "liminals" have no guarantee of the resolution of their ambiguous state; and (3) "Structural inferiority" means occupying the lowest rung of a class-oriented social structure.

Tricksters, like "communitas," a modality of social relatedness central to both art and religion, may, in their various guises, emerge from or imply any or all of these "antistructural" states, generally shifting from one to another in the course of the narrative. With regard to the shift from "structural inferiority" to "outsiderhood," Hobsbawm has delineated one character-type who shares much with the trickster: the "social bandit." Like trickster, the bandit is often regarded as primitive form of social protest and is defined in terms of his marginal and deviant behavior. But unlike trickster, the social bandit is a real person who operates in a real situation, combating the oppression of authority to protect the existence of a peasant group — a person whose antinomian behavior is a necessity rather than a whim. In both fact and fiction, however, the idea that "sometimes oppression can be turned upside down" is "a powerful dream, and that is why myths and legends form around the great bandits."[10] Even when their is no definable historical counterpart, the character of the literary trickster and the narratives about him recreate the pattern of social banditry.[11]

Another relevant dimension of marginality is Mary Douglas's notion of "peripheral" as defined in her recent book, *Natural Symbols*. In her "academically respectable" sense, "a peripheral class is one which feels less the constraints of grid [i.e., rules relating ego-centered individuals] and group [i.e., the sense of a bounded unit] than other classes of people within its social ambit, and expresses this freedom in the predicted way, by shaggier, more bizarre appearances."[12] The peripheral, as Douglas uses it, is related to her conception of "dirt" as formulated in *Purity and Danger*. Dirt is "matter out of place" that "implies two conditions: a set of ordered relations and a contravention of that order. Dirt, then, is never a unique isolated event. Where there is dirt there is system. Dirt is the by-product of a systematic ordering and classification of matter in so far as ordering involves rejecting inappropriate elements. . . . Dirt is a kind of omnibus compendium which includes all the rejected elements of ordered systems. It is a relative idea."[13] In this sense "peripheral" people such as tricksters, are the "dirt" of the social system.

This does not mean (as it might seem to imply) that the marginal or deviant is simply "a bit of debris spun out by faulty social machinery."[14] Rather, as Durkheim pointed out regarding crime in *The Division of Labor in Society*, deviant forms of behavior are a natural and necessary part of social life without which social organization would be impossible. More generally, all semiotic systems are defined in terms of what they are not. Marginality is, therefore, universal in that it is the defining condition as well as the by-product of all ordered systems. We not only tolerate but need "a margin of mess."[15]

II

Some further qualifications and discriminations of marginality are needed to understand the uses of such boundary-making and boundary-breaking in both social and literary contexts. For instance, it is important to note a basic discretion between volitional and nonvolition marginality, between those individuals who deliberately opt from the center (i.e., from a "structural" position) for outsiderhood and those who are consigned to that status, or, as David Buchdahl has stated, the difference between Abbie Hoffman and Bobby Seale. Lest this seem a static opposition, I note that society continually creates "marginal" figures, if not the reasons for the deliberate assumption of a marginal stance. Most marginality is of the mandatory or nonvolitional type, and the mandatory in the form of enforced initiation rituals, for example, is generally a phasic or periodic condition of marginality. Conversely, the purely nonvolitional in terms of birth, class, and so on, *or* the mandatory non-volitional in terms of consignment and prescribed status subsequent to a more or less volitional act, in the sense of a crime against society, tends to be a permanent condition with no guarantee of escape. In the latter case, there is a rite of transition which transfers the individual into a special deviant position, but there is no reentry ceremony to mark a return to normalcy.[16]

"Marginality" may also be distinguished into its comic and tragic modalities in both life and art. Given the tragic emphasis of the Judaeo-Christian tradition, the focus generally falls on the tragic type and pattern. In this modality, the individual who violates the boundaries of what is generally conceived as the social or human structure is punished, and the social order is preserved by the projection of evil onto the victim, by what Kenneth Burke calls the "sacrificial principle of victimage."

In contrast to the scapegoat or tragic victim, trickster belongs to the comic modality or marginality where violation is generally the precondition for laughter and communitas, and there tends to be an incorporation of the outsider, a levelling of hierarchy, a reversal of statuses. It could be said that "fools are characteristically unperturbed by the ignominy that comes of being irresponsible. They have a magical affinity with chaos that might allow them to serve as scapegoats on behalf of order; yet they elude the sacrifice or banishment that would affirm order at their order at their expense. They reduce order to chaos in a way that makes a farce of the [serious] mythical pattern."[17] In short, every society has some form of institutionalized clowning, yet surprisingly little systematic attention has been paid to this phenomenon. One exception is Enid Welsford's study, *The Fool: His Social and Literary History*, wherein she defines the Fool or Clown and summarizes the difference between him and the tragic hero as follows:

> . . . the Fool or Clown is the Comic Man, but he is not necessarily the hero of comedy, the central figure about whom the story is told, nor is he a mere creature of the poetic imagination whom the final drop-curtain consigns to oblivion. . . . As a dramatic character he usually stands apart from the main action of the play, having a tendency not to focus but to dissolve events, and also to act as an intermediary between the stage and the audience. As an historical figure he does not confine his activities to the theater but makes everyday life comic on the spot. The Fool, in fact, is an amphibian, equally at home in the world of reality and the world of imagination. . . . The serious hero focusses events, forces issues, and causes catastrophies; but the Fool by his mere presence dissolves events, evades issues, and throws doubt on the finality of fact.[18]

The obvious question this definition raises is what happens when the fool becomes central to the action and still retains the ability to "dissolve events" and "throw doubt on the finality of fact?" Furthermore, how can we account for innumerable ambiguous "comitragic"[19] forms which involve both laughter and punishment? For example, in such recent films as *Bonnie and Clyde, Easy Rider,* and *Butch Cassidy and The Sundance Kid,* criminal acts and violations of the social order provoke laughter and empathy, and yet the films conclude with the punishment in the tragic demise of the heroes, implying a seriousness to such reversals and inversions that the social fabric cannot sustain without disintegration.

In addition to the violations of social and cultural boundaries, the marginal figure tends, both literally and symbolically, to violate temporal and spatial distinctions. Temporally, there is a violation of the diurnal pattern of expectation in that the individual conducts his activities at night and sleeps or hides away during the daylight hours. Violation of temporal cycles extends to the violation of even the cycle of life and death. Granted, this latter violation applies especially to mythic or legendary figures, but the source of the legend is that even in "real" life such characters do not seem to die when they are supposed to and, like Vautrin in *Le Père Goriot,* collect epithets such as "trompe le mort." In sum, such fictional marginals are independent of our time and of the modes of conscious thought and action dependent upon it.

The marginal figure effaces spatial boundaries in several distinct ways: (1) he is a vagabond who lives beyond all bounded communities and is not confined or linked to any designated space; (2) he lives in cells, caves, ghettos, and other "underground" areas — like the spider inhabiting the nooks and crannies of social spaces. Both of these residence patterns imply what is made explicit in myth and folktale: that is, he lives above or below ground but not as normal mortals *on* the earth. Marginal figures also tend to be associated with marketplaces, crossroads, and other open spaces which are "betwixt and between" clearly defined social statuses and spaces or in which normal structures or patterns of relating break down — with places of transition, movement, and license. Temporally and spatially, he tends to confound the distinction between illusion and reality, if not deny it altogether. In fact, he casts doubt on all preconceived and expected systems of distinction between behaviors and the representation thereof.

Despite his peripheral and interstitial pattern of residence, the marginal figure often appears as "intruder." The most notable example is the *alazon* of classical comedy who, having been rejected (or by virtue of being rejected) from the group or society, in turn interferes with our normal schema of classification. Symbolically he certainly interferes, and again and again one is confronted with the paradox that that which is socially peripheral or marginal is symbolically central and predominant.

The blithe or deliberate ignorance of this paradox has resulted in curious confusions and major theoretical distortions or misapprehensions. Most notably, the tendency to read such symbolic embodiments in terms of dominant social structures makes the marginal seem to be a "residual category, rejected from our normal scheme of classifications." Negative categories such as antistructure, ritual reversals, tricksters, and hippies are consigned to the periphery, as in Mary Douglas's discussion in *Natural Symbols*. This seems surprising, especially in light of the convincing argument she makes in *Purity and Danger* against defining and analyzing dirt as a "residual category." Thus, we ironically "peripheralize" considerations of symbolic marginality and ritual reversal. Why should this be the case? Perhaps in trying to focus on negative categories, we run counter to our strongest mental habits. Yet by ignoring or minimizing negative representations, we fail in some basic sense to get at what symbolic processes are all about and, more importantly, how they function in any given social context.

This failure is all too obvious in considerations of the relationship of narrative or dramatic structure to social structure or of the role of narrative forms in society — be they by literary critics, folklorists, or anthropologists. Literary critics in large part adopt a formalist or autotelic view of literature and eschew or ignore the social dimension altogether. Those who do concern themselves with extraliterary matters are prone to various types of determinism in that they posit psychological, social, or religious variables and concepts and read the literary form (or, more generally, the content) in terms of them.

Most folklorists who have gotten beyond collecting and classifying either treat the tales they collect in the manner of a formalist critic or relate narrative content to the social dimension in terms of a rather rudimentary form of psycho-social functionalism. This type of interpretation is particularly obvious in discussions of trickster-type tales or other narrative forms which tend to be antisocial rather than normative. (I reserve my specific criticisms for the discussion of tricksters proper.) Finally, between these extremes are a number of socially-minded literary critics who admit the social dimension into their analyses of literature but in a very impressionistic fashion and with little if any social theory.

Despite structuralism's claim to mediate between humanism and empiricism, and despite frequent reference to Durkheim's emphasis upon symbolic systems as structures mediating social authority and the individual consciousness, most anthropological considerations of literature are subject to the same criticisms previously made of literary and folkloristic analysis. Structural considerations of narrative in fact tend to become highly formalistic and the notion of mediation is either confined to binary oppositions within the work itself or abstracted by a leap of faith (if not logic) to a general mediation between nature and culture and to universal structures of mind. Those structural accounts which explicitly include the social dimension usually posit an isomorphism between two structures (i.e., the social and the narrative) and make one-to-one mechanical comparisons, glossing over or explaining away those elements which negate, reverse, or are in some way not a charter for or a direct reflection of social structure. (I note in passing that many structural considerations of narrative have consisted of an analysis of content in the form of summary of action rather than of narrative structure.)

On the other hand, most traditional approaches to narrative of the "structural-functionalist" sort run the risk of teleological interpretation. Symbolic forms, notably those which fall into the myth-ritual complex, are simply means to an end and are analyzed in terms of the function they play in maintaining the social system — as mechanisms of social control in the form of "ritualized rebellion," "licensed aggression," or some other steam valve. In the end, the complexities of the symbolic process and the form itself are reduced to either a direct reflection or an aberrant inversion of the social system.

The problem with any of the preceding approaches is that they tend to minimize and, consequently, not account for the ambiguity, the paradox that is at the center of any symbolic form. And, as I mentioned, they thus avoid the entire thorny problem of symbolic inversions, negations, and reversals. Symbolic inversions are not simply logical reciprocals; if you consider them as such you tend to neglect both the transformations which occur with such inversions as well as the comic dimension of many such reciprocal forms.[20] And you avoid *the* question: what happens when such marginal figures as fools and tricksters become central to the action and still retain the ability to "dissolve events" and "throw doubt on the finality of fact?" I offer the premise that another reason for the neglect of symbolic negation or inversion is the tendency to focus on ritual and, lately, narrative structure as irreversible processual forms in the *rite de passage* sense and to view marginality or any sort of antistructure as a temporary phase which an initiand or hero passes through — one which will terminate with the conclusion of the ritual or narrative. This point of view for all its theoretical validity and basis in empirical fact is but part of the whole story. Much of ritual, especially that associated with seasonal and domestic cycles in contrast to developmental cycles, and even to some extent *rites de passage* (at least the liminal phase as discussed by Victor Turner), and of narrative deals with impossible possibilities, with endless caricatures, with reversals, negations, violations, and transformations.

The importance of "marginality" or "liminality" in symbolic processes, of negative patterns of culture, and of antistructure as well as structure has been emphazised in recent discussions both by Clifford Geertz and Victor Turner (and the Mary Douglas of *Purity and Danger*). Geertz has pointed to the necessity of analyzing "counteractive patterns" in culture, or "the elements of a culture's own negation which, in an ordinary, quite un-Hegelian fashion are included within it,"[21] and has recently analyzed one such counteractive pattern in his study of the Balinese cockfight.[22] In his 1968 essay on myth Turner went so far as to say that "possibly the best approach to the problem of cracking the code of myth is the *via negativa* represented by the liminal phase in initiation rites."[23] I would like to continue "marginally" this attempt at redressing the balance by examining one class of narrative which throws into sharp relief many aspects of marginality, the widely distributed trickster tales.

III

The tale of the trickster, picaro, or rogue is one of the oldest and most persistent cultural patterns of negation and one of the oldest of narrative forms. For centuries he has, in his various incarnations, run, flown, galloped, and most recently motorcycled through the literary imagination and much of the globe. Examples are legion. Hermes, Prometheus, Ture, Maui, Eshu-Elegba, Anansi, Wakdjunkaga, raven, rabbit, spider, and coyote are but a few from ancient and native mythology and folktale.[24] And, in Western literature, one could cite Lazarillo de Tormes, El Buscón, Gil Blas, Felix Krull, Augie March, and of late the Butch Cassidys and Easy Riders of film.

The term "trickster" has, unfortunately, become established in the literature, for it would perhaps be better to call both this type of tale and persona by the literary term "picaresque" which combines with the notion of trickery and roguish behavior the idea of the uncertain or hostile attitude of an individual to existing society and an involvement in narrative focussed on movement, within and beyond that society. The main interests of picaresque fiction are social and satirical, and the picaro or rogue whose adventures it relates in episodic fashion tends to be peripatetic because he is "fleeing from, looking for, or passing through" some aspect of society. Through his trickery, that is, his negations and violations of custom, he condemns himself to contingency and unpredictability. As Victor Turner describes it, "in the liminal period we see naked, unaccommodated man, whose nonlogical character issues in various modes of behavior: destructive, creative, etc. . . . but always unpredictable . . ." "and tricksters are clearly liminal personalities."[25]

In almost all cases, and to a greater or lesser degree, tricksters

1. exhibit an independence from and an ignoring of temporal and spatial boundaries;

2. tend to inhabit crossroads, open public places (especially the marketplace), doorways, and thresholds. In one way or another they are usually situated between the social cosmos and the other world or chaos;

3. are frequently involved in scatological and coprophagous episodes which may be creative, destructive, or simply amusing;

4. may, similarly, in their deeds and character, partake of the attributes of Trickster-Transformer-Culture Hero;

5. frequently exhibit some mental and/or physical abnormality, especially exaggerated sexual characteristics;

6. have an enormous libido without procreative outcome;

7. have an ability to disperse and to disguise themselves and a tendency to be multiform and ambiguous, single or multiple;

8. often have a two-fold physical nature and/or a "double" and are associated with mirrors. Most noticeably, the trickster tends to be of uncertain sexual status;

9. follow the "principle of motley" in dress;

10. are often indeterminant (in physical stature) and may be portrayed as both young and old, as perpetually young or perpetually aged;

11. exhibit an human/animal dualism and may appear as a human with animal characteristics or vice versa; (even in those tales where the trickster is explicitly identified as an animal, he is anthropomorphically described and referred to in personal pronouns);

12. are generally amoral and asocial — aggressive, vindictive, vain, defiant of authority, etc.;

13. despite their endless propensity to copulate, find their most abiding form of relationship with the feminine in a mother or grandmother bond;

14. in keeping with their creative/destructive dualism, tricksters tend to be ambiguously situated between life and death, and good and evil, as is summed up in the combined black and white symbolism frequently associated with them;

15. are often ascribed to roles (i.e., other than tricky behavior) in which an individual normally has privileged freedom from some of the demands of the social code;

16. in all their behavior, tend to express a concomitant breakdown of the distinction between reality and reflection.[26]

These different kinds of anomalousness are obviously interrelated. One might, for example, posit trickster's creative/destructive dualism as the basic binary opposition which implies or generates the others, such as order/disorder, life/death, cosmos/chaos, etc. Moreover, these various dualisms are all relative to the attitudes and behavior of the *non*fools with whom the trickster or fool stands in dynamic relation — they are expressive of the social contexts in which they occur and depend upon social experience for perception.

The most important characteristic of these related dualisms, however, is their expression of ambiguity and paradox, of a confusion of all customary categories. The clown or trickster epitomizes the paradox of the human condition and exploits the incongruity that we are creatures of the earth and yet not wholly creatures of the earth in that we have need of clothing and spiritual ideals to clothe our nakedness, of money, and of language — of human institutions. Further, he embodies the fundamental contradiction of our existence: the contradiction between the individual and society, between freedom and constraint.

In Trickster we find a "coincidence of opposite processes and notions in a single representation [that] characterizes the peculiar unity of the liminal:

that which is neither this nor that, and yet is both."[27] Trickster is "at one and the same time, creator and destroyer, giver and negator, he who dupes and who is always duped himself."[28] Following Mikhail Bakhtin, Julia Kristeva has called such coexistence of opposites "dialogic." Interestingly enough, she sees the dialogical tradition originating in Menippean satire and carnival that are characterized by a plurality of languages (sign systems), a confrontation of types of discourse and ideologies with no conclusion and no synthesis — a polyphony which makes monologue impossible.[29]

Dialogic phenomena such as tricksters, as the scholarship amply demonstrates, are also singularly resistant to monological interpretation. Despite Katharine Luomala's observation twenty-five years ago regarding Maui that "a monistic theory of any kind is inadequate for understanding the nature of the hero's character and exploits,"[30] scholars have persisted in trying to explain away this paradoxical coincidence of opposites. It would seem that we would rather do away with contradiction than try to understand it, and we have continued, as Makarius rightly criticizes,[31] to obscure trickster's dialogues with a variety of functional monologues (single-goal approaches or arguments).

The characteristic duality which has given interpreters the greatest difficulty and has engendered the most debate is the coincidence of a trickster *and* a culture-hero *or* the merging of the human or animal *and* the divine, the secular *and* the sacred in a single figure, particularly in the tribal mythology of North American Indians. While in some societies both attributes are, as mentioned, combined in a single figure, in some there is a division into pure culture-hero and purely secular trickster; and in others such as the Winnebago there are two figures, both of whom have trickster attributes, but one of whom is more predominantly a culture-hero and the other more a trickster who performs but a few beneficent acts for mankind. Despite the sacred/secular distinction which some groups make more strongly than others, the trickster figure is in no case simply human and a "well-built-in" member of society. He is always conceived of as more or less than human, and usually the former despite his animal-like attributes. In fact, he may be portrayed as an ignoble, secular character in tribal narrative and yet be ascribed a sacred status and central importance in the rituals of the same group.

For over a century, American scholars have attempted to explain both the trickster/culture-hero coincidence in a single figure and the varying distribution of these characteristics into two or more personae and classes of narrative. The nineteenth-century folklorist, Daniel Brinton, believed that the trickster elements of the Algonkian figure were late and foreign accretions to the character of an originally high and noble deity of light. Influenced no doubt by Max Müller's theories about the development of Indo-European Gods, he postulated a "disease of language" theory to account for the degeneration of the "Great God of Light" into the ignoble trickster, the "Great Hare." In 1891 Boas rejected this theory on the ground that it does not at all "explain why there should be such a uniform tendency to attribute coarse buffoonery or moral deliquencies of the worst sort to an ideal culture-hero. The apparent difficulty, he indicated, 'vanishes with the misconception that actions which benefit mankind must have proceeded from an altruistic disposition.' In reality, the heroes of Indian mythology are very often self-seekers, whose deeds have only incidentally contributed to man's comfort as well as their own."[32] Lowie concurs with Boas that "when the data are fairly considered, there is no valid reason for regarding the buffoon as a mythological being of later origin than the more dignified hero," and makes the further interesting point that the serious culture-hero does not exist at all in the mythologies of some tribes.[33]

Given the absence of a distinct culture-bringer and the "overshadowing literary importance of the trickster," both Boas and Lowie conclude that the trickster may be an older type of character in any given mythology than a properly so-called culture-hero, that he evolves into a trickster-culture-hero, and then in more advanced cultures becomes two separate and distinct figures. Radin further explains the bifurcation in the Winnebago case as the opposition of a popular folklore trickster-hero with the spirits and gods of the shamans but concurs on the primacy of the trickster type.

This view, at times augmented by psychologically-informed interpretations, was and is generally accepted by American folklorists. What Boas's conclusion implied and what Jung formulated in "The Psychology of the Trickster" in Radin's *The Trickster*, was that "the crude primitivity of the trickster cycle makes it all too easy to see the myth as simply the reflection of an earlier, rudimentary stage of consciousness, which is what the trickster obviously seems to be."[34] The popularity of the Radin book has assured the currency of this point of view and, unfortunately, has produced a plethora of psychologically reductive interpretations.

Paul Radin shared Jung's view and regarded the Winnebago trickster as the symbol of an "undifferentiated" psychic state in the process of attaining differentiation and orientation:

> The symbol which Trickster embodies is not a static one. It contains within itself the promise of differentiation, the promise of god and man. For this reason every generation occupies itself with interpreting Trickster anew. No generation understands him fully but no generation can do without him. Each had to include him in all its theologies, in all its cosmogonies, despite the fact that it realized that he did not fit properly into any of them, for *he represents not only the undifferentiated and distant past, but likewise the undifferentiated present within every individual.* This constitutes his universal and persistent attraction.[35]

I would argue, however, with Laura Makarius[36] that the ambivalence and the contradictions with which Trickster's tales abound are *not* proof, as Radin and others imply, of an incapacity to differentiate true from false, good from evil, beneficence from malevolence. Rather, they express the genera-

tive situation of ambivalence and contradictions that the very basis of culture engenders. Seeming undifferentiation and ambivalence are
characteristic of mediating figures, and it may well be that the mediating
figure of Trickster does not represent a regression to a primal, undifferentiated unity but is created in response to a present and constant perception of
opposition, of difference essential to human constructs (viz., Lévi-Strauss).

In this regard, Laura Makarius' interpretation of Trickster is much less
reductive and goes beyond the controversy over the unity or duality of this
contradictory being. She sees Trickster as the mythic projection of the magician violating taboo, the ritual violator of interdiction and, therefore, as the
embodiment of the contradictory power attendant upon the violation of
fundamental taboos. It is this vocation of violator that "overloads his tales
with acts of rebellion, disobedience, defiance, transgression, and sacrilege,"[37] and constitutes his essence and reason for being. If one begins with
the principle that the "sacred" is precisely the result of the violation of taboo
(which is made explicit in myth through profanation and sacrilege), there is
no longer a contradiction between the quality of the "sacred" being of trickster and the secular profaner.[38] Trickster is a sacred being and the founder of
the ritual and ceremonial life of his society precisely because he violates taboos for the profit of his group.[39] In sum, this interpretation (based implicitly on Robertson-Smith's notion of the "ambiguity of the sacred") comes
much closer than previous accounts to understanding Trickster's ambivalent and mediating role and his symbolic significance.

If, however, one insists on a psychological interpretation of Trickster's
behavior, Freud and Bergson's notion of the joke as an attack on control
would seem more appropriate in that it accounts for the laughter produced
whenever Trickster is discussed. "For both the essence of the joke is that
something formal is attacked by something informal, something organized
and controlled by something vital, energetic, and upsurge of life for
Bergson, of libido for Freud."[40] The implications of this notion are both
valid and obvious, and have been perhaps over-exploited in discussions of
this particular "spirit of disorder" and "enemy of boundaries." While this
interpretation is attested, it is limited and too easily becomes but another
functionalist "steamvalve" interpretation.

Finally, the tales themselves present investigators with a related classificatory problem. Like Trickster himself, the tales tend to confound sacred/
secular distinctions for they may be classed as sacred myths, secular tales, or
as an intermediate mixed category. Then, too, actual performance may
confound theoretical distinctions. As Barre Toelken points out about the
Navaho, "secular" trickster tales are often told in the middle of "sacred"
myths. Similarly, trickster tales tend not to conform with anthropologists'
and folklorists' favored tripartite division into myth, legend, and folktale
(viz., Malinowski, Bascom, et al.). Previous discussions have generally
erred in two respects crucial to classification: (1) a failure to take the specific indigenous "emic" categories into account and (2) a failure to consider

specific contexts of performance.[41] Consideration of these factors may resolve the classification problem, but then again it may not, for the distinctive feature of trickster tales (like Trickster himself) may well be their ability to confound classification, including their *and* our traditional narrative categories.

IV

The Winnebago divide their narratives into three classes: myth, (*waika*, meaning "what is old"), tale (*worak*, meaning "that which is told" in the sense of "that which has happened"), and a myth-tale mixed category.[42] Like most Trickster narratives, the Winnebago tales pose a classificatory problem. The tales of both Hare (*wacdjmgega*) who is more trickster than culture-hero and Trickster (*wakdjunkaga*) are classed as sacred myths, *waika*. *Waika* could be told only under certain prescribed conditions and by a few people in the group who possessed the traditional right to narrate them. These conditions, as observed by Radin's informant Sam Blowsnake in obtaining this Wakdjunkaga text in 1912, consisted of offerings of tobacco and gifts to the narrator commensurate with the traditionally accepted value of the myth. It is, therefore, to the best of Radin's knowledge, "an authentic text obtained in an authentic manner."

Waika were also distinguished by formulaic introductions, other various formulae and commonplaces relating to character and action throughout the myth, and plots that consisted of more or less well-coordinated motifs, themes, and episodes. "In the pure trickster cycles such as those of the Trickster and of the Hare, this co-ordination is poor and there is little relation between episodes. Episodes are held together only by the vague theme of a person journeying from place to place."[43] This type of organization tends to be characteristic of all trickster tales: the trickster's effacing of spatial, temporal and social boundaries is embedded in the very structure of the narrative that violates commonly held parameters such as unity of time, place, and action or plot. And, on the level of action and language, such tales frequently exceed the bounds of both decorum and credibility. In short, the peripatetic, "marginal," and antistructural character of the Trickster is reiterated in the episodic, serial quality and the linear simplicity of the narrative.

The most important effect of the violation of credibility and the break with external probability is to focus attention on the wandering hero and to emphasize the internal growth of this central character, as is certainly the case in the tales of Wakdjunkaga. This seeming lack of unifying elements other than character in this and other trickster cycles is so pronounced that some critics, notably Alan Dundes, have argued that trickster tales have no structure beyond the level of episode or, in Dundes's terms, "motifeme" — that there is "no discernible, non-arbitrary manner in which to link such segments into an integrated whole which can be subjected to 'structural analysis.' " Appearances to the contrary, I would argue that as with the "marginal" hero, so too with narrative structure: antistructure implies structure and order. While they express disorder and appear disordered, many trickster cycles, especially that of Wakdjunkaga, are highly structured with respect to both individual episodes and the total cycle.

There has, however, been considerable debate whether collections such as the tales of Wakdjunkaga constitute cycles at all or if "their inclusion into one united narrative [represents] the outlook of the Western systematizing scholar."[44] Evidence indicates that what we describe as a cycle—"a number of narratives centering about a hero or group of heroes and forming a continuous series"[45]—exists as an unperformed and *ideal* work "whose overall form and parts are well known, but which can never be realized in a single performance."[46] This *ideal* work is simply the total understanding that a community has of a group of episodes centering on one character (or group) and those with whom they come into contact. Such an organization is characteristic of oral narratives in which there are usually situational limitations on the amount of time an audience can and will give to any one performer or performance. Everyone in the audience has a sense of the outer perimeters of the cycle, and where the various episodes essentially fit. This doesn't mean that there is a total agreement as to which will follow which, but rather an overall sense of structuring. In analyzing this cycle, then, I will be using these texts as one man's unusually full rendering of these episodes in a situation in which he was given the opportunity to spell out the entire pattern of movement of the cycle.

What we have then in the Winnebago trickster cycle is a circumstantial rendering of one narrative *ideal* in a form which arises from the collaboration between the native narrator, Sam Blowsnake and the anthropologist Paul Radin. I have analyzed it as a whole much as one would analyze the *Iliad* or *Odyssey*, attempting to show that there is structuring beyond the level of the episode and that what we call trickster cycles are not simply random collections of his exploits, just as the works of Homer could hardly be called random.

While the tales of Wakdjunkaga may not conform to the developmental pattern that Radin posits and while different versions of the cycle (if available) might give a different number and different ordering of the tales, there is nonetheless some deep structure, some basic syntax to this rendering of the "ideal" work which is not simply the fortuitous and idiosyncratic arrangement of a given narrator or anthropologist. I would postulate, but cannot prove, that all such cycles have a syntagmatic arrangement, that different classes of episodes may be substituted in certain narrative "slots" and, though only one tale may be told at a given time, both narrator and audience are aware of its place in an unlying, "ideal" syntagm.

Trickster tales generally begin with a statement of order followed by its dissolution and, thereafter, by an examination of forms of disorder. The examination of disorder in the forty-nine-tale cycle of Wakdjunkaga consists of approximately nineteen episodes or discrete units of action that might be summarized as follows:

(Note: W. indicates Wakdjunkaga; → indicates a causal or formal connection between episodes; **indicates temporary re-aggregation.)

Episode 1. (Tales 1–3): Chief prepared to go on warpath, leaves village, and, by sacrilegious actions, deliberately separates self from all human society.

2. *(4–5)*: W. kills and dresses buffalo; right arm fights with his left. First explicit identification as "Trickster" by birds. W. professes ignorance of what they are saying.

3. *(6–8)*: W. meets man who kills and eats bear. He borrows his two children with interdiction to feed them only once a month, upon pain of death if they die. W. breaks rules; children die; father pursues him to the "end of the world." W. jumps in ocean and is given up for dead.

↓

4. *(9–10)*: W. swims in ocean, can't find shore, finally does with help of whitefish. Tries unsuccessfully to catch fish, makes soup from water, buries dead fish for future meal.

5. *(11)*: "Again he wandered aimlessly about the world." Comes to edge of lake, mimes man pointing, realizes it is a tree stump. Acknowledges epithet, "the Foolish One" — first indication of self-awareness.

6. *(12–14)*: W. comes to shore of another lake; catches and kills ducks. Tells anus to keep watch over roasting ducks while he sleeps; foxes steal ducks; W. awakens, punishes anus with burning stick, eats part of own intestines. Again, acknowledges correctness of epithet.

7. *(15–16)*: W. awakens with erection holding up blanket. Mistakenly identifies as chief's banner. Speaks to penis, and when it softens, coils it up and puts in a box which he carries on his back. Sends penis across water and has intercourse with chief's daughter. Thwarted by old woman.

8. *(17–18)*: W. gets turkey buzzard to carry him; buzzard drops Trickster in hollow tree. W. pretends to be a raccoon and thereby dupes women into rescuing him.

9. *(19–21)*: W. and three animal companions decide to live together. Snow falls; they become hungry and at W.'s instigation decide to live in Indian village for the winter. W. disguises self as woman with elk's liver and kidneys, marries chief's son, has three sons. In course of teasing by mother-in-law, loses false vulva; identity discovered, forced to flee.

*****   ↓

10. *(22)*: Tired of wandering, W. goes across lake to real wife and remains in village until son is grown. He tires of sedentary life and the demands of social existence and again succumbs to wanderlust.

*****   ↓

11. *(23–25)*: Encounters and, despite admonition, eats talking laxative bulb. Goes to place where people live, breaks wind and scatters them and

their belongings. Laughing, proceeds onward, begins to defecate and buries self in own excrement. Blinded by own filth, begins to run, bumps into trees, seeks direction to water, and because trees speak to him, he finally reaches water and barely saves himself.

↓

12. (26–31): While washing himself, W. mistakes plums reflected in water for actual plums. Goes ashore, eats actual plums. Comes to oval lodge with two women and many children. Gives them some plums and sends the women in search of more while he stays with the children. He then kills and eats the children who are raccoons. Puts head of one on stake sticking out of door of lodge. Goes to nearby hill and persuades female skunk to dig hole through hill. Lures mother raccoons into hill and kills them. Meal interrupted by squeaking tree, climbs tree, gets caught in fork, wolves come by and eat trickster's food. W. frees himself from the tree and runs in the direction which the wolves had gone.

↓

13. (32–33): Trickster gets head caught in elk skull, walks along river to place inhabited by people. Disguises self with raccoon skin blanket, impersonates an elk and water spirit and dupes people into bringing offerings and splitting skull. People make efficacious medicinal instruments from skull and W. leaves.

14. (34–37): W. transforms self into deer by donning carcass of dead buck-deer and takes revenge on hawk. Traps hawk in rectum. Meets *bear* who envies his "tail." W. breaks wind and frees hawk who emerges without any feathers. W. then deceives bear and kills him. Mink outwits W. in race and gets bear meat. W. vows revenge and goes to village where previously married, gets hunting dog and pursues mink in vain. Again, swears revenge. (↔ Episode 18)

15. (38–39): W. continues wandering. Chipmunk taunts him; W. probes hollow tree with penis; chipmunk gnaws off all but a small piece of his penis. W. kicks log to pieces, kills chipmunk, and finds gnawed off pieces of his penis which he throws into lake and turns into plants "for human beings to use." He then discards the box in which he'd carried his penis. "And this is the reason that our penis has its present shape and size."
*****

16. (40): In scenting contest, coyote leads W. to human village. W. remains, marries, and a child is born to him. When tribe goes on fall move, W. leaves for another place where he lived alone. "There he remained and there he made his permanent home. He never went back to the village where he had first married. One day he decides to go and pay a few visits."
*****

↓

17. (41–44): (Series of visits to various animals and imitations of their methods of obtaining food — Variations on the "bungling host"-type tale) Departed wife inexplicably reappears on the scene. (41) Visits and imitates muskrat who turns ice into lily-of-the-valley roots. (42) When family eats up all of the roots, he visits snipe and imitates his method of

fishing. (43) When all the fish are gone, W. visits another "younger brother," the woodpecker, and imitates his way of getting *bear*. After a long time, when all the bear meat is eaten, W. visits polecat and learns his method of killing deer.

*****   ↓

18. (45–46): Desirous of showing off all his game, W. decides to return with his wife to the village. Long lodge built for W. in center of village next to chief's and he entertains young men with his stories at night. Mink visits village, and W. dupes him into soiling the chief's daughter, thereby getting his revenge. Coyote had married into the village and W. is desirous of revenging himself on coyote and vice versa. W. succeeds and shames coyote who thereupon ceases to live among people.

*****   ↓

19. (47–48): W. stays in village a long time and raises many children. Decides to go around the earth again, for "I was not created for what I am doing here." Travels down Mississippi, recollects the purpose for which he had been sent to earth by Earthmaker and removes all obstacles to the Indians along the river, kills beings that were molesting people, and pushes waterspirit roads farther into the earth. After moving waterfall, he eats his final meal on earth, leaving imprint of buttocks. He leaves earth, goes first into the ocean, and then up to the heavens to the world under Earthmaker's where he, Wakdjunkaga, is in charge.

The overall structure of these episodes resembles the tripartite form of the *rite de passage*: separation (Episode I), margin or *limen* (Episodes 2–17), and reaggregation (Episode 18). (See Fig. 1 for a diagram of the overall structure.) The long period of marginality during which Wakdjunkaga "wanders aimlessly about the earth" breaks down further into two secondary tripartite patterns, two temporary periods of reaggregation and stasis (Episodes 10 and 16) during which Wakdjunkaga returns to his wife or remarries and lives within village society for some greater or lesser period of time. In each case, he voluntarily separates himself from the human community and continues his wanderings. On a third level, there are at least seven incidents of contact with other human beings or opportunities for reaggregation that fail to materialize either because of Wakdjunkaga's inauthentic and asocial behavior (e.g., notably Episode 9 which is a situation of reaggregation on false premises and in the role of Trickster), or because he chooses not to act upon the incident in the direction of reintegration (e.g., Episode 13).

If one ignores Radin's claim that the concluding episode (Tales 47–49) is a formal appendage and not an integral part of the cycle, the overall structure might be viewed somewhat differently. In this episode Wakdjunkaga remembers what he was created to do, performs a series of beneficent deeds for mankind, crosses the ocean, and ascends to the world below Earth maker of which he is in charge. His extended sojourn on earth, the world of Hare, could, therefore, be termed an extended period of "marginality" — a truly ontological rite of passage — in relation to this final reaggregation to his rightful domain in Winnebago cosmology. Radin states that this conclusion was tacked on to justify Wakdjunkaga's role as culture-hero in the "Myth of the Origin of the Medicine Rite" and his position in the sacred Medicine Rite. Whether or not this conclusion is a formal appendage and inconsistent with the character of Trickster as portrayed in the preceding 46 tales, Wakdjunkaga *did* have these positive and reintegrative roles to enact in the central myth and ritual of the Winnebago. With or without this ending to make it explicit, he has the dual character of Trickster and Culture Hero with the emphasis on the former. In the context of Winnebago myth and cosmology (see Fig. 1), his time spent on earth either playing tricks upon or helping mankind is a "marginal" state during which he is separated from his true realm and role. On the other hand, one *could* argue that rather than reaggregation to a true domain of structure, his final departure from human society is a separation to a permanent, sanctioned state of "marginality." In either case, the period spent on earth as described in Episodes 1–18 follows a tri-partite pattern in which he volitionally leaves and returns to the boundaries and structure of human society. Wakdjunkaga's wanderings may be diagrammed as in Fig. 1.

In addition to conforming to this overall pattern, the individual episodes are not discrete and discontinuous segments of action unrelated to one another, but are often causally, if not formally, connected (see summary of

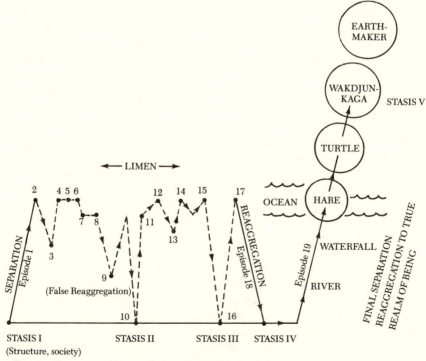

Fig. 1. Diagram of Overall Structure of Episodes

episodes). Their arrangement in relation to the subjective pattern of Wakd-junkaga's increasing awareness of self and others is anything but fortuitous or haphazard, and few if any of the episodes are interchangeable. More-over, Wakdjunkaga's violations of tribal law and custom follow a relatively consistent pattern of satire on the rituals and practice of war; social struc-ture, especially the division into "upper" and "lower" moieties and the op-position between and reciprocal functions of the Thunderbird and Bear chiefs and clan members, sexual taboos and sex-related rules of conduct, especially female; and proper behavior in respect to eating and excreting, in that order of emphasis.

The violations of tribal law and custom whereby Wakandja separates himself from his fellow men and places himself outside social boundaries begin with the first sentence of the first episode: "Once upon a time there was a village in which lived a chief who was just preparing to go on the warpath."[47] Given that the use of the word chief in isolation usually implied tribal chief and given the similarity between Trickster's name and that of the Thunderbird, "Wakandja," this is flagrant satire, for the tribal chief, who was selected from the upper moiety and from the clan generally regarded as most important, the Thunderbird, could not under any circum-stances go on the warpath. He was the locus of peacekeeping and his most important functions were to succor the needy and plead for clemency in all cases of infractions of tribal law and custom, even murder, in which cases he not only interceded for the life of the murderer, but actually if need be offered to take the place of the malefactor. His lodge was a sacred asylum and absolutely inviolable.[48] This satiric inversion is also directed at the chief of the lower moiety who belonged to the Bear clan, who was the center of police, disciplinary, and war powers; who inflicted punishment for viola-tion of law and custom; and who did, indeed, lead the tribe on the war-path. This initial usurpation of the Bear Chief's role establishes the negative, antinomian pattern of Wakdjunkaga's actions and reflects opposi-tion between the upper and lower moieties in Winnebago tribal society and antipathy between perspectives represented in the two chiefs, which ex-tends throughout the cycle in Wakdjunkaga's encounters with bears. The Winnebago clans were organized in accordance with moiety affiliations and reciprocal "bond-friendship" relations as follows:

I. *Wangeregi* Moiety: the upper moiety

Sky Clans
- a. Thunderbird
- b. War-people or Hawk
- c. Eagle
- d. Pigeon

II. *Manegi* Moiety: the lower moiety

Earth Clans
- a. Bear
- b. Wolf
- c. Deer
- d. Buffalo

Water Clans
- e. Water Spirit
- f. Elk
- g. Fish
- h. Snake

The four feasts which the chief gives before he finally picks up his war-bundle plus the slaughter of bears as well as and rather than deer on the latter three occasions are clearly a parody of the War Bundle Feast which was one of the prime ceremonies of the Winnebago and which was given on four different days. Four, moreover, is their sacred number and prime ceremonial unit. The satire of war and the Bear chief are here quite explicit, for the Warbundle Ritual was the greatest glorification of the successful warrior and of the viewpoint of the chief of the lower moiety. Wakdjunkaga compounds his initial violation on the first three occasions by leaving the feast before his guests and by cohabiting with a woman, for the host of a feast must be the last to leave and sexual intercourse was strictly forbidden for men starting on the warpath.

He leaves the fourth and final feast insisting, "It is I, I, who am going on the warpath," and descends to "where there was a boat" accompanied by "those capable of fighting." Insistent, however, upon a solitary venture, he turns his boat back to shore and smashes it. Some continue to accompany him across a swamp, and to discourage them he commits the ultimate sacrilege of trampling on his warbundle and throwing away his arrowbundle. He insures his solitary and antisocial pursuits by desecrating this most prized of all Winnebago possessions, which was carefully concealed and guarded. "From there on he continued alone," outside the bounds of human society and in a naked, unaccommodated situation of lacking almost everything. But, as the conclusion of this episode indicates, he is still in close contact with nature. He calls "all the objects in the world younger brothers when speaking to them," and "he and all objects in the world understood one another, understood, indeed, one another's language."[49] That the Winnebago trickster cycle should begin with what is essentially a satiric inversion of the warbundle ritual and the ideology and practice of warfare is, as Radin has pointed out, "deeply significant both psychologically and culturally."[50] And, despite his assertions about going on the warpath, it certainly aligns Trickster with nonviolence which Makarius sees as a characteristic trait of the blood taboo and characteristic of those who violate it such as clowns and tricksters. The denigration of violence and, therefore, the ability to defend oneself leads in turn to the insitution of the custom of "ritual plunder,"[51] seizing the possessions of others with impunity, which Trickster unquestionably proceeds to do.

When Wakdjunkaga leaves the village, he descends to a large body of water and finally discourages the last of his companions in the middle of a swamp. In terms of the action of the narrative, Wakdjunkaga is crossing or throwing himself into bodies of water, especially lakes, or standing on the edge between land and water in almost every episode. Both when he leaves his village and when he jumps off the end of the earth (Episode 3), he lands in the water. It would seem therefore that both separation from the human community and his anomalous "betwixt and between" nature are associated with water, as indeed they are if one considers both Winnebago cosmology and patterns of habitation. According to Winnebago cosmological notions (see Fig. 1), the four worlds of Earthmaker, Wakdjunkaga, Turtle, and Hare are islands. The world of Hare, Earth, is surrounded by water; the other three worlds are surrounded by sky. Sky and water (especially the latter) are conceived of as anomalous and unstable areas lying between the spiritual realm and the earthly, human realm and partaking of both. Similarly, Wakdjunkaga is both man and spirit, both trickster and culture-hero, both of this world and another, and *in toto* unstable and anomalous.

In legend, the Winnebago originated at a place called Red Banks (Green Bay, Wisconsin); and, in fact, the majority of their villages were located on the shores of lakes and rivers in Wisconsin. Given this pattern of habitation, one would in some sense have to cross bodies of water to leave and to approach human settlements, as Wakdjunkaga does. Historically, the Water Spirit clan was the most powerful of the "lower" moiety, standing in opposition to and outranked only by the Thunderbird clan. And, in myth and ritual, the most powerful spirits were the Thunderbird and the Water Spirit, the latter generally portrayed as a water monster and as a mixed deity, partly good and partly evil, and, in the older myths, identified with malevolent spirits. Most importantly, with regard to Trickster's association with water, the traditional enmity between Thunderbird and Water Spirit was associated with the theme of the human being who has been deceived. This is explicitly borne out in Episode 13 where Wakdjunkaga deceives the woman and the people of her village by impersonating the Water Spirit and in his actions as culture-hero in the final episode when he kills "all beings that were molesting people" and pushes the "roads" of the waterspirits farther into the earth, making it possible for boats to navigate the rivers.

Wakdjunkaga's first act of trickery in Episode 2 consists of trapping and killing an old buffalo. Like the majority of such acts involving animals, this exhibits cruelty and disrespect toward a totemic creature — a clan emblem and guardian spirit explicitly identified with the physical mammal. This episode is also significant in that in dressing the buffalo, Wakdjunkaga's right hand fights with and cuts up his left. This is the first indication of the physical dualism and uncertainty fundamental to trickster and clown figures and occasions the first explicit identification in the text of him as "Trickster" by birds.

In conjunction with Episode 3, this initial act of trickery illustrates the simple as opposed to the extended pattern of Lack (L) — Lack Liquidated (LL) which Dundes has pointed out as the fundamental episodic or "motifemic" structure of trickster tales. Between the situation of Lack and the liquidation thereof, there is usually an intervening paired sequence of "Deceit/Deception" followed by "Interdiction/Violation," and "Consequence/Escape Attempted."[52] Episode 2 follows the simple "L.,D.,D.,LL." pattern, whereas Episode 3 concerning the borrowing of children expresses the extended pattern culminating with Trickster's escape into the ocean. Once more he is in a situation of need and the pattern begins again. This is in fact the manner in which many of the episodes are linked together, for in the majority of his encounters with men, he violates rules or boundaries, thereby necessitating escape and forcing himself to again wander aimlessly. One should be wary in using this deprivation model, for it is trickster himself who creates situations of need—almost it would seem to incur more violations in the process of fulfilling his need. In other words, this pattern is strangely perverted in Trickster's tales. The human need to confuse categories is a curious inversion of our need to fill in what is lacking.

Episode 3 also provides the first indication of self-awareness in the statement, "Trickster got frightened," for, as Radin points out, "being frightened in Winnebago symbolism is generally indicative of an awakening consciousness and sense of reality, indeed, the beginning of a conscience."[53] This is borne out in Episode 5 when he realizes that the man pointing, whom he has been imitating, is nothing but a tree stump and acknowledges the correctness of the epithet, "Foolish One." By the end of Episode 5 (Tale 11), Wakdjunkaga is beginning to have some idea of who he is, and in the telling of Episodes 2–5, the audience has certainly learned that this Trickster is indeed a foolish one who doesn't know right from left, who knows no principles of order and control, who has no sense of direction, and who has few if any skills.

Episode 6 concerning the ducks and his anus is, in the first place, an elaborate travesty of Winnebago festal dancing and singing. Secondly, this and the following episode concerning his penis, are the beginning of Wadkjunkaga's biological education and the first instances of physical definition of character. Wakdjunkaga's misapprehension of his erect penis and blanket for the chief's banner is another piece of explicit satire, here directed at "one of the most important of the Winnebago feasts, that given by the chief of the tribe once a year, at which he raises his emblem of authority, a long feathered crook. It is his obligation at this feast to deliver long harangues admonishing his people to live up to the ideals of Winnebago society."[54] Once again Trickster's actions flaunt and call into question these ideal ceremonial behaviors. His misapprehension of his penis is followed by his correct use of it when he sends it across the river to copulate with the chief's daughter. But he still has no sense of the reality of coitus and he again violates tribal rank and mores. This furtive act of intercourse expresses, nonetheless, the need for society which is borne out in Episode 8 where he solicits the aid of women to extricate himself from a hollow tree.

The satire of tribal systems of rank and kinship and of sexual mores reaches its culmination in Episode 9 when Wakdjunkaga disguises himself as a woman, enters a village and marries the chief's son, bears three sons, has a joking relationship with "his" mother-in-law, and is finally discovered and forced to flee. The entire episode is ridiculous and Rabelaisian at base given the unsavory and inane character of Trickster's disguise and the fact that the children of a chief were of very high social position and did not marry strangers. The episode is also an explicit parody of a conventional type of folktale familiar to the Winnebago that always has an old woman living at the end of the village who assists heroes in their mission or quest and who plays a serious and crucial role in the narrative. Trickster's violations are of an even more severe nature when "her" true sexual identity is revealed in the process of joking with "her" mother-in-law, for this means that he has engaged in homosexual practices with the chief's son, that as a potential "son-in-law," he has violated the strict mother-in-law avoidance, and that he has violated prescribed joking relationships.

Following this false phase of reaggregation, Wakdjunkaga is again separated from the human community. Tired of wandering, he crosses the lake to his real wife and child, and reintegrates himself into village life (Episode 10). He stays until his child is grown and again departs — once more reversing proper behavior in that it is the boy who should start traveling. His concluding words, "I will go around the earth and visit people for I am tired of staying here. I used to wander around the world in peace. Here I am just giving myself a lot of trouble," are another explicit protest against domestication and society with all its obligations.

His first action after leaving society of eating the talking laxative bulb despite admonition to the contrary and the resultant near disaster resumes his biological education and "illustrates the consequences when one defies nature even in a minor fashion." It also illustrates the dangers of Wakdjunkaga's solipsistic course of action and the necessary interdependence of man and nature, for if the trees had not answered and guided him, Trickster would have perished in his own excrement.

Episode 12, which follows from his plunge into the water in the preceding episode, epitomizes Wakdjunkaga's propensity for confusing illusion and reality. He then uses the "real" plums to deceive the mother raccoons and enable himself to eat their children. "When he was finished, he cut off the head of one of the children, put a stick through its neck and placed it at the door as though the child were peeping out and laughing."[55] This is another bitter satire of a Winnebago war custom — one which they tended to deny and ascribe to their enemies. And, here as elsewhere in the cycle, the brunt of his trickery and much of the parody falls upon women.

In Episode 13, he again dupes a woman by impersonating first an Elk Spirit and then a Water Spirit. Trickster's actions here satirize puberty fasting and the acquisition of a guardian spirit. This is one of the most pointed satires of the entire cycle, for every Winnebago child, male and female, fasted between the ages of nine and eleven and tried to acquired a guardian spirit upon whom he could call in any critical situation throughout life. "This acquisition of a guardian and protective spirit at puberty was one of the fundamental traits of Winnebago culture as it was that of numerous other American tribes. According to Winnebago ideas, without it a man was completely unanchored and at the mercy of events, natural and societal, in their crudest and most cruel forms."[56] It is, therefore, highly significant that of all Winnebago religious beliefs and practices, the only one Trickster satirizes is the acquisition of a guardian spirit.

The central action of Episode 14, the race between Trickster and Mink to determine who will be chief and how the bear meat Wakdjunkaga has just butchered will be divided, involves a double satirizing of the Bear Clan. Not only has Wakdjunkaga duped and killed Bear, the race he runs with Mink to divide the meat and decide the chieftainship is, as Radin notes, a "parody of the myth explaining how the Thunderbird clan obtained the chieftainship of the tribe. In that myth a member of the Thunderbird clan, representing the upper phratry, races with a member of the Bear clan, representing the lower phratry, for the chieftainship."[57]

I would also venture to guess that the "reciprocal" trick played on the hawk at the beginning of this episode is similarly a parody of an origin myth. It is at least reflective of the opposition of specific political functions and of perspectives between the Thunderbird and the Hawk Clan. The Hawk or Warrior Clan (or Bad Thunders as it is sometimes called), possessed specific political functions relating to war. Moreover, in what exists of a Warrior Clan Origin Myth, we are told that when the warriors or hawks entered the lodge of the Thunderbirds at Green Bay, they began to look different and that their feathers were worn off, as indeed hawk's are when he is expelled from Wakdjunkaga's rectum.

Episode 15 concerning the diminution of Trickster's penis to normal size is but one, albeit the most important, of several "explanatory motifs" in the cycle. Such preposterous explanations of the present physical and social state of affairs on earth and among men are characteristic of trickster tales, especially those involving culture-heroes. Following this reduction to physical normalcy, Wakdjunkaga again enters a human village (Episode 16), remains there, gets married, and has a child. But when the tribe goes on their fall move, Trickster leaves for another place where he lived alone. In one of the few inconsistent and inexplicable turns of the narrative, he is here described as living apart but with his wife. Desirous of showing off the game he has obtained, he decides to return to the village. While he is well received and is portrayed as a thoroughly integrated member of society, "something of the old unregenerate self still adheres to him," for he tricks and takes revenge on both Mink and Coyote.

After staying in the village a long time and raising many children, Trickster remembers the role for which Earthmaker created him. He leaves, performs a series of beneficent acts for mankind, largely connected with waterways, and ascends to the world below Earthmaker where he is in charge. This final realization of his true identity and role is the culmination of a long and rather convoluted process of increasing self-awareness.

The sum total of these nineteen episodes of rejection, reversal, and transformation, of ahistorical, abiological, and asocial acts is a developmental process. This process of increasing biological, psychic, and social awareness to the point where he returns to society and appears as an almost thoroughly socialized individual and, further, to a realization of his role and identity as culture-hero, is similar in structure to the *Bildungsroman* or developmental novel. Dealing as it does with an individual at odds with society, the seeming antistructure of picaresque narrative implies or assumes this structure or a developmental pattern. The *Bildungsroman* persists as one of the classic patterns of narrative, especially in the tradition of the novel, because it enables the audience to experience the confrontation between the undifferentiated ego of the protagonist and various psychological, moral, and social norms of the author and his period.

The tales of the trickster reflect another process as well. As Trickster travels through the world, develops self, and creates for mankind haphazardly, by chance, by trial and error without advance planning, he reenacts the process that is central both to perception and creation, to the constant human activity of making guesses and modifying them in light of experience — the process of "schema and correction." Picaresque narrative, as exemplified here in the Winnebago cycle of Wakdjunkaga, expresses in both form and content this rhythm of schema and correction, of stasis and process, of structure and antistructure, of creation and recreation. It is indeed "an aboriginal literary masterpiece." That the trickster and the clown have become major metaphors for the artist in this century with its increasing self-consciousness of the creative process is no accident. They have been artists for a long time.

V

The question of what role or function this type of narrative plays in society remains to be answered. The various explanations proffered by many literary critics, psychologists, historians of religion, and anthropologists can be reduced at least to six basic propositions. They are all necessary, but no one of them is a sufficient and complete answer to the question of the social role of narrative in general, or of trickster tales in particular.

Those who adhere to the *first* of these propositions view narrative as entertainment pure and simple, as a "time-changer" that offers temporary respite and relaxation from the tedious business of daily life and social reality. For these critics narrative fictions are "frivolous," "unreal," "artificial," and, therefore, of little or no social importance — at least, none worth analyzing.[58]

Most religious historians, socialist literary critics, and anthropologists of the "myth as social charter" approach explain the functions of narrative as operative, iterative, and validatory or explanatory. "Operative" refers here to narratives, be they myth or legend, which tend to be repeated regularly on ritual or ceremonial occasions; "iterative" to narrative interpreted as model or charter, and "validatory or explanatory" to narratives that are etiological. This *second* type of explanation is valid and obvious when dealing with narratives that positively reflect and are consistent with laws, customs, and values of a given society, but it meets with difficulty in trying to explain negative, "antisocial" tales.

As a result, many critics come to the unsatisfactory conclusion, as did Radin in his 1926 discussion of the "Literary Aspects of Winnebago Mythology," that such myths which portray unthinkable, unmentionable conduct "signally fail, in the most fundamental principles of ethics and morals, to reflect the cultural standards." Most critics of this persuasion, however, tend to explain away, rather than explain, these antinomian tales as satire, "ritualized rebellion," "licensed aggression," etc., and shift into the *third* mode of psychological explanation in terms of projection and sublimation. Specifically, this type of interpretation is evident in Radin's characterization of the trickster tales as an "outlet for voicing protest against many, often onerous, obligations connected with Winnebago social order and with their religion and ritual," and, in Kerényi's statement that "the function of his mythology, of the tales told about him, is to add disorder to order and so make a whole, to render possible, within the fixed bounds of what is permitted, an experience of what is not permitted."[59] In short, the trickster tale becomes little more than a functional steam-valve, be it social or psychological.

A *fourth* point of view sees the function as evaluative, as contributing to a reexamination of existing conditions and possibly leading to change — as is quite likely with all social criticism and satire, whether humorous or not, if taken seriously. Any form of symbolic inversion has an implicitly radical dimension. By effecting an inversion of our assumed values, it exposes "the arbitrary quality of social rank and enables people to see that things need not always be as they are." "From the oppressor's point of view satire can always get out of hand or give people ideas, so it is better not to have it at all"[60] — as is indeed the case in modern totalitarian states.[61]

Related to this view is the *fifth* and perhaps most important type of explanation. This type, which might be termed the "reflective-creative" function, has only been seriously considered in recent years. As Victor Turner has pointed out in "Betwixt and Between," the exaggeration to the point of caricature of natural and cultural features represented in Ndembu initiation masks and costumes, with the grotesqueness and monstrosity of half-human, half-animal monsters, is a primordial mode of abstraction. The exaggerated figure becomes an object of reflection, teaching the neophytes to distinguish between the different "factors" of reality. Abstract or creative thought is provoked by what William James called the "law of dissociation" and what has more recently been termed "cognitive dissonance" — a property which the "marginal" trickster certainly manifests.

This notion is somewhat amplified in Arthur Koestler's discussion in *The Act of Creation* of the "bisociation of two matrixes" which he sees as a pattern fundamental to the act of creation, be it the creation of laughter, of a new intellectual synthesis, or of an aesthetic experience. Briefly, this

means the perception of a situation or idea in two self-consistent but mutu-
ally incompatible frames of reference—what he calls the "bisociation of
two matrices." In contrast to routine thinking, the creative act of thought is
always "double-minded, i.e., a transitory state of unstable equilibrium
where the balance of both emotion and thought is disturbed."[62] In his famous essay on laughter, Henri Bergson similarly defined a situation as creative and comic if it belongs simultaneously to two independent series of
events and is capable of being interpreted in two entirely different meanings at the same time.

Caricature, parody, and other dialogic literary forms operate similarly
by juxtaposing two or more incompatible frames of reference. By calling
attention to the artificiality of literary expression and by being itself a play
upon form, parody of other myths and serious narratives stimulates the perception of the *as if* nature of social forms and structures and the necessity,
but not the supremacy, of control. Like the joke, the picaresque narrative or
the trickster tale affords an opportunity for realizing that an accepted pattern has no necessity. Its excitement lies in the suggestion that any particular
ordering of experience may be arbitrary and subjective. It is frivolous in
that it produces no real alternative, only an exhilarated sense of freedom
from form in general, though it may well provoke thought of real alternatives and prompt action toward their realization.

The *sixth* and perhaps the last function of this sort of narrative is, as
variously expressed by comic theorists, the creation of *communitas*. As defined by Victor Turner, *communitas* is a model of "society as an unstructured or rudimentarily structured and relatively undifferentiated
comitatus, community, or even communion of equal individuals . . . [who]
confront one another integrally, and not as 'segmentalized' into statuses and
roles."[63] It is that modality of social relatedness which prevails in carnival
and the marketplace, where hierarchies are levelled, distinctions dissolved,
and roles reversed, *and* when trickster appears on the scene. Not only does
communitas "obtain symbolic expression in the attributes of liminality,
marginality, and inferiority,"[64] but also recent research has shown a high
positive correlation between creativity and fantasy *and* marginality and deviance—imagination freed from the constraints of social structural roles.

Finally, I would like to address myself to the question, "What happens
when the fool or trickster becomes central to the action" and still retains the
ability to "dissolve events" and "throw doubt on the finality of fact"—what,
in short, happens in this negative dimension of symbolic action? The first
symbolic inversion startles one into fresh views of his contemporary reality.
The second inversion leads to a rediscovery of essential truths, a transvaluation of values, and the affirmation of a primal order (e.g., Wakdjunkaga's
final severing of human ties and his return to the world of which he was
given control at the creation of the cosmos).

Trickster's connection with nothingness, with negativity, and often
with the introduction of death into the world is a threat both to reality and

to our ways of seeing it complexly. But, this relationship may also transform if not "reality," then our modes of perceiving it. Or, as Victor Turner has expressed it: "Liminality may perhaps be regarded as the Nay to all positive structural assertions, but as in some sense the source of them all, and more than that, as a realm of pure possibility whence novel configurations of ideas and relations may arise."[65] Trickster is similarly a "creative negation"[66] who introduces death and with it *all* possibilities to the world. In short, by throwing doubt on the finality of fact by holding the social world open to values which transcend it, Trickster "reveals to us our stubborn human unwillingness to be encaged forever within the boundaries of physical laws and social proprieties."[67]

Trickster's negations and his problematic relationship with reality reflect the problems of the poet or the ruler (or of any nonfool) intent upon knowing and expressing certain elusive but important qualities, upon "expressing that which cannot be thought of." It is, moreover, a given of modern linguistics and structural anthropology, not to mention logic and mathematics — a given which merits more serious discussion and examination than it has been subject to — that definition and differentiation, in short, the very essence of "structure," imply and of necessity involve negation. Things "are" by virtue of and in relation to what they "are *not*"; structure implies antistructure and cannot exist without it; the king creates and needs the fool, for one who actually reigns and holds power has little capacity for irony or self-caricature.

Trickster, "the foolish one" — the negation offering possibility — stands in immediate relation to the center in all its ambiguity. Owing to the ambiguity and autonomy of the unknown, "a point at the periphery of our awareness may begin to develop attributes of the center, at first dividing our attention, but then claiming it completely, and for a while keeping its magical character."[68] And for this we not only tolerate this "margin of mess," this "enemy of boundaries," we create and re-create him.

Notes

1. "The good life can only be lived in a society in which tidiness is preached and practised, but not too fanatically, and where efficiency is always haloed, as it were, by a tolerated margin of mess." Aldous Huxley, *Prisons: The "Carceri" Etchings by Piranesi* (London: The Trianon Press, 1949), p. 13.

2. The original version of this article was reached and written during the tenure of postdoctoral grants from the department of Anthropology, the University of Chicago and the Wenner-Gren Foundation for Anthropological Research, which are hereby gratefully acknowledged. I would also like to thank Terence Turner, Raymond Fogelson, and Paul Friedrich for innumerable suggestions and occasional library loans, and Raymond Firth and Victor Turner and the members of their seminars for invaluable comments and discussions. Finally, I am indebted to my husband, Roger D. Abrahams, for his generous assistance in the painful process of revision.

3. See Claude Lévi-Strauss, *The Raw and the Cooked* (New York: Harper and Row, 1969) and Edmund R. Leach, "Anthropological Aspects of Language: Animal Categories and

Verbal Abuse," in: *New Directions in the Study of Language*, ed. Eric H. Lenneberg (Cambridge: The M.I.T. Press, 1964).

4. See Orrin E. Klapp, "The Clever Hero," *Journal of American Folklore* 67 (1954): 21–34, and Orrin E. Klapp, *Heroes, Villains, and Fools* (Englewood Cliffs: Prentice-Hall, 1962), pp. 1–24.

5. Everett V. Stonequist, "The Marginal Man: A Study in the Subjective Aspects of Cultural Conflict" (doctoral dissertation, Department of Sociology, University of Chicago, 1930), p. 74.

6. Everett V. Stonequist, *The Marginal Man: A Study in Personality and Culture Conflict* (New York: Charles Scriber's Sons, 1937), p. xvii.

7. Stonequist, pp. 3–4.

8. Stonequist, p. xviii.

9. Turner's merging of the notion of a static, synchronic social or personality type and/or situation with a "processual or diachronic profile" is particularly important in the present context because the "trickster" may be defined as a static or synchronic type that occurs cross-culturally *and* which reoccurs in certain liminal cultural situations and historical phases, and because specific literary representations of tricksters combine both this synchronic type and situation(s) *and* a diachronic and developmental *Bildungsroman* narrative structure of events. These events (and often their humor) are specific to and determined by that culture and moment in history.

10. E.J. Hobsbawm, *Primitive Rebels: Studies in Archaic Forms of Social Movement in the 19th and 20th Centuries* (New York: Frederick Praeger, 1959), pp. 24–25.

11. For the delineation and discussion of this pattern see Hobsbawm, *Primitive Rebels*, pp.1–25. For the literary uses of social banditry see my "Liberty's a Whore: Inversions, Marginalia and Picaresque Narrative," in: *Forms of Symbolic Inversion*, ed. Barbara Babcock-Abrahams (in press).

12. Mary Douglas, *Natural Symbols: Explorations in Cosmology* (New York: Pantheon Books, 1970), p. 84.

13. Mary Douglas, *Purity and Danger: An Analysis of Concepts of Pollution and Taboo* (London: Routledge & Kegan Paul, 1966), p. 48.

14. Kai T. Erikson, *Wayward Puritans: A Study in the Sociology of Deviance* (New York: John Wiley and Sons, Inc., 1966), p. 19.

15. For more on deviance as a necessary and universal social phenomenon, see Erikson, *Wayward Puritans*.

16. Erickson, pp. 15–16.

17. William Willeford, *The Fool and His Scepter: A Study of Clowns and Jesters and Their Audience* (Evaston: Northwestern University Press, 1969), p. 101.

18. Enid Welsford, *The Fool: His Social and Literary History* (London, 1935; reprint Massachusetts, 1966), p. xii.

19. I take this term from John Velz's recent paper, "Shakespeare's Comitragedy," ms.

20. Gregory Bateson, Clifford Geertz, Edmund Leach, and Victor Turner *have* indeed addressed themselves directly to the problem of reciprocal forms and have significantly violated the avoidance taboo that most of the anthropological literature seems to obey.

21. Clifford Geertz, *Person, Time, and Conduct in Bali: An Essay in Cultural Analysis* (Cultural Report no. 14, Southeast Asia Studies, New Haven: Yale University Press, 1966), p. 65.

22. Clifford Geertz, "Deep Play: Notes on the Balinese Cockfight," *Daedalus* 15 (1972) pp. 1–38.

23. Victor W. Turner, "Myth and Symbol," in: *International Encyclopedia of the Social Sciences* (New York: Macmillan, 1968), p. 578.

24. See Monroe Edmonson, *Lore: An Introduction to the Science of Folklore* (New York: Holt, Rinehart and Winston, 1970), for a listing of representative trickster figures and their respective traditions.

25. Turner, "Myth and Symbol," p. 578.

26. See Laura Makarius, "Ritual Clowns and Symbolic Behavior," *Diogenes* no. 69 (1970): 66, for a related list of characteristics she sees as common to both clown and trickster. Cf. Turner, "Myth and Symbol," p. 578.

27. Victor W. Turner, "Betwixt and Between: The Liminal Period in *Rites de Passage*," in: *The Forest of Symbols: Aspects of Ndembu Ritual*, ed. V.W. Turner (Ithaca: Cornell University Press, 1967), p. 98.

28. Paul Radin, *The Trickster: A Study in American Indian Mythology* (New York: Philosophical Library, 1956), p. ix.

29. See Julia Kristeva, "Bakhtine, le mot, le dialogue et le roman," in: *Semeiotike: Recherches pour une sémanalyse*, ed. Julia Kristeva (Paris: Editions du Seuil, 1969), pp. 143–173 for a discussion of the term "dialogic" and of dialogical narrative.

30. Katherine Luomala, *Maui-of-a-thousand tricks: His Oceanic and European Biographers* (Bernice P. Bishop Museum Bulletin 198, 1949), p. 27.

31. Laura Makarius, "Le Mythe du 'Trickster,'" *Revue de l'Histoire des Religions* 175: 1 (1969) pp. 17–46; "Ritual Clowns and Symbolic Behavior," *Diogenes* no. 69 (1970) pp. 44–73; and "The Crime of Manabozo," *American Anthropologist* 75:3 (1973) pp. 663-675.

32. Robert H. Lowie, "The Hero-Trickster Discussion," *Journal of American Folklore* 22 (1909) p. 431.

33. Lowie, pp. 431–32.

34. Radin, *The Trickster*, p. 201.

35. Radin, pp. 168–69.

36. Makarius, "Le Mythe du 'Trickster'," p. 45.

37. Makarius, "Le Mythe," pp. 25–26, my translation.

38. Makarius, p. 41.

39. For further discussion of the trickster/culture-hero conjunction, see Norman O. Brown, *Hermes the Thief: The Evolution of a Myth* (New York: Random House, 1969), Chapter 1. Like Makarius, Brown also relates trickster and magician, viewing trickery as the manifestation of magical power (p. 11 ff.).

40. Mary Douglas, "The Social Control of Cognition: Some Factors in Joke Perception," *Man* 3:3 (1968) p. 364.

41. For a discussion of the classification problem in general, see Ruth Finnegan, *Oral Literature of Africa* (London: Oxford University Press, 1970), pp. 366ff. For a discussion of these problems in relation to Trickster tales, see Allen F. Roberts, "The Myths of Son, the Sara Trickster: Structure and Anti-Structure in the Content and Context of Prose Narratives" (M.A. thesis, Department of Anthropology, University of Chicago, 1972), Chapter 3.

42. Paul Radin, "Literary Aspects of Winnebago Mythology," *JAF* 39 (1926) pp. 18–19.

43. Radin, "Literary Aspects," pp. 19–20.

44. Finnegan, p. 360.

45. Luomala, p. 21.

46. Robert Kellogg, "Oral Literature," *New Literary History* 5: 1 (1973) 55–66.

47. Radin, *The Trickster*, p. 4.

48. See Radin, "The Social Organization of the Winnebago Indians, an Interpretation," *Anthropology Series of the Canada Geological Survey* no. 5, Museum Bulletin no. 10 (Ottawa, Canada, 1915); "The Winnebago Tribe," *Thirty-Seventh Annual Report of the United States Bureau of American Ethnology* (Washington, D.C., 1923), pp. 35–550; and *The Trickster*.

49. Radin, *The Trickster*, p. 7.

50. Radin, *The Trickster*, p. 117.

51. For a discussion of the relationship between violation of taboo, nonviolence, "ritual plunder," and clowns and tricksters, see Laura Makarius, "Ritual Clowns and Symbolic Behavior," pp. 58–60.

52. Alan Dundes, *The Morphology of North American Indian Folktales* (= FF Communications no. 195) (Helsinki, 1964), pp. 101ff.

53. Radin, *The Trickster*, p. 134.

54. Radin, *Trickster*, p. 152.

55. Radin, *Trickster*, p. 29.

56. Radin, *Trickster*, p. 115.

57. Radin, *Trickster*, pp. 58–59, n. 87.

58. For an argument *against* regarding trickster tales as simple amusement, see Barre Toelken, "The 'Pretty Language' of Yellowman: Genre, Mode and Texture in Navaho Coyote Narratives," *Genre* 2:3 (1969) p. 231.

59. Radin, *The Trickster*, pp. 152, 185.

60. Harvey Cox, *The Feast of Fools: A Theological Essay on Festivity and Fantasy* (New York: Harper and Row, 1969), p. 5.

61. In this regard, see James Peacock, "Symbolic Behavior and Social History: Transvestites and Clowns in Java," in *Forms of Symbolic Inversion*, ed. Barbara Bacock-Abrahams (in press), for a discussion of the suppression of transvestite clowns by totalitarian Indonesian regimes.

62. Arthur Koestler, *The Act of Creation* (New York: Dell Publishing Co., 1964), pp. 35–36.

63. Victor W. Turner, *The Ritual Process: Structure and Anti-Structure* (Chicago: Aldine, 1969), pp. 96, 177.

64. Turner, *The Ritual Process*, p. 130.

65. Turner, "Betwixt and Between," p. 106.

66. See Cox, *The Feast of Fools*, for a discussion of this concept in radical theology. For a discussion of Trickster as the principle of all possibilities see Barre Toelken on the Navaho Coyote trickster.

67. Cox, p. 141.

68. Willeford, *The Fool and His Scepter*, p. 132.

[Eskimo Poetry] Tom Lowenstein*

In editing the notes to the poems, my motive was partly to provide some idea of their context, but it was also to indicate the individuality of the singers. Possibly as a result of current interest in ethnic poetry, there is a tendency to think in terms of cultures, at the expense of the individual artists within them. It would be a pity if, putting down this book, the reader should only be conscious of having read some Eskimo poems and not, spe-

*Reprinted from Tom Lowenstein, ed. and trans., *Eskimo Poems from Canada and Greenland*, by Knud Rasmussen, © 1973, by permission of the Univ. of Pittsburgh Press.

cifically, the songs of Kibkarjuk, Uvavnuk, Orpingalik, Tatilgak, Netsit, etc. — all of whom seemed to have raised the language of individual expression to a pitch of remarkable intensity.

In any anthology there is a danger of reifying poets into categories, and there is a particular danger of this when it comes to the poetry of so-called primitive people. One of Rasmussen's unusual qualities as an anthropologist was his interest in people, as well as in *the* people. Since he was a Greenlander himself, his work among the Eskimos involved association and identification as well as pure research into "the other." Not only did this enable him to distinguish between individual and group characteristics, but he saw the group largely through the experience of individuals, rather than merely by means of information they provided. As a result of this, he is able to give us a picture of Eskimo song that does not just add up to a generalised aspect of a homogeneous folk-culture, where the singer subordinated his style and subject-matter to the norms of the group. The group norms were manifestly there but, rather than determining what should be sung, they provided opportunities and encouragement for individual expression.

Of course, the common environment and the available range of experience limited the variety of subjects that could be used in song: but even in the hunting songs the theme is almost always dealt with in its particulars, and in response to fresh personal experience. Moreover, the forms built into the culture which the singer could exploit were very loose. For example, the songs of derision and the two-part form the Copper Eskimos used were altogether open for the poet's inspirational handling, and in most cases the received structure gets lost in that of the singer. The struggle to create form was therefore largely the poet's own responsibility: an imperative which was keenly and often crushingly felt, as is indicated by the frequent allusions to the difficulties of composition and a fear of failure — failure to perfect the song itself, and then to perform it in the feasting-house without forgetting the words:

> It's wonderful to make up songs,
> but all too many of them fail . . .
> (Piuvkaq, *Delight in Singing*)

And in another song, which is part of a sequence not included in this volume, Piuvkaq continues:

> I recognise what I want to put into words,
> but it does not come well-arranged,
> it does not become worth listening to.
> Something that is well-arranged,
> something well worth hearing
> hastily to put *that* together
> *that* is often difficult.
> An awkward one — maybe so — I have put together.
> (*Report of the Fifth Thule Expedition*, Vol. 8, part 2)

A successful song, then, is one that is "worth listening to," so a singer's feeling about his work is often expressed as an anxiety that he will bungle the performance in the *quagsé* (the feasting-house where the songs were publicly performed), that he will forget the *words* when the moment comes to sing:

> It was always hard
> to join the happy company
> that sang in the feasting-house:
> for I could never remember
> the words of my little song
> in the drum-dance . . .
>   (Qerraq, *Song of a Diffident Man*)

> Life was wonderful
> when you danced in the feasting-house;
> but did this make me any happier?
> No, I always worried
> I'd forget my song . . .
>   (Netsit, *Dead Man's Song*)

It is significant that in the whole complex activity of performance—i.e. simultaneous singing, dancing, drumming and "conducting"—it is to the words that the anxiety, and therefore the greatest importance, is attached. There are no songs expressive of despair about the drumming or the dance, or failure to bring in the chorus properly. The words were always at the root of the anxiety. Forgetting the words, in a culture without paper, would be like losing the song. No one would be there to prompt. It would be as if the words no longer existed at all, even though, in an earlier, private stage of its evolution, the song had been painstakingly memorised. In the feasting-house performance, the word was the only one among the other cultural variables (costumes, dancing, drumming, refrains) that was not a shared and indestructible certainty. It was almost as if the words had a life of their own, the power of whose presence, or the gap left by whose absence, confirmed or threatened the very being of the singer.

This relationship between language and life itself is suggested by the Eskimo word *anerca*, with its double meaning of breath and poetry. As Orpingalik says about his death-bed song: "This is what I call my song because it is as important to me to sing it as it is to draw breath." The hard-won strength of the finished song, with its often elusive but essentially life-giving qualities, remains very much a part of the singer's private experience: it is only at that moment when the singer adds to it the drumming and the dance, and brings the as yet uninitiated chorus-audience into participation, that the compositional process blends with the general culture. The new becomes familiar—though, as a rule, the song remains the poet's property, and no one else is entitled to sing it.

It will be noticed, however, that there are no songs that concern themselves exclusively with composition. All of them weave it into their treatment of practical matters, such as hunting and survival. *Delight in Singing*, for example, proceeds from the subject of singing to that of hunting:

> It's wonderful
> to hunt reindeer,
> but all too seldom
> one succeeds,
> standing like a bright fire
> over the plain.

In *Dead Man's Song*, the first three verses of the second section are about the problems of getting enough hides for clothing and bed-wear, etc. Similarly, in *Song of a Diffident Man*, Qerraq compares his incompetence as a hunter with other men's success. And at the end of the poem he comes to the problem of remembering his song in the feasting-house. Finally, Ikinilik, an old man of the Utkuhikjalik Folk, who partly out of listlessness no longer catches all the fish he needs, concludes his song:

> For I'm just an ordinary hunter,
> who never inherited singing
> from the bird-song of the sky.

It will be noticed that ideas surrounding the process of composition coincide at some points with those about hunting: a man's survival, his self-esteem and his reputation all hang on his skill as a hunter. In the latter two cases, the same could be said of him in his singer's role. This isn't to suggest that the two activities were of equal importance: it would be impossible to measure this, and one might too easily arrive at an oversentimental or too hard-headed conclusion. But the two activities were parallel in their effect, both for what they meant to the individual and in the amount of soul and skill that went into either pursuit. To be sure, both hunting and composition were attended by a certain mystery (hunting was controlled universally by a system of taboos, and singing, an equally everyday pursuit, was also somehow charmed, as Kilimé says: "We do not know how songs arrive with our breath, in the form of words and music and not as ordinary speech . . ."), but the Eskimos could hardly have survived had they relied on their spells and not developed a hunting-technology; nor would their songs have attained such sophistication had they depended on their spirits to make them up for shamans in moments of unpredictable inspiration. Just as the physical life of the group was sustained by survival-techniques, so it was a craft and discipline in song-composition that brought the poetry into existence. A conscious application of skill was as necessary for the composition of a successful song as a knowledge of sealing techniques was to the same man in his capacity as a hunter.

Rasmussen gives us several vivid pictures of the laborious and self-conscious process that composition was. Vatic exuberance like the shaman Uvavnuk's certainly existed, and non-shamans would also burst spontaneously into song — like the Iglulik woman Takornaq, in the middle of relating her autobiography:

> At this point in Takornaq's story the meat in the pot began to boil, and she interrupted her narration to serve up a meal. Tea was made from our own supply, and the old woman was so pleased at this little trivial courtesy that she at once improvised a song, the words of which were as follows:
>
> Ajaja — aja — jaja,
> The lands around my dwelling
> Are more beautiful
> From the day
> When it is given me to see
> Faces I have never seen before.
> All is more beautiful,
> All is more beautiful,
> And life is thankfulness.
> These guests of mine
> Make my house grand,
> Ajaja — aja — jaja.

But in most cases, a quasi-Wordsworthian process took place, in which the poet retired into the solitude of nature, and struggled to fit words to the tune he had previously composed. The struggle, like that of any poet, was hopefully relieved by the kind of "spontaneous overflow of powerful feelings" that Orpingalik so beautifully defines in his statement at the beginning of this book. Through a combination of method, imagination perseverance, a confluence of inspiration and technique, the song eventually achieved the shape which made it suitable for performance.

Lastly, the internal evidence of the songs themselves very clearly demonstrates an awareness of the craftmanship that went into composition. I have drawn an analogy between hunting and composing skills. But certain recurring phrases and images suggest an even closer connection between the songs and yet another set of techniques. Jenness's comments on the incoherence of many of the songs he collected is, in a sense, quite accurate — for the European reader of his versions. But it begs the question of whether the Eskimos were aware of this, and wanted it any other way. As Heq told Rasmussen, there are some songs that "ordinary people do not have to understand. The wisdom in them is often concealed . . ." Whether the song can be reduced to a prose meaning or not, it will always have emerged from a process in which the poet is searching, above all, for structure. The phrase "putting words together" that so frequently recurs, not only implies structure in itself, but it suggests that the manipulation of words is strongly associated with the exercise of power over concrete objects: objects and materials which are very often associated with the crafts:

I, aya, am arranging
I am trying to put together song this one,
taking it apart, I aya
why I wonder is it always on the tip of my tongue!
(Nakasuk, *Report of the Fifth Thule Expedition*,
                    Vol. 7. Not included in this book)

never heaping evil words
on men . . .

                        (Umanatsiaq, *World*)

My tongue can only put together words
to make a little song.
A mouth, a little mouth,
can that be dangerous?

                    (Netsit, *Men's Impotence*)

A bit of song comes back.
I draw it to me like a friend.
                    (Uvlunuaq, *Song of a Mother*)

I put some words together,
I made a little song,
I took it home one evening,
mysteriously wrapped, disguised . . .
                    (Angmagssalik, *Song to a Miser*)

I weave together
bits of song to answer you . . .
                    (Pivukaq, *The Wide Road of Song*)

Let me cleave words,
sharp little words.
like the fire-wood
that I split with my axe.

                    (Kilimé, *The Abduction*)

The analogy with the crafts is implicit in the language. Words (like snow, or bones, or reindeer skin) are part of the material environment, and they have the sort of concrete property which can be woven, wrapped up, carved and put together, for either functional or aesthetic purposes. The Eskimos' perception of the power and malleability of words would seem to provide something of a clue as to how they raised their poetry to a level beyond that of local interest. The interaction between the singer, the experience and the language is externalised and made real in the activity of composition; the words are carved at a distance from the self, thus preserving what the self would otherwise lose. That the Eskimo poet knew he was doing this was a condition of his doing it well. I hope that the translations in this collection will do justice to my belief that this is so.

On Literature in English

American Indian Authors, 1774–1899

A. LaVonne Brown Ruoff*

The history of literature written in English by American Indians, which begins prior to the Revolutionary War, parallels the history of white migration across the continent. White exploration and settlement were followed inevitably by the arrival of missionaries who converted Indians to Christianity and educated them in religious schools. Consequently the early history of American Indian literature in English reflects the religious education received by Indian authors.

The first American Indian writer to publish in English was Samson Occom (Mohegan; 1723–92). The son of Joshua Tomocham and Sarah, who was reputed to descend from the famous Mohegan chief Uncas, Occom led the life of a typical Mohegan boy. Inspired by missionaries, sixteen-year-old Samson began to study English in order to read the scriptures and was converted a year later. In 1742, at the age of twenty, he enrolled at the Reverend Eleazar Wheelock's Indian Charity School at Lebanon, Connecticut, where he remained for four years. When Occom was forced by ill health and eye strain to leave school, he became a schoolmaster to Indians. In 1751 he married Mary Fowler, a Montauk, who subsequently bore him ten children. During the next few years, Occom served as a missionary among New England Indians. He was so successful as a preacher and fund raiser that he was selected to journey to Great Britain to raise money for Wheelock's school. During his last two years in Great Britain, Occom preached over three hundred sermons and raised over £12,000. He returned home in 1768.

In September 1771 Occom entered the limelight again when he preached a sermon at the execution of a fellow Mohegan, Moses Paul. While drunk, Paul, a Christian Indian, had killed prominent citizen Moses Cook. Occom's fire-and-brimstone sermon so thrilled his audience that he was urged to publish it immediately. His *A Sermon Preached at the Execution of Moses Paul, an Indian* went through nineteen editions, including a translation into Welsh. One of the few temperance sermons published during that period, it was especially timely because of its application to Indi-

*This essay was written specifically for this volume and appears here by permission of the author. © A. LaVonne Brown Ruoff, 1984.

ans, whose drunkenness whites feared. Occom first contrasts the dangers of sin with the joys of eternal life achieved through accepting Christ and then directs his remarks to his "poor kindred, describing the miseries they bring on themselves through alcoholism: "Alas, alas! What will become of all such drunkards? Without doubt they must go to hell, except they truly repent and turn to God. Drunkenness is so common among us, that even our young men and (what is still more shocking) young women are not shamed to get drunk."[1]

The only other book Occom published was *Collections of Hymns and Spiritual Songs* (New London, Conn.: Green, 1774), prepared for use by Christian Indians. Occom devoted the remainder of his life to assisting the Mohegans and other New England tribes with land-claim settlements and to raising funds to support the resettlement of Christian Indians from New England to Oneida lands in New York. He also served informally as minister to the New England and the Stockbridge Indians.

The genre in which most Indian authors of the nineteenth and twentieth centuries have written is autobiography. This choice represents a break with oral tradition because the personal narrative is not part of American Indian oral literatures. Many tribes consider talking about oneself inappropriate. As Christian converts, American Indian authors of the first half of the nineteenth century consciously modeled their personal narratives on the spiritual confessions and missionary reminiscences popular then. They also used some of the themes and devices of the slave narratives, whose popularity coincided with the publication of Indian autobiographies. Because both exslave and Indian authors felt Christianity represented the opportunity for nonwhites to achieve equality in God's love, they graphically portrayed the injustices inflicted upon their peoples by Christian whites. Both ex-slave and Indian authors frequently authenticated their narratives by tracing their family histories and including, either in the narrative or in the appendices, letters from prominent whites attesting to the authors veracity and achievements.[2]

The Indian was a popular subject in the 1820s and 1830s because of both the continued popularity of captivity narratives, which depicted the Indian as a "red devil," and Cooper's Leatherstocking Tales (1823–41), which depicted him as a "noble-but-doomed" red man. Interest in Indians increased during the debate over the 1830 Indian Removal Bill, designed to move Indians from the Southeast and Midwest to Indian Territory (now Oklahoma) and other locations. In the midst of the Removal debate, William Apes (Pequot, b. 1797) published the first autobiography written by an Indian, *A Son of the Forest. The Experience of William Apes, A Native of the Forest. Written by Himself* (New York: Author, 1829), which appeared in an expanded and revised edition in 1831.[3] In his narrative, Apes traces both the growth of his religious beliefs and his sense of Indian identity. Apes's autobiography is especially interesting because he was only raised among Indians until he was four years old. When he was around three, Apes and his siblings were left in the care of his alcoholic maternal grandparents. A year later, his intoxicated grandmother viciously beat young Apes, breaking his arm. Apes uses the incident to demonstrate how whites destroyed Indians by introducing them to alcohol — a dominant theme in nineteenth-century Indian autobiographies. Taken from his Pequot grandparents, Apes was bound out at age five as a servant to white families. The six years of schooling received during his stay with his first master was all the education he ever had. At fifteen, he converted to Christianity and became a Methodist. After a series of conflicts with his third white master, Apes ran away and enlisted in the American army during the War of 1812. His experiences as a bound servant sold at the whim of his masters and as a victim of racial prejudice aroused him to denounce the injustice to which white Christians subjected Indians.

Apes's narrative follows the structure of the spiritual confessions of the period: growing awareness of God's power, conversion, questioning of faith, fall from grace, and recovery. Like most writers of these narratives, he focuses on his religious development and gives little information about his personal life. Regarding his marriage, he indicates only that his wife was a pious woman "nearly the same colour as myself" (p. 98) but does not give her name. Apes's fall from grace occurred shortly after he ran away and met white soldiers, who introduced him to liquor. When the war ended, he struggled to regain his faith and to fight off alcoholism. Baptized in 1819, he became a lay Methodist preacher and was ordained by the Methodist Society in 1829. In his autobiography, Apes's writing style ranges from straightforward narrative to rhapsodic description of conversion to powerful rhetoric in his commentaries on the importance of living a religious life and his attacks on white injustice to Indians.

Apes published a shorter autobiography in *Experience of Five Christian Indians of the Pequot Tribe*.[4] Here Apes is far more critical of whites than he was in *A Son of the Forest* — a pattern repeated by other Indian authors who published more than one autobiography. Apes's last two books focus on Indian-white relations. His struggle from 1833–35 on behalf of the Mashpee (or Marshpee), a mixed-blood group of Wampanoags, is chronicled in *Indian Nullification of the Unconstitutional Laws of Massachusetts Relative to the Marshpee Tribe* (Boston: Howe, 1835), a powerful work of protest literature. His final work was the eloquent *Eulogy on King Philip*.[5] Originally delivered as a series of lectures in Boston, this book traces white abuse of New England Indians in the seventeenth and eighteenth centuries. After the publication of this book, Apes disappeared from public view, leaving no record of his later life and death.

Not until 1847 was another full autobiography written and published by an Indian author. Caught in the struggles to retain tribal lands, to obtain just compensation for land cessions, or to gain civil rights, educated Indians had little leisure to write personal narratives. Interest in the "noble-but-doomed" Indian continued through the 1850s, strengthened by scientific books published during this period, such as Thomas Rowe Schoolcraft's *Algic Researches* (1839) on the Ojibwe.[6] Schoolcraft's studies of that tribe particularly created a literary climate favorable to the appearance of the writer George Copway (Ojibwe; 1818–69). The public eagerly embraced Copway, who cast himself in the role of the "noble red man" possessing both the virtues of his savage past and the religion and education of his civilized present. Copway's *Life, History and Travels of Kah-ge-ga-gah-bowh* (George Copway)[7] was so popular, it went through six editions in one year.

Descended from Mississauga chiefs, Copway was born near the mouth of the Trent River in Upper Canada and raised as a traditional Ojibwe until 1827, when his parents converted to Christianity. In 1830 Copway became a Christian and later occasionally attended the Methodist Mission School at Rice Lake. During 1834–36 he helped Methodist missionaries spread the gospel among the Lake Superior Ojibwe. In 1838 he was sent to Ebenezer School in Jacksonville, Illinois, where for the next nineteen months he received his only formal education. After leaving school, Copway travelled in the East before returning to Rice Lake, where he met and married Elizabeth Howell, a white woman. Copway subsequently served as a missionary to the tribes of Wisconsin and Minnesota and in Upper Canada. In 1845, he was elected vice president of the Ojibwe General Council, but was accused of embezzlement and imprisoned briefly in the summer of 1846. Expelled from the Canadian Conference of the Wesleyan Methodist Church, Copway left Canada for the United States, where he was befriended by American Methodists, who launched him on a career as a lecturer and writer.

Copway established a pattern in his autobiography followed by other Indian authors: blending mystic, historic, and recent past and combining tribal ethnohistory and personal experience. He uses episodes from his own life to teach his audience about his tribe, culture, and Indian-white relations. However, like Apes, he gives little information about his personal life.

In his discussion of Ojibwe life, Copway adopts a highly romantic and nostalgic tone, appealing to his reader's affection for the stereotype of the Indian as a child of nature: "I would much more glory in this birth-place, with the broad canopy of heaven above me, and the giant arms of the forest trees for my shelter, than to be born in palaces of marble studded with pillars of gold! Nature will be nature still while palaces shall decay and fall in ruins" (p. 18). The ethnographic sections are designed to persuade his audience of the value of tribal culture and the essential humanity of Indian people, goals of later Indian autobiographers as well. Quoting Ojibwe maxims that emphasize kindness, generosity, and respect, Copway stresses that such precepts brought Indians peace and happiness before they were seduced by the white man's whiskey.

Copway's sketches of his life with his parents are particularly effective. His characterizations of them as loving, patient, and self sacrificing counter the stereotypical bloodthirsty Indian of the captivity narratives. His descriptions of his own and his family's conversions exemplify Christianity's power to uplift all Indians from what Copway considers is the darkness of tribal religion and from the degradation of white-induced alcoholism. The climax of his narrative is his conversion, which provides a transition from his life as a traditional Ojibwe to that as an emissary between the red and white worlds. His chronicle of his missionary experiences replace the fall from grace and rediscovery of faith in conventional spiritual narratives. Like Apes, he uses a variety of styles; journalistic in the narrative, rhapsodic in the religious and philosophical sections, and rhetorical in the race relations sections.

Copway's second book was *Traditional History and Characteristic Sketches of the Ojibway Nation*.[8] In this book, he clearly sees himself as a transmitter of Ojibwe oral history and tradition, which he enlivens with personal anecdotes. However, he is far more critical of whites here than in his autobiography. In 1850, Copway wrote a pamphlet entitled *Organization of a New Indian Territory, East of the Missouri River*. . . . (New York: Benedict), a plan to establish a separate Indian state. After representing Christian American Indians at the Third General Peace Congress held in August 1850 in Frankfort, Germany, Copway lectured and travelled widely throughout Europe. He recounted his experiences in *Running Sketches of Men and Places, in England, France, Germany, Belgium, and Scotland* (New York: Riker, 1851). One of the first travel books written by an Indian, it is primarily interesting for the novelty of an Indian's commenting on European people and places. Between July and fall 1851 Copway established the short-lived journal Copway's *American Indian*. This year marked the end of his successful career as a writer and of his relations with such eastern intellectuals as Cooper, Irving, Longfellow, Morgan, Parkman, and Schoolcraft, who had supported his various endeavors. Copway disappeared until 1867, when he advertised himself as a healer in the Detroit Free Press. In 1869, he converted to Catholicism and was baptized at Lac-des-deux Montagnes, an Algonquin-Iroquois mission northwest of Montreal. He died shortly after his baptism.

The few Indians who published autobiographies in the next three decades were primarily from the East and Midwest. Not until the 1880s and 1890s did Indian authors from the Plains and Far West begin to publish. After the end of the Civil War, the government turned to the final pacification of the western tribes. By the end of the 1870s, almost all the Plains and western tribes had been forced onto reservations and concerted efforts were made to send their children to white-run schools. As they mastered English, Indians from these areas began to write autobiographies. However, there was far less interest in Indians as subjects of serious literature than there had been earlier in the century. White audiences were more interested in reading about the Civil War or about the conquest of the West by whites than about the impact of this conquest on Indians.

One of the earliest and most colorful personal and tribal histories by an Indian from the Far West was Sarah Winnemucca Hopkins's *Life Among the Piutes*, edited by Mrs. Horace [Mary] Mann (1885; rpt. Bishop, Calif.: Chalfant, 1969). Born near the sink of the Humboldt River in Nevada, Winnemucca (Paiute; c. 1844–91) was the granddaughter of Truckee, whom she claimed was chief of all the Paiutes, and the daughter of Old Winnemucca, who succeeded his father as chief. Because she and her family followed Truckee's policy of peaceful coexistence with whites, Winnemucca spent much of her life as a liaison between Paiutes and whites, both in her people's native Nevada and in Oregon, where they moved to escape white encroachment on their Pyramid Lake Reservation. When the 1878 Bannock Indian War ended, in which many Paiutes participated after leaving the Malheur Reservation in Oregon, Winnemucca accompanied her father and brother Naches to Washington, D.C., to obtain from Secretary of the Interior Carl Schurz permission for the Paiutes to return to the Oregon reservation. Unfortunately, the government provided neither supplies nor transportation for the tribe's return.

Winnemucca's disillusionment with federal Indian policy and with its agents aroused her to take the Paiute case to the public. Encouraged by the success of her first lecture in San Francisco in 1879, she toured the East delivering more than three hundred lectures. Both in these and in her book *Life Among the Piutes*, Winnemucca strongly supported the General Allotment Act,[9] then before Congress. By the time the act was passed in 1887, much of the land on the Malheur Reservation to be allotted to the Paiutes had already been seized by whites. Winnemucca, who had earlier witnessed white seizure of lands at the Pyramid Lake Reservation, lost faith in the power and desire of the government to protect Indian land. Consequently, in 1884, she returned to Nevada to found a school for Paiute children that was located on her brother's farm near Lovelock. Forced by ill health and lack of funds to abandon the school in 1887, she died four years later.[10]

In *Life Among the Piutes*, Winnemucca uses the narrative technique of mixing personal experience and tribal ethnology and the authenticating device of including letters from well-known whites to document her moral character and her achievements, both methods used by earlier Indian autobiographers. Whereas these writers made conversion to Christianity and the spiritual journey central to their narratives, Winnemucca never alludes to these. When she wrote her narrative, the spiritual confession and missionary reminiscence were no longer popular. Instead, Winnemucca makes Indian-white relations her central themes. The impact of white contact on Paiute life is depicted through Winnemucca's descriptions of her experiences as a child and adult. Especially moving is her description of her terror when as a small child, she was buried alive temporarily by parents to hide her from whites, reputed to be cannibals. Winnemucca reveals more of her childhood and of her adult personality than do earlier Indian autobiographers. Both in her valuable Paiute ethnography and in her exciting accounts of her service as a liaison between Paiutes and whites, Winnemucca empha-

sizes the roles played by women in traditional Paiute culture and by Winnemucca herself in achieving peace for her people. Her own role was unusual
for any woman of her day. Her daring exploits as she raced back and forth
between enemy lines, risking rape by white males or murder by hostile
whites and Indians, rival those of the heroines of the dime westerns of the
period.

Winnemucca's style is particularly effective because she dramatizes
important episodes. Margot Liberty suggests that Winnemucca's recreation
of dialogue derives from the quotative style of the Northern Paiute narratives (p. 40–41). The technique enables Winnemucca to dramatize scenes in
which she successfully confronts government officials about their unjust
treatment of her people. She displays considerable narrative skill in her
dramatization of her grandfather Truckee's death in 1859, in which she
weaves together the threads of autobiography, ethnography, and Indian-
white relations that dominate the book. Winnemucca also uses her oratorical power to arouse the sympathy of her audience, exemplified in her final
exhortation for justice for Indian people: "For shame! for shame! You dare
to cry out Liberty, when you hold us in places against our will, driving us
from place to place as if we were beasts. . . . Oh, my dear readers, talk for
us, and if the white people will treat us like human beings, we will behave
like a people but if we are treated by white savages as if we are savages, we
are relentless and desperate; yet no more so than any other badly treated
people. Oh, dear friends, I am pleading for God for humanity" (pp.
243–44). Winnemucca's *Life Among the Piutes* was the only book she ever
published. However, in 1882, the year before this volume appeared, she
published an article on Paiute ethnography entitled "The Pah-Utes," which
appeared in the *Californian* (6:252–55).

Not until the early twentieth century did Indian authors from the
Plains begin publishing autobiographies. Although Indian authors primarily wrote autobiographies in the nineteenth century, they also wrote fiction
and poetry as well. Among the most prolific Indian writers of that century
was John Rollin Ridge (Cherokee; 1827–67), who was a journalist, novelist,
and poet. The grandson of the highly respected Cherokee leader Major
Ridge and the son of John and his white wife Sara Northrup, John Rollin
accompanied his family on the Cherokee Removal from their native Geor-
gia to Indian Territory in 1837. Two years later, both Major and John Ridge
were assassinated for their roles in selling tribal lands. Twelve-year-old
Ridge and his family witnessed his father's murder. Shortly thereafter, the
family moved from Indian Territory to Arkansas. Late in his teens, Ridge
shot a man, presumably in self defense, and fled in 1850 from Arkansas to
the California gold fields. There he began to contribute regularly to such
San Francisco periodicals and journals as *Golden Era, Hesperian*, and *Pioneer*, writing under the name of "Yellow Bird," the translation of his Cherokee name Cheesquatalawny.

Ridge's most famous work is *The Life and Adventures of Joaquín Mu-*

rieta (1854),[11] the first novel published by an American Indian. This fictionalized biography established Murieta's image as a folk hero, precipitating the stories, dramas, and films that have kept him such a popular figure in the folklore of California and Mexico. Ridge's portrayal of Murieta as a social outcast hero who defeats his enemies by using both his keen mind and blazing pistols links the book both to the Gothic romances and to Byron's narrative poems in English literature and to the frontier romances and dime-novel westerns of American literature. Murieta is characterized as a handsome gallant who only became an outlaw to revenge himself against the Anglos who beat him, raped his mistress before his eyes, hanged his brother, and stole his land. Though fearless in battling his enemies, Murieta is gentle with fair maidens in distress.

The novel vividly portrays the anti-Mexican prejudices of gold-hungry Anglos eager to dispossess Mexicans of their land — a situation all too familiar to Ridge, whose Cherokee people were similarly dispossessed. His half-Indian hero achieved the revenge for the outrages against his family and people that Ridge often plotted but never executed. At the end of the novel, Ridge underlines the lesson of Murieta's life and death as an outlaw: "He also leaves behind the important lesson that there is nothing so dangerous in its consequences as injustice to individuals — whether it arise from prejudice of color or from any other source; that a wrong done to one man is a wrong to society and to the world" (p. 158). Clearly Ridge chose to deal indirectly with the injustices suffered by Indians. The decreased interest of the public in the Indian as a subject for serious literature undoubtedly dictated this choice as did their increased interest in stories about the gold fields of California. This shift in popular taste undoubtedly explains the lack of emphasis on Indian subjects in Ridge's works because his letters reveal his commitment to the cause of the Cherokee people. The novel is a forerunner of the western local color movement, which in the coming decades brought acclaim to such writers as Bret Harte, Joaquín Miller, Ambrose Bierce, and Samuel Clemens. In addition to basing his plot on the recent California manhunts for bandits known only as "Joaquín," Ridge also filled his novel with descriptions of local places and landscapes, such as those portrayed in his Shelleyan poem "Mount Shasta." Ridge's *Collected Poems* (San Francisco: Payot, 1868), published posthumously, reveal his interest in the local color movement. "Rainy Season in California," strongly influenced by James Thomson's *Seasons*, colorfully describes the impact of a rainstorm on the hills and valleys. His "Humboldt River" is a powerful description of this Nevada river, whose banks are strewn with the bones of dead pioneers. One of his best poems is the "Arkansas Root Doctor," a character sketch enlivened by dialect. The only poems in this collection that reflect his Indian background are the sentimental "Cherokee Love Song" and "Stolen White Girl." Included in the *Poems* is Ridge's autobiography of his life to age twenty three.

The first American Indian novel devoted to the subject of Indian life is

Simon Pokagon's *O-gi-maw-kwe Mit-i-gwa-ki (Queen of the Woods). Also a Brief Sketch of the Algaic Language by Chief Pokagon* (1899; rpt. Berrien Springs, Mich.: Hardscrabble, 1972). Pokagon (1830–99) was the son of the Potawatomi chief Leopold, whose territory near South Bend, Indiana, once included Chicago. Pokagon attended preparatory programs at Notre Dame, Oberlin, and Twinsburg Institute (near Cleveland, Ohio). Though praised for his knowledge of Greek and Latin and known as the "Longfellow" of his race, Pokagon did not attend college. He married Lonidaw Sinagaw, who bore him four children before dying at the age of 35 in 1871. Pokagon reared his children alone but remarried when they left home to attend school.

White treatment of Indians in the 1890s undoubtedly stimulated Pokagon to write *Queen of the Woods.* Hysteria over the possibility of renewed Plains Indian uprisings during the Ghost Dance Movement culminated in 1890, when soldiers massacred Big Foot's Sioux band at Wounded Knee. White fears of hostile Indians were replaced by indifference both to the Indians' problems and to their contributions to American culture. This indifference was vividly demonstrated at the World Columbian Exposition held in Chicago in 1893, when Indians were not given equal prominence with other American ethnic groups. Pokagon was deeply offended that this fair, held on land his band had ceded sixty years earlier (for which they had not yet been paid) offered educated Indians no opportunity to demonstrate their achievements. He expressed his anger in a pamphlet printed on birch bark and sold at the fair. Originally titled *The Red Man's Rebuke*, it was published as *The Red Man's Greeting* (Hartford, Mich.: Engle, 1893). In response to Pokagon's protest, Mayor Carter Harrison invited Pokagon to attend the fair as the guest of the city of Chicago and to participate in the ceremonies, an invitation Pokagon accepted.[12]

Queen of the Woods, published a few months after Pokagon's death, contains many autobiographical elements. Pokagon uses himself as the narrator and gives his wife's name to the heroine. His description of the separation of Lonidaw's parents during the 1838 round-up of the Potawatomis for removal, of her mother's escape with her young daughter into the swamp, and of the childhood friendship of Pokagon's and Lonidaw's mothers is factual. However, the dramatic deaths suffered by the character Lonidaw and her daughter are fictional.

The novel reflects Pokagon's dedication to educating his audience about traditional Potawatomi life before the coming of whites and about the tragic changes in this life suffered by his people after whites dispossessed them and debauched them with alcohol. As the hero of the romance, Pokagon represents the plight of an Indian torn between desire for the idyllic Potawatomi forest life and his recognition that he must become educated in order to cope with the dominant white culture. In the novel, Pokagon returns to the Potawatomi woodlands after several years in white schools. On a trip deep into the forest, he meets Lonidaw, who is so beautiful and so in harmony with nature that she seems to be a woodland goddess. Able to communicate with all the creatures of nature, Lonidaw is constantly followed by a jealous snow-white deer (sacred in Potawatomi mythology). Although Pokagon returns to school, he is drawn back home by his love for Lonidaw and for traditional Potawatomi life in the forest. Pokagon's romanticization of Lonidaw as a symbol of the Indian's harmony with nature is exemplified in the scene in which she decorates Pokagon's hair with evergreens and calls to wild pigeons with "musical chattering" (p. 127). When Lonidaw and Pokagon marry, the white deer abandons them. Secluding themselves in the forest, Pokagon and Lonidaw rear two children. Renewed contact with the white world destroys this idyllic life. Pokagon sends their twelve-year-old son to school despite his wife's objections. The child returns three years later as an alcoholic, an episode that introduces the anti-liquor theme that dominates the last part of the novel. Shortly after the boy returns, Pokagon's daughter is drowned when her canoe is rammed by a boat operated by two drunken whites. Lonidaw herself almost drowns when she vainly tries to save her daughter. Weeks later, dying of a broken heart, Lonidaw urges her husband to dedicate his life to fighting alcohol abuse, which destroyed first her father and then her children. The novel ends with a strong attack on liquor and a horrifying description of delirium tremens. The dominance of this theme reflects not only Pokagon's knowledge of what liquor had done to his people but also the popularity of temperance literature during this period.

In his idealization of love in nature, Pokagon follows the tradition of Longfellow's *The Song of Hiawatha* (1855), Byron's Haidee episode in *Don Juan* (1818–23), and Chateaubriand's *Atala* (1801). Pokagon's rhapsodic style in describing the beauties of nature is exemplified by the following passage: "Slowly, but surely, the curtain of night was lifted from the stage of the woodland theater: above me, one by one the stars hid themselves, the moon grew pale; while all the warblers of the woods opened their matinee, free to all, chanting from unnumbered throats, 'Rejoice and praise Him! Rejoice and be glad! Rejoice! Rejoice!' " (p. 58). As David H. Dickason has noted, Pokagon begins his novel in ordinary prose but shifts to comparatively regular iambics. Much of the novel could have been printed as blank verse (p. 131).

Although Pokagon did not publish another novel, he did publish several essays on Potawami subjects during the 1890s: "The Future of the Red Man," *Forum*, 23 (Aug. 1897), 698–708; "Indian Superstitions and Legends," *Forum*, 25 (July 1898), 618–29; "Massacre at Fort Dearborn at Chicago," *Harper's*, 98 (Mar. 1899), 649–56; and "The Pottawatomies in the War of 1812," *Arena*, 26 (July 1901; posthumous), 48–55. Two posthumous pamphlets were printed on birchbark: "*Algonquin Legends of South Haven* (Hartford, Mich.: Engle, 1900) and *Pottawatomie Book of Genesis* . . . (Hartford, Mich.: Engle, 1909).

After the turn of the century, American Indian authors published in ever increasing numbers. Although autobiography remained the genre in which they wrote most frequently, they also became highly sophisticated writers of fiction and poetry. The Indian authors of the 1930s and of the late 1960s and 1970s have demonstrated a sophistication that marks them as some of the best writers of these periods. As Indians became authors, they increased the power of the word always present in oral tradition by adding to it the force of the written word.

Notes

1. 1772; rpt. with intro. by A. LaVonne Brown Ruoff (New York: Assn. for Study of American Indian Literatures, 1983), p. i–iv. Biographical information taken from Harold Blodgett, *Samson Occom*, Dartmouth College Manuscript Series, III (Hanover, N.H.: Dartmouth College Press, 1935).

Research for this article was completed under a grant from the National Endowment for the Humanities.

2. See Ruoff, "Nineteenth-Century American Indian Autobiographers: William Apes, George Copway, and Sarah Winnemucca," *New American Literary History*, ed. Jerry W. Ward, Jr. (New York: MLA, forthcoming).

3. Republished as *A Son of the Forest. The Experience of William Apes, a Native of the Forest. Written by Himself* (New York: Author, 1831). Additional biographical information taken from Kim McQuaid, "William Apes, Pequot: An Indian Reformer in the Jackson Era," *New England Quarterly*, 50 (1977), 605–25.

4. Subtitle: *Or, The Indian's Looking-Glass for the White Man* (Boston: Dow, 1833). Republished as *The Experience of Five Christian Indians of the Pequod Tribe* (Boston: Printed for the Publisher, 1837).

5. Although Joseph Sabin suggests that William J. Snelling was the actual author, I find no evidence either to substantiate or refute this. See *A Dictionary of Books Relating to America, from its Discovery to the Present Time* (New York: Savin, 1868), 1:229.

6. Spellings of tribal names are those in current use rather than those used by the authors: *Ojibwe* rather than *Ojibway* or *Ojibwa*; *Paiute* rather than *Piute*.

7. Subtitle: *A Young Indian Chief of the Ojebwa Nation, With a Sketch of the Present State of the Ojibwa Nation, in Regard to Christianity and Their Future Prospects . . .* (Albany, N.Y.: Weed and Parsons, 1847; Philadelphia: Harmstead, 1847). Republished as *The Life, Letters and Speeches of Kah-ge-ga-gah-bowh or G. Copway . . .* (New York: Benedict, 1850), and as *Recollections of a Forest LIfe; or, The Life and Travels of Kah-ge-ga-gah-bowh, or George Copway* (London: Gilpin, 1851). Additional biographical information taken from Donald B. Smith, "Kahgegagahbowh," in *Canadian Dictionary of Biography*, 9 (1861–70), 419–21.

8. Republished as *Indian Life and Indian History, by an Indian Author, Embracing the Traditions of the North American Indians Regarding Themselves, Particularly of that Most Important of All the Tribes, the Ojibways* (1858; rpt. New York: AMS, 1977).

9. The General Allotment Act of 1887 was designed to end the reservation system by alloting Indian land in severalty.

10. See Gae Whitney Canfield, *Sarah Winnemucca of the Northern Paiutes* (Norman: Univ. of Oklahoma Press, 1983), and Margot Liberty, "Sarah Winnemucca, Northern Paiute, 1844–1891," in *American Indian Intellectuals* ed. Margot Liberty, 1976 Proceedings of the American Ethnological Society, ed. Robert F. Spencer (St. Paul: West, 1978), 33–42.

11. Rpt. with intro. by Joseph Henry Jackson (Norman: Univ. of Oklahoma Press, 1977). Additional biographical information taken from Angie Debo, "John Rollin Ridge," *Southwest Review*, 17 (1932), 57–65, and Carolyn Thomas Foreman, "Edward W. Bushyhead

and John Rollin Ridge, Cherokee Editors in California," *Chronicles of Oklahoma*, 14 (1936), 295–311.

12. Biographical information taken from David H. Dickason, "Chief Simon Pokagon: The Indian Longfellow," *Indiana Magazine of History*, 52 (1961), 127–40, and Cecilia Bain Beuchner, *The Pokagons* (1933; rpt. Berrien Springs, Mich.: Hardscrabble, 1976).

The Transformation of Tradition: A Study of Zitkala Sa and Mourning Dove, Two Transitional American Indian Writers

Dexter Fisher*

The nineteenth century marked a period of dramatic upheaval for many American Indian tribes, who, within a brief span, suddenly found themselves dispossessed of their ancestral lands, depleted in numbers, and confined to reservations in the wake of America's great expansion westward. Fearful that their oral traditions would disappear forever as the tribal community became more and more fragmented under the demoralizing conditions of reservation life, some American Indians began to write down the legends and folktales of their tribes, as well as their own personal narratives, in an effort to preserve their history and culture for posterity. Writing became a means to perpetuate tradition in the face of cultural disintegration.

For those early Indian writers, the movement from an oral mode of cultural expression to a written form was difficult and challenging. Not only did authors have to choose which traditions should be written down and then struggle with the problem of how the act of writing might transform those traditions, but they also had to translate their stories into English because, with few exceptions, English was the language of literacy for Indians. Zitkala Sa, a Dakota Sioux of the Yankton band, and Mourning Dove, an Okanogan, are two of the early Indian writers who attempted to make the transition from oral to written form and to bridge the gap between tradition and assimilation.

Zitkala Sa (1876–1938) published most of her work at the turn of the century. Her collection of traditional Sioux tales, *Old Indian Legends*, appeared in 1901, and the autobiographical essays that were collected later in *American Indian Stories* (1921) were initially published in *Harpers* and the

*Parts of this essay appear in "Zitkala Sa: The Evolution of a Writer," *American Indian Quarterly*, 5 (1979), 229–38; "Introduction" to *Cogewea, The Half-Blood*, by Mourning Dove (Lincoln: Univ. of Nebraska Press, 1981); and "The Transformation of Tradition: A Study of Zitkala Sa and Mourning Dove, Two Transitional American Indian Writers" (Dexter Fisher, Ph.D. Diss.). This essay was written for this volume, including parts of the author's previous work; all appear here by permission of the author. © Dexter Fisher, 1984.

Atlantic Monthly in 1900 and 1901. Mourning Dove (1888–1936) published *Co-ge-wea; the Half Blood*, perhaps the first novel by an American Indian woman, in 1927, and *Coyote Stories*, a collection of traditional Okanogan tales, in 1933.

Both women were born and reared during their childhood years in traditional ways on or near reservations, and though they received their education in English primarily at off-reservation schools, both had a first-hand knowledge of the language, stories, and traditions of their respective tribes. Each published a collection of legends written for a children's audience that they gathered from the tribal storytellers. Both *Old Indian Legends* and *Coyote Stories* offer an opportunity for examining the transformation of traditional oral tales into written form.

Conscious of their role in preserving their culture, yet searching for their own individual voices, Zitkala Sa and Mourning Dove anticipate the liminal position of the Indian that will later be reflected in the theme of alienation in contemporary Indian literature. Moving between the remembered past and the alien present, the Indian and white worlds, tradition and change — Zitkala Sa and Mourning Dove attempt to record their experiences and cultural traditions and in doing so become early pioneers of an emerging American Indian literary tradition.

Zitkala Sa

In a letter to Carlos Montezuma dated 20 February 1901, Zitkala Sa writes:

> As for my plans, — I do not mean to give up my literary work — but while the old people last I want to get from them their treasured ideas of life.[1]

Later on that spring, she writes again to Montezuma from the Yankton Agency, saying,

> This place is full of material for stories but I am so uncertain . . . I am quite well and hope I may soon find a good writing mood — to do justice to the abandoned material around me. (June 1901)

Zitkala Sa had every right to feel nervous about her mission to become the literary counterpart of the oral storytellers of her tribe because she felt compelled to live up to the critical expectations of her white audience. She had already become the darling of a small literary coterie in Boston whose members were enthusiastic about the autobiographical sketches and short stories she had begun to place in *Harper's* and the *Atlantic Monthly* the year before. Ginn and Company had given her a contract for *Old Indian Legends* which would appear in the fall of 1901 and were anxiously awaiting material for a second book that would be, in their words, ". . . a fine series of Indian legends, the greatest that the world has ever known." And in its April issue of 1900, *Harper's Bazaar* had included her in a column entitled "Persons Who Interest Us."

Also an accomplished violinist, Zitkala Sa had studied at the New England Conservatory of Music and appeared both as a soloist and an orator with the Carlisle Indian Band to the critical acclaim of the *New York Musical Courier*. As early as 1898, she had been singled out of a group of Sioux visiting New York by Joseph T. Keiley who made a number of photographic portraits of her that would be exhibited over the next few years in New York and abroad and eventually would become part of Alfred Steiglitz's collection. Clearly it would seem, Zitkala Sa had arrived.

But into what world? To her mother and the traditional Sioux on the reservation where she had grown up, she was highly suspect because in their minds, she had abandoned, even betrayed, the Indian way of life by getting an education in the white man's world. To those at the Carlisle Indian School where she had taught from 1898–99, on the other hand, she was an anathema because she insisted on remaining "Indian," writing embarrassing articles such as "Why I Am A Pagan" that flew in the face of the assimilationist thrust of their education.

Born as Gertrude Simmons on the Yankton Reservation in South Dakota in 1876, she spent her first eight years of life on the reservation with her mother in a seemingly idyllic state of harmony, as she describes in "Impressions of an Indian Childhood," published in the *Atlantic Monthly* in 1900. When Gertrude's father, a white man named Felker, deserted the family before his daughter's birth, the mother decided to return to the Yankton agency to live. She also determined to give Gertrude the name of her second husband, Simmons.[2] Gertrude christened herself Zitkala Sa, Red Bird, when she had a falling out with her sister-in-law. As Zitkala Sa, she would try to recreate the spirit of her tribe in her collection of legends.

Like many Native Americans, Zitkala Sa suffered tremendous cultural conflicts during her education at off-reservation schools. From age eight to eleven, she studied at White's Manual Institute in Indiana. The difficulty of learning English and trying to assimilate to American customs seemed insignificant in comparison to the alienation she felt when she returned to her mother's home at the Yankton Agency. Eventually, she left home to complete her education at White's and to study two years at Earlham College. This was the beginning of a schism with her mother that would only widen over the years and would become one of the subjects in her autobiographical sketches.

While at Earlham from 1895 to 1897, Gertrude Simmons distinguished herself as an orator and poet, publishing essays and highly formal poems in the school's newspaper and winning several debating honors. It is during this period that her literary talents begin to take shape, and as she became more and more fluent in English, language became the tool for articulating the tension she experienced throughout her life between her heritage with its imperative of tradition and the inevitable pressure of acculturation. In her early essays, despite their stiff formality, the pattern of ambivalence is already there, as she alternates between a controlled rage over the mistreatment of Indians and a desire to convince America of the Indian's humanity.

In 1900, Zitkala Sa published three autobiographical essays in the January, February, and March issues of the *Atlantic Monthly*: "Impressions of an Indian Childhood," "The School Days of an Indian Girl," and "An Indian Teacher Among Indians." In December of 1902, the *Atlantic Monthly* published her essay, "Why I Am a Pagan." During this same period, she published two short stories, "The Trial Path" and "The Soft-Hearted Sioux," respectively in the March and October 1901 issues of *Harper's* magazine. "A Warrior's Daughter," another short story, appeared in a 1902 issue of *Everybody's Magazine*. These essays and stories were later published in 1921 in a collection entitled *American Indian Stories* by Hayworth Press of Washington, D.C. *Old Indian Legends*, published by Ginn and Co. of Boston, appeared in 1901. With the exception of some scattered poems and short stories that appeared in various Indian rights magazines, as well as the Carlisle Indian School newspaper, these two books constitute Zitkala Sa's published literary output. Within a brief three-year period, her career as a creative writer blossomed for a moment and then declined.

The decline of her "literary" career coincided directly with her marriage on May 10, 1902, to Raymond T. Bonnin, also a Sioux, with whom she moved to the Uintah and Ouray reservation in Utah. They lived there for the next fourteen years and had one son, Raymond O. Bonnin, born in 1903. As the wife of a government employee for the Bureau of Indian Affairs, Zitkala Sa became Mrs. Gertrude Bonnin, working in various capacities among the Utah Indians.

Her creative impulse was not dormant for long, however, and during this period she collaborated quite intensely with William Hanson on the composition of "Sun Dance," an Indian opera that premiered in 1913 in Vernal, Utah. Zitkala Sa contributed substantially to the composition of the opera by telling Hanson in minute detail the rituals surrounding the Sun Dance and sharing with him numerous tales and legends that are woven into the opera's story. She also played tribal songs for him upon her violin which he then transcribed in order to keep both the music and content of the opera as authentic as possible.

In 1916, the Bonnins moved to Washington, D.C., as Gertrude had been elected secretary of the Society of the American Indian. Under the auspices of the SAI, Bonnin launched her life's work in Indian reform, lecturing and campaigning across the country for Indian citizenship, employment of Indians in the Bureau of Indian Affairs, and equitable settlement of tribal land claims. Her temporary post as editor from 1918–19 of the society's publication, the *American Indian Magazine*, gave her the opportunity to reach an even wider audience in print.

In 1926, Bonnin founded her own political organization, the National Council of American Indians, of which she was the single president until her death in 1938. As described in *Indian Truth*, the organization was designed to "create increased interest in behalf of the Indians, and secure for them added recognition of their personal and property rights."[3] Armed with her oratorical skills and her literary ability, Zitkala Sa worked as an independent reformer on behalf of suppressed Indians across the country. She became known to Indians and government officials alike as a persuasive public speaker and an effective mediator.

In one biographical sketch, Bonnin is described thusly:

> The literature of Indian reform gives much attention to the maladjustments suffered by white-educated Indians who returned to their own people. Less well known is the role of these educated Indians in pressing for "progressive" reforms both on and off the reservation. Gertrude Simmons Bonnin was an Indian progressive; her career indicates both the achievements and frustrations attendant upon that role.[4]

It is not surprising at all that Zitkala Sa subsumed her creative energy into a life work of progressive reform for Indians. The wonder is that she wrote at all and in so doing became one of the first Native Americans to bring to the attention of a white audience the traditions of a tribe, as well as the personal sensibilities of one of its members.

Though Zitkala Sa's literary output is modest, it is significant because she is one of the first writers to articulate the tension between the two worlds of her existence — the Indian and the white. She is also one of the first women to write her own story without the aid of an editor, an interpreter, or an ethnographer. In her autobiographical sketches, she describes what it is like to live divided between tradition and assimilation. She is not reaffirming the role of the woman in tribal life, though she does give a great deal of information about that role through her description of her mother's life and traditions. Nor is her purpose to praise the educational opportunities afforded her through governmental policies. Rather, she presents carefully and, at times, sentimentally, the pain and difficulty of growing up Indian in a white man's world. She is not showcasing her life as yet another artifact to be preserved, but rather she is revealing a personality and identity that is uniquely hers.

It would be false to say that Zitkala Sa launched an American Indian literary tradition, but it is possible, in examining the cameo of her life and literature, to say that she struggled toward a vision of wholeness in which the conflicting parts of her existence could be reconciled. That she did not fully succeed is evident in her work, which is a model of ambivalences, of oscillations between two diametrically opposed worlds, but is also a model of retrieved possibilities, a creative, human endeavor that stands at the beginning of many such endeavors eventually to culminate in the finely crafted work of contemporary American Indian writers.

MOURNING DOVE

To study the work of Mourning Dove, an Okanogan and perhaps the first American Indian woman to write a novel, is to observe one of the more fascinating collaborative efforts that exists in the history of American Indian literature. The person who would become Mourning Dove's literary mentor and co-author, as well as personal friend and confidant for twenty years, was Lucullus V. McWhorter, a pioneer of encyclopedic interests and founder of *The American Archaeologist*, who had left his native West Virginia to homestead in the state of Washington in 1903.[5] It was there in 1914 at a Frontier Days Celebration in Walla Walla that Mourning Dove and McWhorter first met.

McWhorter's genuine compassion for the homeless condition of many of the Indian tribes of the Pacific Northwest had already led him to fight tirelessly on their behalf. He had, for example, defended the Yakimas in their struggle to protect their water rights and had published several books and pamphlets on Yakima history and culture. Adopted by the Yakimas into their tribe, he became known as the "Big Foot" of the Yakima because of his size. That name was to stick with him throughout his life and to be used consistently by Mourning Dove in all her correspondence with him.

Like Zitkala Sa, Mourning Dove was very conscious of the passing of an era and the disappearance of age-old customs and traditions of her tribe which she wished to hold on to in some way. But unlike her predecessor, and especially unlike her mentor McWhorter, Mourning Dove had none of the advantages of education, having barely achieved more than three years of formal schooling. Born near Bonner's Ferry, Idaho, in 1888, Mourning Dove moved back and forth between her relatives in British Columbia and those on the Colville Reservation near Omak, Washington. The daughter of Joseph Quintasket (Okanogan) and Lucy Stukin (a full-blood Colville), she was given the English name of Christal Quintasket and the Indian name of Hum-ishu-ma, or Mourning Dove. Her paternal grandfather had been an Irishman who worked with the Hudson Bay Company and who apparently had "married" her Indian grandmother under false pretenses in a tribal ceremony. Mourning Dove later based much of the plot of her romantic novel, *Cogewea; the Half Blood* (Boston: Four Seas, 1927), on the betrayal of Indian women by white men.

Mourning Dove's education consisted of a scant three years in the Sacred Heart Convent at Ward, Washington, which was frequently interrupted by trips home to take care of her younger brothers and sisters. In 1912, when she was twenty-four, Mourning Dove enrolled in a business school in Calgary, British Columbia, to learn typing and to improve her English.

Her first husband was Hector McLeod, a Flathead Indian. In 1919, she married Fred Galler, a Wenatchee. She had no children by either marriage. Continually plagued by poverty, the Gallers worked as migrant laborers, traveling with the seasons, picking hops and thinning apples, pitching tents and camping out under every imaginable condition. And everywhere they traveled, Mourning Dove took her battered old typewriter and tried to work after long hours in the field or orchards.

But even more than the physical hardships, Mourning Dove's greatest obstacle to gathering the material which she continually referred to as the "folklores" that would later be published in *Coyote Stories*, were the Indians themselves. In her correspondence with McWhorter, she repeatedly laments the fact that the Indians are suspicious of her and will not share any legends if they think they are to be published.

Because of the work of anthropologists such as James Teit among the Salishan tribes, McWhorter and Dean Guie, whom McWhorter had asked to edit Mourning Dove's "folklores," were very anxious that Mourning Dove be as accurate as possible in collecting her material. She frequently refers to the difficulty of writing those "brain teasers," Okanogan words and names for various characters in the coyote tales. Not only was the English alphabet incapable of phonetically representing sounds in Okanogan, but there was no standardized dictionary of the language to which she could turn. These handicaps were further compounded by her own difficulties with English. Thus, Mourning Dove faced enormous challenges in trying to render a work in Okanogan that would "sound" right and approximate at the very least the spelling adopted by anthropologists. The process was agonizing for her and often infuriating as Guie compared her work continually to the ethnographic texts he read, asking her to verify again and again spellings, translations, and even basic beliefs of the Okanogans.[6]

What was particularly frustrating for Mourning Dove was that it had never been her idea to write "folklores" exclusively, though she did eventually become extremely dedicated to that task. Rather, she aspired to write novels based on the material of her tribe. Indeed, when Mourning Dove first met McWhorter in 1914, she had already drafted a version of her novel that would eventually be published thirteen years later under the title *Co-ge-we-a, The Half-Blood — A Depiction of the Great Montana Cattle Range* (Boston: Four Seas, 1927). Encouraged by McWhorter's interest in her, she apparently sent him her manuscript for his comments. Unfortunately, there is no record of that initial correspondence, nor is there an extant copy of Mourning Dove's original manuscript (though she does state in one letter that she had saved her first pencil version), but subsequent correspondence indicates that Mourning Dove agreed to let McWhorter "fix up" the story of that "little squaw" and eventually to act as her business manager as well, handling all negotiations for its publication.

McWhorter was extremely optimistic about the potential for success of *Cogewea* because he was convinced that Mourning Dove was the first Indian woman to write a novel of any sort, which alone should tweak the curiosity of the reading public, and certainly the first to incorporate the oral traditions of her tribe into a literary form. But because there was no precedent for an Indian woman writing romance, McWhorter felt compelled to "strengthen the statements" of Mourning Dove, as he put it, by providing ethnographic notes on the stories and traditions that she had woven into the narrative line. At the same time, he had argued to be the Sho-pow-tan of the title page and allow the story to be "told through him." This dual role as editor and annotator unquestionably gave McWhorter a tremendous amount of control over Mourning Dove's manuscript.

Mourning Dove's intention from the beginning had been to write a romance about the half-breed Cogewea, whose name means the little chipmunk in Okanogan, that was based on her own experience and that would preserve in novel form some of the stories of her tribe that had not been recorded. Despite the inclusion of the Okanogan elements, Mourning Dove regarded *Cogewea* as fiction. McWhorter, on the other hand, felt, and perhaps rightly so, that the uniqueness of the novel lay in its explication of those elements informing the Indian point of view. Unfortunately, he could not stick just with his explanatory footnotes, but felt compelled to insert into the narrative innumerable didactic passages about the injustices suffered by Indians at the hands of government agencies, as well as historical facts about other tribes that are hardly relevant to the story. The result is that the narrative, which is very much within the tradition of the western romance with its stock characters and measures of melodrama, becomes overburdened in parts with platitudinous moralizing that does not always mesh with other sentiments in the novel.

If Mourning Dove relied heavily on McWhorter's assistance in the writing of *Cogewea*, she had much more control over the material that would be published under the title of *Coyote Stories* (Caldwell, Idaho: Caxton Printers, 1933). From the inception of their friendship, McWhorter had encouraged Mourning Dove to gather as many of the traditional Okanogan folktales and myths as she could before they disappeared into oblivion with the death of the older storytellers. Unfamiliar with the Okanogan language, McWhorter left Mourning Dove to her own devices in collecting and writing the tales, offering to edit the language as she would complete a tale and remaining available to her for moral support and assistance. They corresponded frequently over the fifteen-year period during which Mourning Dove collected the legends she always referred to as "folklores." When she had recorded a sufficient number of tales to be published, McWhorter arranged for Heister Dean Guie to edit the stories and provide illustrations. McWhorter again provided the notes to the text. The result was the publication in 1933 of *Coyote Stories*, a collection of twenty-seven traditional Okanogan folk tales, eighteen of which center on the adventures of the peripatetic coyote.

The publication of *Coyote Stories* was unquestionably a major event, because it introduced into the public imagination the concept that Indians did indeed have a long and rich cultural tradition of distinct literary merit that was as "American" as anything white Americans had written.

The influence of the white reading audience upon the early Indian writers cannot be exaggerated because within the American imagination, Indians have always been regarded as "exotic," "primitive," or "romantic." If Zitkala Sa and Mourning Dove felt like the observers of their respective

Indian cultures, they were the observed when it came to the white world. Zitkala Sa fascinated the eastern literary world because she had been "a veritable little savage, running wild over the prairie and speaking no language but her own . . ." How remarkable that she could also learn to read and write and *publish* in English. And though Mourning Dove enjoyed the support of McWhorter, her attraction for him was no different. She would be the *first* American Indian woman to write a novel, that is, if she were nurtured properly. Perhaps, such attitudes were inevitable; certainly, they created a situation in which each writer tried to live up to certain literary expectations and in the process began to shape the oral traditions into forms that would be recognizable to their reading audience.

Mourning Dove initially chose the western romance as her form because it was a popular genre and it was fiction. Zitkala Sa, on the other hand, selected autobiography and the short story. In both cases, these choices are extraordinary because they are so far removed from the Indian storytelling tradition. Within the oral tradition, stories exist to explain the way things are and to record history, and they are considered to be true because they have been passed from one generation to the next. Oral storytelling is a communal event; it cannot exist without the dynamic between the teller and his audience. But writing is individual and isolated. The writer by necessity stands apart from the subject and comments on it. Writing goes beyond the domain of the spoken word into a world that must be recreated and contextualized.

Both Zitkala Sa and Mourning Dove felt a profound sense of responsibility to their cultures and both knew that they were pioneers in a transitional moment in history. Zitkala Sa writes of her need to collect as many of the stories as she can "while the old people last," a sentiment that Mourning Dove echoes in letter after letter to McWhorter. One consequence of such self-consciousness is the tendency of both women to over sentimentalize or over romanticize their subjects. Theirs is a literature of polarities — Indian versus white, tradition versus change, primitive versus civilization, even oral versus written.

Because writing was such a different mode of expression from oral storytelling, it is not unusual that so many of the early Indian writers worked with collaborators such as Mourning Dove did with McWhorter. As they moved into a new language and unfamiliar genres, the collaborator was a welcome guide to help in the translation of experience. We may wish that Mourning Dove had worked with someone less zealous than McWhorter, but that relationship was important in illuminating Mourning Dove's own fears and insecurities, aspirations and goals as a writer. Her extensive correspondence with McWhorter begins to suggest the ways in which collaborators were most apt to influence the literature written. There is no question, for example, that McWhorter romanticized Mourning Dove, viewing her as the pioneer that she was but also burdening her with the responsibility for preserving an entire culture. Though Mourning Dove often wrote of the inconveniences of living a nomadic and primitive existence and wondered how her ancestors had done it on a regular basis, McWhorter preferred to envision her early life as idyllic and pastoral, much as Zitkala Sa portrays her childhood self as a "little sportive nymph on that Dakota sea of rolling green."

The key is in remembering, but too often, it seems, the collaborators chose to encourage those memories that reflected their own notions of the pastoral state. But as romanticized as were the visions of the collaborators and those of the Indian writers themselves, the world had changed, an era had passed, and we must be grateful that Zitkala Sa and Mourning Dove were there to record even a moment of that transition and to transform their traditions into a permanent form that has enriched both our literary history and our imagination.

Notes

1. Carlos Montezuma Papers, Microfilm 151, Reel #1, Division of Archives and Manuscripts of the State Historical Society of Wisconsin. Carlos Montezuma was a Yavapai who became quite famous as one of the first Indians to become a doctor. He and Zitkala Sa were engaged to be married for a brief time and exchanged numerous letters which have been included in the Carlos Montezuma Papers.

2. The family history of Ellen Simmons' three marriages may be found in Record #10–1622–09 — Yankton 312 of Record Group No. 75, National Archives, Washington, D.C.

3. Vol. 3, No. 3 (March 1926), 3.

4. *Notable American Women* — 1607–1950 — *A Biographical Dictionary*, ed. Edward T. James (Cambridge, Mass.: Belknap Press of Harvard Univ. Press, 1971), p. 200.

5. For more biographical information on McWhorter, see Nelson A. Ault, *The Papers of Lucullus V. McWhorter* (Friends of the Library, State College of Washington, 1959).

6. The tales that Teit collected were published as "Okanogan Tales" in *Folk-Tales of Salishan and Sahaptin Tribes*, collected by James A. Teit, Marian K. Gould, Livingston Farrand, Herbert J. Spinden; ed. Franz Boas (Lancaster, Pa.: American Folklore Society, 1917), pp. 65–97.

Words and Place: A Reading of
House Made of Dawn   Lawrence J. Evers[*]

In order to consider seriously the meaning of language and of literature, we must consider first the meanings of the oral tradition.[1]

I

Native American oral traditions are not monolithic, nor are the traditions with which Momaday works in *House Made of Dawn* — Kiowa,

*Reprinted from *Western American Literature*, 11 (1977), 297–320, by permission of the author.

Navajo, and Towan Pueblo.[2] Yet, there are, he suggests, "common denominators."[3] Two of the most important of these are the native American's relations to the land and his regard for language.

By imagining who and what they are in relation to particular landscapes, cultures and individual members of cultures form a close relation with those landscapes. Following D. H. Lawrence and others, Momaday terms this a "sense of place."[4] A sense of place derives from the perception of a culturally imposed symbolic order on a particular physical topography. A superb delineation of some such symbolic order is offered by Tewa anthropologist Alfonso Ortiz in his study *The Tewa World* from which the following prayer is taken:

> Within and around the earth, within and around the hills, within and around the mountains, your authority returns to you.[5]

The Tewa singer finds in the landscape which surrounds him validation for his own song, and that particular topography becomes a cultural landscape, at once physical and symbolic. Like Ko-sahn, Momaday's grandmother, the native American draws from it "strength enough to hold still against all the forces of chance and disorder."[6]

The manner in which cultural landscapes are created interests Momaday, and the whole of his book *The Way to Rainy Mountain* may be seen as an account of that process.[7] During their migration journey the Kiowa people "dared to imagine and determine who they were. . . . The journey recalled is among other things the revelation of one way in which these traditions are conceived, developed, and interfused in the human mind."[8] The Kiowa journey, like that recounted in emergence narratives of other tribes, may be seen as a movement from chaos to order, from discord to harmony. In this emergence the landscape plays a crucial role, for cultural landscapes are created by the imaginative interaction of societies of men and particular geographies.

In the Navajo emergence narrative, for example, First Man and First Woman accompanied by Coyote and other actors from the animal world journey upward through four underworlds into the present Fifth World.[9] The journey advances in a series of movements from chaos to order, and each movement takes the people toward greater social and symbolic definition. The cloud pillars of the First World defined only by color and direction become in the Fifth World the sacred mountains of the four directions, the most important coordinates in an intricate cultural geography. As with the Tewa and the Kiowa, that cultural landscape symbolizes the Navajo conception of order, the endpoint of their emergence journey. Through the emergence journey, a collective imaginative endeavor, the Navajos determined who and what they were in relation to the land.

The extraordinary interest in geography exhibited in Navajo oral literature then may be seen as an effort to evoke harmony in those narratives by reference to the symbolic landscape of the present world.[10] Significantly, a

major test theme in Navajo oral literature requires identification of culturally important geographic features. Consider the Sun's test of the Hero
Twins in one of the final episodes in the emergence narrative:

> He asked them to identify various places all over the surface of the earth.
> He asked, "Where is your home?" The boys knew where their home was.
> They pointed out Huerfano Mountain and said that was where they lived.
> The Sun next asked, "What mountain is that in the East?"
>
> > "That's *Sis Naajiní* (Blanca Peak)," replied the boys.
> > "What mountain is down here below us?"
> > "That's *Tsoodzi* (Mount Taylor)," said the boys.
> > "What mountain is that in the West?"
> > That's *Dook'o'oosííd* (San Francisco Peak)."
> > "Now, what mountain is that over in the north?"
> > "Those are the *Dibé Nitsaa* (La Plata Mountains)."
>
> Because all the boys' answers were correct, the Sun said goodby to
> them as they were lowered down to the earth at the place called *Tó Sidoh*
> (Hot Springs).[11]

Through their knowledge of the Navajo cultural landscape the Twins
proved who and what they were to the Sun.

The pattern of the emergence narrative — a journey toward order sym-
bolized by a cultural landscape — is repeated in Navajo chantway rituals. A
patient requires a chantway ritual when his life is in some way out of order
and harmony. In order for that harmony to be restored he must be taken
through a ritual re-emergence journey paralleling that of the People. It is
important to note the role of the singer and his ritual song here, for without
songs there can be no cure or restoration of order.[12] Through the power of
the chanter's words the patient's life is brought under ritual control, and he
is cured.

We come round, then, to another of the "common denominators"
Momaday finds in oral traditions: attitude toward language. Of Kiowa oral
tradition Momaday writes: "A word has power in and of itself. It comes
from nothing into sound and meaning; it gives origin to all things."[13] It is
this concept, remarkably like one text version of the Navajo origin giving
"One Word" as the name of the original state of the universe, which forms
the center of Tosamah's sermon on St. John's gospel in the novel.[14] But more
germane to our discussion of oral tradition generally is the related notion
that "by means of words can a man deal with the world on equal terms."[15] It
is only through words that a man is able to express his relation to place.
Indeed, it is only through shared words or ritual that symbolic landscapes
are able to exist. So it is that the Tewa singer, the Navajo chanter, and the
Kiowa "man of words" preserve their communities through their story and
song. Without them there would be no community. One contemporary
Navajo medicine man suggests that loss of ceremonial words will signal the
end of the world: "The medicine men who have knowledge in the Blessing

Way (*Hozho ji*) will all evidently be lost. The words to the song will vanish from their memory, and they will not know how to begin to sing."[16]

In this context we can better appreciate Abel's dilemma in *House Made of Dawn*. As Momaday suggests: "One of the most tragic things about Abel, as I think of him, is his inability to express himself. He is in some ways a man without a voice. . . . So I think of him as having been removed from oral tradition."[17]

II

House Made of Dawn opens and closes with the formulaic words which enclose all Jemez pueblo tales—*dypaloh* and *qtsedaba*, placing it consciously in that oral tradition.[18] As many oral narratives, the novel is shaped around a movement from discord to harmony and is structurally and thematically cyclic. The prologue is dominated by the race, a central theme in the novel as Momaday has suggested:

> I see [*House Made of Dawn*] as a circle. It ends where it begins and it's informed with a kind of thread that runs through it and holds everything together. The book itself is a race. It focuses upon the race, that's the thing that does hold it all together. But it's a constant repetition of things too.[19]

Parsons tells us that racing is a conspicuous feature of Jemez ceremonialism.[20] The winter race Abel runs in the prologue and at the end of the novel is the first race in the Jemez ceremonial season, an appropriate ceremonial beginning. But the race itself may be seen as a journey, a re-emergence journey analogous to that mentioned in connection with Navajo and Kiowa oral tradition. Indeed, the language echoes a Navajo re-emergence song sung in the Night Chant, from which the title of the book is taken.[21]

These journey and emergence themes begin to unfold in the following scene as Francisco goes in his wagon to meet the bus returning Abel to Walatowa after WWII. The wagon road on which he rides is parallel to the modern highway on which Abel rides. The two roads serve as familiar metaphors for the conflicting paths Abel follows in the novel, and Momaday reinforces the conflict by parallel auditory motifs as well. As the wagon road excites in Francisco memories of his own race "for good hunting and harvests," he sings good sounds of harmony and balance.[22] At the same time the recurrent whine of tires on the highway is constantly in the background until "he heard the sharp wheeze of the brakes as the big bus rolled to a stop in front of the gas pump. . . ." (p. 13) The re-emergence theme is suggested in the passage by the presence of the reed trap (p. 10) — recalling the reed of emergence, and the fact that Abel returns "ill" (p. 13).[23] He is drunk, of course, but he is also ill, out of balance, in the manner of a patient in a Navajo chantway.

Abel's genealogy, the nature of his illness, and its relation to the auditory motifs mentioned above are further defined in the seven fragments of memory he experiences as he walks above the Cañon de San Diego in the first dawn following his return. At the same time these fragments establish a context for Abel's two prominent encounters in Part I with Angela Grace St. John and with the albino Juan Reyes Fragua.

Abel's genealogy is complicated. He did not know who his father was. "His father was a Navajo, they said, or a Sia, or an Isleta, an outsider anyway," which made Abel "somehow foreign and strange" (p. 15). The ties Abel does have to Walatowa are through his mother whose father, Francisco — both sacristan and kiva participant — is the illegitimate son of the consumptive priest Fray Nicolas V. (p. 184). Through Francisco, Abel is a direct descendant of the Bahkyush, a group of Towan-speaking pueblos who immigrated to Jemez in the mid-nineteenth century.[24] He is a "direct [descendant] of those men and women who had made that journey along the edge of oblivion" (p. 19), an experience which gave them a "tragic sense." Abel, as his Bahkyush ancestors, is on just such a "journey along the edge of oblivion" in the novel.

Abel's journey in Part I is a journey of return to Walatowa and his illness is most explicitly related to a WWII experience. At the end of his seven memory fragments in the first dawn of his return Abel recalls:

> This — everything in advance of his going — he could remember whole and in detail. It was the recent past, the intervention of days and years without meaning, of awful calm and collision, time always immediate and confused, that he could not put together in his mind. (p. 25)

In the confusion of war among soldiers who recognized him only as a "chief" speaking in "Sioux or Algonquin or something" (p. 108), Abel lost both the sense of place which characterized his tribal culture and the very community which supports that sense of place. "He didn't know where he was, and he was alone" (p. 26). Incredibly, he doesn't even recognize the earth: "He reached for something, but he had no notion of what it was; his hand closed upon the earth and the cold, wet leaves" (p. 26).

Mechanical sounds are associated with Abel's disorientation. The "low and incessant" (p. 26) sound of the tank descending upon him reaches back in the novel to the "slow whine of tires" Francisco hears on the highway and looks ahead to the sound of Angela's car intruding on his vision in the first dawn above the valley as it creeps along the same highway toward the Jemez church (p. 27). These are the same mechanical sounds Abel tried "desperately to take into account" as the bus took him away to the war — again on the same highway (p. 25). They are the sounds that reminded him as he left the pueblo to go to war that "the town and the valley and the hills" could no longer center him, that he was now "centered upon himself" (p. 25).

That Angela Grace St. John, the pregnant wife of a Los Angeles physician who comes to Walatowa seeking a cure for her own ailments, will become an obstacle in Abel's re-emergence journey is first suggested by the extensive auditory motifs of Part I. Yet her perceptions of his problems and of the Indian world generally have earned the sympathy of some readers.[25] Perhaps her most seductive perception is that of the significance of the corn dancers at Cochiti Pueblo:

> Their eyes were held upon some vision out of range, something away in the end of distance, some reality that she did not know, or even suspect. What was it that they saw? Probably they saw nothing after all, . . . nothing at all. But then that was the trick, wasn't it? To see nothing at all, . . . nothing in the absolute. To see beyond the landscape, beyond every shape and shadow and color, *that* was to see nothing. That was to be free and finished, complete, spiritual. . . . To say "beyond the mountain," and to mean it, to mean, simply, beyond everything for which the mountain stands of which it signifies the being. (pp. 37–38)

As persuasive as Angela's interpretation of the Cochiti dancers may seem, it is finally a denial of the value of the landscape which the novel celebrates. Angela's assumption that the Cochiti dancers possess a kind of Hindu metaphysics which rejects phenomena for noumena is a projection of her own desires to reject the flesh.[26] Her attitude toward the land is of a piece with her attitude toward her own body: "she could think of nothing more vile and obscene than the raw flesh and blood of her body, the raveled veins and the gore upon her bones" (p. 36). We become almost immediately aware of the implications of that denial she craves in two following scenes: the *corre de gaio* and Abel's second reflection on the Cañon de San Diego.

We view the *corre de gaio* through Angela who again projects feelings about her own existence on the ceremony. For Angela the ceremony like herself is "so empty of meaning . . . and yet so full of appearance" (p. 43). Her final impression of the ceremony is sexual. She senses some "unnatural thing" in it and "an old fascination returned upon her" (p. 43). Later she remarks of the ceremony: "Like this, her body had been left to recover without her when once and for the first time, having wept, she had lain with a man" (p. 45). In the albino's triumph and Abel's failure at the *corre de gaio* she finds sexual pleasure.

The etiological legend of Santiago (St. James) and the rooster is told by Fr. Olguin appropriately enough for his "instinctive demand upon all histories to be fabulous" (p. 68).[27] The legend explains the ceremonial game which follows in the novel. Just as the sacrifice of the rooster by Santiago produced cultivated plants and domesticated animals for the Pueblo people, so too does ritual re-enactment of the sacrifice promote fertility at Walatowa. While ethnographers suggest that the *corre de gaio* is of relatively minor ceremonial importance in Pueblo societies, in the context of the novel the rooster pull affords Abel his first opportunity to re-enter the ceremonial functions of the village.[28] It is, we are told, the first occasion on which he has taken off his uniform. Though the ceremony itself seems efficacious, as rain follows in the novel, Abel is "too rigid" and "too careful" (p. 42) at the game and fails miserably.[29]

Abel's failure at the rooster pull demonstrates his inability to reenter the ceremonial life of the village, as he realizes in his second reflection at dawn, July 28, 1945. The section opens with an explicit statement of the relation of the emergence journey and the landscape: "The canyon is a ladder to the plain" (p. 54), and is followed by a description of the ordered and harmonious existence of life in that landscape. Each form of life has its proper space and function in the landscape, and by nature of that relation is said to have "tenure in the land" (p. 56). Similarly, "man came down the ladder to the plain a long time ago. It was a slow migration . . ." (p. 56). Like the emergency journeys of the Kiowa and the Navajo mentioned earlier, the migration of the people of Walatowa led to an ordered relation to place which they express in their ceremonial life. As Abel walks in this landscape in the dawn he is estranged from the town and the land as well. "His return to the town had been a failure" (pp. 56–7) he realizes because he is no longer attuned to its rhythms. He has no words to express his relation to the place. He is "not dumb," but "inarticulate" (p. 57).

Despite his inarticulateness, the rhythm and words are still there "like memory, in the reach of his hearing" (p. 57). We recall that on July 21, seven days before, "for a moment everything was all right with him" (p. 32). Here however;

> He was alone, and he wanted to make a song out of the colored canyon, the way the women of Torreón made songs upon their looms out of colored yarn, but he had not got the right words together. It would have been a creation song; he would have sung lowly of the first world, of fire and flood, and of the emergence of dawn from the hills. (p. 57)

Abel is at this point vaguely conscious of what he needs to be cured. He needs a re-emergence. He needs words, ceremonial words, which express his relation to the cultural landscape in which he stands. He needs to feel with the Tewa singer quoted earlier his authority return to him. But here out of harmony with himself and his community he needs most of all the kind of re-emergence journey offered in a Navajo chantway.

Significantly, the passage closes, as did the dawn walk of July 21, with an emblem of Angela St. John intruding on Abel's vision: "the high white walls of the Benevides house" (p. 58). The house itself is another symbol of Angela's denial of the land or more particularly the landscape of the Cañon de San Diego.[30] In contrast to Francisco and the other native residents of Walatowa who measure space and time by reference to the eastern rim of the canyon, Angela measures hers in relation to this "high, white house:"

> She would know the arrangement of her days and hours in the upstairs and down, and they would be for her the proof of her being and having been. (p. 53)

His re-entry into the village spoiled, Abel turns not to the ceremonial structure of the pueblo for support but to Angela. And it is the Benevides house, not the land, which provides "the wings and the stage" for their affair (p. 53). Abel's first sexual encounter with Angela is juxtaposed in the novel with Francisco's encounter with the albino witch in his cornfield. Indeed, Angela, who "keened" to the unnatural qualities of the albino during the *corre de gaio*, echoes the auditory symbols of evil mentioned earlier. Just as Nicolas *teah-whau* "screamed" at him (p. 15), and the moan of the wind in the rocks (p. 16) frightened him earlier, as Angela and Abel make love "she wanted to scream" and is later "moaning softly" (p. 62).[31]

Earlier in his life Abel found physical regeneration through a sexual experience with Fat Josie (pp. 93, 106–7). His affair with Angela has just the opposite effect. Lying physically broken on the beach in Part II Abel reflects:

> He had loved his body. It had been hard and quick and beautiful; it had been useful, quickly and surely responsive to his mind and will. . . . His body, like his mind, had turned on him; it was his enemy. (p. 93)

The following couplet in the text implicates Angela in this alienation:

> Angela put her white hands to his body.
> Abel put his hands to her white body. (p. 94)

Later Abel tells Benally that "she [Angela] was going to help him get a job and go away from the reservation, but then he got himself in trouble" (p. 161). That "trouble" derives in part from Abel's separation from his land.

Auditory symbols follow Abel directly from his affair with Angela to the climactic scene of Part I, the killing of the albino. Just before the murder the albino laughs "a strange, inhuman cry" (p. 77). Like the sound of Nicolas *teah-whau* it is "an old woman's laugh" that issues from a "great, evil mouth" (p. 77). At the very scene of the murder the only sound that breaks the silence is "the moan of the wind in the wires" (p. 77).

That Abel regards the albino as evil, as a witch (*sawah*), is clear enough even without the explicit statements of Father Olguin, Tosamah, and Benally later (pp. 94–5, 136–7). Moreover, it is clear at the time of the murder that Abel regards the albino as a snake. He feels "the scales of the lips and the hot slippery point of the tongue, writhing" (p. 78). But that Abel is "acting entirely within the Indian tradition" when he kills the albino is wrong.[32]

Abel's compulsion to eradicate the albino-snake reveals an attitude toward evil more akin to the Christian attitude of Nicolas V.: "that Serpent which even is the One our most ancient enemy" (p. 50). The murder scene is rife with Christian overtones. The killing takes place beneath a telegraph pole which "leaned upon the black sky" (p. 77); during the act "the white hands still lay upon him as if in benediction" (p. 78); and after the albino's death "Abel knelt" and noticed "the dark nails of the hand seemed a string of great black beads" (p. 79). Abel appears to kill the albino then as a frustrated response to the White Man and Christianity, but he does so more in accordance with Anglo tradition than Indian tradition. Indeed, he has been trained in the Army to be a killer.

We recall here that the murder takes place squarely in the middle of the fiesta of Porcingula, the patroness of Walatowa, and that a central part of the ceremony on that feast is a ritual confrontation between the Pecos bull and the "black-faced children, who were the invaders" (p. 73). Parsons describes the bull-baiting at Jemez during the fiesta of Porcingula, August 1, 1922, as follows:

> An hour later, "the Pecos bull is out," I am told and hasten to the Middle. There the bull-mask is out playing, with a following of about a dozen males, four or five quite young boys. They are caricaturing Whites, their faces and hands painted white; one wears a false mustache, another a beard of blond hair. "U.S.A." is chalked on the back of their coat or a cross within a circle. . . . They shout and cry out, "What's the matter with you boy?" or more constantly *"Muchacho! Muchacho!"*
>
> .   .   .   .   .   .
>
> The bull antics are renewed, this time with attempts of his baiters to las-soo. Finally they succeed in dragging him in front of their house, where he breaks away again, to be caught again and dragged into the house. From the house a bugler steps out and plays "Wedding Bells" and rag-time tunes for the bull-baiters to dance to in couples, "modern dances," ending up in a tumble. Two by two, in their brown habit and sandalled feet, four of the Franciscan Fathers pass by. It grows dark, the bugler plays "taps" and this burlesque, reaching from the Conquistadores to the Great War, is over for the night.[33]

The very day then that Abel kills the albino the community from which he is estranged could have provided him with a way of ritually confronting the white man. Had his return not been a failure, he might have borne his agony, as Francisco had "twice or three times" (p. 76), by taking the part of the bull. "It was a hard thing," Francisco tells us, "to be the bull, for there was a primitive agony to it, and it was a kind of victim, an object of ridicule and hatred" (p. 75). Hard as that agony was, Abel as Francisco before him might have borne it with the support of his community. Separated from that community, he acts individually against evil and kills the white man.

Momaday forces us to see the murder as more complicated and subtle in motivation despite Benally's sympathetic reflections on the realities of witchery (p. 137), Tosamah's reference to the murder as a legal conundrum (p. 136), and Abel's own statement that the murder was "not a complicated thing" (p. 95). Death has not been a simple thing for Abel to cope with earlier in the novel, as shown by his emotional reactions to the deaths of the doe (pp. 16–17), the rabbit (p. 22), the eagle (pp. 24–25), as well as the deaths of his brother Vidal and his mother. More to the point is the fact that the White Man Abel kills is, in fact, a white Indian, an albino. He is the

White Man in the Indian; perhaps even the White Man in Abel himself. When Abel kills the albino, in a real sense he kills a part of himself and his culture which he can no longer recognize and control. That that part should take the shape of a snake in his confused mind is horribly appropriate given the long association of the Devil and the snake in Christian tradition (cf. Fray Nicolas V.) and the subsequent Puritan identification of the American Indians as demonic snakes and witches in so much of early American litera- ture.[34] In orthodox Pueblo belief the snake and the powers with which it is associated are accepted as a necessary part of the cosmic order: "The He- brew view of the serpent as the embodiment of unmitigated evil is never elaborated among the Pueblos; he is too often an ally for some desired end."[35]

Yet, the whiteness of the albino suggests something more terrible than evil to Abel. As the whiteness of the whale does to Ishmael, it suggests an emptiness in the universe, a total void of meaning. It is an emblem comple- mentary to Angela's philosophizing over the Cochiti dancers. The albino confronts Abel with his own lack of meaning, his own lack of a sense of place.

This reading is reinforced by the poignant final scene in Part I. Fran- cisco stands alone in his corn field demonstrating the very sense of place Abel has lacked on his return. We recall that in this very field Francisco too had confronted evil in the shape of the albino, but that he responded to the confrontation very differently:

> His acknowledgement of the unknown was nothing more than a dull, in- trinsic sadness, a vague desire to weep, for evil had long since found him out and knew who he was. He set a blessing upon the corn and took up his hoe. (p. 64)

Because of Abel's act, Francisco is for the first time separated from the Wa- latowa community. He stands muttering Abel's name as he did in the open- ing of the chapter, and near him the reed trap — again suggesting the reed of emergence — is empty.

III

Part II of the novel opens with Abel lying broken, physically and spiri- tually, on the beach in Los Angeles. Like the helpless grunion with whom he shares the beach, he is out of his world. Abel's problem continues to be one of relating to place. As in Part I at Walatowa he fails to establish a sense of place in Los Angeles because of a failure to find community. Not only is he separated from other workers at the factory, but even Tosamah and the In- dian men at the Silver Dollar reject Abel. That rejection is a major cause of Abel's second futile and self-destructive confrontation with evil in the per- son of Martinez, a sadistic Mexican policeman.[36] The pattern of the second confrontation is a repetition of the first. Just as Abel kills the albino at Wala- towa after he has failed to find community there, so too he goes after Martinez, also perceived as a snake (*culebra*), after he has failed utterly to find community in Los Angeles. Implication of Anglo society in this failure is again explicit and powerful, as Abel has been sent to Los Angeles by the government on its Relocation Program after serving time in prison for killing the albino.

On the beach Abel "could not see" (p. 92). This poverty of vision, both physical and imaginative, is akin to the inability of one-eyed Father Olguin to "see" and is related to Abel's prison experience: "After a while he could not imagine anything beyond the walls except the yard outside, the lavatory and the dining hall — or even walls, really" (p. 97). Yet it is by the sea that Abel gains the insight required to begin his own re-emergence. For the first time he asks himself "where the trouble had begun, what the trouble was" (p. 97), and though he still cannot answer the question consciously, his mind turns again to the mechanical auditory images noted earlier:

> The bus leaned and created; he felt the surge of motion and the violent shudder of the whole machine on the gravel road. The motion and the sound seized upon him. Then suddenly he was overcome with a desperate loneliness, and he wanted to cry out. He looked toward the fields, but a low rise of the land lay before them. (p. 97)

The bus takes Abel out of a context where he has worth and meaning and into a context where "there were enemies all around" (p. 98). From the cultural landscape of the Cañon de San Diego to the beach where "the world was open at his back" (p. 96), Abel's journey has taken him, as his Bahkyush ancestors, to "the edge of oblivion": "He had been long ago at the center, had known where he was, had lost his way, had wandered to the end of the earth, was even now reeling on the edge of the void" (p. 96). On the beach, then, Abel finally realizes that "he had lost his place" (p. 96), a realization accompanied by the comprehension of the social harmony a sense of place requires. Out of his delirium, as if in a dream, his mind returns to the central thread of the novel, the race, and here at last Abel is able to assign meaning to the race as a cultural activity:

> The runners after evil ran as water runs, deep in the channel, in the way of least resistance, no resistance. His skin crawled with excitement; he was overcome with longing and loneliness, for suddenly he saw the crucial sense in their going, of old men in white leggings running after evil in the night. They were whole and indispensable in what they did; everything in creation referred to them. Because of them, perspective, proportion, design in the universe. Meaning because of them. They ran with great dignity and calm, not in hope of anything, but hopelessly; neither in fear nor hatred nor despair of evil, but simply in recognition and with respect. Evil was. Evil was abroad in the night; they must venture out to the confrontation; they must reckon dues and divide the world. (p. 96)

We recall that as Abel killed the albino "the terrible strength of the hands was brought to bear only in proportion as Abel *resisted them*" (p. 78, emphasis added). The murder is an expression of Abel's disharmony and imbalance. As Abel here realizes "evil is that which is ritually not under control."[37] In the ceremonial race, not in individual resistance, the runners are able to deal with evil.

Tosamah's description of the emergence journey and the relations of words and place serve as a clue to Abel's cure, but the role he plays in Abel's journey appears as ambiguous and contradictory as his character. He is at once priest and "clown" (p. 165). He exhibits, often on the same page, remarkable insight, buffoonery, and cynicism. He has then all the characteristics of Coyote, the trickster figure in native American mythologies.[38] Alternately wise and foolish, Coyote in native American oral tradition is at once a buffoon and companion of the People on their emergence journey. As Coyote, a member of "an old council of clowns" (p. 55), the Right Reverend John Big Bluff Tosamah speaks with a voice "full of authority and rebuke" (p. 55). As Coyote, "he likes to get under your skin; he'll make a fool out of you if you let him" (p. 165). Note how Momaday describes Tosamah:

> He was shaggy and awful-looking in the thin, naked light; big, lithe as a cat, narrow-eyed, suggesting in the whole of his look and manner both arrogance and agony. He wore black like a cleric; he had the voice of a great dog. (p. 85)

The perspective Tosamah offers Abel and the reader in the novel derives not so much from his peyote ceremonies, for which Momaday seems to have drawn heavily on La Barre's *The Peyote Cult*, but rather from the substance of the two sermons he gives.[39] The second sermon, "The Way to Rainy Mountain," which Momaday has used in his book by the same title and several other contexts, addresses the relation of man, land, community, and the word. In it Tosamah describes the emergence of the Kiowa people as "a journey toward the dawn" that "led to a golden age" (p. 118). It was a journey which led the Kiowa to a culture which is inextricably bound to the land of the southern plains. There, much in the manner of Abel looking over the Cañon de San Diego in Part I, he looks out on the landscape at dawn and muses: "your imagination comes to life, and this, you think, is where Creation was begun" (p. 117). By making a re-emergence journey, Tosamah is able to feel a sense of place.

That coherent native relation to the land described so eloquently by Tosamah is counterpointed in the novel not only by Abel's experiences but also by the memories of Milly, the social worker who becomes Abel's lover in Los Angeles. Milly, like Tosamah, is from Oklahoma. There her family too had struggled with the land, but "at last Daddy began to hate the land, began to think of it as some kind of enemy, his own very personal and deadly enemy" (p. 113). Even viewed in the dawn her father's relation to the land was a despairing and hopeless one:

> And every day before dawn he went to the fields without hope, and I watched him, sometimes saw him at sunrise, far away in the empty land,

very small on the skyline turning to stone even as he moved up and down the rows. (p. 113)

The contrast with Francisco, who seems most at home in his fields, and with Tosamah, who finds in that very landscape the depth of his existence, is obvious. The passage also recalls Angela's denial of the meaning of the land and Abel's own reflections on "enemies."

In his first sermon in the novel, Tosamah addresses the crucial role of words and the imagination in the re-emergence process. The sermon is a bizarre exegesis of St. John's gospel which compares Indian and Anglo attitudes toward language. As participants in oral traditions, Indians, Tosamah tells us, hold language as sacred. They have a childlike regard for the mysteries of speech. While St. John shared that sensibility, he was also a white man. And the white man obscures the truth by burdening it with words:

> Now, brothers, and sisters, old John was a white man, and the white man has his ways. Oh gracious me, he has his ways. He talks about the Word. He talks through it and around it. He builds upon it with syllables, with prefixes and suffixes, and hyphens and accents. He adds and divides and multiplies the Word. And in all of this he subtracts the Truth. (p. 87)

The white man may indeed, Tosamah tells us, in a theory of verbal overkill that is wholly his own, "perish by the Word" (p. 89).

Words are, of course, a problem for Abel. On the one hand, he lacks the ceremonial words — the words of a Creation song — which properly express his relation to community and place. He is inarticulate. On the other, he is plagued by a surfeit of words from white men. The bureaucratic words of the social worker's forms effectively obscure his real problems. At the murder trial, he thinks: "Word by word by word these men were disposing of him in language, *their* language, and they were making a bad job of it" (p. 95). Again when Benally takes him to the hospital after the beach scene bureaucratic words get in the way. Indeed, Benally perceives Abel's central problem as one of words, as he equates finding community with having appropriate words:

> And they can't help you because you don't know how to talk to them. They have a lot of words, and you know they mean something, but you don't know what, and your own words are no good because they're not the same; they're different, and they're the only words you've got. . . . You think about getting out and going home. You want to think you belong someplace, I guess. (p. 144)

Tosamah perceives a similar dislocating effect of words on Abel, though he relates it to religion. Scorning his inarticulateness and innocence, he sees Abel as caught in "the Jesus scheme" (p. 136). Beyond his sermons, there is a special irony in the fact that Tosamah doesn't understand Abel and his problems, for he is described several times in Part II as a "physician."

Though they put Abel's problems in a broader and clearer perspective, Tosamah's words are of little use to Abel.

IV

Part III is told from the point of view of Ben Benally, a relocated Navajo who befriends Abel in Los Angeles. Roommates in Los Angeles, Ben and Abel share many things in their backgrounds. On his one visit to Walatowa, Benally finds the landscape there similar to that in which he grew up. Like Abel he was raised in that landscape without parents by his grandfather. Benally even suggests that he is somehow related to Abel since the Navajos have a clan called Jemez, the name of Abel's pueblo. Moreover, we recall that Abel's father may have been a Navajo, and that Francisco regards the Navajo children who come to Walatowa during the Fiesta of Porcingula as "a harvest, in some intractable sense the regeneration of his own bone and blood" (p. 72). This kinship gives Benally special insight into Abel's problems and strengthens his role as Night Chanter.[40]

Benally's childhood memories of life with his grandfather near Wide Ruins reveal a sense of place very like that Abel groped for on his return to Walatowa:

> And you were little and right there in the center of everything, the sacred mountains, the snow-covered mountains and the hills, the gullies and the flats, the sundown and the night, everything — where you were little, where you were and had to be. (p. 143)

Moreover, this sense of place gives him words: ". . . you were out with the sheep and could talk and sing to yourself and the snow was new and deep and beautiful" (p. 142).

In Los Angeles, however, Benally's sense of place is lost in his idealism and naïveté. Return to the reservation seems a pale option to the glitter of Los Angeles. "There would be nothing there, just the empty land and a lot of old people, going noplace and dying off" (p. 145). Like Milly, Benally believes in "Honor, Industry, the Second Chance, the Brotherhood of Man, the American Dream. . ." (p. 99). Theirs is a 50s American Dream of limitless urban possibilities. Benally believes you can have anything you want in Los Angeles and that "you never have to be alone" (p. 164). Yet in the very scene following his reflection on this urban cornucopia, we find Benally excluded even from the community of The Silver Dollar, counting his pennies, unable to buy a second bottle of wine. Idealism obscures Benally's vision, even as Tosamah's cynicism obscures his.

Nevertheless, Benally is the Night Chanter, the singer who helps restore voice and harmony to Abel's life. In the hospital having realized the significance of the runners after evil, Abel asks Benally to sing for him:

> "House made of dawn." I used to tell him about those old ways, the stories and the songs, Beautyway and Night Chant. I sang some of those things, and I told him what they meant, what I thought they were about. (p. 133)

The songs from both the Beautyway and the Night Chant are designed to attract good and repel evil. They are both restorative and exorcising expressions of the very balance and design in the universe Abel perceived in the runners after evil. Ben's words from the Night Chant for Abel are particularly appropriate, since the purpose of the Night Chant is to cure patients of insanity and mental imbalance.[41] The structure and diction of the song demonstrate the very harmony it seeks to evoke. Dawn is balanced by evening light, dark cloud and male rain by dark mist and female rain. All things are in balance and control, for in Navajo and Pueblo religion good is control. Further note that a journey metaphor is prominent in the song ("may I walk. . . .") and that the restorative sequence culminates with "restore my voice for me." Restoration of voice is an outward sign of inner harmony. Finally, note that the song begins with a culturally significant geographic reference: *Tségihi*. One of its central messages is that ceremonial words are bound efficaciously to place. No matter how dislocated is Benally or idiosyncratic his understandings of Navajo ceremonialism, the songs he sings over Abel clearly serve a restorative function.

Angela also visits Abel in the hospital and offers him words. She tells Abel the story her son likes "best of all" (p. 169). It is a story about "a young Indian brave," born of a bear and a maiden, who has many adventures and finally saves his people. Benally marvels at the story which reminds him of a similar story from the Mountain Chant told to him by his grandfather.[42] Yet unlike the Navajo legend and the Kiowa bear legend told by Tosamah earlier (pp. 120–21), both etiological legends tied firmly to cultural landscapes, Angela's story is as rootless as a Disney cartoon. Abel seems to realize this, if Benally does not, for he does not respond to Angela. Benally couldn't tell what he was thinking. He had turned his head away, like maybe the pain was coming back, you know" (p. 170). Abel refuses to play Angela's game a second time.

V

Part IV opens with a description of a grey, ominous winter landscape. Olguin is reflecting on his seven years' service at Walatowa. He claims to have grown "calm with duty and design," to have "come to terms with the town" (p. 174). Yet he remains estranged from the village; it is not his place. He measures his achievement in the language of commerce, noting with his predecessor Nicolas V what good works "accrued to his account" (p. 174). Like Angela who was offended that Abel "would not buy and sell" (p. 35), Olguin seeks to at least make good the "investment" of his pride.

Whereas Abel looks to Benally's Night Chant for restoration Olguin seeks and claims to find restoration from the journal of Nicolas. In that same journal we recall Nicolas V himself sought restoration of his Christian God:

> When I cannot speak thy Name, I want Thee most to restore me. Restore
> me! Thy spirit comes upon me & I am too frail for Thee! (p. 48)

The passage leaves off in a fit of coughing and seems a singularly ineffectual
request.

At the same time Abel sits with his dying grandfather. Though Francisco's voice had been strong in the dawn, it now grows weaker and fades as it
has on each of the six days since Abel's return to Walatowa. The few words
Francisco does speak, in Towa and Spanish, juxtapose in the manner of
Parts I and II the memory fragments which Abel seeks to order in his own
mind. Francisco is here, as Momaday suggests, "a kind of reflection of
Abel."[43] The passage translates:

> Little Abel . . . I'm a little bit of something . . . Mariano . . . cold . . . he
> gave up . . . very, very cold . . . conquered . . . aye [exclamation of
> pain], Porcingula . . . how white, little Abel . . . white devil . . . witch
> . . . witch . . . and the black man . . . yes . . . many black men . . . run-
> ning, running . . . cold . . . rapidly . . . little Abel, little Vidal . . . What
> are you doing? What are you doing?

As the seventh dawn comes these words grow into coherent fragments in
Francisco's memory and serve as a final statement of the realizations about
the relation of place, words, and community Abel has had earlier in the
novel.

Each of the fragments is a memory of initiation. In the first Francisco
recalls taking Abel and Vidal to the ruins of the old church near the Middle
to see "the house of the sun."[44]

> They must learn the whole contour of the black mesa. They must know it
> as they knew the shape of their hands, always and by heart. . . . They
> must know the long journey of the sun on the black mesa, how it rode in
> the seasons and the years, and they must live according to the sun appear-
> ing, for only then could they reckon where they were, where all things
> were in time. (p. 177)

This is the sense of place Abel lost in "the intervention of days and years
without meaning, of awful calm and collision, time always immediate and
confused" (p. 25). As he is instructed to know the shape of the eastern mesa
like his own hands, it is appropriate that in the *corre de gaio* the albino
should first attack his hands (p. 44), that in the murder scene (and Abel's
memory of it) hands should be so prominent (pp. 77–79, 94), and finally
that as he lies on the beach after Martinez's brutal beating of his hands, Abel
should think of Angela's effect on him in terms of hands (p. 94). The relation to place taught him by Francisco is broken by each, as are his hands.
Now through Francisco's memory Abel is re-taught his ordered relation to
place and how it is expressed in "the race of the dead" (pp. 185–86). Abel
similarly participates in Francisco's memories of his initiation as a runner
(in the race against Mariano pp. 187–88), as a dancer (from which he
gained the power to heal pp. 186–87), as a man (with Porcingula, "the child

of the witch" pp. 184–85), and as a hunter (as he stalks the bear pp. 178–84).

All signs then point to a new beginning for Abel as he rises February 28, the last day of the novel. His own memory healed by Francisco's, for the first time in the novel he correctly performs a ceremonial function as he prepares Francisco for burial and delivers him to Father Olguin.[45] He then joins the ashmarked runners in the dawn. Momaday comments on that race in his essay "The Morality of Indian Hating:"

> The first race each year comes in February, and then the dawn is clear and cold, and the runners breathe steam. It is a long race, and it is neither won nor lost. It is an expression of the soul in the ancient terms of sheer physical exertion. To watch those runners is to know that they draw with every step some elementary power which resides at the core of the earth and which, for all our civilized ways, is lost upon us who have lost the art of going in the flow of things. In the tempo of that race there is time to ponder morality and demoralization, hungry wolves and falling stars. And there is time to puzzle over that curious and fortuitous question with which the people of Jemez greet each other.[46]

That very question — "Where are you going?" — must ring in Abel's ears as he begins the race. The time and direction of his journey are once again defined by the relation of the sun to the eastern mesa, "the house made of dawn." Out of the pain and exhaustion of the race, Abel regains his vision: "he could see at last without having to think" (p. 191). That vision is not the nihilistic vision of Angela — "beyond everything for which the mountain stands." Rather, Abel's "last reality" in the race is expressed in the essential unity and harmony of man and the land. He feels the sense of place he was unable to articulate in Part I. Here at last he has a voice, words and a song. In beauty he has begun.

Notes

1. "The Man Made of Words," in *Indian Voices: the First Convocation of American Indian Scholars* (San Francisco: Indian Historian Press, 1970), p. 55.

2. For surveys see Ermine Wheeler-Voegelin, "North American Native Literature," *Encyclopedia of Literature*, Vol. II, ed. Joseph T. Shipley, pp. 706–21; Mary Austin, "Aboriginal," in *The Cambridge History of American Literature*, ed. William Petefield Trent et al. (New York: Macmillan, 1945), pp. 610–34; and more recently Alan Dundes, "North American Indian Folklore Studies," *Journal de la société des Américanistes*, 56 (1967), pp. 53–79.

3. "A Conversation with N. Scott Momaday," *Sun Tracks: An American Indian Literary Magazine*, 2, No. 2 (1976), p. 19.

4. See Momaday's column "A Special Sense of Place," *Viva, Sante Fe New Mexican* (May 7, 1972), p. 2; D. H. Lawrence, *Studies in Classic American Literature* (1923; rpt. New York: Viking, 1964), pp. 1–8; Aldo Leopold, *A Sand County Almanac: With Essays on Conservation from Round River* (1949; rpt. New York: Ballantine, 1970), pp. 238–40; Eudora Welty, "Place in Fiction," *Three Papers on Fiction* (Northampton, Mass.: Metcalf, 1955), pp. 1–15; etc. The Autumn 1975 issue of the *South Dakota Review* is given entirely to a symposium and commentaries on "The Writer's Sense of Place."

5. *The Tewa World: Space, Time, Being, and Becoming in a Pueblo Society* (Chicago: Univ. of Chicago Press, 1969), p. 13.

6. Momaday, "An American Land Ethic," *Sierra Club Bulletin*, 55 (February 1970), p. 11.

7. *The Way to Rainy Mountain* (1969; New York: Ballantine, 1970). See also Momaday's "A First American Views His Land," *National Geographic*, 150, No. 1 (1976), pp. 13–18.

8. *Rainy Mountain*, p. 2.

9. Ethelou Yazzie, ed., *Navajo History* (Many Farms, Ariz.: Navajo Community College Press, 1971).

10. See Margot Astrov, "The Concept of Motion as the Psychological Leit-motif of Navajo Life and Literature," *Journal of American Folklore*, 63 (1950), pp. 45–56; and Gladys A. Reichard, *Navajo Religion: A Study of Symbolism*, 2nd ed. (1950); Princeton: Princeton Univ. Press, 1974), p. 19.

11. *Navajo History*, p. 57.

12. Leland Wyman, *The Windways of the Navajo* (Colorado Springs: The Taylor Museum, 1962), pp. 27–28; and the whole of Reichard's *Prayer: the Compulsive Word* (Seattle: Univ. of Washington Press, 1944).

13. *Rainy Mountain*, p. 42.

14. See P. E. Goddard, "Navajo Texts," *Anthropological Papers of the American Museum of Natural History*, 34 (1933), p. 127.

15. *Rainy Mountain*, p. 42.

16. Curley Mustache, "Philosophy of the Navajos," (Navajo Community College: mimeo, 1974), p. 11. Compare *Navajo Religion*, p. 289.

17. "A Conversation with N. Scott Momaday," p. 19.

18. Walatowa, "Village of the Bear," is the Jemez name for their village. See Frederick Webb Hodge, ed., *Handbook of American Indians*, Part I (1907; rpt. New York: Roland and Littlefield, 1965), p. 630. See Elsie Clews Parsons, *The Pueblo of Jemez* (New Haven: Yale Univ. Press, 1925), p. 136, for the formula; and Dennis Tedlock's discussion of the convention in "Pueblo Literature: Style and Verisimilitude," in Alfonso Ortiz, ed., *New Perspectives on the Pueblos* (Albuquerque: Univ. of New Mexico Press, 1972), pp. 219–42.

19. "An Interview with N. Scott Momaday," *Puerto del Sol*, 12 (1973), p. 33.

20. Parsons, p. 118.

21. The song first appeared in Washington Matthews, *The Night Chant: A Navajo Ceremony*, Memoirs of the American Museum of Natural History, 6 (1902); and in another version in Matthews, "Navaho Myths, Prayers, and Songs," University of California Publications in American Archaeology and Ethnology, 5 (1907), which was posthumously edited by Pliny Earle Goddard.

22. N. Scott Momaday, *House Made of Dawn* (1968; New York: New American Library, 1969), p. 11. Subsequent citations refer to the NAL edition and appear parenthetically in the text.

23. Compare the emergence log in *Rainy Mountain*, p. 1, and the reed in *Navajo History*, p. 9.

24. See Parsons' account of the Pecos migration in *Pueblo of Jemez*, p. 3. Note that one of the five Bahkyula making that journey was named Francisco. The genealogical relations of Abel are further defined in Part I by the journal of Nicolas V., through which the incidence of albinism at Walatowa is also established. See Parsons, pp. 49–50. Again note the name of one albino mentioned there, Juan Reyes Fragua, is also the name of the albino in the novel.

25. Carole Oleson, "The Remembered Earth: Momaday's *House Made of Dawn*," *South Dakota Review*, 11 (1973), p. 63; Harold S. McAllister, "Incarnate Grace and the Paths of Salvation in *House Made of Dawn*," *South Dakota Review*, 12 (1975), pp. 115–25.

26. See Mark Porter, "Mysticism of the Land and the Western Novel," *South Dakota Review*, 11 (Spring, 1973), p. 82. Angela is closely associated with the Roman Church throughout. She shares a brand of piety with Father Olguin and his predecessor Fray Nicolas V. which emphasizes the denial of the flesh. The links between Angela and Olguin appear even closer in an earlier version of parts of the novel where Angela appears with her mother and brother, one Fr. Bothene (Olguin?). See "Three Sketches from *House Made of Dawn*," *Southern Review*, 2 (1966), p. 941. Bothene reappears in "Cryptic Tale from the Past," a column in *Viva, Sante Fe New Mexican* (April 1, 1973), p. 7. There Momaday writes of Ellen Bothene, "an elderly matron;" Raoul Bothene, "a man of the cloth;" and Angela, "the less said about her the better."

27. San Diego is the patron of Jemez pueblo. Stories of him abound in Mexico and the American Southwest. Compare "The Adventures of San Diego," in Leslie White, *The Acoma Indians*, 47th ARBAE (Washington: G.P.O., 1932), pp. 180–89.

28. See Parsons, p. 95; and Edward Dozier, *The Pueblo Indians of North America* (New York: Holt, Rinehart, and Winston, 1970), p. 199. Parsons observed the *corre de gaio* on July 25, 1922. Note the corresponding day of the month in the novel. Another description of the rooster pull appears in Albert Reagan's novel *Don Diego* (New York: Alice Harriman Company, 1914) which is also set at Jemez.

29. Of the rooster pull at Acoma, Leslie White writes "It is said that rooster blood is 'good for rain,' " *The Acoma Indians*, p. 106.

30. The Benevides name seems to have come to the area with the Franciscan Fray Alonso de Benavides, author of a detailed report on the missionary effort in New Mexico. Benavides brags that "from the house of one old Indian sorcerer I once took out more than a thousand idols of wood, painted in the fashion of a game of nine pins, and I burned them in the public plaza." Frederick Webb Hodge, George P. Hammond, and Agapito Rey, eds. and trans. *Fray Alonso de Benavides' Revised Memorial of 1634* (Albuquerque: Univ. of New Mexico Press, 1945), p. 46.

31. *Teah-whau* means "people-hair" or "mustache."

32. Marion Willard Hylton, "On a Trail of Pollen: Momaday's *House Made of Dawn*," *Critique*, 14 (1972), p. 62; Oleson, p. 62.

33. Parsons, pp. 96–97.

34. See Leslie Fiedler, *The Return of the Vanishing American* (New York: Stein and Day, 1968), pp. 116–19; and Roy Harvey Pearce, *Savagism and Civilization: A Study of the Indian Mind and the American Mind*, revised ed. (Baltimore: Johns Hopkins Press, 1965), pp. 13–16.

35. Hamilton A. Tyler, *Pueblo Gods and Myths* (Norman: Univ. of Oklahoma Press, 1964), p. 226. See also the serpent as an integral part in Jemez iconography in Parsons, Plates 3, 5, 7, and elsewhere; and Reagan, pp. 4–5. Of Navajo witchery Kluckhohn writes: "several informants volunteered remarks such as 'witches are needed for rain — just as much as the good side' which would indicate that such malevolent activities are actually necessary to the natural equilibrium." See *Navajo Witchcraft* (1944; rpt. Boston: Beacon, 1967), p. 60.

36. There is slight evidence suggesting that Momaday based Abel's confrontations with evil in part on an actual case history. On Good Friday in 1952 two Acoma Pueblo men, Willie and Gabriel Felipe, killed Nash Garcia, a Mexican state policeman, near Grants, New Mexico. A part of their defense at the subsequent trial was the contention, supported by psychotherapist George Devereaux, that they perceived Garcia as a witch. See *Albuquerque Journal*, February 27, 1953. The killing is the basis for short stories by Simon Ortiz and Leslie Silko printed in Kenneth Rosen, ed., *The Man to Send Rain Clouds* (New York: Viking, 1974).

37. *Navajo Religion*, p. 5; see also Dozier, p. 200.

38. See my note "Further Survivals of Coyote," *Western American Literature*, 10 (1975), pp. 233–36.

39. Weston La Barre, *The Peyote Cult* (1964; rpt. New York: Schocken, 1969). Compare, for example, La Barre, p. 7, and Tosamah, p. 101.

40. Benally may once have framed the whole novel. Note the unmistakable diction which introduces "The Sparrow and the Reed" in "Three Sketches from *House Made of Dawn*," p. 933.

41. *Navajo Religion*, p. 12.

42. The very suggestive system of elder brother/younger brother analogies which runs through the novel — and is implicit here in the legend from the Mountain Chant — is worked out provocatively in relation to Navajo and Pueblo twins legends in Joseph E. DeFlyer's doctoral dissertation *Partition Theory: Patterns and Partitions of Consciousness in Selected Works of American and American Indian Authors* (Nebraska, 1974). See especially p. 231.

43. "An Interview with N. Scott Momaday," p. 34.

44. See Parsons, pp. 59–60, and figure 5.

45. See Parsons, p. 50.

46. *Ramparts* 3 (1964), p. 40.

Alienation and Broken Narrative in *Winter in the Blood*

Kathleen M. Sands*

The narrator of James Welch's *Winter in the Blood* suffers the malaise of modern man; he is alienated from his family, his community, his land, and his own past. He is ineffective in relationships with people and at odds with his environment, not because he is deliberately rebellious, or even immaturely selfish, but because he has lost the story of who he is, where he has come from.

Welch's narrator is an American Indian, but one who suffers more than the tensions of living on the margins of conflicting societies. He is an Indian who has lost both tribal identification and personal identity because he is cut off from the tradition of oral narration which shapes consciousness, values, and self-worth. He is a man whose story is confused, episodic, and incomplete because he has never received the story of those who came before and invested the landscape and the people with significance and meaning. Storytelling keeps things going, creates a cultural matrix that allows a continuum from past to present and future; but for the deliberately nameless narrator of *Winter in the Blood*, there is no past, no present, and certainly no future, only the chaos of disconnected memories, desperate actions, and useless conversation.

His dilemma is clear from the beginning of the novel. Welch is blunt as he reveals the barrenness of the narrator's perceptions of himself and his environment. As he walks toward his mother's ranch the narrator reflects, "Coming home was not easy anymore" (p. 2). The land he crosses is empty and abandoned: "the Earthboys were gone" (p. 1). The ranch buildings have caved in. Even at this own ranch, there is a sense of emptiness, especially in his relationships with his family: "none of them counted; not one

*Reprinted from *American Indian Quarterly*, 4 (1978), 97–106, by permission of the author.

meant anything to me. And for no reason. I felt no hatred, no love, no guilt, no conscience, nothing but a distance that had grown through the years" (p. 2). In fact, he reveals he no longer has feelings even about himself.

There is little for him to feel but pain. His injured knee aches; he is bruised and hung over; his woman has run off, taking his rifle and razor; his mother is abrupt and self-concerned; his ancient grandmother is silent. His memories give him no comfort: his father drunk and grotesquely frozen to death, his brother mangled on the road, his own bitter realization that his red skin, not his skill, had been the reason he got a job in the Tacoma hospital. Memory fails him totally as the events of the past stream through his mind in a nightmare collage. The story of his life is disordered, chaotic, and finally, to him, meaningless. As the narratives are broken, so is the man.

Welch develops the intensity of the narrator's sense of dislocation and alienation through the episodic nature of the narrative. In the first encounter between Lame Bull and the narrator, they recall a flood on the stream where the narrator is fishing. Lame Bull insists that it occurred when the narrator was not much more than a gleam in his father's eye. The narrator counters, "I remember that. I was almost twenty" (p. 8). The story is brief and terse; conflicting versions result in separation of the men rather than a sharing of a common event. The story does not work because it does not grow out of a shared perception. Other such episodes in the novel demonstrate the emptiness and distance created by separate stories or conflicting versions of the same one. Teresa and the narrator tell variants of the story of Amos, the one duck that survived the neglected water tub. Teresa's version is skeletal and the narrator becomes confused, mixing up Amos and the turkey. The retelling of the events creates confusion rather than clarity. Then, when the narrator asks his mother why his father stayed away so much, she is defensive and abrupt, switching the focus of the discussion to a recollection of First Raise's death. The narrator admits limply that he has little recollection of the event. The episode results not in shared grief or comfort but in Teresa's accusing her son of being a drifter too. The narrator is alienated again: "I never expected much from Teresa and I never got it. But neither did anybody else. Maybe that's why First Raise stayed away so much" (p. 21). This is a bitter resolution to the question which prompted the brief story.

The stories that might make the narrator understand his family and his history are either incomplete or contradictory. They increase his discomfort, frustrating his attempts to confirm his past and create a continuity of events from which to operate in the present. Even when recollections from the family past nudge his memories to the surface, he is unable to patch together satisfactory narratives within his own mind: "Memory fails" (p. 19).

The one story that he does recall, as he sits in the living room facing his grandmother, is her story. Memory does not fail the narrator here as he recalls in rich detail the circumstances of the telling and the events of the narrative: "When the old lady had related this story, many years ago, her eyes were not flat and filmy; they were black like a spider's belly and the small black hands drew triumphant pictures in the air" (p. 36). Traditional story-telling devices are themselves memorable to the narrator: gesture, animation, drama. And as Welch spins out the memory in the narrator's mind, he enriches the language with detailed images and melodious rhythms. The narrator's memories take on the color, logical sequence, and vitality of the traditional tale, all stylistic characteristics which are deliberately absent from the disturbing episodes which create conflict and further alienate the narrator. In recalling his grandmother's story of her youth he is struck with a kind of awe because "she revealed a life we never knew, this woman who was our own kin" (p. 34). He is caught up in the mystery of the past, in a yearning to know the complete story, and in a fear that he might lose what part of it he still holds. The memory is incomplete but it is not cause for confusion or recrimination. It is the single intact thread in the torn fabric of his history. It holds a promise of some continuity with the past, of pride in his Blackfeet ancestry. His grandmother, however, is silent now, lost in her own memories and physical frailties, and the narrator's memories of the story she told years before slip away, too fleeting to affect the practiced chaos of his life.

When the narrator heads for town, his confusion and misdirection intensify even more: "Again I felt that helplessness of being in a world of stalking white men. But those Indians down at Gable's were no bargain either. I was a stranger to both and both had beaten me" (p. 120).

The structure of the novel reflects the increased sense of disorientation in the terseness of the language and the separation of incidents. As the narrator's life lacks motivation, direction, continuity, the novel apparently does too. This merging of narrative and form allows the structure of the work to carry the theme as effectively as the narration itself. The airplane man becomes a key figure in the effectiveness of the episodic technique. He is a man with no past, no identity, no future, and, more importantly, no story to tell. "Well, that's another story," he says (p. 45), but he never tells the story. His hints and contradictions only puzzle the narrator further. The airplane man is the radical extreme of disorientation, dislocation, distrust, disillusionment, and disgust. The narrator is mildly fascinated by his wild plots, but he is also repulsed, instinctively aware of the severity of the man's disorder. The appearance of the airplane man marks the narrator's most frustrating and isolated period in the novel, so that even his encounters with women are without intimacy or emotion. They provide drunkenness without relief or elation, fights without victory. And all the while there are snatches of stories, traces of memories. The incompleteness of the stories and memories that disturbed him acutely at home has intensified so that life becomes a confusing and sterile nightmare: "There were the wanted men with ape faces, cuffed sleeves and blue hands. They did not look directly into my eyes but at *my mouth, which was dry and hollow of words.* They seemed on the verge of performing an operation. Suddenly a girl loomed before my face, slit and gutted like a fat rainbow, and begged me to turn her loose, and I found my own guts spilling from my monstrous mouth. Teresa hung upside down from a wanted man's belt, now my own belt, crying out a series of strange warnings to the man who had torn up his airplane ticket" (p. 52 italics added). The nightmare goes on; images and stories melt into one incomprehensible vision of chaos and mute desperation. The elements of a dozen stories have merged into a bizarre and terrifying reality that follows the narrator from sleep into consciousness. Not until the airplane man is arrested, still without having told his story or revealed his identity, has the narrator had enough of the town, and of himself: "I wanted to lose myself" (p. 125).

The time he has spent in the towns has not been without some benefit, however, for it is there that he is confronted again and again with the memory of his brother's death. The story of Mose's death is crucial to his confrontation with his personal past and the landscape that defines him. The story unfolds slowly in his mind. It is too painful to recall at once, so he pieces it together slowly. It too is episodic, but as with his grandmother's story, it is set apart from the alien world of the present by a detailed narrative and a richness of style absent from the action concerned with his search for his girl friend. The story, however, is left unfinished in the city. Not until the narrator returns to the reservation and cleanses himself of the town dirt and corruption can he face the pain of the remembered sequence of events that preceded Mose's death.

The final episode in the story is precipitated by two events that enable the narrator to complete the story. First, his grandmother has died during his absence and he shares the task of digging her grave with Lame Bull. As they rest he notices the grave of his father, with its headstone which tells only part of a story: "A rectangular piece of granite lay at the head of the grave. On it were written the name, John First Raise, and a pair of dates between which he had managed to stay alive. It said nothing about how he had liked to fix machines and laugh with the white men of Dodson, or how he came to be frozen stiff as a plank in the borrow pit by Earthboy's" (p. 137).

First Raise had been a man who told stories. Granted, they were stories to entertain the white men in the bars, but he had one story which had given him hope, a reason to live from year to year. Every fall he had planned to go hunting, had made elaborate preparations in his mind, and had told his sons of the deer he would shoot. It was a story to live on, but no gravestone could carry First Raise's story. That was up to the narrator. And Mose, the only other man the narrator was not alienated from, did not even have a grave marker. All that was left was the narrator's memory. Awareness of the grave and his recollection of the bone-chilling cold of winter send his memory back over the last few minutes of his brother's life. Even then, so close to the end, the memory breaks off as the narrator walks out to look at his brother's unmarked grave, returns to the house, picks up the nearly-full bottle of wine, and goes to the corral to saddle Bird. Then, as though some unconscious understanding of the power of the story still permeates his mind, he invents a story for Bird, surmising the terror the horse must have felt when it had been broken, empathizing with the animal fear and sympathizing with the age and loyalty of the animal, which in its terror of man had been conquered only by its comprehension of death: "You ran and ran for what must have seemed like miles, not always following the road, but always straight ahead, until you thought your heart would explode against the terrible constriction of its cage. It was this necessity, this knowl-edge of death, that made you slow down to a stiff-legged trot, bearing side-ways, then a walk, and finally you found yourself standing under a hot sun in the middle of a field of foxtail and speargrass, wheezing desperately to suck in the heavy air of a summer's afternoon . . . A cow horse" (pp. 145–46). In the invention of the story, Bird, the same horse he was riding when his brother was struck and killed, is forgiven for its part in the death through the narrator's comprehension of its instinctive acceptance of its role as cow horse: "No, don't think it was your fault — when that calf broke, you reacted as they trained you." The forgiveness allows the narrator to resume and complete Mose's story, "I didn't even see it break, then I felt your weight settle on your hind legs" (p. 146). At last there is no blame. He has forgiven the horse, helpless to reverse its instincts, and he has forgiven him-self in the process. Finally, he can grieve: " 'What use,' I whispered, cried for no one in the world to hear, not even Bird, for no one but my soul, as though the words would rid it of the final burden of guilt, and I found my-self a child again" (p. 146). A burden does remain, but it is the burden of grief, not guilt; the story has created a catharsis. The pain has been con-fronted and endured, and again, in the eloquence of the language and the merging of emotion, landscape, and tragedy, Welch has demonstrated that this story, as the story of his grandmother's youth, is essential to the narra-tor's comprehension of himself and his relationship to all that is past. The narrator's telling of his brother's death has been long and painful, a kind of logo-therapy, at least in part curative of the alienation and bitterness and distance he feels. True, the tears he sheds are solitary, but they are a demon-stration of feeling for his brother, and more importantly, for himself.

Having unburdened himself, the narrator moves on toward the iso-lated cabin Yellow Calf inhabits to tell the blind Indian of his grandmoth-er's death. He had been there twice before, once when he was a child, riding behind First Raise through a snow storm, and again before his trip to town. The first trip had seemed significant at the time, but his understand-ing of it was incomplete. He had known the old man was important, but he had been too young then to ask the right questions. The questions had lin-gered all those years though, and now on the third visit, he begins, "Did you know her at all?" (p. 151). Slowly, with prompting from the narrator, Yellow Calf tells the story of the bitter winter, the starvation, the shunning of the then-beautiful young wife of Standing Bear, the bad medicine the people associated with her after the chief's death. Finally, with the right questions, Yellow Calf tells how someone became her hunter and protector. The half-formed questions that the narrator has carried over two decades are suddenly answered. At the end of Yellow Calf's story, he thinks for a moment and in that moment the old horse farts: "And it came to me, as though it were riding one moment of the gusting wind, as though Bird had had it in him all the time and had passed it to me in that one instant of corruption. 'Listen, old man' I said. 'It was you — you were old enough to hunt!' " (p. 158). Now he knows: Yellow Calf and his grandmother were both Blackfeet; for twenty-five years they had met and loved; Teresa was their child; he was their grandson. The story that his grandmother had told meshed with the one completed by Yellow Calf, and with the completion the narrator knows himself.

The narrator laughs at Bird's fart, at the revelation of truth, at the amazing simplicity of the mystery of his beginnings which had eluded him for so long: "I began to laugh, at first quietly, with neither bitterness nor humor. It was the laughter of one who understands a moment in his life, of one who has been let in on the secret through luck and circumstance" (p. 158). Yellow Calf joins in the laughter, the laughter of relief that the story is finished and the mystery revealed, that he has lived long enough to pass his memory on to his grandson. It is the mutual laughter of the understanding of just one moment in time, but it is a beginning.

The story has done more than give the narrator a personal identity. It has given him a family, a tribal identity. It has invested the land with history and meaning, for Yellow Calf still lives in that place of the bitter winter, dwelling in harmony with the earth. The old man makes explicit the continuity of human history and the land: "Sometimes in the winter, when the wind has packed the snow and blown the clouds away, I can still hear the muttering of the people in their tepees. It was a very bad time" (p. 153). But it was also a memorable time, a time of such suffering that the land has taken on a sacred meaning for the old hunter, and in turn for the young man. The oral tradition of the people has been passed on to the alienated, isolated Blackfeet man and given him a continuity of place and character. The images that have lived for decades in the old man's mind have been transferred to the younger man: "And so we shared this secret in the presence of ghosts, in wind that called forth the muttering tepees, the blowing snow, the white air of the horses' nostrils. The cottonwoods behind us, their dead white branches angling to the threatening clouds, sheltered these ghosts as they had sheltered the camp that winter. But there were others, so many others" (p. 159). The story merges the past with the present, and the language is detailed and descriptive, at times poetic, meant to make the images indelible in the narrator's mind. Like his grandmother's story, Yellow Calf's story is "literary" in style. This rich style is used by Welch only in the two complete narrations in the novel, Mose's story and the combined stories of the old ones.

The two most important narratives in the novel come to completion in one day, both of them on the land where they began in real experience, and they offer the narrator a balanced and curative release of both tears and laughter, a sense of harmony with the earth, and an understanding of himself. But the reintegration of man into family, society, and the land is not accomplished in a moment, not even a moment of intense revelation; the rent fabric of life is not so easily repaired. Even as the secret of Yellow Calf is revealed, the narrator realized "there were others, so many others" (p. 159). Yet that very realization is in itself a sign of insight, and what he has learned gives him the capacity for imagination for the first time in the novel: "I tried to imagine what it must have been like, the two of them, hunter and widow. If I was right about Yellow Calf's age, there couldn't have been more than four or five years separating them . . . It seemed likely that they had never lived together (except perhaps that first winter out of need). There had never been any talk, none that I had heard . . . So for years the three miles must have been as close as an early morning walk down this path I was now riding" (pp. 160–61). His imagination crosses the boundaries of time, but it is linked to the land as he ponders the knowledge he has gained: "It was a good time for odor. Alfalfa, sweet and dusty, came with the wind, above it the smell of rain. The old man would be lifting his nose to this odor, thinking of other things, of those days he stood by the widow when everyone else had failed her. So much distance between them, yet they lived only three miles apart. But what created this distance? And what made me think that he was Teresa's father? After all, twenty-five years had passed between the time he had become my grandmother's hunter and Teresa's birth. They could have parted at any time. But he was the one. I knew that. The answer had come to me as if by instinct, . . . as though it was his blood in my veins that had told me" (p. 160). Inevitably there must be doubts left for the narrator, but one crucial question had been asked and firmly answered, opening the possibility for reintegration. If Yellow Calf and his grandmother had closed the distance, perhaps his feelings of distance from his family, his past, his people, his land were not unconquerable.

Two events at the end of the novel demonstrate the positive effect of the narrator's new comprehension of himself and his place within the social and physical environments. As he returns to the ranch, he is met by family friends who have come ostensibly to offer condolences but really to question him about the woman who had run away from him. In response to the query the narrator invents a story, saying that his "wife" had returned from Havre and is in the house. "Do you want to see her?" he challenges (p. 165). His imagination, once engaged, allows him to create a story of his own, one which at the end of the novel, he seems determined to turn from lie to fact when he says, "Next time I'd do it right. Buy her a couple of cremes de menthe, maybe offer to marry her on the spot" (p. 175). The projection is somewhat tentative, but the intent is to close the literal and emotional distance between himself and the girl and to make his story true.

The other event which dramatizes the effect of his new knowledge is the cow-in-the-mud scene. Despite the fact that he wants to ignore the stupid animal, he does not. He enters into a frantic struggle to save the cow, committing all his strength and energy to the task. In the process the pent up anger that has cut him off from his family and the land is spent. "What did I do to deserve this?" he asks (p. 169), meaning not just the job of saving the cow but all the suffering he has been through. He goes on, "Ah, Teresa, you made a terrible mistake. Your husband, your friends, your son, all worthless, none of them worth a shit . . . Your mother dead, your father—you don't even know, what do you think of that? A joke, can't you see? Lame Bull! The biggest joke—can't you see that he's a joke, a joker playing a joke on you? Were you taken for a ride! Just like the rest of us, this country, all of us taken for a ride" (p. 169). The narrator's anger is directed at himself, at everyone around him, at society, at the country. It is a bitter anger, but it is anger tempered by a sympathy and passion he had not demonstrated before. Earlier, he could say dryly that he never expected or got much from Teresa, but now he feels something for her, a mixture of anger and sympathy. He sees that she is a victim too. He sees beyond himself. His fury purged, he begins to move again saying, "I crouched and spent the next few minutes planning my new life" (p. 169). Having discovered the distant past in Yellow Calf's and his grandmother's story, having resolved the crucial event in his own past by reliving Mose's story, and now intently engaged in the physical present, he projects into the future. He verbalizes no projections and the dilemma of the moment re-engages him, but the very ability to consider the future is encouraging; coupled with his determination to find the girl who had left him, it signals a coming to terms with life that he has not been capable of before.

On another level the cow-in-the-mud scene reintegrates the narrator with the natural environment in a dramatic way. He has walked and ridden the land but has not been a part of it. Now he is literally sucked into it. As the earth has sucked First Raise and Mose into it, it now draws the narrator, so that symbolically he is linked with those who are now past, those for whom he feels the strongest emotional ties. In triumphing over the earth, he had become one with it. As the rain begins to wash the mud from his face, he wonders "if Mose and First Raise were comfortable. They were the only ones I really loved, I thought, the only ones who were good to be with. At least the rain wouldn't bother them. But they would probably like it; they were that way, good to be with, even on a rainy day" (p. 172). Though again he is alone, he is also at one with the earth and at peace with himself and his place on it.

James Welch's use of oral tradition in *Winter in the Blood* is a subtle one. He has adapted the traditional form to suit the needs and style of modern fiction. He has transformed it from an essentially narrative mode to one that carries the theme of reintegration of the alienated contemporary Indian. It is not, however, a simply thematic device to facilitate a positive ending in an essentially ironic, even cynical novel. The function of storytelling in Indian communities is to keep life going, to provide a continuum of the past into the present, to allow for the predication of a future. The narratives in *Winter in the Blood* are broken. Those which do come together are painful for teller and reader alike, and they do not promise a happy future. What they do provide for the narrator is knowledge and insight into the past, a painful acceptance of the present, and maybe, just maybe, the strength and understanding to build a future.

An Act of Attention: Event Structure in *Ceremony*   Elaine Jahner*

After reading Leslie Silko's novel *Ceremony*, many readers know the novel possesses an energy that engages their sense of themselves as persons. That energy seems to elude discussion because the labeling required in any kind of analysis appears more than usually inadequate for describing the act of attention that is an essential part of the reader's experience. But then there are those like myself who sense that trying again and again to talk about the quality of attention evoked by the book can be an important part of developing more sensitive understanding not only of Leslie Silko's own work but of other Native American writers who might also require of readers a particular attention directed toward matters that their previous experience of novels may not have demanded. Perhaps one way of describing the magnetic field of attention is to say that the lodestone in this field is the experience of event[1] rather than sequentially motivated action as the determinant of plot coherence; but that is too cryptic a statement to have much meaning without explanation.

In this context the word "event" has a specific meaning that is best described through looking at Silko's novel. Once event has been defined, we can contrast the nature of its structuring force with that of other, more commonly experienced ways of developing coherence within any novel. Since giving event structure priority over temporal structure seems to be a characteristic of art that is intimately related to an ongoing oral tradition, progress made toward understanding event may be progress toward understanding relationships between oral and written literatures.

One of the pivotal events in *Ceremony* is that which describes the protagonist Tayo singing the sunrise song after his first encounter with the mys-

*Reprinted from *American Indian Quarterly*, 5 (1979), 37–46.

terious woman. If we examine that passage, we can identify the essential features of Silko's sense of event:

> He stood on the steps and looked at the morning stars in the west. He breathed deeply, and each breath had a distinct smell of snow from the north, of ponderosa pine on the rimrock above; finally he smelled horses from the direction of the corral, and he smiled. Being alive was all right then: he had not breathed like that for a long time . . .
>
> Coming closer to the river, faintly at first, faint as the pale yellow light emerging across the southeast horizon, the sounds gathered intensity from the swelling colors of dawn. And at the moment the sun came over the edge of the horizon, they suddenly appeared on the riverbank, the Ka't-'sina approaching the river crossing. He stood up. He knew the people had a song for the sunrise . . .
>
> He repeated the words as he remembered them, not sure if they were the right ones, but feeling they were right, feeling the instant of the dawn was an event which in a single moment gathered all things together — the last stars, the mountaintops, the clouds, and the winds — celebrating this coming. (pp. 181–82).

Almost every aspect of the long quotation is significant. Tayo's experience of event is precisely realized in language replete with the most exact sensuous detail. There are distinct smells, sounds and colors, all qualities of definite and real places. Each detail shapes the way Tayo experiences this particular intersection of life and story. Ostensibly alone, Tayo does not experience the moment as isolation. He senses the presence of the Ka't'sina and knows he is in touch with very fundamental life forces. In this place, at this time, he gives them full recognition. His own act of attention is complete. We know from earlier developments in the novel that the place where he finds himself able to sing the sunrise song is a specific place, marked by the stars themselves. It is Tayo's center of the world, using that phrase in the sense in which it is used in American Indian ceremony. It is also an emergence place for him because he moves into a new level of experiencing his role in an all-encompassing story.

Tayo's participating in the sunrise event is both convergence and emergence. Past understandings of the meaning of experiences converge and permit emergence to new levels of comprehension, new parts of the story and new aspects of ceremonies. Events are boundary experiences marking stages of life for the protagonist. They also mark stages of the story for the reader who can experience their impact by relating to their significance as primary human experiences that are at one and the same time, acts of recognition and experiences of renewal of energies. As recognition, event implies pattern, form that is enduring yet specific as to time and place. As experience, it implies conscious participation in the dynamic energies that generate and perpetuate life and form. Both the pattern and the experience are, by their very nature, culturally specific; and it is at this level that a reader must bring his or her own cultural experiences into relation with those of the protagonist.

There is nothing of chance or absurdity in the meaning and experience of event which can only be experienced by one who knows how to recognize its signs. Such knowledge is by no means universal and the novel *Ceremony* has as its theme, the gaining of that knowledge. Furthermore, the novel itself is shaped by the processes that lead to the capacity to experience event in life or in art. The ebb and flow of narrative rhythm in the novel creates an event in the process of telling about event. The entire process is ceremonial, and one learns how to experience it ceremonially by achieving various kinds of knowledge attained not through logical analysis but through narrative processes that have their own epistemological basis.

Although many types of narrative function in *Ceremony*, jokes, personal experience stories, rumor, gossip, two major types of narrative shape the events of the novel and affect the way the other types interweave as they lead to different kinds of perception. These two types are the contemporary and the mythic tellings, the timeless and the time-bound narratives. The two are not independent of each other in that they constantly shape each other, but finding out how they interact is complicated by the fact that all which occurs in the time-bound framework is confused because the ways of knowing, the various kinds of narrative are all entangled. Reader and protagonist alike must learn to untangle, and the reader can follow Tayo from event to event by moving from poetry to prose and back again to poetry. Silko juxtaposes the mythic portions of the novel and the story of Tayo's efforts by stating the myth in poetic form to contrast with the prose that carries forward contemporary realizations of the meaning stated in poetic sections.

The first event of the novel occurs while Tayo is a soldier. The dense jungle rain, so different from rain in the desert, appears malevolent and Tayo curses it. When he returns home, there is drought and Tayo assumes responsibility for it, believing that his curse caused it. His belief derives from the fact that he knows or intuits the power of words in relation to myth but he follows the results of his powerful words to the wrong mythic prototypes. His experiences at this stage are like those of the character Auntie whose feelings are "twisted, tangled roots, and all the names for the source of this growth were buried under English words; out of reach. And there would be no peace and the people would have no rest until the entanglement had been unwound to the source" (p. 69). As the first poetic portion tells us, the mythic story is the source and it gives rise to ritual and ceremony, situations in which words bring things into being:

> See, it is moving.
> Thee is life here
> for the people.

> And in the belly of this story
> the rituals and the ceremony
> are still growing. (p. 2)

At the beginning of the novel, Tayo is sufficiently in touch with the nature of mythic life to recognize the potential significance of the first event of the novel—his cursing the rain. What he can not understand is the event's actual significance. Silko's description of the event clearly indicates both the convergence and the emergence aspects of its meaning. When Tayo acts out of a firm sense of event, he knows that his actions can not be insignificant; there is the experience of gathering together and moving on-ward:

> He started repeating 'Goddamn, goddamn!'; it flooded out of the last warm core in his chest and echoed inside his head. He damned the rain until the words were a chant, and he sang it while he crawled through the mud to find the corporal and get him up before the Japanese saw them. He wanted the words to make a cloudless blue sky, pale with a summer sun pressing across wide and empty horizons. The words gathered inside him and gave him strength. (p. 12)

What Tayo can not understand is the literal effect his words will have so he can not emerge from this first event into new levels of understanding without help from medicine men — help he receives later in the novel. Alien ways of looking at the world prevent a full understanding of the event experience. Entanglement is Silko's main metaphor for describing obstacles to the event experience, and its use in early sections of the novel helps readers sense the feeling and meaning of Tayo's need to truly understand the connections among acts that will lead him to full event experience. "He could feel it inside his skull — the tension of little threads being pulled and how it was with tangled things, things tied together, and as he tried to pull them apart and rewind them into their places, they snagged and tangled even more" (p. 7).

Reader and protagonist alike go from event to event trying to learn the connection between contemporary action and the mythic prototype. To perceive the wrong bonds is to be caught up in the wrong boundaries of experience and to misunderstand the nature of cause and effect. After the first event, the main patterns of imagery in the novel have to do with vaguely understood or false boundaries and relationships. Tayo knows he is caught between different ways of seeing relationships, and he senses that the real boundaries have to do with mythic prototypes: "Years and months had become weak, and people could push against them and wander back and forth in time. Maybe it had always been this way and he was only see-ing it for the first time" (p. 18). False boundaries lead to death and while he is in a state of confusion about the meaning of relationships, Tayo lives a kind of death in life: "He inhabited a gray winter fog on a distant elk mountain where hunters are lost indefinitely and their own bones mark the boundaries" (p. 15).

As he struggles with various conflicts and watches the drought-stricken land, Tayo remembers the actions narrated in the second poem of the novel which tells of the argument between Reed Woman and her sister Corn Woman, an argument that results in Reed Woman abandoning the present world and going to an earlier one so that the rain disappears. Because he knows that his actions have something to do with myth, Tayo blames himself for the drought. The relationship between cause and effect, though, is more complex than Tayo realizes; and the second section of the novel emphasizes what it means not to know the connections. In this section, the medicine man Ku'oosh helps Tayo understand both the fragility and the complexity of the connections and relationships. Both the imagery and the plot elements having to do with boundaries come together in the event that is the medicine man's ceremony. As always, Silko's description of time and place are specific. It is a windy afternoon: Tayo is at home but he must remember and mentally enter a cave near Laguna that he knows well. After the medicine man has led Tayo to an understanding of the meaning of his ceremony by making him remember the meaning of a particular place, he brings Tayo to a profound experience of not knowing. He explains the fragility of the world, the need for the telling of the story behind each word and he asks Tayo for his own story of the war—a story that Tayo can not convey to him. According to the medicine man, telling the entire story is the human responsibility; Tayo realizes the difficulties of the responsibility and becomes ill once again.

The imagery and action that cluster in the third section of the novel have to do with trying to evade responsibilities seemingly too big to be understood. Tayo has learned that the medicine man does not know the right bonds anymore. Tayo himself must search for them because, as the medicine man says, "It is important to all of us. Not only for your sake, but for this fragile world" (p. 36). With the theme of responsibility for searching for new links between prototype and contemporary action, there is also concentration on the meaning of the process of transmission of stories. Silko shows us that the transmission of such knowledge is a far more complicated process than scholars usually describe. Transmission involves not only the sharing of knowledge but the sharing of how the knowledge has been shaped through one's living with it. Any event by event analysis of the entire novel is impossible in a short paper but since all the specific events have to do with the learning process that is part of the transmission of knowledge about stories, I will simply sketch the learning process for subsequent events.

Some characters, like Harley, evade the responsibility that goes with the entire learning process. They accept quick solutions, quick magic, but they can not perceive the right relationships and boundaries. As one of the poems says,

They thought they didn't have to worry
about anything
They thought this magic
could give life to plants
and animals.
They didn't know it was all just a trick. (p. 48)

Unlike Harley, Tayo has known and loved people who knew how to make the right stories relate to the right points in the ongoing movement of life. One important teacher was his uncle Josiah. The phrase, "Josiah said," introduces the many sections of the novel that narrate Tayo's childhood learning about the meaning that event can have: " 'You see,' Josiah had said, '. . . there are some things worth more than money.' He pointed his chin at the springs and around at the narrow canyon. 'This is where we come from, see. This sand, this stone, these trees, the vines, all the wildflowers. This earth keeps us going' " (p. 45). Josiah understood the importance of the conjunction between the right place and the right time. Such respect for place and its relation to time is an important element in learning how to experience mythic knowledge which, in turn, leads to the event experience.

There was also a woman called the Night Swan who understood the need to seek for real boundaries in the life process. She understood too the need to relate one's understanding of real boundaries to one's capacity to feel. Her experiences with her first lovers had taught her only that some paths can not lead to emergence from anything: "She kept him there for as long as she could, searching out the boundary, the end to the power of the feeling. She wanted to prowl those warm close places until she discovered the end because at that time she had not yet seen that the horizon was an illusion and the plains extended infinitely; and up until that final evening, she had found no limit" (p. 85). The Night Swan taught Tayo that the experience I am calling event is the key to maintaining every form of life because it relates change and continuity. Some people, like Tayo and herself, are different. These people are part of change and the way in which these "different ones" experience event is a fundamental part of the way the prototypical myths remain a vital part of human life. She says to Tayo, " 'You don't have to understand what is happening. But remember this day. You will recognize it later. You are part of it now' " (p. 100).

Tayo does recognize it later when the teacher Betonie finally prepares him for the full experience of event and brings home to him the fact that learning the transmission process of myth involves learning to bring the meaning of all the changes he has experienced in life to the way he feels the stories. If he can bring the meaning of his actions to the way he feels the stories, then he will be attentive enough to sense the subtle shifts and movements that define the way the story takes shape through the people who allow it to come into their lives. When the story comes into lives, it sets the important boundaries because it shapes events that relate past to present, prototype to immediate experience. Through the ceremonies that Betonie performs for him, Tayo realizes a little more about how to allow story to shape his experience as event so that both he and the story remain alive. Through ceremony he begins to learn to feel the gathering of meaning that occurs in story: "He remembered the black of the sand paintings on the floor of the hogan; the hills and mountains were the mountains and the hills they had painted in sand. He took a deep breath of cold mountain air; there were no boundaries; the world below and the sand paintings inside became the same that night. The mountains from all the directions had been gathered there that night" (p. 145). In any event, space and time, inner and outer come together. The significant boundaries are between what and who are or are not part of the event; between what is gathered together and what is scattered.

Betonie also teaches Tayo that an important part of the experience of events is the experience of transitions: " 'There are balances and harmonies always shifting, always necessary to maintain. . . . It is a matter of transitions, you see; the changing, the becoming must be cared for closely. You would do as much for seedlings as they become plants in the fields' " (p. 130). Transitions are a part of the emergence phase. During the transitional times, Tayo must nourish the feelings that enable him to respond fully to events when their time and place has come. That there is a right time and right place and that these are specific, real places is something that Silko carefully establishes. One could document references to the right time and the right place for all the event experiences of the book, but the major ones are set with special care.

Betonie explains to Tayo that he must watch for the right mountain, the right stars and the right woman before he will be able to finish the Ceremony. When he finds the right conjunction of all, he is able to sing the sunrise song, the event quoted at the beginning of this paper. Once he comes to this intersection of time, place and story, Betonie's teachings become "a story he could feel happening—from the stars and the woman, the mountain and the cattle would come" (p. 186). Once Tayo has come to this realization, he is a conscious participant in the development of the story. He can shape the story because he understands something about the real boundaries that relate and separate actions and persons. He has many kinds of new strength when he can untangle the twisted roots of his thoughts and he knows that some things outdistance death and destruction:

> The mountain outdistanced their destruction, just as love had outdistanced death. The mountain could not be lost to them, because it was in their bones; Josiah and Rocky were not far away. They were close; they had always been close. And he loved them then as he had always loved them, the feeling pulsing over him as strong as it had ever been. They loved him that way; he could still feel the love they had for him. . . . This feeling was their life, vitality locked deep in blood memory, and the people were strong, and the fifth world endured, and nothing was ever lost as long as the love remained." (pp. 219–20)

Understanding and participating in event is knowing that vitality and love endure. This is Tayo's healing experience. He re-creates himself in creating the new boundaries in his life, not those of logic, but the traditional ones of story. Even witchery can be handled within the boundaries of story. It is only those events that do not seem part of any pattern at all which are utterly destructive. They intrude upon lives without preparation and rearrange them so that there can be no transitions among events and all pattern seems irrelevant; even ceremony appears irrelevant. But once the true pattern is perceived by those participating in it, the story goes on and the right ceremonies are in the belly of the story. The story perpetuates life and love; and people experience the story as event.

Through the narrative events of the novel, protagonist and reader gradually learn to relate myth to immediate action, cause to effect; and both reader and protagonist learn more about the power of story itself. The reader seeks to learn not only what happens to Tayo but how and why it happens. The whole pattern of cause and effect is different from most novels written from a perspective outside the mythic mode of knowledge. To employ myth as a conscious literary device is a quite different thing from employing the mythic way of knowing as the basic structural element in a novel as Silko does. But as they read the story, readers are not likely to analyze what kind of energy is at work; they continue reading because Silko is a skilled storyteller. Then, in direct proportion to the degree of their belief in mythic reality, critical readers are likely to distance themselves from the novel's world and begin to consider the nature of its impact. It is at this stage of inquiry that the concept of event structure can have meaning. Perhaps the experience of event is something all people have but the novel poses interesting questions. What constitutes the experience for different people in different cultures and how is it shaped by different kinds of narrative? More specifically, how does the novel as a particular kind of narrative function in shaping and describing event experience?

The critic Irving Buchen says that "the novel is not a defined but a discovered form."[2] In the context of Silko's writing we can carry this statement further and say that a certain type of novel is becoming a form (and forum) for re-discovering narrative potential in a contemporary context. For the traditional tribal artist, narrative forms have always had to do with particular ways of knowing and learning; they have not been mere objects of knowledge. The novel is a narrative genre well-suited for examining how the traditional ways of knowing function in a multi-cultural world where the meanings of narrative are often twisted and tangled. The novel can accommodate enough detail and can juxtapose enough different kinds of narrative to show how it is possible to untangle our responses to different ways of knowing and follow them to their experiential roots.[3] For that is what event is, a primary experience of sources of knowledge shaped not by logical concepts but by the action of story. Such an experience requires of readers a special act of attention that combines the oldest mode of attentiveness — the mythic mode—with a contemporary one shaped by our successive experience with novels. If we accept Dan Ben-Amos' characterization of any genre as a cluster of thematic and behavioral attributes,[4] then we can easily focus on the concept of event as a cluster of both thematic and behavioral attributes that are shaping an emerging type of American Indian novel, one that has interesting differences from other types of American novels because its emphasis is less on what is known than on how one comes to know certain things and because it demands an attentiveness from the reader that has less to do with grasping what the action is than it does with feeling how actions have meanings that live and grow according to the many different ways human beings have of knowing about them.

Notes

1. The term "event" has a long history in the criticism of narrative but it has no single, critical meaning. It is often used to refer to the duration of a given state of being. The following definition is typical. ". . . events are . . . complex structures consisting of states and a (change) relation over these states." Teunis van Dijik, *Some Aspects of Text Grammars* (The Hague, 1972) p. 308. The term, as defined in this paper, requires that particular elements be part of a state before that state is defined as event. But as in previous uses of the term, mine assumes that event is a basic unit of narrative structure.

2. "The Aesthetics of the Supra-Novel," in *The Theory of the Novel*, ed. John Halperin (New York, 1974) p. 102.

3. The whole concept of narrative modes as epistemological models that function in the novel is one that Barbara Hardy explores: "Narrative, like drama, lyric, or dance, cannot be regarded simply as an aesthetic invention used by artists in order to control, manipulate, order and investigate the experiences of that life we tend to separate from art, but must be seen as a primary act of mind transferred to art from life. The novel does not invent its structures but heightens, isolates and proceeds to analyze the narrative forms, methods and motions of perception and communication. Sometimes explicitly, always implicitly, the novel is concerned to analyze the narrative forms of ordinary life. *Tellers and Listeners* (London, 1975) p. 1.

4. "Analytical Categories and Ethnic Genres," in *Folklore Genres* ed. Dan Ben-Amos (Austin, 1976) p. 231.

The Killing of a New Mexican State Trooper: Ways of Telling an Historical Event
Lawrence J. Evers*

Do you see what happens when the imagination is superimposed upon the historical event? It becomes a story. The whole piece becomes more deeply invested with meaning.
                                        —N. Scott Momaday, "The Man Made of Words"

*This essay appears here in print for the first time by permission of the author. © Lawrence J. Evers, 1984.

On Good Friday in 1952 New Mexico state trooper Nash Garcia was killed and burned in his patrol car twenty miles from McCartys, New Mexico, deep in the Acoma reservation, and the following Monday two Acoma brothers, Willie and Gabriel Felipe, were arrested and charged with the murder. From the outset the killing stirred imaginations. Willie Felipe's confession printed on the front page of the *Albuquerque Journal* appeared a forced and inadequate explanation for the charred pile of bones and St. Christopher medal pictured sensationally above on the same page. Motive was the most persistent question in press coverage, the long hearings and trial, through the final psychiatric testimony in the case which gained the brothers a reduced sentence of life imprisonment early in 1953. The press, the court, the psychiatrists all looked for meaning in the event before they allowed it to sink into some slight chapter in the history of New Mexico. The small meanings they found were colored by the expectations of their professions and the majority community which they shared, and it remained for two Pueblo writers, in fictions published some twenty years after, to turn that small line segment of history into circles of form.

As fictions, Leslie Silko's "Tony's Story" and Simon Ortiz's "The Killing of a State Cop" have been noticed and praised.[1] Their editor writes: "It is interesting, and perhaps noteworthy, that two stories in this volume, by two different authors, deal with this same theme of violence and death of the white intruder."[2] The similarities of the stories *are* remarkable, all the more so against the background of N. Scott Momaday's *House Made of Dawn*. And it was initially an attempt to understand the curious relations of these imaginative accounts which took me back round to examine the records of the case on which they were based.[3] Records of the "United States vs. William R. Felipe and Gabriel Felipe" help us to see the role of the individual imagination in the creation of fiction, but they are of interest in their own right as well. Like Browning's Old Yellow Book, they preserve an intriguing variety of perspectives on a single event.

I

The barest account of the events of Friday, April 11, 1952, come to us through confessions wrung by F.B.I. agents from the Felipes early in the morning of April 14.[4] Both Willie, thirty-two at the time of the killing, and Gabriel, twenty-eight, were born at Acomita, New Mexico, where they were living then—Willie with his wife, Gabriel with his mother and step-father, Mariano Vicente. According to Gabriel's confession, the brothers borrowed their step-father's pickup, bought two pints of Tokay wine at Los Ritos bar on Highway 66, and drove with their 30-30s north of Acoma toward Mount Taylor to hunt deer the morning of the killing. After an eerie hunt, Willie returned with a small deer, put it on the floor in the cab, and they returned to Los Ritos to buy sandwiches and more wine. There they turned west to Grants. It was about 2:00 P.M.

We headed west on Highway 66 and I was driving. We had driven about 10 miles west from Los Ritos when I saw Nash Garcia parked in his state patrol car beside the highway. We drove on west about one mile and decided we had better not go to Grants with the deer in the pickup. William had deer blood on his pants so we decided to go home instead of going to Grants. I turned around and headed east on Highway 66, and I was driving about 65 or 70 miles per hour when we passed Nash Garcia still parked beside the highway. Garcia honked at us when we passed, and I stepped on the gas. And when we were about 1/2 mile east of where we passed Garcia, William looked back and said, "that patrol is following us." I looked and could see the state police car in the mirror. I drove on east to the McCarty road and turned south on McCarty road. Garcia followed us at a high rate of speed for about 7 or 8 miles, and I told William that Nash Garcia was the patrol chasing us and that he was the son-of-a-bitch that had put me in jail for drunk driving and for us to ambush Garcia and kill him. William said, "O.K., let's kill him, but not here as this is not a good place to ambush him." We drove on about five miles with Garcia following us until we came up to a hill which had rocks and trees on it, and I said to William, "This is it." I drove the pickup off the road toward the hill and hid it behind a cedar tree. William jumped out of the pickup, took a 30-30 rifle and ran into the ditch about 15 feet from the pickup. Just as Garcia stopped I heard William shoot one shot and then three fast shots and Garcia yelled, "I give up. Don't shoot." Garcia opened the car door and stepped out of his car and fell beside his car.[5]

Loading the body into the patrol car, the brothers drove the car deeper into the backcountry, hid it in a grove of pinyons, and returned to spend the night at their mother's home. In the morning, Gabriel, carrying Garcia's revolver in his suitcase, went to Albuquerque with his mother and stepfather. Willie returned to the hidden patrol car, piled the front seat with dry cedar, and set the wood on fire. The following evening—Easter Sunday—he was arrested at Acomita. Gabriel remained free another day until, ironically, he was arrested on the streets of Albuquerque by a cousin of Garcia's.

The circumstances under which these confessions were obtained were questionable as their very language suggests, a matter I shall return to. However, in terms of the above reconstruction, the central motivation for the killing was clearly an old grudge given circumstantial intensity by alcohol and guilt at poaching a deer. Later in a statement given to psychiatrist Robert Navarre, Gabriel recalled the source of the grudge. He had been working for the railroad near Lincoln, Kansas, and had returned home.

All of us Acoma Indians come home. I went to Grants to pick up a mattress, I got drunk, and I sit in a car with three other Indian boys. A patrolman come to where we were parked on the side of the street. This is the same patrolman I got in trouble with later [Garcia]. He asked us what we were doing. We say, "nothing." He say, "drinking?" We say, "no." He search us and find bottle. He arrest us for drunk driving. This patrol always bother Indians. We were by road, not driving.[6]

Garcia's prior record with Indians in general and Gabriel in particular was of scant interest to the Albuquerque press as they rushed to report the sensational killing and eulogize the first officer slain in line of duty in the state. Garcia, it was reported, had been a popular officer in Grants, and in the pages of the *Albuquerque Journal* and *Star* his stature grew. He entered law enforcement as a deputy sheriff in Albuquerque, joining the state police force about eight years before the killing. Garcia advanced to the rank of Captain and for a time was in charge of state police detachments in the Sante Fe area. Ben Chavez, an Albuquerque city patrolman, former neighbor, and friend of Garcia, praised him to the *Albuquerque Journal*: "When Nash was made Captain in 1948, he won it through merit. He was one of the best men in the district. A good man, a sincere man, faithful to his superiors, he believed in policework as a profession."[7] The remark punctuated two large pictures on the same front page which bore the caption:

> Held in ambush killing—Willie Felipe shows State Police Chief Joe Roach the remains of Patrolman Nash Garcia near Grants. Roach lowers his head and chokes back tears as he views the ashes—all that was left of his fellow officer when Garcia was shot down in a hail of bullets and then burned.

Garcia seems to have come to Grants in exile, though, after being demoted to patrolman. His brother Pete blamed the demotion on politics and jealousy and recalled that Garcia "was broken hearted when he was demoted and transferred two years ago."[8] Yet the press was mute about the circumstances surrounding the demotion and transfer, focusing rather on such comments from Garcia's superior officer as "He didn't have a chance to use his gun. They shot him down like a dog."[9] On April 15, a front page picture in the *Albuquerque Journal* showed Garcia with two small children. The caption read: "Nash was their godfather and hero." On April 17, the papers report a hero's funeral for Garcia. His bronze casket approached the church in a 1300 car procession while fifty uniformed state policemen and thirty city policemen and sheriff's deputies gave the final salute. "Hushed citizens along the street removed their hats at the passing of the bier," and "the crowd at the church overflowed onto the front steps." Joseph Montoya spoke at the graveside as the State of New Mexico buried a hero.

Heroes are not created idly. More often than not, they come to being to serve some political cause. So too in this case, though the emotional force generated by the death and memory of Nash Garcia, "godfather and hero," diffused in surprising directions. Sixties liberals might predict lynch mobs and a rebirth of Kit Carson style Indian control programs. But response was not so clear cut, a reflection of wavering federal Indian policy of the time. Indians were viewed with increased regard then, we recall, following their dramatic performances in World War II. Navajo was our unbreakable secret code, Ira Hayes toured the country with a Medal of Honor, even Willie Felipe wore a Bronze Star. And federal efforts to reward them with admission to the urban splendors of the fifties through relocation programs were well underway. Yet Indians remained wards. "I have lived with them. I know them. They are children," said one prospective juror during jury selection for the Garcia case.[10] More consistently in the documents of the case the brothers and all Indians are called "boys." They are viewed as possessing a kind of cultural immaturity, so that in assigning responsibility for the killing, the press looked not to the Felipes but rather to those who influenced them, their legal guardians.

Alcohol provided a convenient focus for the search. Early reports of the killing give the bottles of Tokay a special prominence, and liquor is clearly blamed for the act. Even "the grim-faced residents of Grants— where Garcia was well-liked—put part of the blame upon persons who sell liquor to Indians."[11] Accordingly, one of Governor Edwin L. Merchem's first responses to the case was to call State Liquor Director Elfego Baca onto the carpet. And Baca responded quickly. On April 18 charges were filed against Nepomucena Sanchez, owner of El Cerritos Bar, for allegedly selling liquor to the Felipes. Manuel Ortiz, operator of La Mesita Bar in the same area, was also charged with bootlegging liquor to Indians as similar investigations spread throughout the state.[12]

The political uses of the murder went well beyond a shakeup in the state liquor commission, however. The *Albuquerque Journal* editorialized in an early news story on the case: "Garcia's brutal slaying flung a challenge at federal and state law enforcement. It boils down to what the officers will do about the problem in Northwestern New Mexico with its complicated troubles of Indian lands and white cities."[13] The problem of course derived from the peculiar legal topography of reservation border area where a muddle of federal, state, private, and Indian allotment lands created jurisdiction troubles. Properly, federal officers had jurisdiction over federal and federal trust lands, while state officers (like Nash Garcia) reigned on state and private lands. Customary agreements with tribal officials (in this case the governor of Acoma Pueblo) allowed state officers to respect or ignore the boundaries as convenience dictated. In any case, the "challenge" posed by the press displaced any racial tensions generated by the murder with bureaucratic ones. Governor Merchem suggested that Bureau of Indian Affairs law enforcement efforts "have been nil," and righteously replaced Garcia with two men.[14] Federal officials reacted defensively and in kind. The memory of a heroic Garcia, the need to find influences that made the "boys" go wrong, and a flurry of political bickering suppressed any attempt by the press to deal with the more complex cultural aspects of the case.

II

The trial of the two brothers opened September 22, 1952, at Sante Fe with the Honorable Carl A. Hatch, U.S. District Judge, presiding in open court. U.S. Attorney Maurice Sanchez represented the government; Albuquerque attorneys Phillip Dunleavy and A. T. Hannett—himself a former governor of the state—represented the Felipes. Prior press treatments of the killing were felt in the courtroom. While a number of prospective jurors were excluded because they objected to the death penalty, each of the twelve Anglo males seated admitted freely to having followed the case in area newspapers. Judge Hatch repeatedly overruled Dunleavy's objections to this knowledge as prejudicial. When jury selection was complete, Hatch summarized: "All the jurors stated that they could and would lay aside anything they had read and decide the case solely upon the evidence."[15]

In all, the evidence presented at the trial from which the jurors were charged to decide the case bore striking resemblance to the newspaper accounts they were instructed to disregard. The prosecution labored to tell the events of the killing with gruesome realism. At one point Sanchez introduced a movie taken from a patrol car following the chase route that led to the scene of the killing, as he attempted to paint the crime as the "blackest in the history of the state."[16] Despite a few sensational remarks of their own and despite frequent objections, the defense brought a weary fatalism to the trial, echoing the apologetic motivations proffered in the Albuquerque newspapers.[17] The brothers had killed Garcia, admitted Dunleavy, but they did so possessing a "very low grade intelligence" and under the influence of alcohol. Therefore they were not responsible for their actions; they were temporarily insane.

To establish patterns of alcohol use and the level of Willie's intelligence, Dunleavy called not only expert professional testimony but also members of Felipe's family. He probed Willie's war record at length, as a key defense strategy appears to have been to establish the profound change service in the war had on Willie. Pabilita Vicente, Felipe's mother, testified that "when he came back, he was a changed boy. I could not understand that he was so different, that his behaviour wasn't good. . . . And it seemed like he learned that [to drink alcohol] in the army."[18] Mariano Vicente, Willie's stepfather, similarly testified to a "tremendous change" in Willie on his return from the war.[19]

Willie himself recalled that he was reluctant to go into the Army: "I was called by the draftboard and I didn't want to join the Army, and they had a little time in hunting me. But I finally got into the service when they found me."[20] Once inducted, Willie served the Infantry in the 37th Division well. His service earned him a Bronze Star awarded April 28, 1944, for meritorious service at Bougainville, Solomon Islands. The citation, introduced as evidence at the trial, reads in part:

> Throughout enemy attack PFC Felipe was a gunner in a light machine gun squad. His pillbox bore the brunt of the enemy's small arms and automatic fire, and was only fifty yards from the nearest enemy held pillbox. PFC Felipe manned his gun throughout the entire battle, delivering steady and murderous fire throughout. He refused all offers of relief. Later he volunteered on ammunition and food carrying parties over a

route through open trenches and was subject to enemy sniper and knee mortor fire.[21]

Discharged in October of 1945, Willie re-enlisted within a year to serve as a truck driver. A superior noted on his papers: "likes Army, and would like to make it a career."

Yet a distinguished warrior does not make a distinguished truck driver. Following his reenlistment, questions were raised about Willie's ability to serve in his new role. In March of 1947 he was discharged for "inaptness." It was on this "inapt" image that the defense rested its case, coupling it with a final attempt to shift accountability to the brothers' guardians: "The real criminal was the bootlegger who gave these boys the liquor."[22] The whole of the defense argument was ruled irrelevant by Judge Hatch. In his instructions to the jury, Hatch ordered them not to consider drunkenness or mental ability as factors in determining temporary insanity, and the jury quickly found the brothers guilty of first degree murder. On October 17, 1952, Hatch sentenced them to die in the electric chair in Sante Fe.

III

In an effort to substantiate an appeal, the defense had the Felipes transferred to the United States Department of Justice Medical Center in Springfield, Missouri, for psychiatric examinations, and it was there that a deeper cultural context for the killing began to unfold. One of the first matters the federal psychiatrists reviewed were the confessions I have quoted. Dr. George Devereux wrote of the confessions:

> It is absolutely certain that this inmate [Willie] is materially unable to understand many of the words contained in his confession and the long sentences it contains. Regardless of whether the confessions are true or not, he signed a document which he did not understand as to content, and whose significance for his fate he was unable to evaluate properly.[23]

Trained in both anthropology and psychiatry, Devereux was unusually qualified to examine the brothers, and he pushed beyond the particular problem of the confessions to larger linguistic and cultural considerations which had been ignored in the trial.[24] He pointed out that one had to know Acoma culture to understand what the brothers meant by any given English word, thereby questioning the validity of previous testing of Willie:

> To us a "bear paw" is just a bear paw. To him this expression, which, I understand, appears in one of his Rorschack tests, has a special meaning: bear paws are used in Acoma curing rituals. If he says "mother," he can mean either his mother or his mother's sister, etc.[25]

But more directly related to the killing, argued Devereux, were the brothers' dreams and witch beliefs. He diagnosed Gabriel as a psychopath, one who compensated for a sense of inadequacy in fantasy through persecutory ideas of "being misunderstood," "picked on," and "envied." Gabriel was convinced that people envied him for his large flocks of sheep and therefore sought to harm him by gossip and by witchcraft. This Devereux notes is an "abnormal attitude for an Acoma Indian" in one important respect: Gabriel's feeling that witches had to be dealt with privately, instead of calling in one of the Acoma medicine societies who are supposed to deal with such matters. Gabriel, for example, told stories of his uncle's behavior that he considered normal:

> His uncle saw one night a large and a small fox — the latter being the "guardian" of the large fox — attack his flock. The uncle pursued them, and found two witches in human shape who had beside them foxskins, showing that they had just resumed human shape. (*Real* transformation, not just casting off a foxskin is meant.) They pleaded to be let off, but the uncle shot them.
>
> His uncle saw three deer: one male, two female, whose actions suggested that they were witches. He pursued them and when he saw them in human shape, despite their pleas, he shot them.[28]

These actions Gabriel considered natural, whereas, according to Devereux, a normal Acoma would have called in a medicine society: "The normal Acoma considers witchcraft a public matter. This inmate considered it a private grievance."[27] In addition to regular persecution dreams Gabriel told Devereux that he was bothered by hearing whistling sounds at night that were not heard by others: "although he was somewhat vague at this point, he seemed to say that ghosts converse by whistling."[28] In view of these factors and his entire examination, Devereux concludes his report on Gabriel with an inferential reconstruction of his state of mind during the killing:

> The evening before [the offense], the inmate was frightened by the ominous hooting of owls — birds of ill omen in Acoma culture. He was also quite drunk. During the hunt [the morning of the killing] he saw at thirty yards a large antlered deer — shot at it — thought he hit it, but the deer disappeared. When he went to the spot he saw no tracks, although he is a good tracker. This suggested to him — quite frighteningly — that he had had an experience with a witch-deer. . . . The pursuit itself [by Garcia] startled and frightened him a great deal, since being pursued is one of his principal nightmares. It is interesting to note that although they had outdistanced the police car, they stopped. One of Gabriel's nightmares is that of being pursued and being unable to get away and, for reasons of internal, neurotic motivation, *could* not get away. By the time he stopped the pick up . . . he was temporarily insane.[29]

As in his examination of Gabriel, Devereux argued that Willie Felipe was psychotic on the basis of his transformations of cultural beliefs about witchcraft into private, personal, and paronoic ideas.[30] People on the Acoma reservation hated and envied him and caused him trouble by witchery. "Sent" illness (witchcraft) killed his child. Fox-witches tore out the throat of several of his sheep but did not eat them. Like Gabriel, he believed that his maternal uncle had trouble with three witch-deer, and that the morning of Garcia's killing Gabriel shot at a witch-deer. But Devereux shows that Willie's problems were more deeply entwined with the psychological history of his family. Willie spoke poignantly of the return of an elder brother from the service:

> He lost his heart. The Indian doctors went out and brought his heart back and he was supposed to swallow it and chew it, but my brother chewed it and he did not get any better. The Indian doctors burned special weeds and my brother swallowed the smoke and then he was supposed to throw up his bad heart and bad spirits and feel better. The Indian doctors did this four times in four days, but he did not get better and he died in the state hospital in Colorado.[31]

Willie believed that his natural father Santiago Felipe, who had died some years before of a fall from a cliff, appeared to his maternal aunt and his sister with the top of his body transformed into a mountain lion, and that the aunt caused his father to die by supernatural means. Willie told Devereux that he knew this because when the corpse of his father was found in the cleft of a rock, he had an "old hole" in his side which had been plugged.

Willie believed that the killing of Garcia was not an act of the free will, but the result of having been witched. He had recurring anxiety dreams about being pursued. Sometime before the killing, he reported to Devereux that he had had a terrible dream of being pushed off a cliff. He considered this dream to be an omen of something terrible to happen.[32] Devereux recreated what did happen in Willie's mind on April 11, 1952, as follows:

> Each human being has a touchy point little related to reality. In this case of this man being pursued was about the worst thing that could happen to him, especially when it came on top of an anxiety dream and an encounter with a witch-deer — and under the influence of alcohol. On top of all this, he was pursued by a *black car,* which he related to the ominous black car which he had hallucinated sometime earlier near a salt lake. At this time the patient was in a state of *insane fear,* to such an extent that he is convinced that the black car was *flying* after him. (I carefully ascertained that he meant "flying" literally, and not in the sense of "going fast.") To the inmate this pursuit was a witch experience, triggering off temporary insanity. In reply to what he saw when he aimed, looking down the barrel, he replied, in obvious confusion: "Something black — just a black car — something black." When asked the color of the trooper's uniform he hesitated and had great trouble recalling that it was black. As far as the inmate knows now, he shot simply at something black: a black car which pursued him.[33]

In sum, Devereux argued in his report to the court that previous legal tellings of the killing were culturally blind, as they ignored the compelling psychic factors which moved the Felipes to kill Nash Garcia. He cautioned that while Indian beliefs are sometimes mistaken for delusions, in this case the danger was the reverse: that the delusional character of Indian beliefs, as held by the Felipes, might be mistaken for "normal" Acoma belief. The degree and manner of the brothers' witch beliefs marked them as psychotic rather than cultural in character.

Devereux's report was offered to Judge Hatch in an effort to obtain another trial for the Felipes. The new evidence of a supernatural context for the murder gained the Felipes not a second trial but a final headline and a reduced sentence.[34] On March, 3, 1953, Judge Hatch spared them the electric chair and sent them to prison for life.

IV

Writers of fiction and storytellers are united in their need to imagine historical events. Even as the pages of the *Albuquerque Journal* yellowed and the Felipe brothers' trial record slipped into the federal storage center in Denver, memories of the Nash Garcia case lived in rumor along Highway 66. The rumors solidified into a legendary image of Garcia very different from the journalistic image I have reviewed. Leslie Silko recalls:

> This one rumor was that he hated Indians and that he'd been transferred to the Laguna area from near Cuba or Sante Fe because his superiors already knew he was psychotic about Indians. Another story was that his own family admitted that there was something haywire with him, and he got what was coming to him.[35]

In a recent visit to Laguna-Acoma High School, Silko found that well over half the children she read to were aware of this image of Garcia. Five years old when the Felipe brothers were sent to prison, what Silko knows of the case is based on these tellings of the killing she heard as she grew up at Laguna. The rumor image of an Indian-hating Garcia is evident in "Tony's Story," as are the bare bones of the event that we have viewed in newspaper accounts and the trial record: the returned veteran, the wine, the chase, the 30-30, the burning of the body. Throughout it is clear that Silko has very consciously shaped the event in her own mold.

A parched summer landscape is integral to Silko's design, and she shifts the time of the action from early spring to San Lorenzo Day late in summer. From the opening of the story, life on the reservation withers as the pueblo awaits overdue summer rains. But it is only as the brutal state trooper appears behind him on the highway that Antonio Sousea "knew why the drought had come that summer."[36] In the story's climactic scene Antonio is moved to act on that recognition, and he shoots the trooper. The sand soaks up the trooper's blood even as it had Leon's on the carnival grounds in the opening scene of the story.

> The tumbleweeds and tall yellow grass were sprayed with glossy, bright blood. He was on his back, and the sand between his legs and along his left side was soaking up the dark, heavy blood — it had not rained for a long time, and even the tumbleweeds were dying. (77)

As the trooper and his car burn, the story closes with rain clouds gathering in the west.

Silko also shapes her characters carefully. The Felipe brothers of fact become types no less a pair for their lack of a blood relation. Tony is the younger, yet a traditionalist, deferential even in his final action. Leon is aggressive, a war veteran. He talks too loudly, shakes hands like a whiteman, and drinks boldly in defiance of the whiteman's law. In conflict with the trooper, Leon looks to his "rights" and "letters to the BIA" for support; Tony to old Teofilo's stories and chants and arrowheads. As the "he" becomes an "it" for Tony, the trooper remains a "big Bastard" and a "state cop" to the end for Leon. Similarly, the historic Nash Garcia undergoes a transformation to become the state cop in "Tony's Story." Silko draws him as purely symbolic as the albino in N. Scott Momaday's *House Made of Dawn*. Like the albino, the state cop hides behind prominent dark glasses and speaks in a high pitched voice. And like the albino he is perceived as a witch.

The witch perception lies at the very center of Silko's telling of the event, giving it an eerie likeness to the Devereux report. The presence of the big cop lingers with Tony as he returns from the San Lorenzo Day carnival:

> Stillness breathed around me, and I wanted to run from the feeling behind me in the dark; the stories about witches ran with me. That night I had a dream — the big cop was pointing a long bone at me — they always use human bones, and the whiteness flashed silver in the moonlight where he stood. He didn't have a human face — only little, round, white-rimmed eyes on a black ceremonial mask. (72)

Later when Tony looks at the cop he sees only "the dark image of a man" which he avoids, remembering his parents' caution "not to look into the masked dancers' eyes because they would grab me, and my eyes would not stop." (73–74) Pursued by the cop in the final scene, Tony must look at the cop and his eyes do not stop until the cop's boy is in flames. Disposal of the witch-cop by burning is one of the few supernatural motifs Silko uses which Devereux does not mention in his analysis of Willie Felipe. Just as Willie Felipe has ominous dreams which foreshadow the killing of Garcia, so too Tony. As Felipe felt pursued by a black object and saw only a black object when he shot, so too Tony doesn't remember aiming and kills not a cop but a witch in a "strange form." But Silko was unaware of the Devereux report until well after publication of the story, and despite similarities, the two accounts of the killing are profoundly different. As I have noted, Devereux interpreted the Felipes' witch beliefs as aberrant by Acoma standards, as evidence of their psychosis. Linking the witch motif with the drought setting, Silko creates a psychological and cultural context in which Tony is drawn irreversibly to the killing. Tony's witch perception gives evidence of the persistence of cultural belief. By force of characterization and setting, Silko casts the act which rises from that belief in an affirmative tone.

V

If Leslie Silko's telling of the event gives form to Devereux's pyschologi-
cal telling, Simon Ortiz's "The Killing of a State Cop" does the same for
journalistic accounts. Twelve years old at the time of the killing and a resident of the reservation on which it occurred, Ortiz's experience with the
event was more immediate than Silko's. Accordingly, his story is more
faithful to the "facts" of the case. "The Killing of a State Cop" reflects the
rumored image of Garcia, but not to the exclusion of the tone of journalistic
accounts. In fact, Ortiz's description of the murder of Luis Baca rivals the
tellings of the *Albuquerque Journal* and prosecutor Sanchez in its graphic
detail. He emphasizes the deliberate fashion in which the brothers lured
Baca to the murder scene and evokes a sort of pathos for Baca as he dies: "He
called something like he was crying. 'Compadre,' he said. He held up his
right hand and reached to us." (107).

But while Ortiz describes the murder with a chilling realism, like Silko
he shapes our reaction to it through his art. One example of this is the way in
which he handles motivation. As in newspaper and trial accounts, blame
for the killing is most explicitly placed on the wine Felipe drank and the
craziness it created in him. Yet Ortiz's Felipe recognizes that in some fey
sense Baca *wanted* to die:

> Aiee, I can see stupidity in a man. Sometimes even my own. I can see a
> man's drunkenness making him do crazy things. And Luis Baca, a very stu-
> pid son-of-a-bitch, was more than I could see. He wanted to die. And I,
> because I was drunken and *muy loco* like a Mexican friend I had from
> Nogales used to say about me when we would play with the whores in
> Korea and Tokyo, wanted to make him die. (106)

The psychological bond between Felipe and Baca suggested here is given a
faint supernatural tone by other details in the story. Felipe sees the same
disguised fear in Antonio while they wait to ambush Baca as when they
"were kids and he used to pretend not to be scared of rattlesnakes" (107).
After they shoot, Baca's car continues on in a preternatural way.

A key device Ortiz uses to mitigate our response to the killing is point of
view. The story is told by a young Acoma who like Ortiz was twelve years
old at the time of the killing. Felipe brothered the narrator. He took him
hunting and fishing and shared his plans with him. More importantly, Felipe told the boy stories, and, as a story, the telling of the killing was special
for Felipe wanted the narrator "to remember what he said always" (101).
Felipe's purpose in telling the killing to the boy was clearly didactic: "[Fe-
lipe] told me I better learn to be something more than him, a guy who
would probably die in the electric chair up at Santa Fe" (103).

Ortiz uses the boy's comments on Felipe to frame his story much as
Silko uses setting to frame hers. The boy's opening comments give depth to
the "inapt" Felipe of press and legal tellings at the same time they place the
killing in another political context entirely: "That was one trouble with him

[Felipe]. He was always thinking about what other people could do to you. Not the people around our place, the Indians, but other people." (101). The remark turns the paranoia assigned the brothers by Devereux into too deep a concern with oppression. Baca's Indian-hating becomes but an explicit and extreme case of a more general and constant pressure, a case answered by an extreme act.

But Ortiz does not let us off so easily. The narrator's closing comments reveal that fact and fiction are blurred in his mind. Did the murder happen or was it but another of Felipe's stories? Even after his parents confirm the story's reality — perhaps the more so — the boy is left with a feeling of vague hopelessness. Appropriately, the narrator's initial response to this malaise is vaguely Christian: "Every night, for quite a while, I prayed a rosary or something for him" (108). The veneer of Christian hope gives little solace, and it is finally the telling of the story itself which is the narrator's best response to his experience with Felipe not as a polemic or an apology, but as a culturally sensitive documentary.

VI

There is one other imaginative account which may be based in part on the Nash Garcia case. N. Scott Momaday has on occasion remarked that portions of the plot of his novel *House Made of Dawn* were loosely based on an actual case history.[37] He recalls reading of a young Indian who when brought to trial for murdering a man testified that he killed the man because he was a witch. Witch murders have occurred periodically throughout the history of the American Southwest and only a speculative link may be made between the newspaper account Momaday noticed and reports on the supernatural aspects of the Garcia case.[38] Nonetheless, links between Momaday's novel and the case are provocative.

Springfield psychiatrist Robert Navarre's "Report of a Neuropsychiatric Examination of William Felipe" contains the following summary of Felipe's psychic history:

> After his discharge he returned to his old life on the Acoma Reservation. The patient was now no longer contented with his old life. . . . He became quite restless and frequently had an urge to leave the reservation, and "go someplace." He became increasingly irritable and found it difficult to control himself. He had difficulty sleeping at night, had nightmares about his Army experiences, and relived his experiences during which artillery shells and mortar shells hit the ground very close to him. At night he would shake and tremble when he heard a sudden noise. His heart would beat fast, his hands would shake, he would develop twitching of his eyes and lips, he would have difficulty in getting his breath, and would sweat all over and feel chilly. At night he would awake suddenly: "It feels like somebody is standing there right beside me, right behind me and I start to get scared after that." He would then have great difficulty in going back to sleep. He became apprehensive of some impending disaster,

and had a strong urge to do something about this, but he did not know what to do. He had dreams in which snakes tried to kill him. . . . The only relief that he was able to obtain from all these difficulties was from drinking alcohol.[39]

The report reads as a summary of Abel's return to Walatowa after World War II in *House Made of Dawn*. The dreamlike memory of combat and a mysterious threatening presence come together for him at the end of Part One of that novel when he kills an albino who he perceives as a snake-witch outside a bar.[40] Momaday turns in the rest of the novel from perspective to perspective to give us glimpses of the motivation of that act. Abel himself views the act as simple: "A man kills such an enemy if he can."[41] Father Olguin, curate at Walatowa, argues at Abel's trial "that in his own mind it was not a man he killed, but something like an evil spirit," and adds: "I believe that this man was moved to do what he did by an act of imagination so compelling as to be inconceivable to us."[42] The court responds to Olguin with facts: "He committed a brutal and premeditated act which we have no choice but to call by its right name."[43] But the cultural enigma posed by the murder is most memorably expressed in the novel by Tosamah, Kiowa Priest of the Sun, in a typically sardonic burst:

> And do you know what he said? I mean, do you have any *idea* what that cat said? A *snake*, he said. He killed a goddam *snake!* *The corpus delicti*, see, *he threatened to turn himself into a snake*, for crissake, and rattle around a little bit. Now ain't that something, though? Can you *imagine* what went on at that trial? There was this longhair, see, cold sober, of sound mind, and the goddam judge looking on, and the prosecutor trying to talk sense to that poor degenerate Indian: "Tell us about it, man. Give it to us straight." "Well, you honors, it was this way, see? I cut me up a little snake meat out there in the sand." Christ, man, that must have been our finest hour, better than Little Bighorn. That little no-count cat must have had the whole Jesus scheme right in the palm of his hand. Think of it! *What's-His-Name v. United States*. I mean, where's the legal precedent man? When you stop to think about it, due process is a hell of remedy for snakebite.[44]

Like Silko and Ortiz, Momaday, through Tosamah, makes painfully visible the tension between the "facts" and the illusive cultural realities in a single murder case. But Momaday makes explicit what is only implied in the short stories. The murder typifies life at the friction point between cultures.

In a tantalizing foreword to his fictionalized account of a Chicago murder, *Compulsion*, Meyer Levin proposes that certain crimes become emblems for the era in which they occur. Dostoevski's *Crime and Punishment* evokes the "feverish soul-searching" of nineteenth century Russia, *An American Tragedy* the "sociological thinking" of Dreiser's America.[45] Similarly, my colleague John Hollowell suggests that "*In Cold Blood* exemplifies the meaningless crime that has become symptomatic of America in the last decade."[46] From a more restricted vantage, journalistic, legal, and psychiatric records, taken together with the imaginative accounts of Silko, Ortiz, and Momaday, refract the killing of Nash Garcia in a varicolored emblem of post-war Indian relations.

Notes

1. The stories were published in Kenneth Rosen, ed., *The Man to Send Rain Clouds: Contemporary Stories by American Indians* (New York: Viking, 1974). Two notable reviews of the book are Peter G. Beidler's published in the *Arizona Quarterly*, 30 (1974), 357–59, and Mick McAllister's in the *American Indian Quarterly*, 1 (1974), 210–11.

2. Rosen, p. xi.

3. I should like to acknowledge the help of my students Kathleen Cohill, Glenn Dick, and Marlene Hoskie in gathering information on the case. Ms. Ann Neff in the Office of the Clerk, United States District Court, District of New Mexico, kindly arranged to have the file of the "United States vs. William R. Felipe and Gabriel Felipe" transferred from the Federal Records Center in Denver, Colorado, to United States District Court in Tucson for my review. The file includes transcripts of the trial, the Court's correspondence regarding the case, and many of the exhibits introduced, which include the Felipe's confessions, reports of their psychiatric examinations, photos of the scene of the killing, and other materials.

4. Plaintiff's exhibits 10 and 16, "U.S. vs. William R. Felipe and Gabriel Felipe," #16902 criminal.

5. Plaintiff's exhibit 16, 4–7.

6. "Report of Neuropsychiatric Examination of Gabriel Felipe," Nov. 11, 1952, Medical Center for Federal Prisoners, Springfield, Missouri. Gabriel Felipe's drivers license was revoked February 1, 1952, following his conviction January 25, 1952, for driving while intoxicated.

7. "Laud Slain Officer," *Albuquerque Journal*, April 15, 1952, p. 1.

8. "Job Came First," *Albuquerque Journal*, April 16, 1952, p. 13.

9. "Nash Garcia is Ambushed," *Albuquerque Journal*, 14 April 1952, p. 1.

10. Transcripts of "United States vs. William R. Felipe and Gabriel Felipe," p. 40.

11. *Albuquerque Star*, April 15, 1952, p. 1.

12. The same issue of the *Albuquerque Star*, April 18, 1952, disclosing Baca's actions reports, for example; that "Farmington's new mayor Tom Bolack vows drive to stamp out bootlegging," 24.

13. *Albuquerque Journal*, April 15, 1952, p. 1.

14. *Albuquerque Star*, April 19, 1952, p. 10.

15. Transcripts, p. 96.

16. Transcripts, p. 221.

17. For example, Dunleavy to Captain White, head of the New Mexico state police: "Are you familiar with the fact that less than two years ago the chief of the state police was convicted of putting a bicycle lock on the testicles of an accused person?" Transcripts, p. 168.

18. Transcripts, p. 362.

19. Transcripts, p. 368.

20. Transcripts, p. 380. Compare Ortiz's "Kaiser and the War," Rosen, pp. 47–60.

21. Citations of military documents are from copies introduced as evidence at the trial.

22. Transcripts, p. 167.

23. "Summary Psychiatric Evaluation of Gabriel Felipe," Dec. 26, 1952, p. 4.

24. One of Devereux's best known contributions in the area is *Reality and Dream: Psychotherapy of a Plains Indian* (New York: International Universities Press, 1951).

25. "Summary Psychiatric Evaluation of William Felipe," Dec. 22, 1952, p. 4.

26. "Evaluation of Gabriel Felipe," p. 1.

27. "Evaluation," p. 1.

28. "Evaluation," p. 3.

29. "Evaluation," p. 5.

30. Unless otherwise noted the following material is taken from Devereux's "Summary Psychiatric Evaluation of William Felipe."

31. Robert Navarre, "Report of Neuropsychiatric Examination of William Felipe," Dec. 16, 1952, p. 2.

32. " . . . we must remember that his father was found dead in a cleft rock, after having fallen from a cliff. . . . Falling into a cleft rock also occurs in a rather terrible contest in one of the chief Acoma myths." Devereux, "Summary Psychiatric Evaluation of William Felipe," p. 3.

33. "Summary," p. 6.

34. " 'Delusions of Witchcraft' Cited in New Psychiatric Report on Felipe Brothers," *Albuquerque Journal*, Feb. 27, 1953, p. 8.

35. Personal communication, Mar. 30, 1976, Laguna, New Mexico.

36. Rosen, *The Man to Send Rain Clouds*, p. 73; hereafter cited parenthetically.

37. Personal communication, Oct. 18, 1971, Omaha, Neb.

38. See Marc Simmons, *Witchcraft in the Southwest: Spanish and Indian Supernaturalism on the Rio Grande* (Flagstaff: Northland Press, 1974).

39. pp. 3–4.

40. For a more extended treatment of the significance of the albino, see my essay "Words and Place: A Reading of *House Made of Dawn*," *Western American Literature*," 11 (1977), p. 296–320.

41. *House Made of Dawn* (New York: New American Library, 1969), p. 95.

42. *House*, p. 94.

43. *House*, p. 94.

44. *House*, p. 136.

45. *Compulsion* (New York: Simon and Schuster, 1956), p. ix.

46. *Between Fact and Fiction: The New Journalism and the Nonfiction Novel* (Univ. of North Carolina Press, 1976).

INDEX